Feminist Methodologies for International Relations

D1448259

Why is feminist research carried out in international relations (IR)? What are the methodologies and methods that have been developed in order to carry out this research? *Feminist Methodologies for International Relations* offers students and scholars of IR, feminism, and global politics practical insight into the innovative methodologies and methods that have been developed – or adapted from other disciplinary contexts – in order to do feminist research for IR. Both timely and timeless, this volume makes a diverse range of feminist methodological reflections wholly accessible. Each of the twelve contributors discusses aspects of the relationships between ontology, epistemology, methodology, and method, and how they inform and shape their research. This important and original contribution to the field will both guide and stimulate new thinking.

BROOKE A. ACKERLY is Assistant Professor in the Department of Political Science at Vanderbilt University. She is the author of *Political Theory and Feminist Social Criticism* (2000).

MARIA STERN is a Lecturer and Researcher at the Department of Peace and Development Research, Göteborg University. She is the author of *Naming Security – Constructing Identity: Mayan Women in Guatemala on the Eve of "Peace"* (2005).

JACQUI TRUE is Senior Lecturer in the Department of Political Studies at the University of Auckland, New Zealand. She is the author of *Gender, Globalization, and Postsocialism: The Czech Republic after Communism* (2003) and co-author of *Theories of International Relations* (third edition, 2005).

Feminist Methodologies for International Relations

Edited by

Brooke A. Ackerly, Maria Stern, and Jacqui True

CAMBRIDGE
UNIVERSITY PRESS

CAMBRIDGE UNIVERSITY PRESS
Cambridge, New York, Melbourne, Madrid, Cape Town, Singapore, São Paulo

CAMBRIDGE UNIVERSITY PRESS
The Edinburgh Building, Cambridge CB2 2RU, UK
Published in the United States of America by Cambridge University Press,
New York

www.cambridge.org
Information on this title: www.cambridge.org/9780521678353

First published 2006

Printed in the United Kingdom at the University Press, Cambridge

A catalogue record for this book is available from the British Library

Library of Congress Cataloguing in Publication data
Feminist methodologies for international relations / edited by Brooke A. Ackerly,
Maria Stern, and Jacqui True.– 1st ed.
p.   cm.
Includes bibliographical references and index.
ISBN-13 978-0-521-86115-1
ISBN-10 0-521-86115-2
ISBN-13 978-0-521-67835-3 paperback
ISBN-10 0-521-67835-8 paperback
1. International relations. 2. Feminism–Methodology. I. Ackerly, Brooke A. II.
Stern, Maria. III. True, Jacqui. IV. Title.
JZ1253.2.F46 2006
327.101-dc22
2005029843

ISBN-13 978-0-521-86115-1 hardback
ISBN-10 0-521-86115-2 hardback
ISBN-13 978-0-521-67835-3 paperback
ISBN-10 0-521-67835-8 paperback

For our children – Aasha, Annlyn, Alexander, Andreas, Hugo, and Seamus – and for all those who care for them.

Contents

Contributors

BROOKE A. ACKERLY (PhD, *Stanford University*, USA) is Assistant Professor, Department of Political Science, Vanderbilt University. Her research interests include democratic theory, cross-cultural human rights theory, feminist theory, social criticism, and feminist methodologies and methods. She integrates into her theoretical work empirical research on democratization, human rights, credit programs, and women's activism. Her publications include *Political Theory and Feminist Social Criticism*; "Women's Human Rights Activists as Cross-cultural Theorists," in *International Journal of Feminist Politics* (2001); and "Is Liberal Democracy the Only Way?" in *Political Theory*. She was previously a Visiting Fellow at the Center for International Studies, University of Southern California, where she and Jacqui True first collaborated on questions of feminist IR methodology. She is currently working on a book manuscript on an immanent and cross-cultural theory of universal human rights.

CAROL COHN (PhD, *Union Graduate School in Social and Political Thought*, USA) is the Director of the Boston Consortium on Gender, Security, and Human Rights, and a Senior Research Scholar at the Fletcher School of Law and Diplomacy, Tufts University. Her research and writing have focused on gender and international security, ranging from work on discourse of civilian defense intellectuals, gender integration issues in the US military, and, most extensively, weapons of mass destruction, including "Sex and Death in the Rational World of Defense Intellectuals," *Signs* 12, 4, and most recently, with Sara Ruddick, "A Feminist Ethical Perspective on Weapons of Mass Destruction," in *Ethics and Weapons of Mass Destruction: Religious and Secular Perspectives*, ed. Sohail H. Hashmi and Steven P. Lee. Her current research, supported by the Ford Foundation, examines gender mainstreaming in international peace and security institutions; a central focus is the passage of UN Security Council Resolution 1325 on women, peace and security, and the on-going efforts to ensure its implementation.

BINA D'COSTA (PhD, *Australian National University*, Australia) is currently a post-doctoral fellow at the University of Otago. In 2003–4 she was the John Vincent fellow in the Department of International Relations at the Australian National University, Canberra, Australia. She has taught in the Department of Women's Studies and International Relations at ANU. Her research interests include feminist theories of International Relations, gender and governance, theories of citizenship, conflict management and peace-building issues, and transnational networking. She is continuing her work on transitional justice and truth and reconciliation in South Asia.

TAMI AMANDA JACOBY (PhD, *York University*, Canada) is Assistant Professor, Department of Political Studies, and research fellow at the Centre for Defence and Security Studies, at the University of Manitoba in Canada. She has done extensive fieldwork in Israel, Palestine, and Jordan. Her publications include *Redefining Security in the Middle East* (co-edited with Brent E. Sasley) and articles on the Arab–Israeli conflict, women's movements in the Middle East, and Canadian foreign policy. She has two books forthcoming: *Women in Zones of Conflict*, and *Maple Sands: Prospects and Legacies of Canada–Middle East Relations*.

ANNICA KRONSELL (PhD, *Lund University*, Sweden) is Assistant Professor, Department of Political Science, at Lund University, where she teaches courses in international relations. Her current research focuses on gender and the new Swedish security context and the changing role of military–civil relations. Her recent publications in English include "Gender, Power and European Integration Theory," in *European Journal of Public Policy*; "Gendered Practices in Institutions of Hegemonic Masculinity: Reflections from Feminist Standpoint Theory," in *International Feminist Journal of Politics*; and, with Erika Svedberg, "The Duty to Protect: Gender in the Swedish Practice of Conscription," in *Cooperation and Conflict*.

FIONA ROBINSON (PhD, *Cambridge University*, UK) is Associate Professor of International Relations in the Department of Political Science, Carleton University, Ottawa, Canada. She has also taught at the University of Sussex, England. Her research focuses on ethics and international relations, normative international relations theory, feminist 'care ethics' and global social policy, and human rights. Her book *Globalizing Care: Ethics, Feminist Theory and International Relations* was published in 1999. Her most recent publications include "NGOs and the Advancement of Economic and Social Rights: Philosophical and Practical Controversies," *International Relations* (2003); and "Human Rights and the Global Politics of Resistance: Feminist Perspectives," *Review of International Studies* (2004).

MARIA STERN (PhD, *Göteborg University*, Sweden) is Lecturer and Research Fellow in the Department of Peace and Development Studies, at the University of Göteborg, Sweden. She also teaches at the Department of Gender Studies at the University of Göteborg. She is currently directing a research project on "Gender in the Armed Forces: Militarism and Peace-building in Congo-Kinshasa and Mozambique," funded by SIDA/Sarec-Sweden. Her recent publications include *Naming Security–Constructing Identity: Mayan Women in Guatemala on the Eve of "Peace"* (2005); and Véronique Pin-Fat and Maria Stern, "The Scripting of Private Jessica Lynch: Biopolitics, Gender and the 'Feminization' of the U.S. Military," in *Alternatives: Global, Local, Political* (2005).

CHRISTINE SYLVESTER (PhD, *University of Kentucky*, USA) is Professor of Women's Studies at the University of Lancaster, UK, and Professorial Research Associate in the Department of Politics and International Relations at the School of Oriental and African Studies (SOAS), University of London. Her books include *Feminist International Relations: An Unfinished Journey*, and *Feminist Theory and International Relations in a Postmodern Era*. An abiding interest in the arts appears in many of her IR writings over the past ten years, including pieces in *Millennium*; *Alternatives*; *International Feminist Journal of Politics*; *Body and Society*; *Borderlands e-journal*; and *Brown Journal of World Affairs*.

J. ANN TICKNER (PhD, *Brandeis University*, USA) is Professor, School of International Relations at the University of Southern California, and the past director of USC's Center for International Studies (2000–3). She is the author of *Gender in International Relations: Feminist Perspectives on Achieving Global Security* (1992) and *Gendering World Politics: Issues and Approaches in the Post-Cold-War Era* (2001).

JACQUI TRUE (PhD, *York University*, Canada) is Senior Lecturer, Department of Political Studies at the University of Auckland, New Zealand. Her research interests include international political economy, global civil society, feminist theory and methods, and gender policy analysis. Her publications include "Transnational Networks and Policy Diffusion: The Case of Gender Mainstreaming," in

International Studies Quarterly (2001), with Michael Mintrom; and *Gender, Globalization, and Postsocialism: The Czech Republic after Communism* (2003), and she is a co-author of *Theories of International Relations*, third edition (2005) She began to reflect seriously on the methodological contributions of feminist IR with Brooke Ackerly while a post-doctoral fellow at the Center for International Studies, University of Southern California. She is currently working on a comparative institutional analysis of regional trade organizations and the pursuit of gender equity.

S. LAUREL WELDON (PhD, *University of Pittsburgh*, USA) is Associate Professor of Political Science at Purdue University. She has published a book, *Protest, Policy and the Problem of Violence Against Women: A Cross-national Comparison* (2002) as well as articles in the *Journal of Politics*; *New Political Science*; and the *International Journal of Feminist Politics*.

MARYSIA ZALEWSKI (PhD, *University of Wales*, UK) is Director of the Centre for Gender Studies at the University of Aberdeen, Scotland. Her primary research interests include feminist theory, gender and international relations, and the politics of theorizing. She has published widely in the area of gender and international relations, feminist theory, and women's studies. Recently published work has appeared in the following journals: *Political Studies* (2005); *International Studies Review* (2003); *Feminist Theory* (2003); *Sexualities* (2003); and *International Journal of Women's Studies* (2003). Books include *Feminism after Postmodernism: Theorising through Practice* (2000). Current research interests include the politics of theorizing the conflict in Northern Ireland; the "failures" of feminism; and gendered epistemologies in war and conflict.

Acknowledgments

This volume, from its inception to its final stages of completion, reflects a collective effort. Besides the many people who contributed directly to its content, there are ever-expanding ripples of people whose work and knowledge have made this book possible.

First of all we owe a vast debt to all whose scholarship, commitment, and hard work have created the field of feminist IR. We (Ackerly, Stern, and True) all began our careers at a time when we were able to benefit from the critical building blocks of so much feminist scholarship within IR. Some feminist scholars had already paved the way for serious engagement with gender; in a field which was notoriously gender-blind and deaf, their ground-breaking work enabled us to draw upon their advancements in the formulation of our research questions, areas of study, and methodologies. We are now joined by more feminist scholars in expanding and developing the field of feminist IR inquiry. Without the efforts of all of these people, this book could not exist. You will see, not all, but many of them cited throughout the volume. Instead of naming them all here individually, we would like to extend our admiration and gratitude to feminist IR scholars as a diverse and dynamic collective. Thank you!

This book also is part of an ongoing dialogue on feminist methodologies for IR that includes many more people than those whose work appear in these pages. The process of putting together this volume has involved discussing feminist methodology with many scholars in diverse forums – discussions that we hope will continue. We also hope new discussions will arise and include many more. Several people, however, deserve special mention.

The idea for this book first took shape in conjunction with a panel on feminist methodologies at the International Studies Association (ISA) annual convention in 2002, in which we, Drucilla Barker, Laura J. Parisi, and Ann Tickner participated. The ISA then generously supported a one-day workshop on feminist methodology in February 2003, during which many of the ideas for this book took further shape. Those participating were Anna Agathangelou, Erin Baines, Gemma M. Carney, Carol

Cohn, Bina D'Costa, Vivienne Jabri, Tami Jacoby, Annica Kronsell, Bice Maiguashca, Rekha Pande, Jan Jindy Pettman, Elisabeth Prügl, Fiona Robinson, Christine Sylvester, J. Ann Tickner, and Marysia Zalewski. Additional panels on feminist methodology at the 2004 annual ISA conference further contributed to the content of the book. Those participating include many already mentioned, as well as Laura Sjöberg and S. Laurel Weldon. Thanks to all of you for your invaluable contributions and to the audiences at those panels for their intellectual curiousity and engagement with methodological issues. We look forward to continuing conversations.

We also are grateful to the ISA for providing the venue and financial support for these discussions.

Special thanks to Lyndi Hewitt for extensive bibliographic work.

We gratefully acknowledge the important roles that John Haslam and three anonymous reviewers played in bringing this many-voiced manuscript to fruition.

Academic endeavors, we believe, are best served by ongoing dialogue. We greatly appreciate the many small (and large) exchanges that help us to think in new ways and that make our daily work lives both more productive and more fun. Therefore, we also thank our students and our immediate colleagues at Vanderbilt University, Göteborg University, and the University of Auckland. We would also like to officially thank each other for each editor's unique contribution, patience, hard work, and commitment.

We have been working on this book over a period of three years and across the span of three continents. Without the help of many people, this book would never have been completed. We therefore would like to thank all who enabled us to pursue and, ultimately, complete this project. Specifically, we want to extend our gratitude to those whose care and work often goes unacknowledged, unthanked and under-remunerated in our globalizing economy. Much invisible labor in the world is labor of love and care that enables so many to do so much. Brooke would especially like to thank Beth Stout, Sarah Huang, Bill Zinke, Katherine Stevenson, Richard Ackerly, Barbara Zinke, and the teachers at West End Day School. Maria would like to thank Eduardo Simón Brynnel, Véronique Pin-Fat, Maria Eriksson Baaz, Ann Gollin, and Kaia Stern, as well as the teachers at the International Preschool and the International School, Gothenburg Region. Jacqui True would like to thank Michael Mintrom, Julia True, and the teachers at the University of Auckland's Park Avenue Infant and Toddler Creche.

1 Feminist methodologies for International Relations

Brooke A. Ackerly, Maria Stern, and Jacqui True

Over the past two decades feminism has made refreshing, often radical contributions to the study of International Relations (IR). Feminism is no longer a rare import but a well-established approach within IR, as its inclusion in the core texts and scholarly collections of the field testifies. IR students today benefit from the theoretical and empirical space opened up by feminist scholars. Since the late 1980s, feminist scholars have paved the way for serious engagement with gender and theory in a previously gender-blind and theoretically abstract IR field.[1] Despite its increasing recognition, however, the progress of feminist international relations scholarship has been far from straightforward. In a state-centric discipline that is notorious for its lack of self-reflection, developing feminist methodologies and conducting feminist research have been major challenges. However, since *all* power relations are essential to feminist perspectives and to the feminist research process, feminist methodologies are highly relevant for the study of global politics.

Feminist Methodologies for International Relations offers students and scholars of international relations, feminism, and global politics practical insight into the innovative methodologies and methods that have been developed – or adapted from other disciplinary contexts – in order to *do* feminist research for IR. Beginning with the first wave of feminist IR, scholars have been making theoretical breakthroughs. Attention to methodology has been vital to the development of feminist IR as a diverse, varied, and *collective* inquiry. While feminist research methods have been the subject of informal discussions, these have been largely unpublished. Most students and scholars are unaware of the methodological rigor underpinning feminist IR research. The *details* of feminist work – details that are necessary to know in order to replicate or further develop a particular IR research agenda – are typically not included in

---

[1] For example, *Gendered States* (Peterson 1992) established feminist IR firmly within the IR discipline by providing a theoretical account of the new subfield and by presenting a coherent, yet diverse, body of feminist scholarship on international relations.

published texts or monographs. Indeed, there is no scholarly work that discusses *how* IR feminist research is conducted. Little attention has been paid to building a body of literature on methodologies that would enable feminist scholars to learn from one another. As a result, the significance of methodology for feminist IR and the study of global politics is not well understood or appreciated.

For the first time, therefore, this volume makes a diverse – albeit necessarily selective – range of feminist IR methodological reflections accessible to students, teachers, and scholars in the (inter)disciplines of IR, feminist IR, and women's studies. The differences and debates within these fields fuel feminist methodological inquiry and make a book such as this possible, necessary, and controversial. We expect that this collection will provoke debate and discussion among new and already established scholars. But we also hope that it will be widely used and consulted by those in search of inspiration and suggestions for how to design their research, and by those interested in the methodological conundrums the book evokes.

Feminist Methodologies for International Relations aims both to demystify and to complicate assumptions about how feminist scholars of international relations do their work. As editors, we are in the ironic position of writing a definitive text for a field that eschews definition. However, we invite readers to join us in appreciating this irony rather than struggling against it. The politics of defining, studying, and being from the margins has been critical to feminist IR scholarship since its inception. In the spirit of this tradition, this volume's focus on methodology brings to the fore issues of marginalization and difference within the field, as well as the challenges of dealing with the politics of being a feminist IR scholar.

Clearly, *Feminist Methodologies for International Relations* contributes to a larger discussion on methodological developments within IR, as well as within feminist inquiry more broadly. Feminist IR scholarship has built upon positivist and mainstream IR methodologies in the service of exploring feminist questions.[2] For example, IR texts, such as True and Mintrom (2001), use a dataset uniquely designed for the study of a feminist IR question: the extent to which transnational feminist networking has influenced national policy change, as indicated by the establishment of new state institutions for the promotion of gender equality. Using regression analysis, also, Caprioli (2000) explores the

---

[2] Partly because of the nature of the feminist research questions being asked by its contributors, this volume includes examples of only qualitatively oriented research designs.

impact of gender inequality on state behaviour internationally, a research question that takes as given the conventional ontology of IR (see also Tessler and Warriner 1997).[3] Inglehart and Norris (2003), Apodaca (1998; 2000), and Poe et al. (1997) study questions that could be framed as feminist IR questions but that are difficult to pursue using datasets that were not designed to study such questions. New quantitative indicators such as the United Nations Development Program's gender development index (GDI) and gender empowerment measure (GEM) facilitate feminist IR research by making it possible to compare the degree of gender equality within and across states. As well, Keck and Sikkink (1998) and Carpenter (2002) develop constructivist theoretical methodologies to analyze issues – women's transnational activism and gender constructs in war respectively – that are integral to feminist IR inquiry.

In addition, feminist IR methodologies build on feminist methodologies from other disciplines. There are many excellent texts that address questions of feminist methodology outside of IR from a range of perspectives. These texts include volumes that show the politics and the practicalities of how feminist scholars conduct their work within different fields and approaches through a myriad of methods including oral history, fieldwork, case study, discourse, comparative institutional, and quantitative data analyses.[4] Some of these works ask whether we can we identify *a* feminist methodology, and if so, what that methodology might entail (Maynard and Purvis 1994; DeVault 1999; D. Smith 1999). Contributions such as these have been useful to feminist IR scholars. Both L. T. Smith (1999) and Basu (1995) draw on feminist postcolonial theorizing and offer a powerful critique of western research traditions and methodologies. L. T. Smith develops counter-practices of research, clearing space for a serious engagement with indigenous knowledges – and ways of knowing; whereas Basu addresses many of the critical problematics of a global feminism that transcends national and cultural boundaries by focusing on women's movements in different contexts. *Feminist Methodologies for International Relations* consciously builds on this earlier, interdisciplinary work.

---

[3] Caprioli (2004) argues that a neofeminist IR based on the quantitative analysis of gender and state behaviour as the dependent variable might make feminism more relevant to IR just as neorealism reinvented classical realist perspectives in the field. But we question this analogy, since, in our reading, neorealism actually reduced the rich historical and philosophical tradition of realism to an ahistorical, scientifically testable set of propositions. This did not result in a diverse or more systematic research agenda as Caprioli assumes.

[4] For instance, see Bowles and Klein 1983; Fonow and Cooke 1991a; Nielsen 1990; Reinharz 1992; Gluck and Patai 1991.

The distinctiveness of feminist methodologies inside and outside IR lies in their reflexivity, which encourages the researcher to re-interrogate continually her own scholarship. Although this volume includes examples of qualitatively oriented research designs only, such self-reflexivity is important not only in qualitative research. Feminist IR scholars learn from and adapt methodologies used in mainstream IR and interdisciplinary feminist studies, but the methodologies they employ are not merely derivative of them. In a variety of ways, IR feminist studies make an original contribution to methodological thinking, useful for IR scholars and feminist scholars in other fields.

There is a gradual realization, especially among critical and constructivist scholars, of the importance of interpretivist methodologies (see Milliken 1999; Goff and Dunn 2004; Checkel 2004). Many feminist scholars, perhaps precisely because of their marginality in the field and their interdisciplinarity, have been at the forefront of the development of constructivist and postmodern methodologies in IR (see Sylvester 1994a; Prügl 1999). They have had to be particularly creative with the tools of a discipline not intended for the questions feminists ask, and notably eclectic in drawing on tools from other disciplines and sites. Feminist IR scholars have developed not just a toolkit of methods but ways of incorporating ontological and epistemological reflection into methodological choices that lead them to rethink the boundaries of the IR discipline.

Taken together, the chapters in this book build on the collective accomplishments of feminist IR methodologies; they demonstrate the value to IR inquiry of studying from multiple locations and of studying the intersection of social relations in any one location. They address both marginalized and non-marginalized subjects. For non-IR feminist scholars, especially those who do transnational research, the feminist IR methodologies presented here provide rich and unique examples of how to study *up* and *down* simultaneously. They engage with the traditional ontology of IR focused on states, conflict, military, and international institutions. They use insights from researching marginalized sites and subjects in order to revision IR concepts of security, sovereignty, nationality, and global politics. Most of the chapters explicitly consider class, race, ethnicity, and other power relations as they manifest themselves within gender inequalities in global politics (Tiberghien-Chan 2004). Indeed, as the volume as a whole shows, feminism is not about studying women and gender exclusively. Just as states, conflict, institutions, security, and globalization cannot be studied without analyzing gender, gender cannot be studied without analyzing these subjects and concepts.

Consequently, feminist methodological approaches not only are innovative but also raise new ethical and political dilemmas that expand methodological inquiry. These dilemmas revolve around the power relations between the researcher and the research subjects and the power inequalities among the research subjects themselves. *Feminist Methodologies for International Relations* shows how such dilemmas are particularly heightened in the research sites where feminist IR scholars are most engaged, including conflict zones, the interstices between civil society and international organizations, and political and economic borders. When engaging with these ethical questions, IR feminism contributes to IR and interdisciplinary feminist debates about the merits of different methodological approaches and the potential abuses of power.

As we look over the contributions to this volume, the logic for each chapter's inclusion may not be obvious to the reader. We have consciously worked to include contributions from feminist IR scholars with a variety of academic homes, national origins, ethnic backgrounds, and years in the field. We have aimed to show a range of contributions to feminist methodologies for international relations in terms of research questions and methods, ontological and theoretical perspectives, and regional and institutional sites of study, without either seeking or claiming to be comprehensive. Far from it: since this is the first published volume devoted to the explicit presentation and discussion of IR feminist methodologies, we could not possibly include the full diversity and potentially vast scope of methodological approaches that currently exist or are under development in the field of feminist IR. Thus each chapter should be read as a unique contribution and as part of a collective conversation about feminist IR methodology. Indeed, none of the authors in this volume had the benefit of such a collection when they were exploring their research questions and designing their research projects.

Although this volume reflects feminist IR scholarship which uses qualitative methods, its attention to methodology is also highly relevant for those scholars and students primarily interested in quantitative methods – or indeed employing a triangulation of methods. What makes the scholarship discussed in this book *feminist* is the research question and the theoretical methodology and not the tool or particular method used (see Ackerly and True, this volume). As illustrated by the contributions to this volume, feminist research cannot be reduced to a particular normative orientation or political, ideological agenda (cf. Carpenter 2003: 299).

In sum, the contributing chapters demonstrate that doing feminist research is extremely demanding theoretically and analytically as well as ethically and politically. Within IR it sets new standards for methodological rigor that could make a difference to scholarship and to the world we live in. Certainly, a normative purpose drives feminist research efforts, as it does all IR scholarship whether or not consciously or explicitly (see Cox 1981). But feminist normative perspectives are often plural, contingent, and relational, since feminist scholarship is highly attuned to and self-reflexive about power and politics. The volume resists the seduction of giving a fixed, substantive definition of feminist methodology. Instead, it offers an entry point from which to consider collectively many different feminist methodologies engaged by scholars who are interested in studying global politics from a stance that gender matters.

Further, the volume offers a form of collective authorship, not yet professionally rewarded in dominant professional norms, but nonetheless important to advancing IR scholarship. (Within contemporary professional and disciplinary norms, single authorship usually "counts" more than co-authorship, and authorship "counts" more than editorship.) We hope that it will encourage future collective efforts that defy the professional norms that demarcate the field of IR.

Defining our terms

In order for this volume's *raison d'être* to be fully grasped, we need to define some of our nomenclature; what we mean by epistemology, ontology, method, ethics, and methodology in particular. For the most part, and unless otherwise indicated, the chapters in this volume share common definitions of key terms associated with knowledge. We consider *epistemology* to refer to an understanding of knowledge – of how we can know – and therefore what constitutes a research question. We use *ontology* to mean an understanding of the world; for instance, what constitute relevant units of analysis (i.e., individuals, genders, states, classes, ethnicities) and whether the world and these units are constant or dynamic and able to be changed through, *inter alia*, research. We see *method* as indicating the kind of tool of research or analysis that a researcher adopts; for example, discourse analysis, oral history, participant observation, and qualitative data collection are all possible methods and are used by the authors in this volume. By *ethics* we mean to highlight the rights and responsibilities that inhere in the relationship between the research subject and the researcher. And we use *methodology* or *theoretical method* to refer to the intellectual process guiding reflections about the relationship among all of these; that is, guiding self-conscious reflections on epistemological assumptions, ontological perspective, ethical responsibilities, and method choices.

Methodologies take *many* forms. For instance, methodological reflections are those that lead us to consider the relationship between ontology and epistemology. How does our understanding of the world affect our understanding of knowledge? What constitutes an IR question and what it would mean to answer that IR question? Methodology involves reflecting on one's epistemology. What does it mean to have inquired about a subject? It also requires consideration of the relationship between ontology and method. How does the researcher's view of the potential for changing the world affect the way she does her research? And between epistemology and method: what is the best way of designing the research project so as to answer the research question? Ethical issues are part of methodological reflection. They compel us to ask how our own subjectivities, that of our research subjects, and the power relations between us affect the research process. Finally, methodologies shape the choice of and development of methods. For instance, feminist methodological reflections are often directed at the redesign of methods that have been used to explore non-feminist questions in fields where feminist inquiry is relatively new.

Unlike those empirical methods that are designed to generate results that can be replicated by different scholars, however, feminist methodologies likely yield different results in the hands of different theorists. Yet, this non-reliability need not be viewed as a weakness of feminist scholarship (cf. King et al. 1996). Rather, it is an important implication that is explicitly recognized and directly addressed by the collective, self-reflective, and deliberative nature of feminist methodologies. As their research questions and the methods used to address them expand, feminist scholars need theoretical methodologies to guide and examine the research process. This ongoing methodological reflection can be seen as an important aspect of feminist scholarship, which, although not unique to feminism, sets most feminist contributions to IR apart from the mainstream.

Feminist ontologies that expand our notions of world politics to include the personal and previously invisible spheres, and that start from the perspective that subjects are relational (rather than autonomous) and that the world is constantly changing (rather than static), demand self-reflective methodologies as well as the innovative methods and postpositivist epistemologies that this volume features.

A number of chapters in this volume invoke Sandra Harding's scholarship on methodology and in particular the categories she introduced to make sense of feminist epistemologies: feminist empiricism, standpoint feminism, and feminist postmodernism (1987). The reader might ask how this volume's approach compares with previous discussions of feminist epistemology in IR that apply Harding's typology. As Laurel Weldon in her chapter clarifies, following Harding, "feminist methodologies are epistemologies in action." In this sense, discussion of methodology may have greater import for feminist research than epistemological debate; and it makes sense that this discussion is occurring after considerable debate about epistemological positions has already taken place within feminist IR. Rather than categorize and divide, our intention in this volume, like Harding's, is to appreciate the coexistence and significant overlap between different epistemological and methodological approaches (for instance, between feminist standpoint and postmodern feminist approaches to international relations). The range of contributions to feminist IR (in this volume and elsewhere) and their creative reinvention of traditional theoretical approaches and methods is a major strength when viewed from the perspective of a collective, self-reflective, and deliberative feminist methodology.

The outline of this volume

Each of the chapters in this volume discusses some aspects of the relationships among ontology, epistemology, methodology, and method, and how they inform and shape their feminist IR research. The volume itself is organized in three main parts that treat different relationships in the methodological process. The first part addresses the methodological conversations between feminist and non-feminist IR, and, in particular, the relationships between ontology and epistemology, and epistemology and methodology. Theoretical engagement with the mainstream discipline leads IR feminists to rethink epistemologies and develop new theoretical and methodological approaches. This engagement with epistemology is itself a methodology for research of relevance to feminist scholars inside and outside of IR. The second part of the volume presents five case studies in which the authors deploy empirical feminist research methods and reflect on the relationships between method and methodology, ontology and method, and ethics and method. Here the feminist researcher takes her theoretical insights to the field to address new research questions; these theories, however, become challenged in the field research process. The third part of the volume offers new methodological frameworks for examining international relations and for further developing feminist international relations. The relationships among epistemologies, ontologies, and method come into focus when the feminist IR scholar turns her inquiry toward engagement with other feminist scholars and is prompted to reexamine her tools of inquiry once again.

Part I: Methodological conversations between feminist and non-feminist IR

Vexed methodological conversations between feminist and non-feminist IR have taken place in recent years, leading scholars to wonder whether there is any common ground.[5] This section comprises three chapters that provide different readings of the intellectual history of feminism's engagements with the International Relations field. Each chapter presents the development of feminist methodologies in IR from a particular stance. The chapters examine the disparities and difficulties surrounding the intersections of feminism "within" IR on the one hand, and feminism "and" IR on the other. The methodological exploration of these intersections contextualizes the contributions in the second and third parts of the volume.

In her chapter, Ann Tickner addresses the question of why feminists do not just adopt mainstream methodologies such as exploring and testing hypotheses about gender hierarchy and state behavior. She argues that feminist scholars ask different research questions from mainstream scholars, questions that have rarely or never been asked before in the field of IR. To answer their questions, moreover, IR feminists have used different methodologies from the social scientific approaches that have dominated the discipline. For Tickner, feminist research is necessarily postpositivist, since positivist methods provide no account of the origin and importance of research questions. While arguing that there is no unique feminist empirical method, she claims that there are perspectives on methodology that are distinctly feminist. Her chapter analyzes two examples of IR feminist empirical research that draw on these perspectives. Thus, the chapter opens the way for a broad diversity of feminist contributions to international relations that are question-driven but not dependent on one methodology or method.

Marysia Zalewski's chapter presents a kind of methodological engagement with IR that is an alternative to Tickner's dialogical approach. Taking a genealogical approach, the chapter reflects on some of the contours and paradoxes of feminist methodologies as they have manifested in the IR discipline over the last two decades or so. The practice and metaphor of "distraction" is employed as a methodological device, one informed by work on "haunting and the sociological imagination" (Derrida and Gordon) along with the "methodology of getting lost"

---

[5] See, for example, Tickner 1997; 1998; Keohane 1998; Marchand 1998; Enloe 2001; Carpenter 2002; *International Studies Review* Forum 2003 (5, 2: 287–302).

(Lather) and the thinking strategies of French feminist, Luce Irigaray. For Zalewski, feminist IR methodology narrates the process of search and research, and in this way demands responsibility without affording the production of "comfort texts." Working with distractions, the chapter itself acts as a performance of a feminist IR methodology by illustrating some of the processes of a deconstructionist feminist approach. Zalewski cautions feminist scholars to be wary of the demands made by mainstream IR, especially in relation to the field's methodological *fetishism*, yet does not deny the importance of reflecting on the IR question, "What is your methodology?" The excesses of feminism and the "feminine" are deeply problematic for the discipline of IR, yet IR feminism is more powerful precisely when its methodologies are manifold and unclassifiable, as illustrated in the chapters in Part II of the book.

In her chapter, Laurel Weldon outlines an IR method that is informed by a standpoint feminist epistemology and emphasizes the collective aspects of scholarship. She argues that the unwillingness of IR feminists to point out the unique, analytic advantages of marginalized standpoints diminishes the significance of feminism's methodological contribution to IR, which is not merely to add another perspective. Opening the IR discipline to feminist criticism improves our understanding of international relations and strengthens the "objectivity" of mainstream knowledge. A field's approach to inquiry and furthering knowledge may be evaluated in terms of both its own internal mechanisms for assessing its knowledge claims *and* its ability to respond to critical scrutiny from other perspectives. Contributing to evaluation of knowledge claims from within and outside the field of IR, feminist perspectives should expect inclusion in IR on *methodological* rather than normative or political grounds. Compared with Zalewski's postmodern method of distraction, Weldon explicitly argues that IR must take feminism seriously.

Part II: Methods for feminist International Relations

The second part of this volume comprises five chapters that offer self-reflective discussions of the authors' own feminist research methods applied to critical IR questions of security, military, the state, international justice, and the global order. These studies are informed by a range of feminist theories – often more than one in each chapter. Their subjects range across familiar and marginal sites of international relations in different parts of the world. They introduce a variety of research methods, including qualitative interviews, ethnography, participant observation, oral history, ethnographic life stories, and discourse analysis, in the service of different theoretical and epistemological approaches.

The first two chapters illustrate feminist methodologies in the familiar sites of International Relations scholarship: military and foreign policy establishments. Feminist scholarship has made significant headway in revealing how gender demarcates the traditional subjects of inquiry within IR and unsettling the sedentary truths of the discipline, such as the distinction between foreign and domestic (Tickner 1992; 2001), and between war and peace (Sylvester 1994a; 2002; Elshtain 1989; Enloe 1990; 1993). The chapters by Carol Cohn and Annica Kronsell show how the well-trodden research terrain of the military changes when hegemonic masculinity is exposed in its barracks. They also reveal just how inadequate traditional IR theory and methodologies are for analyzing the power of gender in national security sites. But what is remarkable about these two chapters is that they explicitly detail and reflect upon their *methods* for unmasking the workings of gender in familiar IR territory.

Carol Cohn reflects on her motives and methods for studying the "moving target" of United States national security across the course of two decades and several research projects. Her methods are multiple given that her object of study – the institutional structures and official discourses of national security – is mobile and multi-sited. They have involved participant observation, discourse analysis, semi-structured interviews using the snowball sampling method, and gender analysis. Cohn refers to her method choice as the juxtaposition and layering of many different windows that allow her to identify telling patterns over time. It is through this multiplicity of methods that Cohn seeks to bring different sites and discourses of national security during the Cold War, the first Gulf War, and the military sex and gender controversies of the 1990s into the same frame of study. Cohn's feminist methodology never leaves out her own subjectivity or story. They have both enabled and inhibited the knowledge that she receives from informants, and inevitably shaped the knowledge that she produces and shares. Yet, as Cohn demonstrates with a stunning account of her lunch with former Secretary of Defense Robert McNamara, when engaged in the research process, she suspends her beliefs and disbelief in order to try to get inside the worldviews of her informants. This process involves momentarily centering her intellectual curiosity and inhabiting the identity of the researcher, while placing her political, ontological, and epistemological values and preconceptions aside.

In her chapter, Annica Kronsell follows Cynthia Enloe's (and Carol Cohn's) example by asking questions about what appear to be normal, even banal, everyday practices in order to make visible the *gender* of international relations practices. Kronsell documents her feminist methods for studying institutions – here the Swedish defense forces – that claim to be gender-neutral but daily reproduce norms of hegemonic masculinity through rituals, routines, and symbols. Studying "silence," she argues, means that the researcher has to rely on methods of deconstruction to study texts and discourses emerging from such institutions. That is, the scholar must look for and study what is not contained within the text but rather is written between the lines or expressed as symbols and in practices. Moreover, through interviews with women inside institutions of hegemonic masculinity, Kronsell contends, it is possible to unmask the gendered nature of the military given the disruption that their presence provokes. Taken together, these research methods help to break the institutionalized silences on gender. As such they are crucial components within a feminist methodology because they enable the IR researcher to connect everyday gendered practices to persistent global patterns of gender power relations.

After Cohn and Kronsell, Part II shifts terrains to address the methodological dilemmas of conducting fieldwork in unconventional sites, such as among activist groups in conflict zones, and with subjects of study that have been traditionally absent from IR, such as women and marginalized communities. Chapters by Bina D'Costa, Tami Jacoby, and Maria Stern discuss the challenges of employing theoretical and methodological tools of the IR discipline, designed for traditional subjects in the study of international security, in sites where the conventional notion of the nation-state is problematic due, for example, to nationalist secession, competing claims to political territory, and ethnic genocide. In this sense, they exhibit the feminist IR practice of researching marginal sites and confronting the field with subjects that have traditionally rendered its gatekeepers uncomfortable. Yet, unlike previous IR studies "from below," these chapters keep the "scaffolding" in place and, importantly, discuss how their authors addressed a number of difficult methodological and ethical issues in the field. They also explicitly explore the challenges of bringing the insights found in marginalized sites and among subjugated peoples to bear on the study of IR.

In her chapter, D'Costa exhibits a methodology by which feminist researchers can provide the opportunity for marginalized women to speak for themselves in order to revise IR concepts and theories. In her fieldwork, she analyzes the experiences of women raped in the 1971 civil war that created Bangladesh from the perspectives of the women themselves. D'Costa confronts some of the challenges she faced carrying out her oral history interviews in the field, where the silence of some of her subjects and her own subjectivity as a young, educated, unmarried Bangladeshi woman both inhibited and facilitated her research, ultimately having a transformative effect on her research question. In this sense, she takes up the theme of studying (the politics of) silences, discussed in Kronsell's chapter. Her methodological self-reflection also takes up Laurel Weldon's challenge to IR feminists by illustrating the transformative impact of bringing marginalized standpoints into the discourse of IR.

Tami Jacoby's chapter also raises methodological questions associated with the implementation of a feminist standpoint epistemology in the field; her research subjects are women in protest movements in Israel/Palestine with whose politics Jacoby often does not agree. Her data collection depends on her negotiating a field of research imbued with political relations. She recounts the challenges of basing one's research of security on the experiences of women. In particular, she addresses the difficulty of translating "experience," so crucial in the forging of a feminist standpoint, through the political encounter between the researched and the researcher. Jacoby understands her research subjects as acting politically through the interview process; in an act of "self-presentation," the research subject speaks in ways that she wants to be heard. As for D'Costa, the process of reconceptualizing her original research questions is as important as finding the answers when researching women on the margins. Thus, for Jacoby, the fact that women may experience insecurity differently from men turns out not to be the fundamental issue that she envisioned at the outset.

Stern's chapter further probes into the challenges and problems of studying security as a gendered concept and practice raised in D'Costa's and Jacoby's pieces. For Stern, the dominant IR conceptualizations of security fail to provide an epistemological framework for understanding Mayan women's insecurity, which is hybrid, contingent, and defined in terms of their sexualized and racialized identities (as Mayan, women, and poor). She asks, "What does (in)security mean from the perspective of Mayan women?" To address her question, Stern develops a feminist post-structuralist textual reading of security as a discursive practice. She explains how she conducted partial life history interviews with Mayan women. This method allowed her to develop an analytical framework for addressing the multiplicity of these women's insecurities, and the intersection of different power relations. Moreover, Stern's methodology required her to use the insights of her study on the multiple and contingent interconnections between security and identity to revise mainstream IR concepts of security.

Self-reflection on methodology and method trumps epistemological or normative stance for the feminist researchers in all of the five case studies featured in this second section. Indeed, without a feminist theoretical methodology, the importance of learning about about the silences and absences in familiar institutions or about marginalized and excluded people's experiences for our understanding of international relations would not be evident. In the final section of the volume we foreground feminist methodologies that provide a framework for self-reflection on ontological and epistemological assumptions, the choice of research questions and methods.

Part III: Methodologies for feminist International Relations

The last three chapters challenge and transgress the boundaries that define and delimit IR scholarship, while also offering new methodologies for feminist IR. Feminist IR scholars have continually contested the confines of the "home" field of IR. They have borrowed methods from other areas of social science to address the silences in the field that attention to gender reveals. In so doing, feminists have contributed to broadening the range of IR methodologies, and continue to search for new methodologies to bring the many different relations of power in global politics into sharp relief.

The chapter by Christine Sylvester argues that feminists studying international relations can increase their visual acuity and expand their capacities to sight IR feminist relevant topics and activities by paying attention to the fine arts. To bring the arts, in any form, into international relations is a border transgression of the usual field, notwithstanding gestures to "the art of war" and "the art of politics" by IR scholars. Feminist IR is far more concerned than the conventional field to improve the capacity to sight, site, and cite salient activities that constitute our world; but feminist IR has not yet explored art as methodologically and substantively relevant to its work. Accordingly, Sylvester introduces methods and sites for feminist IR consideration, including portraiture, still life, abstraction, sculpture, urban architecture, and the developmental art museum. She explores a way of knowing by reflecting on art. And, inspired by new insights on knowing, she explores ways of thinking about art for knowing about and doing IR.

Fiona Robinson draws on the theoretical resources of a critical feminist approach to argue for a normative theory in IR that is characterized by an epistemological and methodological commitment to relationality. Relationality is evident in at least three distinct areas: ontology, epistemology, and in feminist views on the relationship between ethics and politics. In the light of these observations, Robinson contends that a feminist methodology for normative IR is characterized by a specific stance on the question of the relationship between theory and practice.

It must involve actually looking at human social arrangements, not just generally, but specifically – that is, in terms of how real people are affected by actual policies, processes, institutions, and structures. Robinson suggests two tools – *critical moral ethnography*, and *mapping geographies of responsibility* – that could be employed by feminist researchers to help achieve this task. These tools allow for normative engagement with feminist IR research and issues of globalization, inequality, conflict and security, human rights and citizenship, international organization, and global civil society. Only through this engagement can feminist IR effectively reflect on, evaluate, critique, and possibly transform the inequalities and exclusions that exist within specific social-moral systems, and among individuals and groups, in the world today.

Concerned with persistent global inequalities, Ackerly and True draw on the diversity of feminist approaches to IR and make extensive use of the examples in this volume to identify a critical feminist methodology and suggest a feminist theoretical method. Such an explicitly *feminist*, critical methodology and its concomitant *method* of theorizing not only help to clarify the struggles for social justice in our globalizing age, but also enable us to do better scholarship and, as theorists, to live up to the goal of informing and transforming practice in order to improve human well-being globally.

Conclusions

The chapters in *Feminist Methodologies for International Relations* emphasize that feminist IR is a collective, open, and ongoing project in which dialogue and diversity are seen as significant strengths. We have deliberately presented a variety of approaches to methodology and examples of methods in this collection. We hope that this range inspires the reader to pick and choose from the methods presented here so as to develop creatively an appropriate methodology and method to address her IR research questions. Rather than devising new categories to determine what feminist IR or feminist methodology *is*, the volume makes explicit the methodological contributions of feminist IR that, taken collectively, are both multi-voiced and self-reflective.

Part 1

Methodological conversations between feminist and non-feminist IR

What do feminist methodologies offer the field of IR and the study of global politics? The first set of contributions, by Ann Tickner, Marysia Zalewski, and Laurel Weldon, respond to (and resist) this question. They consider the place, meaning, value, and politics of feminist methodologies in the field of IR. Without offering conclusive answers, the chapters in this section evoke crucial questions about the centrality of methodology to the production of all forms of knowledge.

2 Feminism meets International Relations: some methodological issues

J. Ann Tickner

Feminist approaches entered the discipline of International Relations (IR) at the end of the 1980s, about the same time as the "third debate," or the beginning of what has been called a "postpositivist era" (Lapid 1989). Postpositivism, which includes a variety of approaches such as critical theory, historical sociology and postmodernism, challenged the social scientific methodologies that had dominated the discipline, particularly in the United States. Most IR feminists situate themselves on the postpositivist side of the third debate.[1] Seeing theory as constitutive of reality and conscious of how ideas help shape the world, many IR feminists, together with scholars in other critical approaches, have challenged the social scientific foundations of the field.[2] Most IR feminist empirical research, which took off in the mid-1990s, has not followed the social scientific path – formulating hypotheses and providing evidence that can be used to test, falsify, or validate them. With some exceptions, IR feminists have employed a variety of methods, most of which would fall within postpositivist methodological frameworks.[3]

An earlier, but substantially different, version of this chapter appeared in *International Studies Quarterly* 49, 1 (2005) under the title "What is Your Research Program? Some Feminist Answers to International Relations Methodological Questions."

[1] I am defining social scientific methodologies as methodologies committed to causality, hypothesis testing, and replicability. Postpositivism challenges social scientific claims that the social world is amenable to the kinds of regularities that can be explained by using causal analysis with tools borrowed from the natural sciences, and that the way to determine the truth of statements is by appealing to neutral facts. "Debate" is probably a misnomer. Social scientific methodologies continue to dominate – in the United States at least – and there has been little real engagement between these very different methodological approaches.

[2] While there is a large transdisciplinary literature on gender issues in global politics, I have chosen to focus on feminist interventions in, and critiques of, the discipline of IR.

[3] There is a body of IR research on gender and women that does use conventional social scientific methodology, although not all of these authors would necessarily define themselves as feminists in the epistemological sense. There have been studies of the effect of gender equality on public opinion, on foreign policy, and on violence, as well as studies of the effect of the gender gap in voting on foreign policy and the use of force. See, for

In this chapter, I undertake three tasks related to IR feminists' methodological preferences with particular emphasis on the state and its security seeking practices. I choose to focus on the state because it is the central unit of analysis in IR, and on security because it is an issue at the core of the discipline. I suggest how these methodological preferences differ from conventional social scientific frameworks. First, I elaborate on four distinctive perspectives of feminist methodology, which I construct by drawing on the work of feminists in the disciplines of sociology, philosophy, history, political theory, and anthropology, disciplines in which feminism has had a longer history than in IR, a history which includes rich and diverse literatures on methodological issues. I distinguish between the term "methodology," a theory and analysis of how research does or should proceed, and "method," a technique for gathering and analyzing evidence (Harding 1987b: 2–3).[4] Following Harding, I argue that there is no unique feminist research method; feminists have drawn upon a variety of methods, including ethnography, statistical research, survey research, cross-cultural research, philosophical argument, discourse analysis, and case study. What makes feminist research unique, however, is a distinctive methodological perspective or framework which fundamentally challenges the often unseen androcentric or masculine biases in the way that knowledge has traditionally been constructed in all the disciplines. I then discuss two examples of IR feminist empirical scholarship which exemplify these methodological perspectives and which are asking questions about the state and its security-seeking practices.[5] As mentioned earlier, few IR feminists have used social scientific methodologies or quantitative methods. Drawing on the previous methodological discussion and the analysis of my chosen studies, the third part of the chapter offers some observations on the problems that feminists have raised with respect to the use of statistics

---

examples, Gallagher 1993; Brandes 1994; Tessler and Warriner 1997; Caprioli 2000; Caprioli and Boyer 2001; and Eichenberg 2003. Caprioli and Boyer (2001) cite a number of studies from political science, business, communications, and psychology as examples of feminist scholarship that uses social scientific methodology. It is, of course, true that feminists from a variety of disciplines have used conventional scientific methodology. However, this is not the methodology used by a majority of IR feminists, much of whose work fits more closely with the methodological perspectives that I discuss in this chapter.

[4] Within what I have defined as "method," discussions do take place of technique-specific methodological assumptions.

[5] Following *The American Heritage Dictionary* (third ed., 1994), I define "empirical" as meaning "guided by practical experience and not theory." I distinguish it from "empiricism," which the dictionary defines as "employment of empirical methods as in science." Feminists, whose methodological perspectives I am describing, generally reject empiricism.

and quantitative methods as well as some of the potential value that statistical indicators might have if used with feminist sensibilities.

Feminist perspectives on methodology

Feminists claim no single standard of methodological correctness or "feminist way" to do research (Reinharz 1992: 243); nor do they see it as desirable to construct one. Many describe their research as a journey, or an archeological dig, that draws on different methods or tools appropriate to the goals of the task at hand, or the questions asked, rather than on any prior methodological commitment more typical of IR social science (Reinharz 1992: 211; Charlesworth 1994: 6; Jayaratne and Stewart 1991: 102; Sylvester 2002). Feminist knowledge-building is an ongoing process, tentative and emergent; feminists frequently describe knowledge-building as emerging through conversation with texts, research subjects, or data (Reinharz 1992: 230).[6] Many feminist scholars prefer to use the term "epistemological *perspective*" rather than "methodology" to indicate the research goals and orientation of an ongoing project, the aim of which is to challenge and rethink what is claimed to be "knowledge," from the perspectives of women's lives (Reinharz 1992: 241). Feminist scholars emphasize the challenge to and estrangement from conventional knowledge-building caused by the tension of being inside and outside one's discipline at the same time. Given that feminist knowledge has emerged from a deep skepticism about knowledge which claims to be universal and objective but which is, in reality, knowledge based on men's lives, such knowledge is constructed simultaneously out of disciplinary frameworks and feminist criticisms of these disciplines.[7] Its goal is nothing less than to transform these disciplinary frameworks and the knowledge to which they contribute. Feminist inquiry is a dialectical process – listening to women and understanding how the subjective meanings they attach to their lived experiences are so often at variance with meanings internalized from society at large (Nielsen 1990: 26). Much of feminist scholarship is both transdisciplinary and avowedly political; it has explored and sought to understand the unequal gender

---

[6] In her biography of biologist Barbara McClintock, Evelyn Fox Keller describes McClintock's method for researching the transmutation of corn as letting the plants speak rather than trying to impose an answer. Keller talks about McClintock's "passion for difference," which she emphasizes over looking for similarities in her data (Keller 1983). This tolerance and, indeed, preference for ambiguity is in sharp contrast with conventional social science.

[7] It is to this skepticism that Reinharz (1992) refers when she suggests that feminists have a distinct "perspective" on existing methods rather than using *a distinct* feminist "method."

hierarchies, as well as other hierarchies of power, which exist in all societies, and their effects on the subordination of women and other disempowered people with the goal of changing them.[8]

I shall now elaborate on four methodological perspectives which guide much of feminist research: a deep concern with which research questions get asked and why; the goal of designing research that is useful to women (and also to men) and is both less biased and more universal than conventional research; the centrality of questions of reflexivity and the subjectivity of the researcher; and a commitment to knowledge as emancipation.[9]

Feminist research asks feminist questions

According to Sandra Harding, traditional social science has typically asked questions about nature and social life that certain (usually privileged) men want answered (Harding 1987b: 6). In her later work, Harding traces the relationship between the development of modern western science and the history of European colonial expansion. Challenging the claim to value-neutrality of modern science with respect to the questions it has asked, she argues that European voyages of discovery went hand in hand with the development of modern science and technology – Europeans who were colonizing the world needed to know about winds, tides, maps, and navigation as well as botany, the construction of ships, firearms, and survival in harsh environments. Research topics were chosen, not because they were intellectually interesting, but in order to solve colonialism's everyday problems. Harding also examines and supports the validity of non-western scientific traditions, such as those originating in China, India, Africa, and the pre-Colombian Americas, thereby offering support for post-Kuhnian and post-colonial claims that there is no one "true" scientific method. While Harding is not arguing for cognitive relativism (since she does not believe that all claims that science makes are equally accurate), she does argue that other cultures have used different methods and assumptions

---

[8] "Third-wave feminism," feminism which began in the early 1990s and which was reacting against treating "woman" as an essentialized universal category, has emphasized the different positionality of women according to class, race, culture, and geographical location. IR feminists who emphasize difference and this type of intersectionality might reject attempts to generalize about knowledge from women's lives as discussed in this chapter.

[9] The following section relies heavily on Harding 1987; Fonow and Cook 1991a; and Bloom 1998; but it is striking to note the extent to which much of the work on feminist methodology and feminist research implicitly or explicitly raises these same issues.

about the world to arrive at equally plausible explanations (Harding 1998: 39–54).

In a different context, Harding argues that conventional western scientific progress is judged not on the merit of the questions that are asked but on how questions are answered. It is not in the origin of the scientific problem or hypothesis, but rather in the testing of hypotheses or the "logic of scientific inquiry," that we look to judge the success of science (Harding 1987: 7). Feminists counter that *the questions that are asked* – or, more importantly, *those that are not asked* – are as determinative of the adequacy of the project as any answers we can discover.

The questions that IR has asked since the discipline was founded have typically been about the behavior of states, particularly powerful states and their security-seeking behavior, given an anarchical international environment. Much of the scholarship in international political economy and international institutions has also focused on the behavior of the great powers and their potential, or lack thereof, for international cooperation. These questions are of particular importance for the foreign policy interests of the most powerful states.

Most IR feminists have asked very different questions. While they may seek to understand state behavior, they do so in the context of asking why, in so many parts of the world, women remain so fundamentally disempowered in matters of foreign and military policy. Rather than speculate on the hypothetical question whether women *might* be more peaceful than men as foreign policymakers, they have concentrated on the more immediate problem of why there are *so few* women in positions of power.[10] On issues of war and peace, feminists have asked why wars have been predominantly fought by men and how gendered structures of masculinity and femininity have legitimated war and militarism for both women and men;[11] they have also investigated the problematic essentialized association of women with peace, an association which, many believe, disempowers both women and peace (Sylvester 1987; Tickner 2001: 59). Rather than uncritically assume the state as a given unit of analysis, feminists have investigated the constitutive features of "gendered states" and their implications for the militarization of women's

---

[10] Speculation on this issue was undertaken by Francis Fukuyama (1998). It is a question frequently asked of IR feminists (see Tickner 1997). Feminists claim that such speculation is a distraction from the real issues facing women. For a critique of Fukuyama's conservative conclusions, which were that men should be kept in power in western democracies in order to be able to stand up to security threats from other parts of the world, see Tickner 1999.

[11] As Joshua Goldstein (2001) claims, it is remarkable how many books have been written on war and how few of them have asked why wars are fought predominantly by men.

(and men's) lives (Peterson 1992a; Enloe 2000). But the basic question that has most concerned IR feminists is why, in just about all societies, women are disadvantaged, politically, socially, and economically, relative to men, and to what extent this is due to international politics and the global economy. Conversely, they have also asked in what ways these hierarchical gendered structures of inequality may actually support the international system of states and contribute to the unevenly distributed wealth and resources of the global capitalist economy.

Feminist questions are challenging the core assumptions of the discipline and deconstructing its central concepts. Feminists have sought to better understand a neglected but constitutive feature of war – why it has been primarily a male activity, and what the causal and constitutive implications of this are for women's political roles, given that they have been constructed as a "protected" category. They have investigated the continuing legitimation of war itself though appeals to traditional notions of masculinity and femininity. Working from the discovery of the gendered biases in state-centric security thinking, they have redefined the meaning of (in)security to include the effects of structural inequalities of race, class, and gender. Similarly, on the bases of theoretical critiques of the gendered political uses of the public/private distinction, they have rearticulated the meaning of democracy to include the participation of individuals in all the political and economic processes that affect their daily lives (Ackerly 2000: 178– 203). While not rejecting in principle the use of quantitative data, feminists have recognized how past behavioral realities have been publicly constituted in state-generated indicators in biased, gendered ways, using data that do not adequately reflect the reality of women's lives and the unequal structures of power within which they are situated. For this reason they have relied more on hermeneutic, historical, narrative, and case study methodological orientations rather than on causal analysis of unproblematically defined empirical patterns. Importantly, feminists use gender as a socially constructed and variable category of analysis to investigate these power dynamics and gender hierarchies. They have suggested that gender inequality, as well as other social relations of domination and subordination, has been among the fundamental building blocks on which, to varying extents, the publicly recognized features of states, their security relationships, and the global economy have been constructed and on which they continue to operate to varying degrees.

Rather than working from an ontology that depicts states as individualistic autonomous actors – an ontology typical of social science perspectives in IR and of liberal thinking more generally – feminists start from an ontology of social relations in which individuals are embedded in, and

constituted by, historically unequal political, economic, and social structures. Unlike social scientific IR, which has drawn on models from
economics and the natural sciences to explain the behavior of states
in the international system, IR feminists have used sociological analyses
that start with individuals and the hierarchical social relations in which
their lives are situated.[12] While social scientific IR has been quite system-
determined or state-focused, feminist understandings of state behavior
frequently start from below the state level – with the lives of connected
individuals. Whereas much of IR is focused on describing and explaining
the behavior of states, feminists are motivated by the goal of investigating the lives of women within states or international structures in
order to change them.

Use women's experiences to design research that is useful to women

A shared assumption of feminist research is that women's lives are
important (Reinharz 1992: 241). "Making the invisible visible, bringing
the margin to the center, rendering the trivial important, putting the
spotlight on women as competent actors, understanding women as
subjects in their own right rather than objects for men – all continue to
be elements of feminist research" (Reinharz 1992: 248). Too often
women's experiences have been deemed trivial, or important only in so
far as they relate to the experiences of men and the questions they
typically ask.

An important commitment of feminist methodology is that knowledge
must be built and analyzed in a way that can be used by women to
change whatever oppressive conditions they face. When choosing a
research topic feminists frequently ask what potential it has to improve
women's lives (Jayaratne and Stewart 1991: 101). This means that
research must be designed to provide a vision of the future as well as a
structural picture of the present (Cook and Fonow [1986] 1990: 80).
Feminists study the routine aspects of everyday life that help sustain
gender inequality; they acknowledge the pervasive influence of gender
and acknowledge that what has passed as knowledge about human
behavior is, in fact, frequently knowledge about male behavior (Cook
and Fonow [1986] 1990: 73). Feminists claim that what is called
"common sense" is, in reality, knowledge derived from experiences of
men's lives, usually privileged men. Importantly, "male behavior" and

---

[12] This evokes a spatial image of a network of connected individuals, rather than states as
billiard balls or autonomous actors (Prügl 1999: 147).

"men's lives" are highly dependent on women and other subordinate groups playing all kinds of supportive roles in these lives and behind this behavior; for if there were only (privileged) men, their lives would surely be different. Designing research useful to women involves first deconstructing previous knowledge based on these androcentric assumptions.

Joyce Nielsen suggests that feminist research represents a paradigm shift in the Kuhnian sense in that it sees women, rather than just men, as both the subject matter and creators of knowledge. This leads to anomalies or observations that do not fit received theory. For example, the periodization of history and our understanding of the timing of progressive moments do not always fit with periods that saw progress for women (Nielsen 1990: 19–21). Nielsen outlines the way in which androcentric theories have been used to explain the origins of human society. In the focus on "man the hunter," man's (*sic*) origins were associated with productive rather than reproductive tasks. Men were seen as responsible for organizing human life, and women's roles as gatherers and reproducers were completely ignored. Nielsen claims that these partial stories are not good science; it follows, therefore, that objectivity depends on the positionality of the researcher as much as on the method used, a claim that contradicts the depiction of science as a foolproof procedure that relies on observation to test theories and hypotheses about the world (Nielsen 1990: 16–18). To this end, Sandra Harding claims that a distinctive feature of feminist research is that it uses women's experiences as an indicator of the "reality" against which conventional hypotheses are tested and unconventional questions are formulated (Harding 1987: 7). Feminists have also claimed that knowledge based on the standpoint of women's lives, particularly marginalized women, leads to more robust objectivity, not only because it broadens the base from which we derive knowledge, but also because the perspectives of "outsiders" or marginalized people may reveal aspects of reality obscured by more orthodox approaches to knowledge-building.[13]

Designing IR research of use to women involves considerable paradigm shifts. While the role of women as reproducers, caregivers, and unpaid workers has been largely ignored in conventional economic analysis, it is central to feminist concerns. Marilyn Waring has documented how national income data ignore reproductive and caring tasks. She describes the daily routine of a girl in Zimbabwe who works at household tasks from 4am to 9pm but who is officially classified as

---

[13] For an elaboration on this idea as it pertains to black feminist thought, see Collins 1991: 36. Collins defines black feminist intellectuals as "outsiders within."

"economically inactive" or "unoccupied" (Waring 1988: 15–16). Yet national income data, which ignore these reproductive and caring tasks, are used by political elites to make public policy. IR feminists have highlighted the role of domestic servants and home workers; although, since the Industrial Revolution, the home has been defined as a feminine space devoid of work, feminists have demonstrated how women in all their various productive and reproductive roles are crucial to the main-tenance of the global capitalist economy (Chin 1998; Prügl 1999). Making visible that which was previously invisible has led IR feminists to investigate military prostitution and rape as tools of war and instru-ments of state policy (Moon 1997; Enloe 2000). This leads not only to redefinitions of the meaning of security but also to an understanding of how the security of the state and the prosperity of the global economy are frequently dependent on the insecurity of certain individuals', often women's, lives. In bringing to light these multiple experiences of women's lives, feminist researchers also claim that the research they conduct cannot and should not be separated from their identities as researchers.

Reflexivity

As Sandra Harding has claimed, most feminist research insists that the inquirer be placed on the same critical plane as the subject matter. "Only in this way can we hope to produce understandings and explan-ations which are free of distortion from the unexamined beliefs of social scientists themselves" (Harding 1987: 9). In contrast to conventional social scientific methods, acknowledging the subjective element in one's analysis, which exists in all social science research, actually in-creases the objectivity of the research. Similarly, Mary Margaret Cook and Judith Fonow reject the assumption that maintaining a gap be-tween the researcher and the research subject produces more valid knowledge; rather, they advocate a participatory research strategy that emphasizes a dialectic between the researcher and the researched throughout the project (Cook and Fonow [1986] 1990: 76). Joyce Nielsen talks about knowledge creation as a dialogic process that re-quires a context of equality and the involvement of the researcher in the lives of the people she studies (Nielsen 1990: 30). Feminists also struggle with the issue of power differentials between the researcher and her subjects.

What Reinharz refers to as a "reflexive attitude" has developed in reaction to androcentric research with its claims to value neutrality. Personal experience is considered an asset for feminist research; many feminist researchers describe in their texts how they have been motivated to conduct projects that stem from their own lives and personal experiences. Often the researcher will reflect on what she has learnt during the research process, on her "identification" with the research subjects, and on the personal traumas and difficulties that the research may have involved. In her research on the (in)security of Mayan women in Guatemala, Maria Stern reflects on her ethical obligation to her research subjects and her attempts to co-create a text in which the narrators can claim authorship of their own stories. This rewriting of (in)security using the voices of marginalized lives constitutes a political act which can challenge dominant and oppressive ways of documenting these lives (M. Stern 2001: 71). Many feminists who conduct interview research acknowledge an intellectual debt to British sociologist Ann Oakley, who proposed "a feminist ethic of commitment and egalitarianism in contrast with the scientific ethic of detachment and role differentiation between researcher and subject" (Reinharz 1992: 27; see also Bloom 1998). Whereas personal experience is thought by conventional social science to contaminate a project's objectivity, feminists believe one's own awareness of one's own personal position in the research process to be a corrective to "pseudo-objectivity." Rather than seeing it as bias, they see it as a necessary explanation of the researcher's standpoint which serves to strengthen the standards of objectivity, resulting in what Sandra Harding has called "strong objectivity" or "robust reflexivity" (Reinharz 1992: 258; Harding 1991: 142; Harding 1998: 189). Many feminists also believe in the necessity of continual reflection on and critical scrutiny of one's own methods throughout the research project, allowing for the possibility that the researcher may make methodological adjustments along the way (Ackerly 2000). For feminists, one of the primary goals of this commitment to experiential and reflexive knowledge-building has been the hope that their research project might contribute to the improvement of women's lives, at least in part through the empowerment of their research subjects.

Knowledge as emancipation

"Feminism supports the proposition that women should transform themselves and the world" (Soares et al. quoted in Ackerly 2000: 198). Since many feminists do not believe that it is possible to separate thought from action, and knowledge from practice, they claim that feminist research cannot be separated from the historical movement for the improvement of women's lives out of which it emerged (Mies 1991: 64). The aim of much feminist research has been the empowerment of women; many feminists believe that the researcher must be actively engaged in political struggle and be aware of the policy implications of her work. Feminist scholarship is inherently linked to action and social change (Reinharz 1992: 175). To this end, feminism focuses on uncovering "practical knowledge" from people's everyday lives. This type of knowledge-building has parallels with Stephen Toulmin's description of participatory action research. Toulmin contrasts participatory action research, which he claims grows out of Aristotelian ethics and practical reasoning, with what he terms the High Science model with its Platonic origins, a model that is closer to social scientific IR. The product of participatory action research is the creation of practical knowledge with the emphasis on the improvement of practice rather than of theory. Toulmin sees the disciplines closest to this type of research as being history and anthropology, with their traditions of participant observation that grows out of local action, the goal of which is changing the situation (Toulmin 1996).

Feminists frequently engage in participant observation. They are generally suspicious of Cartesian ways of knowing, or the High Science model, which depicts human subjects as solitary and self-subsistent and where knowledge is obtained through measurement rather than sympathy. Feminists tend to believe that emotion and intellect are mutually constitutive and sustaining rather than oppositional forces in the construction of knowledge (Code 1991: 47). Maria Mies contrasts feminist research, which she claims takes place directly within life's processes, with what she calls an alienated concept of empiricism where "research objects" have been detached from their real-life surroundings and broken down into their constituent parts (Mies 1991: 66). She describes her research among rural women workers of Nalgonda, India, as sharing as far as possible their living conditions and allowing them to carry out their own research on the researchers. Her findings were translated into Telugu so that they could be used for betterment of the society. Mies claims that this reciprocal exchange of experiences gave these women so much courage that they could tackle problems of sexual violence in new ways and come up with different solutions, thereby getting beyond their victim status (Mies 1991: 73; see also Ackerly 2000: ch.1). She claims that she would never have gained these insights about how these practical solutions emerged from her project by using conventional research methods. While social science IR would rightly claim that its knowledge-building is a contribution to the betterment of society, the research model to which it aspires is to remain detached and, to the greatest extent possible, value-free and separate from political action.

Evidence of these methodological perspectives in feminist IR

While most of these methodological predispositions that I have outlined are drawn from the work of scholars in disciplines, such as anthropology and sociology, whose subject matter is focused on studying human social relations rather than statist international politics, it is, nevertheless, striking the degree to which many IR feminists have used similar methods and expressed similar methodological sensibilities. Starting their research from women's lives has taken IR feminists well outside the normal boundaries of the IR discipline.

With this background in mind, I shall now discuss two "second-generation" feminist IR texts, exploring their methodological orientations as well as the research methods they use.[14] While I realize that I cannot do justice here to a very rich and diverse literature, I have chosen these two as exemplary of the kind of methodological orientation I have outlined and because each is concerned with theorizing the state and its security-seeking practices. Katharine Moon's *Sex Among Allies* deals with national security policy, an issue central to IR, but through the lens of military prostitution, a subject not normally considered part of IR. Christine Chin's *In Service and Servitude* deals with issues of development and global political economy, but it does so through an examination of the lives of female domestic servants in Malaysia and state policies with respect to regulating their lives.[15] Both these scholars start their research from the lives of some of the most marginalized, disempowered women and demonstrate how their lives and work impact on, and are impacted by, national security and the global economy. Both use ethnographic methods and participant observation to conduct in-depth case studies, methods not typical of IR. Both express the hope that their research will help to improve the lives of the women they study as well as expose hierarchical exploitative social structures upon which states and their security policies are built.[16]

---

[14] "Second-generation" is a term that has come to be used in feminist IR to refer to empirical case studies that have followed from "first-generation" feminist critiques of IR theory which challenged the assumptions, concepts, and methodologies of the IR discipline from feminist perspectives. Second-generation feminist IR has also undertaken empirical research on men and masculinity. See, for example, Hooper 2001 and True 2002.

[15] I take one study which focuses on security and one which focuses on international political economy (IPE). The majority of IR feminist research has focused on IPE. See, for example, Prügl 1999; Marchand and Runyan 2000; and Peterson 2003.

[16] As this volume demonstrates, second-generation feminist research uses a wide variety of methods. Not all of it is dependent on studying women in local settings.

Sex Among Allies

In *Sex Among Allies*, Katharine Moon takes up a little-examined subject and one not normally considered part of the discipline of International Relations: prostitution camps around US military bases in the Republic of Korea during the early 1970s. She argues that the cleanup of these camps by the Korean government, which involved imposing health standards on and monitoring of women prostitutes, was directly related to establishing a more hospitable environment for American troops at a time when the United States was in the process of pulling its troops out of Korea as part of the strategy, articulated in the Nixon Doctrine, to place more of the US security burden on regional allies. Through an examination of relevant United States and Republic of Korea government documents and interviews with government officials and military personnel in both states, Moon links efforts to certify the health of prostitutes to policy discussions between the two states about the retention of military bases at the highest level. The challenge for Moon is to show how prostitution, a private issue normally considered outside the boundaries of international politics, is linked to national security and foreign policy. In so doing, she asks questions not normally asked in IR, such as: what factors helped create and maintain military prostitution, and for what ends? She also questions the accepted boundaries that separate private sexual relations from politics among nations and shows how prostitution can be a matter of concern in international politics and a bargaining tool for two alliance partners who were vastly unequal in conventional military power (Moon 1997: 13). Moon demonstrates how private relations among people and foreign relations between governments inform and are informed by each other (Moon 1997: 2).[17]

Moon's analysis leads her to rethink the meaning of national security. Claiming that it was the desire of the Korean government to make a better environment for American troops, rather than an effort to improve the conditions under which prostitutes lived and worked, that motivated the government to improve the conditions of the camps, Moon demonstrates how the government's weakness at the international level *vis-à-vis* the United States caused it to impose authoritarian and sexist control at the domestic level. Moon's evidence supports the feminist claim that the security of the state is often built on the insecurity of its

---

[17] Moon describes her work as being at the intersection of IR and comparative politics. In a personal observation she noted that her research has been more widely recognized in comparative politics. She attributes this to the fact that comparative politics asks questions different from those asked by IR.

most vulnerable populations and their unequal relationships with others, in this case on the lives of its most impoverished and marginalized women. While many of these women felt betrayed by the Korean government and its national security policies, ironically many of them saw the state as their only possible protector against the violence they suffered at the hands of US soldiers. They believed that the lack of protection was tied to the weakness of their own state.[18] Moon concludes that the women saw national sovereignty, or the ability to stand up to the United States, as a means to empower their own lives (Moon 1997: 158). In their eyes, Korea had never been treated as a sovereign state by the United States or other big powers; international institutions were deemed even more distant and difficult to deal with. Moon's study challenges the conventional meaning of national (in)security; it also challenges us to think about how the relational identities of states are constituted and how often policies deemed necessary for national security can cause insecurity for certain citizens.

Moon's choice of research topic carried considerable personal risk. In reflecting on her role as researcher, Moon speaks of how her frequenting of shanty towns during her research meant that she herself became morally suspect. She was cautioned about publishing her work, lest people would question her moral character. Getting women to speak was difficult and Moon frequently had to use intermediaries because of the feeling of shame that talking about their experiences evoked in many of these women. Many of them had little concept about the structure of a research interview and frequently expressed the view that their opinions were unimportant and not worth recording. Moon states that she did not aim to provide likely-to-be-distorted statistical evidence but to show, through narrating the women's lives, how heavily involved they were in US – Korean relations and thus of importance to international politics. While she aims to say something new about state security practices and international politics, one of her principal goals is to give voice to people who were not considered having anything worthwhile to say, thereby helping to improve their lives. She talks of her work as helping to lift the

---

[18] Moon notes that this finding is quite at odds with feminist suspicions of the state, which she dates back to Virginia Woolf's famous indictment of the state's role in war-making. Moon claims that Woolf's indictment is quite middle-class and western. Those who challenge sovereignty and talk about being world citizens live in wealthy countries and are socially, intellectually, and economically empowered enough to talk about opting out of the state (Moon 1997: 158). The high level of awareness of Moon's subjects about the national security policies of the Korean state supports the claim that marginalized people have a deep level of understanding of the privileged world of which they are not a part. See footnote 13.

curtains of invisibility of these women's lives and to "offer these pages as a passageway for their own voices," thus allowing them to construct their own identities rather than having them imposed on them by societal norms and taken-for-granted definitions – definitions that are often imposed when conventional data are used (Moon 1997: 2). Moon concludes that the expansion of the definition of political actor to include individuals without significant resources or control over issues – those not normally defined as actors by IR – can challenge governments' claim to their exclusive definitions of national interest and national security (Moon 1997: 160).

In service and servitude

Christine Chin's text examines the importation of Filipina and Indonesian female domestic workers into Malaysia, beginning in the 1970s, and how their labor supported a Malaysian modernization project based on an export-led development model in the context of the neoliberal global economy. Chin asserts that the global expansion of neoliberalism has gone hand-in-hand with the free trade in migrant female domestic labor throughout the world. She asks two basic questions of her study, both of which are linked to women's lives. First, why is unlegislated domestic service, an essentially premodern social institution with all its attendant hardships, increasingly prevalent in the context of constructing a modern developed society by way of export-led development? And second, why is there an absence of public concern regarding the less-than-human conditions in which some domestic servants work (Chin 1998: 4)? To answer these questions, Chin rejects a "problem-solving" approach, which, she claims, would focus on explaining foreign female domestic labor as a consequence of wage differentials between the labor-sending and labor-receiving countries; instead, she adopts what she terms a critical interdisciplinary approach.[19] According to Chin, problem-solving lacks historicity and divides social life into discrete, mutually exclusive dimensions and levels which have little bearing on one another. Chin's preference for a critically oriented methodology is based on her desire to examine the relationship between domestic service and the developmental state and its involvement with all levels of society from

---

[19] Chin is following Robert Cox's famous distinction between problem-solving theory (which, according to Cox, accepts the prevailing order as its framework), and critical theory, which stands apart from that order and asks how it came about, with the goal of changing it. See Cox 1981: 129–30.

the household to the transnational, the goal of which is to expose power relations with the intention of changing them (Chin 1998: 5).

Chin asks how is it that paid domestic reproductive labor, usually performed by women, supports and legitimizes the late twentieth-century developmental state. As she notes, there has been much work on the Asian "developmental state" and its mechanisms of coercive power, but little on how the state has used policies that regulate transnational migrant domestic labor as part of this coercive strategy. Coming out of a Gramscian framework, Chin claims that the developmental state is not neutral but an expression of class, ethnic, racial, and gender-based power, which it exercises through both coercion and cooptation of forces that could challenge it. The state's involvement in regulating domestic service and policing domestic workers in the name of maintaining social order is not just a personal, private issue but one that serves this goal, as the state can thereby provide the good life for certain of its (middle-class) citizens through repressing others. Since proof of marriage and children is necessary in order for middle-class families to be eligible for foreign domestic workers, domestic service is an institution through which the state has normalized the middle-class adoption of the nuclear family (Chin 1998: 198). Winning support of the middle class family by promoting policies that support materialist consumption, including the paid labor of domestic servants, has helped to lessen ethnic divisions in Malaysia and increased loyalty to the state and hence its security.

Chin questions the assumption, implicit in economic theory, that capitalism is the natural order of life; she claims that critical analysis is designed to deconstruct this objective world and reveal the unequal distribution and exercise of power that inheres in and continues to constitute social relations, institutions, and structures (Chin 1998: 17–18). Thus, the questions that Chin asks in her research are primarily constitutive rather than causal. She rejects causal answers that rely solely on economic analysis of supply and demand about why the flow of foreign domestic servants into Malaysia in the 1970s and 1980s increased, in favor of answers that examine the constitution of the developmental state as a coercive structure that gains its legitimacy through seeking support of the middle classes for its export-oriented development at the expense of poor women's lives. It is these poor women's lives that remain at the center of her research and concern.

Chin is explicit in positioning herself in the context of her work. She tells us that she came to her study through her own background, which was that of an "upper class Malaysian Chinese extended family . . . whose family members were served twenty-four hours a day by nannies, housemaids and cooks" (Chin 1998: xi). Having been motivated to do this research after witnessing the abuse of a neighbor's Filipina servant, Chin lived in various neighborhoods of Kuala Lumpur, where she could observe working conditions and where she heard many stories of mistreatment and abuse; she spoke with activists who counseled these workers and began to reflect on her own privileged status and the tensions between her class status and being an academic researcher. She had to confront the relationship between domestic service and the political economy of development; a relationship made irrelevant by the dominant discursive practices that characterized a western, mainstream-based education on global politics.

Chin's research grew out of her reflection on her own privileged status, her witnessing of the exploitation of those she studied, and her determination to do something about it. She observed how her subjects' everyday lives helped shape decision-making at the national level as well as how their lives were affected by transnational forces beyond their control (Chin 1998: 22). While many of the employers with whom she spoke did not see how the research could be of intellectual interest, some of the workers asked Chin to publish her work so that the world could know about the harsh conditions under which they worked and lived. Chin acknowledges that coming to know this world forced her to rethink the relationship between theory and practice (Chin 1998: xvii). She also speaks of constructing her own identity as a scholar as the interviewing stage of the project progressed. Questioning "common sense," Chin suggests that the ultimate objective of the study is to help ascertain potentialities for emancipation from the constraints of seemingly natural social relations, institutions, and structures (Chin 1998: 27). She defines her project as emancipatory also insofar as it attempts to undo received epistemological boundaries and "social data" collection practices that ignore or silence marginalized voices and fail to present social change in all its complexities (Chin 1998: 29).

Chin describes her research method as "a nonpositivist manner of recovering and generating knowledge." She contrasts this with feminist empiricism, which, as discussed earlier, may correct for certain androcentric biases but risks distilling the complexities of social life into a series of hypotheses that can be labeled as truth (Chin 1998: 20). While acknowledging the usefulness of attitudinal surveys, Chin worries that they may constrain an understanding of the complexities of various forces that shape the performance and consumption of reproductive labor. Chin conducted her research through archival analysis and open-ended interviews, relying on fieldwork notes as evidence. This narrative method allowed Chin's subjects, like Moon's, to recount their lives in their own words and speak about any issue they pleased, thereby constructing their own identities and challenging identities that had been constructed by others. Chin reflects critically on the interview process as it proceeds; she notes how frequently employers would try to coopt her by establishing a common relationship. She also reflects on the need to be continually questioning what she had previously taken for granted in everyday life, lending support to the feminist position that there is no social reality out there independent of the observer.

Like many IR feminists doing empirical research, Chin and Moon have rejected basic social science methodology in favor of qualitative (single) case studies which rely on more interpretive methodologies.[20] They use open-ended ethnographic research that relies on narrative accounts of the lives of women at the margins of society, accounts which they prefer over statistical analysis of government-generated data. In that data on national security, development, and modernization, the experiences which Chin and Moon documented are barely reflected. Indeed, no state agency could be convinced to acknowledge the systematic existence of such problems associated with prostitution and the maltreatment of women, let alone collect and publish comparable data on their magnitude. With the goal of making certain women's lives more visible, Chin and Moon begin their analysis at the micro level and study issues not normally considered part of IR. Looking for meaningful characterizations rather than causes, they have sought to understand the foreign policies of states and international politics more generally through the telling of stories of lives rendered insecure by states striving to increase their own security or wealth. Moon documents the Republic of Korea's authoritarian behavior with respect to certain of its citizens as a necessary response to its weak and dependent position *vis-à-vis* the United States. Looking to promote internal stability and economic growth, Malaysia sought to increase the material welfare of certain of its citizens, including certain middle-class women, at the expense of the security of other women's lives. These are nuanced findings that could not be discovered through the use of conventional indicators.

Both Chin and Moon deny the possibility of a reality independent of the researcher, and both attempt to have their research subjects claim their own identities through the telling of their own stories. They see this as a way of rejecting the identities that society has bestowed upon these women, identities that often form the basis of state policies that may render their lives more insecure. Both authors use gender as a category of analysis to help them understand how individuals, families,

---

[20] Of course, qualitative case studies are also an important part of social scientific IR.

states, societies, and the international system are constituted through, and in resistance against, hierarchical and often oppressive power relations. While neither of them make specific reference to the literature on methodology that I outlined in Part I, the degree to which their methodological sensitivities parallel these feminist research practices is striking.[21]

Feminist reservations about quantitative research

These two cases, as with most feminist IR research, have avoided quantitative methods. As my case studies have demonstrated, fitting women and other marginalized people into methodologically conventional quantitative frameworks has been problematic. Many of the experiences of women's lives have not yet been documented or analyzed, either within social science disciplines or by states. The choices that states make about which data to collect is a political act. Traditional ways in which data are collected and analyzed do not lend themselves to answering many of the questions that feminists raise. The data that are available to scholars and, more importantly, the data that are not, determine which research questions get asked and how they are answered. Marilyn Waring describes how national accounting systems have been shaped and reshaped to help states frame their national security policies – specifically to understand how to pay for wars.[22] In national accounting systems no value is attached to the environment, to unpaid work, to the reproduction of human life, or to its maintenance or care, tasks generally undertaken by women (Waring 1988: 3–4). Political decisions are made on the basis of data that policy elites choose to collect (Waring 1988: 302). Waring goes on to assert that, under the guise of value-free science, the economics of accounting has constructed a reality which believes that "value" results only when (predominantly) men interact with the marketplace (Waring 1988: 17– 18).

Maria Mies also argues that quantitative research methods are instruments for structuring reality in certain ways; she claims that she is not against every form of statistics but rather against its claim to have a monopoly on accurately describing the world. Statistical procedures serve to legitimize and universalize certain power relations because they

---

[21] The one exception is that Chin does make reference to Sandra Harding's work on methodology.

[22] Waring makes reference to a claim by statistical historians Joseph Duncan and William Shelton that a 1941 paper entitled "Measuring National Income as Affected by War," by Milton Gilbert, was the first clear, published statement of the term "Gross National Product" (GNP) (Waring 1988: 55).

give a "stamp of truth" to the definitions upon which they are based (Mies 1991: 67).[23] For example, the term "male head of household" came out of a definition of a traditional, western, middle-class, patriarchal family, but does not correspond with present reality, given that a majority of women either work in the waged sector to supplement family income or are themselves heads of households. However, it is a term that has been used, either explicitly or implicitly, in national accounting procedures and by international aid agencies, and thus has had significant consequences for women's classification as workers, receivers of social benefits, and refugees. Women's work, often unpaid, as farmers, workers in family businesses, and caregivers is frequently overlooked in the compilation of labor statistics. Crime statistics under-report women's victimization in the private sphere, where most violent crimes go unreported. Feminist rejection of statistical analysis results both from a realization that the questions they ask can rarely be answered by using standard classifications of available data and from an understanding that such data may actually conceal the relationships they deem important.[24]

These concerns, along with the methodological predispositions that I discussed in the first part of this chapter, raise important issues concerning statistical measures of gender (in)equality. Standard measures of gender inequality, such as women's participation in politics and the percentage of women in the workforce, do not adequately capture the fact that states have been constituted historically as gendered entities with all the attendant problems that this has created for women. Feminists claim that the lack of gender equality, which they believe exists in all states, albeit to widely varying extents, cannot be understood without reference to these historical, gender-laden divisions between public and private spheres. As Spike Peterson and other feminists have pointed out, at the time of the foundation of the modern western state, and coincidentally with the beginnings of global capitalism, women were not included as citizens but consigned to the private space of the household; thus, they were removed both from the public sphere of politics and from the economic sphere of production (Peterson 1992a: 40–44). As Carole Pateman (1988) has documented, women were not included in the original social contract by most contract theorists in the western tradition; rather, they were generally subsumed under male heads of households with no legal rights of their own. Feminists would claim that this

---

[23] It is of course the case that qualitative methods can also be power-laden.

[24] For example, even if cross-national aggregate conventional measures of wages and work conditions were available, they would not give an adequate picture of the degree of gender inequality and gender oppression demonstrated in the Chin and Moon studies.

public/private distinction, upon which the modern state was founded, has set up hierarchical gendered structures and role expectations which impede the achievement of true gender equality even today in states where most legal barriers to women's equality have been removed. For example, when women enter the workforce they do so with the expectation that they will continue to perform necessary reproductive and caring tasks, thus increasing their workload significantly because of the double burden. More importantly, this reinforces an expectation which may carry over into the types of paid employment, such as childcare and social services, considered most suitable for them. When women enter politics, particularly in areas of foreign policy, they enter an already constructed masculine world where role expectations are defined in terms of adherence to preferred masculine attributes such as rationality, autonomy, and power. It is for these reasons that women continue to be under-represented in positions of political and economic power, even in societies long committed to formal equality and equal opportunity legislation.

It is for such reasons that many feminists have chosen the qualitative case-study methods of the type that I have described – as well as other methods that can be generally subsumed under a postpositivist label. However, this should not mean that feminists are averse to using quantitative data in appropriate ways as indicators of gender inequality and gender oppression. Thanks to the efforts of women's international organizing, especially around the United Nations Decade for Women (1975–1985), the UN began to disaggregate data by sex, thus helping to bring the plight of women to the world's attention. The United Nations *Human Development Report* of 1995 (UNDP 1996) focused specifically on women and gender issues. In that report, the United Nations Human Development Programme first introduced its gender development index (GDI), based on gender differences in life expectancy, earned income, illiteracy, and enrollment in education. It also introduced the gender empowerment measure (GEM), based on the proportion of women in parliament and in economic leadership positions (Benería 2003: 19–20; Seager 2003: 12–13). While they are crude indicators, the GDI and the GEM do give us comparative, cross-national evidence about the status of women relative to men.[25] It is data such as these, which go beyond traditional categorizations of national accounting, that can support feminists' claims about gender inequality and provide support for efforts to

---

[25] Joni Seager's *Atlas of Women in the World* (Seager 2003) provides a wide range of data on gender inequality in map form, much of it from UN and other international and regional organizations' data.

pressure states and international organizations to design and support public policies that are better for women and other disadvantaged people. They also provide evidence for transnational movements lobbying for the improvement of human rights. Economic data have also provided important evidence for the growing field of feminist economics and the large body of literature on gender in development (see for example Benería 2003).

Subject to critical scrutiny and sensitivity to some of the problems I have mentioned, statistical measures of gender inequality can provide important evidence of women's subordination. Jayaratne and Stewart (1991: 93) emphasize the potential value of quantification while rejecting traditional procedures – such as bias toward male subjects, male selection of topics, false claims of objectivity and universality, and over-generalization of results – that are antithetical to feminist values. Nevertheless, feminists must continue to ask questions about, and be skeptical of, the ways in which knowledge based on statistical evidence has been constructed. They must also continue to emphasize the ways in which the privileging of such knowledge, under the guise of objective, value-free science, has worked to hide oppressive hierarchies of power and strategies designed to overcome them.[26]

Conclusion

In this chapter I have offered some reasons why most IR feminists have chosen to conduct their research outside positivist social scientific frameworks. I have suggested that many of the questions they have posed are not answerable within such frameworks. While there is no such thing as a feminist method, there are distinct feminist perspectives on methodology which have emerged out of a deep skepticism of traditional knowledge, knowledge that is based largely on certain privileged men's lives and experiences. The two case studies that I discussed illustrate the parallels between IR feminists' methodological sensitivities and these methodological perspectives from other disciplines. These IR feminists are asking questions about the linkages between the everyday lived experiences of women and the constitution and exercise of political and economic power at the state and global level. Specifically, they seek to understand how gender and other hierarchies of power affect those at the margins of the system. Their findings reveal states constituted in

---

[26] By this I refer to the fact that knowledge with an explicit emancipatory message is frequently judged to be "political" and, therefore, not objective. Of course, all knowledge is political and what is judged as "objective" frequently supports the status quo.

gendered ways, whose security-seeking practices frequently render the lives of their most powerless citizens more insecure.

IR feminists more generally are asking questions that have rarely or never been asked before in IR; moreover, they are questions that probably *could not* be asked within the epistemological boundaries of positivist social scientific approaches to the discipline. For this reason, and others that I have discussed, in the foreseeable future at least, IR feminists are likely to favor methods that allow women to document their own experiences in their own terms. Frequently, these are experiences about which there is little available data, since they have been either ignored or categorized in ways that deny their subjects their own identities. Constructing knowledge from the standpoint of the outsider provides us not only with a wider perspective but also with a unique perspective on knowledge about insiders. Since it offers us a more complete picture of reality, it has the potential to enrich and even transform the discipline in ways that are beneficial for everyone.

3   Distracted reflections on the production, narration, and refusal of feminist knowledge in International Relations

Marysia Zalewski

> Local women said: no matter
> How you sprinkled it, every time
> You'd sweep a concrete floor,
> You'd get more off it.
> As if, deep down,
> There was only dust.[1]

I was on my way to a conference with an abstract and a promise. But then I got distracted. (A. Gordon 2001: 32)

Methodology: a personal story

"What method have you adopted for this research?"

This is a persistent question. One asked within a certain tone of voice, an almost imperceptible sigh of relief that the one asking is not the one answering; the sound also of a powerful demand to know, a distanced usually firm utterance capturing in its delivery the authority of the interrogator. (Weston 2002: 39)

When I was a graduate student the question "What method have you adopted for your research?" made me very nervous, especially in its recurrent manifestation: "Is there a distinct feminist methodology?" – a question to which I found it very difficult to provide a definitive answer especially when I suspected that only the answer, "Yes," followed up with a robust, rationalistic, and conventionally acceptable defense, would suffice. Of course, I could speak at length about the absence of women and considerations of gender in traditional texts in the field of International Relations (IR), and point to the violence that this both does and masks, but this did not convince my questioners. What was it, they wanted to

I would like to thank the three editors of the volume for their thoughtful comments, hard work, and patience.
[1] Second stanza from the poem "Wings," by John O'Donohue, in O'Donohue 2000.

know, that made feminist methodology manifestly *different* from other methodologies, and was that difference sufficient to justify it as legitimate academic research in the discipline of International Relations?

There seemed to be a great deal at stake if I got the answer "wrong." This was of great concern to me, as it seemed to be the case that the only possible responses I could give were *always* (going to be) wrong or unacceptable because what ended up being left, which might be claimed as amounting to "a distinct feminist methodology," was something relating to "women's experiences" and/or some form of (perhaps) essentialized femininity which was clearly not conventionally acceptable in IR as a methodological tool or practice. If the label "feminist" could not be attached to the usual tools of social science research[2] (and if it could, this, tautologically, seemed to imply the superfluity of feminist approaches), one was left making arguments about the validity and originality of connections between women's experiences and theorizings and claims to social scientific knowledge. The subsequent bemused look on the faces of more traditionally minded colleagues on hearing arguments prioritizing new knowledge claims based on women's daily and bodily experiences – the "messiness" of everyday life (D. E. Smith 1987) – provides a reminder of how easy it seems to have been to place feminist work at the bottom rung (Enloe 1996) of the ladder as far as legitimate knowledge claims in IR go. As Sylvester suggests, to many conventional analysts within IR "feminism rings in the ears but is not an enterprise to be rung in as a full partner" (2002: 11).

The interrogative, probing questions continued, both in the context of my own work and more generally in the area of feminist IR:

> How have feminists contributed to the discipline?
> Why is a feminist approach necessary?
> What difference will feminism make?
> Do you think this work is really doing anything on a significant scale to transform the way people think?

It is, perhaps, reasonable to ask questions about how feminists in IR have methodologized. Employing the understanding that "thinking methodologically is theorizing about how we find things out; it is about the relationship between the process and the product of research" (Letherby 2003: 5), feminist scholars have consistently scrutinized the bases on which their methodological decisions have been made. Feminists have never wanted exemption from such scrutiny, given the historical and

---

[2] This might include inductive argument, logical deduction, critical theory, participant observation, interviewing techniques, rational choice theory, and so on.

logical desire for the authority and legitimacy of feminist knowledge claims. Put another way, feminists want their work to be accepted and effective. Thus, questions about feminist methodology are not unreasonable, but the stock of acceptable and credible answers held by the discipline of IR (especially but not exclusively the mainstream of the discipline) potentially renders such questions inequitable. This is because feminist work does not measure up to the conventional standards used by the discipline. Why and how this is the case is a matter of great dispute, but it has led to something of a dilemma for feminists, because, while it implicitly and explicitly works to destabilize the epistemological, ontological, and methodological master-narratives of the discipline, there is a simultaneous draw towards the traditional measures of legitimacy and authority, and the rewards of offering a convincing and acceptable defense of feminist methodologies that the powerful disciplinary questions demand. As a consequence, after more than fifteen years of work in this area, feminist scholars can still conclude that "in spite of the substantial growth and recognition of feminist scholarship in the last ten years, it still remains quite marginal to the discipline" (Tickner 2001: 3); and "it is evident that feminist IR still faces considerable obstacles in gaining acceptance within [the] mainstream" (Steans 2003: 448).

This chapter will reflect on some of the contours and paradoxes of feminist methodologizing as they have manifested themselves in the discipline of International Relations over the last two decades or so. My title claims that these reflections are distracted ones, which is something I need to explain. I use the practice and metaphor of "distraction" as a methodological device which works both with and against its implications of disruption and diversion. It is an approach which is partly inspired by Avery Gordon's work on "haunting and the sociological imagination" (2001) and Patti Lather's work on the "methodology of mess" (2001). My discussion is also overlaid with the thinking strategies of Luce Irigaray (1985) and Jacques Derrida's deliberations on "spectral secrets" and "hauntology" (1994). My aim is not to "apply" their work and thus entertain a "positivistic return to a more exact form of science" (Foucault 2001: 71), but rather to weave the insights gained from their work through my discussion. Let me explain further.

Avery Gordon was on her way to a conference with an "abstract and a promise," a promise to deliver the paper she had pledged when she submitted her abstract, and to speak professionally about what kinds of methods could adequately study important issues. But on her way to the conference she got distracted "by a photograph and had to take a detour in order to follow the traces of a woman's ghost" (2001: 32). Gordon discovered the woman only by the "photographic evidence of her absence" (32), suggesting that the woman's presence was revealed by virtue of "not being there." The story concerns the history of psychoanalysis and the Third Psychoanalytic Congress which took place in Weimar, Germany, in 1911. The woman, Sabina Spielrein, was not in the photograph taken of the conference delegates (overwhelmingly a picture of men), despite her role in changing the early history of psychoanalysis through her relationship with Carl Jung and Sigmund Freud. The invisibility of Spielrein alerted Gordon to "the systematic exclusions produced by the assumptions and practices of a normalized social science. These normal methods foreclose the recognition of exclusions and the sacrifices required to tell a story as the singularly real one" (42).

As I read Gordon's book, I was contemplating how I would write this chapter but I kept getting distracted. I had tentatively envisaged a perusal of the different approaches feminist scholars in IR had taken, which implied that I had to make at least two foundational decisions before I could write anything. One involved the choice of how to categorize feminist work in IR; a second concerned making a decision about the relationship between the disciplinary demands of IR and feminist scholarship. In other words, it seemed that in order to satisfactorily address the question of the character and status of feminist methodologizing in IR and offer a tolerably acceptable story of the associated production of feminist IR knowledge, I had to implicitly or explicitly work with the discipline's broad position on methodologizing.[3] The form that such an engagement took might vary; yet I became increasingly troubled, especially in the context of the term – the word – the practice – of *methodology*.

Methodology; the "ology" of method. It is a hard word; a scientific word. It suggests problem-solving solutions and advice in the service of delivering "better accounts" (Lather 2001: 203). It offers the possibility or the hope of an answer to the question of "how to study social reality" (Corbetta 2003: 13). Yet as a feminist scholar I was aware, as Gordon's distraction implies, that conventional social science methodologies inhibit recognition of all the exclusions and sacrifices required in order to tell a singular story. I was very uncomfortable with this. But then I got distracted by a (non-)scientific story.

Methodology: a "fairy tale"

What types of knowledge do you want to disqualify in the very instant of your demand: "Is it a [social] science?"   (Foucault 2001: 72)

---

[3] And not "forget" IR; see Bleiker 1997.

Banu Subramaniam tells a story about "Snow Brown and the Seven Detergents," in which Snow Brown travels across the seas to the "Land of the Blue Devils" to become a scientist. On arrival, she locates the "Department of the Pursuit of Scientific Truth," and in the "Room of Judgment" she is instructed by the "Patriarch" to ask, "'Mirror, mirror on the wall, who is the fairest scientist of them all?' 'You are, O Supreme White Patriarch!' said the mirror. The Patriarch laughed . . . 'You should [all] aspire to . . . find Scientific Truth.'" (Subramaniam 2001: 36).

But, in her pursuit of Scientific Truth, Snow Brown kept asking the "wrong questions," and pursuing the "wrong paths." Yet her obedient desire to become a scientist impelled her to avail herself of the "Seven Detergents," which eventually "washed" her away, and she became Snow White. Still she failed. "How could she ever have been the fairest scientist? How could she have been anything but last when judged by a mirror that wanted to produce clones of the Supreme White Patriarch?" (39).

My distraction by this story suggested that too closely following the methodological path determined by the discipline of IR was, perhaps, not appropriate. I did not aspire to repeat the work of what Irigaray (1985: 203) calls "your eternal instructors in social science" and become a "mainstream clone"; nor did I want to represent or position feminist IR in this way. Much advice has been offered to feminist scholars in IR as to the best way to operationalize their research questions and interests and thus to have some hope of adequately answering the disciplinary question, "What method have you chosen for your research?" Although Keohane's articulation might seem extreme (on the social scientistic continuum) and even parodic (Bleiker 1997), some version of it is implicit in most requests of feminists by the discipline (see Tickner, this volume).

Specifying their propositions, and providing systematically gathered evidence to test these propositions, will be essential: scientific method, in the broadest sense, is the best path toward convincing current nonbelievers of the validity of the message that feminists are seeking to deliver. We will only "understand" each other if IR scholars are open to the important questions that feminist theories raise, and if feminists are willing to formulate their hypotheses in ways that are testable – and falsifiable – with evidence. (Keohane 1998: 197)

From this, it is clear that, broadly conceived, the practice and pursuit of methodology in IR still relies quite heavily on the putative objectivity of the natural sciences. This remains something of a puzzle, given that "real" scientists long ago gave up on the illusion of the production of clean knowledge and the idea of a "real world" of unsullied objects and data (Funtowicz and Ravetz 1997). But still more curious is the drive to pursue social research in this manner in the wake of contemporary political and intellectual destabilizations of foundational metanarratives; said differently, in "a post-foundational era characterized by the loss of absolute frames of reference" (Lather 2001: 221). Or, as Avery Gordon (2001: 10) articulates it, the poststructural imagination "has bequeathed an understanding that the practices of writing, analysis, and investigation, whether of social or cultural material, constitute less a scientifically positive project than a cultural practice that organizes particular rituals of storytelling by situated investigators."

Similarly, Patti Lather's work on the "methodology of getting lost" takes seriously the responsibilities of ethical research practices in the context of the contemporary ruins of a confident social science, a field destabilized by postmodern doubts about the use of methodology as a route to some "noncomplicitous place of knowing" (Lather 2001: 204). Lather's approach distances itself from the demand and temptation to produce what she calls a "comfort text" – one that maps easily on to our usual ways of knowing, as most (neo)mainstream narratives in IR do – and suggests that the task in social research involves counter-practices of knowing and telling, and calling into question the construction of authoritative narrations, "even while one's confidence is troubled" (Lather 2001: 214) or one finds oneself without an "alibi" (Irigaray 1985: 203).

Yet I had a chapter to write about feminist methodologies in IR; a task invoking responsibilities, especially given feminist scholars have justifiably wanted to acquire the condition of believability in IR – to "sound truthful" (A. Gordon 2001: 145) – and *en route* have worked assiduously to deliver feminist knowledge. For example, an early classificatory strategy in feminist IR revolved around the philosophical foundations of feminist theory and the ensuing associated political manifestations. Scholars committed to explicitly explaining the bases of feminist methodologizing typically utilized Sandra Harding's philosophical/political typology (sometimes via Hawkesworth's lucid rearticulation of this); empiricist/ liberal, standpoint/radical, postmodern/postmodern.[4] A later classificatory schema tracked the disciplinary positivist/postpositivist debate, with most feminists placing themselves, or being placed, in the latter camp.[5] The orbit of constructivism has materialized as one of the most recent manifestations of disciplinary methodological skirmishes, in which feminist work is variably placed but not usually (if ever) credited with having

---

[4] A small sample of these includes: Harding 1986; 1987; 1991; Hawkesworth 1989; Sisson Runyan and Peterson 1991; Sylvester 1994a; Zalewski 1993a; 1993b; and Whitworth 1994.
[5] A small sample of these includes Tickner 1997 and in this volume; Peterson and Sisson Runyan 1993; and Peterson 1992a.

an originary contribution (Locher and Prügl 2001). As Sylvester muses, "all-embracing constructivism, therefore, comes out as fathered, like most IR" (2002: 11), thereby, once again, positioning feminism in a subordinate or helpmeet role (Zalewski 1998b).

Other ways in which feminist scholars in IR have conducted their work include the following. First, some feminists have responded to overt critical inquiries about feminist approaches in IR which have been expressed in varying tones of approval and disapproval by scholars whose primary area of scholarly expertise is not feminism. Secondly, feminists have explained, reviewed and also, perhaps logically, disciplined the work of other feminists. Thirdly, others have produced a broad range of textbooks and edited books, along with the accretion of many chapters in more generic text books in the discipline.[6] Inevitably, given the character and demands of the academic profession – perhaps especially IR, given its masculinist aspirations – a canon has emerged involving the creation of a number of experts or at least leading authorities in the generic field of feminist IR. There might be some dispute over who and what work legitimately counts in the latter; but one might use some of the traditional benchmarks of the academy, which currently include published work (particularly single-authored books and journal articles), alongside acknowledgment of "expert" status, which, in IR (or more specifically in US-led IR) includes eminent scholar panels and representation on high-status panels at the annual convention. Responses and reactions to this large body of work has been varied. In the more visible echelons of hegemonic IR, this has sometimes taken the form of an engagement with self-defined defenders/supporters of the discipline, a debate which some feminist scholars become involved with and which others studiously ignore. Yet, while narrating this story, I got distracted by a feeling of *déjà vu*.

Methodology: a feminist Groundhog Day?

[We have] the spectacle of an endlessly repeatable . . . temporality framed within the repetition of an annual event that serves to predict the specific future of the infinitely repeatable cycle.   (O'Donnell 2000: 1)

---

[6] A small sample of these includes Ackerly 2001; Carver, Cochran, and Squires 1998; Cohn 1988; 1993; Elshtain 1987; Enloe 1989; 1993; 1996; 2000; Grant and Newland 1991; A. Jones 1996; Hooper 2001; Marchand and Parpart 1995; Marchand and Sisson Runyan 2000; Sisson Runyan and Peterson 1993; Peterson 1992b, 2003; Pettman 1996; Sharoni 1994; Steans 1997; M. Stern 2001; Stienstra 1994; Tickner 1992; 1997; 2001; True 2001; Carver, Zalewski, Kinsella, and Carpenter 2003; Sylvester 1994a; 1994b; 2002; Weber 1994; Zalewski and Parpart 1998; Zalewski 1994; 1995; 2002.

There is abundant evidence of a large mass of feminist scholarship in IR; yet this is counterposed by a backdrop of regular disciplinary marginalization, disapproval, and rejection, as the comments by Steans and Tickner quoted earlier bear out. Are the fortunes of feminist IR locked into an endless cycle of "suspended animation" (Kinsella 2003b: 295), analogous to having recurrent nightmares of defending one's graduate thesis over and over again? Like Phil Connors in *Groundhog Day*,[7] will feminists IR scholars "succeed" and satisfy only by transmuting into something the discipline, in its traditional and neo guises, demands: "a small-town good guy content to live within the ritualistic, rigid confines of Punxsutawney [IR]"? (O'Donnell 2000: 1).

The customary narration of feminist IR tends to reinforce the homogenized bond between feminism and the discipline of IR (recent examples include Steans 2003 and Sylvester 2002[8]). This story habitually begins and ends with the discipline. As has been suggested, one consequence of this disciplinary framing is that answers that do not resonate with disciplinary understandings will rarely seem good enough, and the answers to the powerful, disciplinary, methodologically inspired questions, "How have feminists contributed to the discipline?", "What difference has feminism made?", and "Why is a feminist approach necessary?" will continue to seem inadequate. Furthermore, the constant waiting for and expectation of a fully authorized (by the discipline) discovery of the "real" nature of feminist contributions to the field of International Relations can, ironically, serve to boost the discipline's own narcissistic sense of itself. In Derridean terms, a center requires a periphery for its existence as the outside organizes the discursive framework of the inside; as such, the mainstream necessarily shapes itself in response to the (peripheral) presence or absence of woman. Methodologically centering woman could fatally dishevel IR's structure, which is not something that the (neo)mainstream desires.

Of course, there are good or at least understandable reasons why disciplines such as IR have developed such bounded methodological systems which resist disruption. The sciences and philosophies

---

[7] A 1993 film directed by Harold Ramis, starring Bill Murray as the narcissistic television weatherman who becomes stranded in Punxsutawney, Pennsylvania. He is sent there to report on the famous festival in which Punxsutawney Phil, the resident groundhog, is brought to the town square every February 2 to see whether or not he casts a shadow, thereby predicting the beginning of spring. The main premise of the film is that Murray's character, Phil Connors, is condemned to wake up each morning to a new February 2 in Punxsutawney until he learns how to overcome his vanity and properly romance the new producer, who accompanies him (see O'Donnell 2000).

[8] Most "first-wave" feminist IR scholars have told the story of feminist IR in this way.

of modernity ushered in hopes of disciplining power with truth. Conventional social science methods were offered up as the best hope of achieving one of the goals of these methods, namely the betterment of human society using objectively driven argument and evidence (Krasner 1996: 124). Yet the institutionalization of these methods has encouraged the development of an increasingly narrow set of acceptable ways of doing research, which Avery Gordon characterizes in the following way: "Bloodless categories, narrow notions of the visible and the empirical, professional standards of indifference, institutional rules of distance and control, barely speakable fears of losing the footing that enables us to speak authoritatively and with greater value than anyone else who might" (A. Gordon 2001: 21). Gordon's bluntness reminds us why feminist and poststructural scholars find conventional social scientific practices objectionable, as these practices tend to result in draining social fields of energy, vitality, and complexity in the search for the illusory "crystalline purity" which scientific objectivity promises (Andrews 1990: 24). It has regularly seemed to be the case that all that (pseudo)scientific methods could offer were bloodless categories and narrow notions of the visible and empirical, which persistently, in IR, have demanded the delivery of a normalized, linear, tidy narrative of feminist scholarship, the exclusionary outcome of which has become an all too familiar marginalization.

As a feminist scholar, I questioned my involvement in the enterprise of looking to tell the story of feminist methodologizing within and through IR, especially as I was concerned that attempting to guarantee the credible status of feminist knowledge claims by authoritatively narrating the story of how feminists have methodologized simply reifies the dilemma that feminists have endeavored to flee. To affirm confidence in the potential of the foundational authority of "master-methodologizing" while simultaneously mired in rejecting them seemed bizarre, tantamount to setting feminist IR up to fail. Then I was reminded of – distracted by – Irigaray's response to the question, "What method have you adopted for your research?"

A delicate question. For isn't it the method, the path to knowledge, that has always also led us astray, by fraud and artifice, from woman's path, and to the point of consecrating its oblivion?   (Irigaray 1985: 150)

A primary motivation behind the "science question" in feminism (Harding 1987), which centrally involves questions about methodology, was to interrupt the way in which feminist politics had attempted to follow mainstream methodologies and tried to guarantee and control the linkage between feminism's normative commitment to emancipation and its practical commitment to social transformation (McLure 1992: 361). This practice of interruption was partly intended to foster skepticism about the worthiness and desirability of the scientific method, not because it was being badly implemented and was therefore amenable to correction, but rather because "scientific method" and the methodologies it bequeaths are the problem. Put more simply, the production and evaluation of knowledge are not an equal-opportunities game (Snider 2003: 369), and the dilemma feminists in IR face raises its head once again. Institutional rewards for confining feminist scholarship within the parameters the discipline offers are appealing, given the scholarly aspiration to successfully accomplish legitimacy in IR. Yet the legitimized methodological tools appear to sponsor feminist failure, as the tools and methods which feminists use, and the ontologies, epistemologies, and methodologies they insist are credible and important, are not ones that conventional social science as practiced in IR deems acceptable. The persistent but fleeting gestures towards the vast majority of feminist scholarship in the mainstream, as well as at its more critical edges, lend continued weight to this perception. Feminist methodologizing continues to remain somewhat inexplicable (echoing the exasperated Freudian lament, "What do women want?"), and is therefore unacceptable to the mainstream, which perhaps explains why there is an "eternal return" to the questions I introduced at the beginning of this chapter and a perpetual dissatisfaction with most feminist answers.

Methodology: working with feminist distractions

The languages used to preserve domination are complex and sometimes contradictory. Much of how they operate to anesthetize desire and resistance is invisible; they are wedded to our *common-sense*; they are formulaic without being intrusive, entirely natural – "no marks on the body at all."

(Hunt 1990: 199, my emphasis)

In haunting, organized forces and systemic structures that appear removed from us make their impact felt in everyday life in a way that confounds our analytic separations and confounds the social separations themselves.

(A. Gordon 2001: 19)

It is only "common sense" that feminists are asked to justify their methodologies in ways that are understandable to the discipline of IR, isn't it? Yet commonly held "sense" is, as several contributors to this volume (Tickner, Kronsell) indicate, the problem. If, as Hunt argues, the "languages" used to preserve domination are "wedded to our common-sense," rendering "invisible" the mechanisms of anesthetization, this suggests that looking for feminist IR *through* IR and from the mold from where it is deemed to have originated and to which it owes allegiance, is problematic. Rather than rummage through feminism's drained and exhausted position at the center/margins of the discipline called International Relations (Zalewski 2002), and taking seriously the methodological devices offered by "hauntology," this suggests expressing feminist IR in the "shape described by absence" (A. Gordon 2001: 6). This approach also takes seriously postmodern (re)articulations that "life is complicated" (2001: 3),[9] along with recognition of the failure of modernity's promise to "deliver us from evil." It also acknowledges the limitations of our prevalent modes of social inquiry and their ineptitude in communicating the depth, density, and intricacies of social life. The complexities, paradoxes, and contradictions therein have been brutally cleansed by conventional approaches.

The "poetic is essentially to make a space for the unthought" (Brossard 1980: 81). This idea, taken up through the metaphor and methodological practice of distraction alongside Gordon and Derrida's use of "hauntology," might assist in the search for an illustration of those things that both confound our analytic separations (and, as such, feel removed from us) yet at the same time make their impact felt. As Avery Gordon suggests, "tracking ghostly or spectral forces by looking at the shape described by absence, captures perfectly the paradox of tracking through time and across all those forces that which makes its mark by being there and not there at the same time" (2001: 6). Thinking about how to articulate the pieces, the lost ideas, the broken thoughts, the puzzles, the curiosities, the silences, the not seen/not there, "the disqualified" (Foucault, 1980: 83), gestures toward some ways through which to articulate how the (un)thought, the (un)imagined, the forgotten, the disliked, the abject, the feared and the (un)remembered are drained and expunged by conventional social science methodologies.

Working with distractions involves hauntings, ghosts, and spectral secrets which make material presences within absences. Being distracted invokes the lost thoughts, the glimpsed insights, the forgotten moments, the things that seemed to matter once, even if fleetingly, the "ghostly signals and flashing half-signs" (A. Gordon, 2001: 204) and the luminous, weighty presences of the apparently invisible. As Hunt contends, the languages used to preserve domination are complex and sometimes contradictory, yet they are wedded to our (social scientific) common

---

[9] Gordon acknowledges that this may seem a banal expression of the obvious; it is nonetheless a profound theoretical statement, perhaps the most important theoretical statement of our time.

sense. As such, looking for the "barely visible" (see Kronsell, this volume), yet solidly felt, in a discipline weighed down by heavily guarded institutional memory/amnesia – as well as anaesthesia – is clearly difficult, yet this is where we might find rigorously pursued feminist methodologizing. When Cynthia Enloe (1989) writes about the deployment of women's sexuality on American bases in Second World War Britain, the ghostly, slippery traces and ominous legacies of centuries of gendered/sexualized notions about "women's worth" begin to materialize, ironically illustrated in the ambiguous title of her chapter, "Base Women." Enloe's paying attention to what she "didn't notice" (Enloe 2001), rather than swatting away conventionally insignificant distractions, has led to the development of her impressive body of scholarship, which is of profound importance to feminist and IR scholars.

When Carol Cohn reimagines the spectral traces flowing between discourse and practice while listening to the speaking and thinking practices of defense intellectuals, she makes material the ways in which beliefs about gender and sex act as a "pre-emptive deterrent to thought," skillfully demonstrating some of the anesthetizing effects of conventional approaches (Cohn 1993: 232). Illustrating the barely visible or "insignificant markers" of local gendered beliefs practiced through recruitment procedures in garment factories, Juanita Elias meticulously displays the synaptic connections and effects between the voracious needs of multinational corporations and "fashioning inequality" (2004). When Kathy Moon discerned a "ghost" of woman's sex or gender in Enloe's *Bananas, Beaches, and Bases* (1989), she followed the distraction and scrupulously traced it to tell a powerful story about the use of Korean women's "sex" to ease relations between soldiers and states (1997). Stirred by an instance of the usually invisible and ignored abuse of domestic servants, Christine Chin investigates the powerful relationship between the domestic labor of Filipina and Indonesian women and the self-serving strategies of the developmental state of Malaysia, exposing deep and disturbing connections (1998).

Sifting through seemingly rock-solid ideologies of state-securitizing practices in western modernity, Spike Peterson finds invisible but hugely effective practices of "forgetting" the human costs of our unreflective reproduction of categories of domination (1992a: 38). Charlotte Hooper (2001) takes on one such unreflective practice of "forgetting" and performs an archaeological dig through the pages of *The Economist* magazine, showing how this publication interpellates its readers into identifying with various models of hegemonic masculinity. Employing a gendered textual reading, Hooper expertly shows how what appears on the surface to be largely gender neutral is instead drenched in a wash of hegemonic masculinity.

Weaving literature (Margaret Atwood's *The Handmaid's Tale*, 1985) and International Relations together, Christine Sylvester asserts that "the power of the abject zone is the contamination it seeps but rarely announces" (2002: 68). Revisiting John F. Kennedy's administration in the 1960s, Sylvester circuitously narrates how the largely invisible and seemingly ineffective and irrelevant activities of women in and around the White House machinery "ooze power with, around, or over those they loyally attended" (2002: 56). Singling out a joke made by Kennedy after his electoral triumph in 1959 (when both his wife and the wife of a friend were pregnant, Kennedy quipped, "Okay, girls, you can take the pillows out now. We won"), Sylvester demonstrates how adult "girls" become "sex-linked pregnant wives," indelibly "married" to their husband's powerful positions.

Jokes are often a site through which the work or presence of the invisible or the silenced appears. My own early reflections on the gendered character of IR include a consideration of a joke told at an international conference in 1994. An American diplomat in Britain was asked what he missed most about home. His answer was, "A good hamburger." His wife's answer was, "My job." Most of the delegates laughed (Zalewski 1996: 347). Yet the joke evidences the powerfully gendered nature of diplomacy and the sacrifices that countless women have made in order to tailor their marriages and lives to fit in with their husbands' careers and the significant (unpaid and overlooked) contribution that such women's activities have made to the workings of governments and interstate relationships (see also Cohn, this volume).

The insignificant, barely visible markers and traces of gender or sex, the "spectral secrets," describe how "that which appears to be not there is often a seething presence" (A. Gordon, 2001: 8). But this "nothingness" is also resisted because it has effects; it matters. Begona Aretxaga's discussion of the physical and conceptual contamination of women's menstrual blood in Irish republican women's dirty protest, and the embarrassment this caused republican men, demonstrates how the (in)significant markers of gender are strictly policed, thereby, ironically, exposing their force.[10] "The interstitial character of women's political

---

[10] Irish republican men took part in the "dirty protest" as a response to the withdrawal of their status as political prisoners in the late 1970s and early 1980s. The men's dirty protest (in which they refused to wash or dispose of bodily waste, such as urine and faeces) gained media, public, and academic attention. Yet republican women in Armagh

practices, the fact that they were situated in the margins of social and political space, places dominant gender discourse *out of place* by introducing slippages of meaning and creating new social fields" (Aretxaga 1997: 78). Consequently, investigating the supposed underside of knowledge – the production and maintenance of "ignorance/forgetting" – is a significant and powerful aspect of feminist research programs and methodologies. As such, feminist methodologizing consists of a constant juxtaposing and layering from different sites, different contexts, and different constituencies (Cohn, this volume).

Methodology: forgetting feminist distractions

Repressive strategies do not aim to eliminate . . . but to preserve the division.
(Seidman 2001: 354)

We might also trace the shape of feminist methodologizing in IR through gaps, breaks and connections shaped by amnesia/anaesthesia and performative, repetitious (un)distracted reflections and spectral (re)deployments of gender/sex in the discipline's reception of feminist IR. These disciplinary activities, most often "thoughtless," or "unreflective/forgetful," might be found in a number of places; here I consider two of these. One is through debates about the "contribution" of feminism to the discipline of IR, specifically looking at Robert Keohane's engagement with J. Ann Tickner in *International Studies Quarterly* (*ISQ*) 1998; a second involves the framing and character of some of the questions asked in this context by reconsidering the interview with Cynthia Enloe in the *Review of International Studies* (Enloe 2001). A brief perusal discloses some of the unreflective exercises of refusal as well as illustrating how distractions engendered by feminist questions and answers are unreflectively misheard, avoided, resisted, and rejected. My attention to the *ISQ* debate and the *RIS* interview involves focusing on how conventional discursive practices work to conserve traditional parameters; in these examples the reinvention of the marginal status of feminist scholarship.[11] This methodological approach illustrates how textual closure around gender and feminism works in a specific text by reading a text against itself so as to expose what might be thought of as the "textual subconscious," where meanings are expressed which may be directly contrary to the surface meaning (Barry 2002: 73), as well as by

---

Prison also deployed a dirty protest, largely in response to an instance of violent body searches by prison officers (see Aretxaga 1997).

[11] As such, the argument about unreflective/forgetting is a discursive/methodological one.

focusing on what, in conventional social scientific terms, would be a very small sample.

The journal *International Studies Quarterly* is one that occupies a distinguished place in the discipline of IR, given its association with the powerful, discipline-defining professional body, the *International Studies Association*. The *ISQ* tenaciously observes the methodological norms of social inquiry, and has had a reluctant relationship with feminist scholarship, one characterized by benign impatience with the apparently inexhaustible feminist propensity to keep questioning (rather than "satisfactorily" answering), both generically and in the context of IR itself. Repeatedly rebuked for not explicitly including feminist work in its "Dissident Voices" issue (1990), the journal has since endorsed a small number of feminist-related articles, including a *Dialogue* section centering on J. Ann Tickner's essay, "You Just Don't Understand: Troubled Engagements Between Feminists and IR Theorists" (Tickner 1997). Presenting himself as a benevolent inquisitor of feminism, if sometimes a seemingly besieged one, Robert Keohane leads the debate. Proclaiming sympathy with Tickner's work, he asserts that it is also necessary to offer criticisms of arguments that "do not seem convincing" (194). Keohane goes on to imply that Tickner has yet to convince him of the worthiness of feminist scholarship. In this process, he reiterates that Tickner, and feminist scholars generally, should aspire to harmonize with preset standards, which are tautologically identified as the (only) legitimate grounds for making authoritative judgments and acceptable claims to IR knowledge production. But in order to reveal the truth of his approach and the overall unacceptability of feminist IR knowledge (except in insipid formulations), Keohane has to maneuver around his own spectral deployments of gender as well as a series of ghostly feminist distractions. Let me elucidate.

Keohane appears anesthetized to the possibility that gender breathes life into ostensibly neutral concepts, practices, and words.[12] Enamored of the scientistic adherence to the retrospective use-value of theory, Keohane "forgets" that "texts come before us as the always-already-read; we apprehend them through sedimented layers of previous interpretations" (Jameson 2001: 101). For example, if we think of gender/sex as a productive system and discourse which is animated by a hierarchical logic, we might look for traces of the work of gender/sex through Keohane's self-assured use of dualistic imagery as part of his justificatory arsenal. Binary formulations that structure Keohane's essay include convincing/incredible; rhetoric/explanation; misleading/truthful.

---

[12] Gender – or beliefs about sexual difference – is not the only source of this oxygenization.

Reading Tickner through a lens which "always-already" writes feminism as "incredible-rhetorical-untruthful," Keohane confidently asserts his authoritative views. Yet Keohane is incapable of adequately theorizing feminist scholarship because feminism always materializes as inferior through his mainstream methodological lexicon, and, as such, he is necessarily drawn into dismissing methods and the ensuing narratives which fall outside the narrow remit of the scientifically positivist project. Consequentially, feminism can only appear as inadequate, because it is tautologically "unconvincing." He dismisses feminist arguments as "rhetorical" (194), concluding with the reprimand that feminist scholarship will lead us down the "wrong" path, that is, one that does not harmonize with (neo)mainstream desires. Reducing feminism's polymorphous cacophony to a "single note" (Kinsella 2003: 294) is summarily demonstrated by Keohane's conclusion that feminist work might be useful insofar as it could tell scholars something about the relationship between "differently gendered states" and the propensity for states to be aggressive (197). Rushing to place "women's" activities and feminist interruptions and distractions within a (neo)mainstream political and intellectual agenda deflates the promise of feminism into a mirage.

The British journal *Review of International Studies* is the official publication of the professional body the British International Studies Association. The *RIS* has a more complexly layered relationship with feminist scholarship,[13] though it notoriously awarded the annual prize for the best article of the year to an essay on gender which a number of feminist scholars deemed inadequate with regard to its feminist scholarship.[14] More recently, the editors conducted an interview with Cynthia Enloe (2001). Interviews, as a research method, are both interesting and problematic. Who qualifies as an appropriate interview subject? What questions should be asked? Which answers are properly included or edited out? Some forms of these questions lie at the heart of all social science research methods, either explicitly or implicitly, and answers to them are not arbitrary but contained within the parameters of disciplinary acceptability. In this brief perusal I focus on two of the questions asked and a fragment of one of Enloe's answers.

"Is the gender and IR project going anywhere?" is one question asked of Enloe, followed up with "Do you think this work is really doing anything on a significant scale to transform the way people think? Is it

---

[13] This may be indicative of some of the differences between North American and British/European IR.

[14] Carpenter 2002; A. Jones 1996. For critiques, see Carver, Cochran, and Squires 1998; Carver, Zalewski, Kinsella, and Carpenter 2003; Zalewski 1998.

a dialogue of the deaf, between specialists in gender and those of a traditional Political Science/IR persuasion?" (661). The use of "the deaf" is intriguing, given that "the deaf" do hear – if "differently" from the ways we have come of think of as "normal". Perhaps there is an analogy here with the debate between feminist IR and (neo)mainstream IR. Notwithstanding, the practice of unreflectively employing hierarchical binaries which are partly structured through and with (ideas about) gender is (barely) evident in the character of these questions. Is the consequence of significantly transforming the way people think a reasonable test of feminist IR? We might trace a subtle spectrally gendered thread here. For example, there is an assumed opposition between specialists in gender on the one hand and Political Scientists/IR scholars on the other (the use of upper- and lower-case letters is indicative). Are gender specialists not IR specialists? Are feminist IR scholars not doing *real* IR? In an interview with Kenneth Waltz in the *RIS*, he was similarly asked about "the feminist contribution to IR theory," as if feminist IR was not already IR theory (Waltz 1998: 386).[15] Further, who are "the people" whose thinking has to be transformed by feminists? Is there faint evidence of another hierarchy here which suggests that academics offer explanatory theory to "people," rather than looking at how "people" theorize?

This point might additionally be illustrated by revisiting a fragment of one of Enloe's answers. If anything *could* encapsulate how feminist methodologies *begin* to work, "I didn't notice it" might be it (651). This barely perceived nugget is offered by way of an answer to a question about Enloe's rethinking what the study of politics meant to her. The interviewers asked what produced the change: "Was it life experience, or was it the result of scholarly reflection – the outcome of reading books?" Yet another gendered (raced, classed) hierarchy hazily materializes; life experience and scholarly reflection (equated with reading books). We can think about this binary in at least two ways. Given that, globally, there are twice as many illiterate women than men (Dowd 1995: 317), scholarly reflection becomes a gendered practice. Enloe's answer emphasizes how feminist scholars have to work very hard, as much of the work involves looking to see what is not there and at what is not considered relevant or significant – at what we "didn't notice." As Carol Cohn reiterates, the defense intellectuals she works with and on shared some of her views and thoughts, yet "didn't think they were something to *think* about" (Cohn, this volume).

---

[15] Waltz said that feminists do not offer a new or revised theory; they only contribute "sometimes interesting interpretations." This despite the fact that ideas about gender, women, and sexuality seethe through Waltz's *Man, the State, and War* (2001)!

Time for feminist methodology?

Conclusions shouldn't sound too satisfied, all the edges rounded off.
(Enloe 2001: 660)

Fifteen years is not a long time in disciplinary terms. Finding feminism "still" on the margins in IR in the midst of copious feminist scholarship perhaps mirrors the fortunes of western feminist work more generally. We are witnessing an abundance of publications in the generic area of feminism and gender, alongside its apparent marginality. This paradox dovetails with a contemporary sense of both the duplicitous power and impotence of feminism. Feminism has become something of a "phantom word" – that which is at the same time fragile and a powerful seething presence. Patricia Williams offers this eloquent description:

They [phantom words] create a confined but powerful room in which to live. The power of that room . . . is deep, angry, eradicated from view, but strong enough to make everyone who enters the room walk around the bed that isn't there . . . they do not even know what they are avoiding; they defer to the unseen shapes of things with subtle responsiveness, guided by an impulsive awareness of nothingness.   (Williams 1997: 49)

Assuming the neutrality of language and concepts, Keohane expresses trepidation at the prospect of engaging in conversations about feminism, given the omnipresent threat of *ad hominem* attacks (1997: 194). For an authoritative, legitimized voice "of" IR to convey such anxiety surely gestures powerfully towards a gendered phantom that "isn't there." Yet, as the ghostly metaphors used in this chapter imply, perhaps the gendered phantom *is* there after all.

I think of feminism as something like a Tardis. The Tardis is the travel machine used in the cult 1960s television show *Dr Who*. On the outside the Tardis looks like an old-fashioned police telephone call box, but, on opening the door, the interior exposes a seemingly infinitely expansive time machine. Similarly, feminism appears to be small, confined, and with a clear, straightforward and manageable purpose, yet alternative readings, *or in use*, suggest that it is not, perhaps, what is meant to be. Feminism might be used for purposes very different from that presumed or assumed, and its capacities – or possibilities – might be infinite in that its boundaries are constantly being reinvented. This idea of infinity is not meant to breathe innocence into feminism, as, like deconstruction, feminism is both remedy and poison (Derrida 1981). Yet the idea of extending to infinity, "which rules out in advance any determination of value" (Irigaray 1985: 108), does not reflect the conventional perception of the contours of feminist IR, especially in terms of its reception outside feminist audiences in IR over the past fifteen years or so. But the traditional record that works to preserve the wealth and fortunes of IR theory tends to leave us with only glimpses of the subjects and processes in which feminists are interested. The task has always been to read or write between and around the lines of the conventional and neoconventional historical markings which are written and read through hegemonic frames.

The neediness of the discipline of IR finds repeated expression, not least in the demand that feminists tell an orderly linear story, that they narrate "a sequence of events like the beads of a rosary." Threats to figure feminism as undecidable (Zalewski 2003), in a space of permanently disputed classification, has always been disturbing for the discipline. In *Groundhog Day*, the main protagonist, Phil Connors, is seemingly doomed to endlessly rehearse the same daily activities. Escape beckons only through appropriate reclassification, which brings with it order, predictability, comfort, and (hetero)normality. Yet feminist undecidability resists this reclassification, constantly foregrounding the idea that contemporary IR is trying too hard to maintain its boundaries. "Daily life is not a tidy house where china ornaments are arranged in tight rows for display. In daily life, china is shattered, the shelves are knocked down, dirt is tracked across the carpet, and screams shatter the mirror" (de Montigny 1995: 223).

The discipline's inabilities to theorize or understand feminism in part illustrate its troubled relationship with problematizations of modernity, which has induced a "wash of insecurity, anxiety and hopelessness across a political landscape formerly kept dry by the floodgates of foundationalism and metaphysics" (Brown 2001: 5). Fear of the specter of "shattered screams" and "dirt [being] tracked across the carpet" gives some voice to the "barely speakable fears of losing the footing that enables us to speak authoritatively" that swarm through the desires of disciplinary methodological security. Setting IR "against itself" and renegotiating and destabilizing the limits of institutional and disciplinary border patrols provide one way to upset the traditional exclusionary narrative. This, however, does not promise the delivery of a "comfort text" about feminist methodology.

But Irigaray counsels, "Women, stop trying" (1985: 203). I am still disturbed by questions about feminist methodology. The point is not to refuse the questions, but rather to refuse the rush to decidability. When Irigaray urges "women" to stop trying, she is surely suggesting an interrogation of and a resistance to such questioning, rather than offering (up) a delivery of (necessarily unsatisfactory) answers. The idea(l) of methodologically supplying "concrete answers to concrete questions" is redolent of IR's disciplinary needs, yet the word – the practice – of methodology, conventionally bounded, offers no security for feminism, as it cannot proceed beyond its own narrow terms. Perhaps telling the story of feminist methodology lies in narrating the process of the search for it, and the practice of it, which, although demanding responsibility, does not allow the comfort of finality or the production of "comfort texts." This obdurate stance finds better expression through the poem which opened this paper, six lines which better illustrate the illusion of secure methodological foundations, perhaps, than twenty pages of prose.

> Local women said: no matter
> How you sprinkled it, every time
> You'd sweep a concrete floor,
> You'd get more off it.
> As if, deep down,
> There was only dust.

So, through all the concretized foundations that IR manufactures, there is, perhaps, only dust deep down. But, as the poem implies, the "dust" piles up and collects into something substantial. Trying to locate and discuss the spaces in between the dust particles and the ways in which the dust sometimes can be seen and sometimes cannot, and sometimes threatens to choke you, is one way to think about feminist methodologizing and what feminists *do*. Asking the questions "Where are the women?", "What are women doing?", "What work are ideas about sex, femininity and masculinity doing?", and the myriad questions which flow from these, evokes imageries, metaphors, and practices of a stirring or sweeping of IR with "feminine" (methodological) tools which disturb and destabilize. Seven more lines of poetry perhaps provide an evocative yet revealing response to the question "What have feminists contributed to the discipline?"

> Often during sweeping,
> A ray of light
> Through the window
> Would reveal
> How empty air
> Could hold a wall
> Of drunken dust.[16]

---

[16] Second and third stanzas from the poem "Wings," by John O'Donohue, in O'Donohue 2000.

4   Inclusion and understanding: a collective methodology for feminist International Relations

S. Laurel Weldon

Mainstream scholars of international relations seem unwilling to incorporate the burgeoning body of feminist work into their analyses (Tickner 1997, 2001; Keohane 1997; Sylvester 1996b; Whitworth 1997; Locher and Prügl 2001). Some feminists have responded to this lack of attention with calls for inclusion (Enloe 1996; Tickner 1997; 2001; Whitworth 1997; Locher and Prügl 2001; Committee on Status of Women in the Profession [hereafter Committee] 2001). Such calls are based on the argument that the marginalization of feminist work is unjust, stemming as it does from the subordination of women in society and in the field itself (Zalewski and Parpart 1998; Enloe 1993; Tickner 1997; 2001; Sylvester 1996b). In addition, feminist scholarship offers substantive insight, improving our understanding of gender inequality and prompting revision of key concepts in mainstream IR (e.g. Tickner 2001; Enloe 1996; Sylvester 1996b; Committee 2001). However, feminist scholars have been hesitant to argue that mainstream scholars who attend to feminist work will have a *better*, more objective view of international relations than those who do not. This hesitation is mainly due to concerns that making such arguments requires invoking a positivist epistemological stance or an essentialist conceptualization of women (Tickner 2001: 13; Enloe 1996: 186, 200).

In this chapter, I aim to show that these concerns are unwarranted. I argue that greater attention to feminist work on the part of mainstream scholars will result in a *better*, less partial view of international relations. Concrete efforts to take account of the perspectives of marginalized groups further our understanding of international relations, and thus constitute a *methodology of inclusion*. This is most clear when we reconstitute *methodology* more broadly to include the collective dimension of research. Indeed, I argue, feminist standpoint theory (to which many feminist IR scholars subscribe) implicitly requires, but does not offer, a collectivist approach to methodology. I propose such a collectivist account of methodology, drawing on a combination of feminist standpoint and pragmatist epistemology. This methodology of inclusion implies that attending to feminist work improves our understanding of international relations while avoiding both essentialism and positivism.

Below I begin by explaining how I understand the terms *epistemology* and *methodology*. Then I argue that feminist standpoint theory requires, but does not offer, a collectivist understanding of methodology. Third, I try to show that pragmatism offers such a collectivist account of method, albeit one that is insufficiently attentive to the importance of power. Next, I combine feminist and pragmatist approaches to develop a collectivist account of epistemology and methodology, and I draw out some implications for how the field of IR organizes itself. I argue that questions of disciplinary self-organization ought to be thought of as methodological issues, since they are critical for advancing our understanding of international relations. I briefly consider some objections that the methodology of inclusion implicitly requires a commitment to some problematic positivist tenets. Last, I give a concrete example of how inclusion produces better analysis by examining a non-academic community of knowers, namely, activists in the global movement against gender violence.

Epistemology and methodology

In this section I plan to illustrate the methodological implications of standpoint epistemology. An epistemology is an account of how we know things (Harding 1987b). I use the word "knowledge" here the way people use it in everyday language, to refer to things that we have reason to believe, to understandings of the world that help to organize or improve our lives. Epistemology is important because it shapes the *practice* of knowing, *how* we know, or methodology. In other words, methodology is epistemology in action (Harding 1987b; Ackerly and True, this volume).

Methodology, our approach to developing knowledge, has generally been understood too narrowly and individualistically. Typically, for example, methodology is thought to be a question of whether a researcher uses qualitative or quantitative methods, or what specific type of method or tool one should use to examine a specific question. But, as the Introduction to this volume points out, the knowledge we develop is even more fundamentally shaped by the questions we ask (and do not ask), by what we consider interesting and important. Even more broadly, being a scholar implies membership in a scholarly public, in a community of scholars striving for understanding. Most scholars acknowledge, for example, that they are building on the work of others, and benefit from dialogue with others, in developing their ideas. No one is developing databases and writing articles for her or his own edification; good scholarship changes minds, and gets people to do or see things differently. Indeed, the process of presenting, critiquing, and revising work is critical to furthering our understanding. This suggests that the structure of the scientific community is critical for enabling scholarly pursuits. Indeed, some argue that all science, but especially social science, can take place only in a democratic context where people can speak and associate freely (see, for example, Dryzek 1990). Others argue that all knowledge depends on communities, that the idea of an individual knower in isolation is a fiction (L. H. Nelson 1993; Dewey 1939). From this perspective, it is critical to recognize that issues of methodology are *collective* decisions, for both feminist and non-feminist researchers alike. In fact, as I argue below, feminist standpoint epistemology *requires* this broader, collectivist definition of methodology.

The need for a collectivist feminist account of science

Current feminist scholarship draws on an epistemological approach that aims to take into account the consequences of cultural differences, gender differences, and power relationships for the development of knowledge.[1] The idea of standpoint theory, or situated knowledge, is at the heart of this approach.[2] Many scholars argue that what we know is importantly shaped by the context in which we find ourselves. Standpoint theory holds that members of dominant and subordinate groups have systematically different experiences deriving from their different social positions (Hartsock 2003).

Standpoint theorists stress the epistemological benefits of examining questions from the perspective of marginalized groups. This theory emphasizes "how positions of political disadvantage can be turned into sites of analytical advantage" (Harding 1998: 91). The position of the

---

[1] Much has been made of the epistemological differences among feminist approaches to IR, leading to an identification of differences between feminist empiricists, postmodernists and standpoint theorists. But if feminist scholarship could ever be so easily divided (see Keohane 1991; Weber 1994 for an early treatment of this question), contemporary feminist work in IR has blurred these categories, melding standpoint epistemology and postmodern approaches, and incorporating many so-called feminist empiricists (Locher and Prügl 2001; Harding 1998; Tickner 1997; Tickner, this volume; True 2001; Sylvester 1996b).

[2] Here I try to characterize debates and tendencies that are most prominent in feminist discourse. Of course, in doing so, I do not deny that there are many nuances and differences among feminist epistemological approaches. But approaches that rely on the idea of situated knowledge, especially standpoint theory, in its many and varied versions, do have the implication I outline here.

subordinate or oppressed groups offers special analytic leverage because some social phenomena are not visible from the position of the powerful group. "In societies stratified by race, ethnicity, class, gender, sexuality, or some other such politics shaping the very structure and meanings of social relations, the *activities* or lives . . . of those at the top both organize and set limits on what persons who perform such activities can understand about themselves and the world around them" (Harding 1998: 150; see also Hartsock 2003). Viewing social relations from the position of the oppressed does not just add another set of experiences to existing accounts; it forces revision of the dominant accounts, since it reveals them as partial and limited (Hartsock 2003; Harding 1998).

Recently, feminist theorists have worked to move beyond the dichotomy of "powerful and powerless" implicit in early accounts of standpoint theory to recognize the multiplicity of "oppressed," marginalized, and/or feminist standpoints.[3] But the core emphasis on the connection between experience and standpoint, and on the role of power in suppressing some standpoints, is retained in current accounts (Harding 1998; Locher and Prügl 2001; Tickner 1997; 2001).

Standpoints are not *innate* in groups but rather arise from a particular political situation, namely a situation of group hierarchy or domination. Standpoints are the perspectives of groups, not of individuals.[4] Standpoint epistemology does not focus on *individual* differences in viewpoints, but rather on issues, values, or styles of discourse, that inform a *group* perspective. "Communities, and not primarily individuals, produce knowledge" (Harding 1993: 65).

Asserting that groups share "standpoints" has raised charges of essentialism (Tickner 2001; Sylvester 1996b). *Essentialism* refers to the analytic mistake of attributing a fundamental, underlying essence to a group that does not, in fact, exist. But asserting that a group shares a standpoint does not suggest that each person in the group has the same opinions or values, or that anything shared derives from some fundamental group essence or nature (cf. Harding 1998). Rather, standpoints are constructed collectively by group members. This means, for

---

[3] I follow Williams (1998: 16) in defining marginalized groups as those groups for whom social and political inequality is and has historically been structured along the lines of group membership, for which group membership is not experienced as voluntary or mutable, and for which negative meanings are assigned to group identity.

[4] Hartsock emphasizes that standpoints are not perspectives or viewpoints, but she means to say that they are not individual points of view and that they are not immediately apparent to individuals. We can use the word "perspective" interchangeably with "standpoint," then, if we stipulate that these perspectives are group perspectives and are the product of discussion among group members.

example, that feminist standpoints can be *adopted* by men, but they are *developed* when women – in all their diversity – interact, discuss, and indeed contest representations of "women," "women's interests," and women's identities. A standpoint, then, is expressed most fully in *collective* products: feminist publications, newspapers, conferences, and the like (Harding 1998).[5]

Finally, standpoints provide only a general guide to those issues that are salient for a particular group. A standpoint is an agenda, not a particular theory or policy position. Standpoints suggest problems, questions, and ideas, not worked-out answers, theories, or hypotheses (Harding 1993). Groups of women might have conflicting interests on a particular issue, but share a concern that the issue itself be discussed. So identifying a standpoint does not suggest that all the members of a group agree on anything or share an interest. A feminist standpoint is a collective product, the *result* of discussions among women seeking to alter their situation of subordination. It is achieved, not given, and must be determined by empirical observation and theoretical reflection.[6]

This discussion suggests that the development of standpoints depends on discussions among the members of marginalized groups about their marginalization: a feminist standpoint can issue only from discussions among diverse women about how best to address their marginalization. Post-colonial standpoints emerge from discussions of post-colonial peoples regarding their subordinated condition. Thus, standpoint epistemology requires that knowers from marginalized groups have the opportunity to form groups within which to develop their distinctive perspectives. Such groupings of marginalized people have been called *subaltern* or *counter*-publics (N. Fraser 1992).

At the same time, for these standpoints to advance collective understanding, they must have some influence on other knowers, especially on those groups that dominate scholarly discourse. Otherwise, the potential insights offered by these standpoints will go unrealized. Standpoint

---

[5] In this respect, a "standpoint" is quite different from the "method of gazing" proposed by Sylvester (this volume). As I understand it, this method of gazing can be undertaken by an individual person, an individual researcher. A standpoint is not something that can be attained by individuals regardless of how long they engage in reflection or discussion. A standpoint emanates from group efforts to collectively define its priorities and concerns. (Note that even if the painting "gazes back" in some sense (as Sylvester suggested in a panel discussion at the ISA in Montreal), this does not constitute a group collectively deliberating or arguing about their priorities.)

[6] As I read Hartsock and Harding, the idea of a standpoint, especially as pluralized in Harding, is quite similar to Iris Young's (2000) notion of a group perspective. Some may notice that connection as I draw on Young's concept a bit here to elaborate the meaning of standpoint and its connection to the diverse experiences of group members.

epistemology offers a corrective to the partial and limited view that is a result of restricting science to knowers from the dominant group. Standpoint epistemology seeks to identify "the assumptions generated by 'ways of life' and apparent in discursive frameworks, conceptual schemes and epistemes, within which dominant groups tend to think about nature and social relations, and to use such schemes to structure social relations for the rest of us, too" (Harding 1998: 150). Considering marginalized standpoints makes the limits of these dominant frameworks more visible.

For example, as Cynthia Enloe (1996) points out, from the dominant perspective in International Relations, the exercise of power and the maintenance of relationships of hierarchy among states look relatively simple. From this perspective, we study the powerful because they are the ones who shape international relations: "To study the powerful is not autocratic: It is simply reasonable" (188). But studying those rendered less powerful and marginalized by international relations reveals that maintaining hierarchy is actually far more complex than this account suggests. If we ask how it is that the less powerful come to participate in and support (for example, through their paid and unpaid labor) an international system that disempowers them, then we discover that the exercise of power is more complex (and perhaps more mutable) than previously thought. Taking the perspective of the marginalized reveals the importance of legitimation processes, processes by which existing political structures are portrayed as just, natural, and rational. It reveals the presence *as well as the limits* of coercive power in the everyday lives of those at the bottom of the hierarchy of power (Enloe 1996; see also Tickner 2001). Indeed, the study of social movements, of activism and resistance on the part of these very people, has resulted in current IR scholarship on "soft power" (Sikkink 2000).[7]

Feminist approaches to method require a collectivist understanding of science; standpoint epistemology implies both the existence of a scientific community and the creation of sub-communities or counter-publics of marginalized people. As Locher and Prügl (2001) note: "Feminist epistemology points away from the solitary human mind toward constituted and politically legitimized groups of knowers" (122; cf. Harding 1993; L. H. Nelson 1993). Apart from critiques of existing scientific collectives, however, feminist work on methodology has not developed a constructive account of how interactions between knowers *should* be

---

[7] See also Locher and Prügl (2001) for a discussion of feminist conceptualizations of power.

structured. Below, I draw on some ideas from pragmatism to flesh out such an ideal.

A pragmatist approach to theorizing the scientific collective

In pragmatist approaches to method, the importance of the community of knowers is primary. Consequently, pragmatists offer a somewhat more worked out account of how scientific communities ought to be organized. This account is somewhat problematic, from a feminist point of view, as I explain below. Nevertheless, the pragmatist model offers some insight into how best to organize scholarly collectives to ensure the development and dissemination of marginalized standpoints. Here I mainly draw on the discussion of scientific communities in the work of pragmatist John Dewey.[8]

For Dewey, the most distinctive feature of science, and the source of whatever value science can contribute to the world, is its *collective* nature, its "organized intelligence" (1939: 346). Knowledge is not possible for isolated, individual knowers. Knowledge of *social* phenomena is particularly dependent on discussion with others. "Knowledge cooped up in a private consciousness is a myth, and knowledge of social phenomena is peculiarly dependent upon dissemination, for only by distribution can such knowledge be obtained or tested" (1939: 394).

A scientific group is distinguished by its collective intelligence. By this Dewey does not mean that scientists are more intelligent than ordinary people. On the contrary, Dewey argues that every person can contribute to the collective intelligence of the groups to which they belong. Rather, Dewey argues that the activity of cooperation, of collective inquiry, is what allows scientific communities to make the contributions to our lives that they do make. (Of course, intelligence may be found elsewhere and may be practiced anywhere). Intelligence, as used here, does not imply the conventional meaning of the term, as individual cognitive ability or the like. Nor does intelligence mean greater apprehension of Truth (with a capital T). Any knowledge produced by scientific communities is fallible, that is, it could be revised at any time. Intelligence is defined in terms of particular contexts and situations, and is not measured in absolute terms. Intelligence, for Dewey, is a collective phenomenon, a

---

[8] Although Rorty is a more contemporary and popular pragmatist theorist, who has explicitly sought to link his ideas to feminist work, there are some problems in Rorty's work that make it more difficult for feminists to appropriate. For further discussion see Cochrane 1999.

method or orientation rather than an attribute. Intelligence refers to an open-minded will to learn. Intelligence is an attitude, and intelligence in action is "inquiry."

Inquiry is the *collective* practice of investigation of problems, confusions, or indeterminacies by a community of scholars who agree on some shared procedures or approaches. Scientific methods, then, are rather broadly defined as those practices that are recognized as valid by the scientific community. These methods must be developed in the practice of trying to confront public problems: "the tools of social inquiry will be clumsy as long as they are forged in places and under conditions remote from contemporary events" (1939: 397). Dewey is explicit about eschewing a narrow view of the scientific method based on stereotypical understandings of current practice: "Experimental method is something other than the use of blow-pipes, retorts and reagents . . . Constant revision is the work of experimental inquiry" (1939: 460). These methods change over time, and the community of scientists constantly seeks to improve them, and to incorporate new ways of obtaining insight. Although these methods are shared, then, none are immune to criticism. Collective intelligence is *fallible*.

For Dewey, the scientific method does not produce Truth, but provides a more useful way of viewing the world than did previous versions. The measure of "truth" in this sense is whether a concept or theory is helpful in understanding some specific question or issue, whether it has some practical application. Traditional epistemological questions, for Dewey, such as "the mind/body problem," do not advance science since they are not tied to practical problems (Deising 1991). We discover the methods and ideas that are most useful by critical reflection on and discussion of our collective practices.[9]

Science requires an openness to and engagement with a community:

No scientific inquirer can keep what he (*sic*) finds to himself or turn it to merely private account without losing his scientific standing. Everything discovered belongs to the community of workers. Every new idea and theory has to be submitted to this community for confirmation and test. There is an expanding community of cooperative effort and of truth. It is true enough that these traits are now limited to small groups having a somewhat technical activity. But the existence of such groups reveals a possibility of the present – one of the many possibilities that are a challenge to expansion, and not a ground for retreat and contraction. (1939: 459)

---

[9] Ideally, on the Deweyan pragmatist view, theory should perform all three functions specified by Zalewski (1996): theory as a tool for furthering understanding of problems, theory as critique, and theory as everyday practice.

The method of inquiry should not be the sole preserve of scientists. Ideally, everyone should have the opportunity to participate in constructing knowledge about society, identifying problems, devising solutions to problems. Collective inquiry should work to improve society. There is no surer way to understand it, on Dewey's view. So science is intrinsically communicative, and it is experimental in the sense that science should design and evaluate efforts to improve society (1939: 459).

For Dewey, inquiry is a process, never completed, an active expression of an openness, a willingness to learn. Inquiry is a socially shared process within critical communities (Cochrane 1999). Inquiry, or intelligence in action, requires that people participate in solving the problems that they confront. The ability to address complex problems is maximized when all affected by a problem are involved in solving it. For this to work, people must have adequate power to affect the problem-solving process. Better problem-solving results, then, from more open, participatory interactions, from more *democratic* processes (Cochrane 1999: 183; Deising 1991: 80).

This understanding of science suggests that methods are the practices that scientists use to advance our understanding and to transform problems, and they are the routines that are collectively accepted, or that eventually come to be accepted, as ways of attaining insight. Science at its best is an open, public endeavor. Complex problems, especially social science's problems, are best dealt with when all of those affected can participate in discussion. Each person participating contributes to greater collective intelligence.

Participation here does not mean mere involvement. It means that individuals are engaged in discussion, and critically reflect on the questions and problems at hand. In order for people to engage in such discussion, we have to be sure that everyone has the support they need to contribute. Collective interactions should serve to develop the capacities of individuals. In order to maximize intelligence, then, we have to ensure that individuals are not prevented from voicing an idea or question because they are intimidated or silenced by the powerful or because they do not have the resources they need to contribute effectively. The results of such inquiry are not answers that are timelessly true, but better understanding of social problems, or perhaps a reframing of the problems. Such insights depend greatly on context, however. They may not apply equally in all times or places or to all people.

Perhaps some version of this collectivist account of science might be adapted to suit feminist social inquiry. This view of science emphasizes the importance of collective critical discussion and deliberation about problems as critical for advancing our understanding of society. It is in *collective* deliberation that new ideas and methods are tested, endorsed or rejected, and emulated. The pragmatist ideal of the scientific community also grounds arguments for a wider and more diverse group of participants. Participation in the community is what makes the individual a scientist. And the community of scholars ought to be oriented towards social change for the better; it is only by trying to change things that social scientists can understand how things work, and the consequences of change. So the method of inquiry, on Dewey's view, does not allow a community of disengaged, impartial, apolitical knowers. Such a community is an *obstacle* to collective intelligence. Finally, Dewey's agnosticism as to what constitutes a scientific method, and his emphasis on collective practice, fit well with feminist principles.[10]

Problems with pragmatist collectivism

Of course, feminist readers have good reason to be suspicious of appeals to community (Cochrane 1999; Locher and Prügl 2001). Indeed, feminists have been critical of the very idea of a "community of scientists," and skeptical that such a community could be a resource for feminists. Indeed, "feminists have pointed out that these communities are rather exclusive, not only in the sense of excluding people who lack power, but even more so in excluding the standpoints of those less privileged, the ways of knowing that make sense from their perspective" (Locher and Prügl 2001: 122). Exclusion refers not only to the physical exclusion of marginalized group members from scholarly activities, meetings, and the like, but also to "internal exclusion" or the effective silencing of those who are nominally participants in a discussion (Young 2000).

Some theorists read Dewey as arguing that critical inquiry, or mere discussion, can counter the power of groups that are systematically privileged by social, political, and economic structures. These theorists read Dewey as arguing that critical inquiry will unearth such privilege and expose it to collective scrutiny, thereby undermining it. But social power is quite resistant to change. Indeed, feminists and others have criticized pragmatism for its underestimation of how resistant power is. Cornel West, for example, has observed that Dewey overestimates the role that inquiry can play in "dislodging and democratizing the economic and political powers that be" (West, in Cochrane 1999: 183). Deising (1991) similarly concludes that Dewey's unified analysis of

---

[10] For further discussion of the possible feminist appropriation of Dewey's ideas see Seigfried 2002.

science and politics was refuted by events, because he underestimated the power of capitalism.

Cochrane (1999) argues that while there is something to these concerns, Dewey does not claim that such inquiry *alone* will be able to counter or neutralize institutionalized power, although he does think it can help to undermine it. Dewey's pragmatism *does* problematize power, but under-theorizes it (Cochrane 1999). A better way of describing the problem for feminists wishing to appropriate Dewey's ideas, then, is that the concept of power does not figure centrally in his account of communities of knowledge. Feminist approaches to social science, in contrast, place power at the center of analysis (Locher and Prügl 2001; Cochrane 1999). As noted, feminist analyses of power emphasize not only the way power is used to physically exclude less powerful groups, but also the way that powerful groups dominate discussions even when less powerful groups are nominally included. This is called internal exclusion, and feminist standpoint epistemology aims to address this problem.

These feminist criticisms of the collectivist vision of science underlying pragmatism are powerful, and point to a major problem with accounts of theory and method that rely on the ideal of free discussion. But without such a collectivist vision of science, standpoint epistemology is incomplete. With a collectivist understanding of science, I suggest, feminist epistemologies are amplified and their methodological implications clarified. Below I suggest that adapting the pragmatist vision of science as a participatory, democratic community of scholars completes standpoint epistemology.

A feminist collectivist approach

Although feminists are critical of power relations in the community of scholars, standpoint epistemologies do require a collectivist basis.[11] Standpoints do not emerge fully formed from the lives of individuals. They are group standpoints. They emerge from interaction among marginalized group members, from discussion of their lives. And the relation between marginalized standpoints and dominant standpoints is critical for advancing our collective understanding of the problems that interest us (Harding 1998). Yet we know little about how knowers should interact to ensure that marginalized standpoints are developed

---

[11] Of course, a collectivist approach to scientific inquiry does not, on its own, require mechanisms to ensure inclusion. It is feminist standpoint epistemology combined with the pragmatist approach that grounds the account of scholarly collectives that I advance here.

and disseminated. How best can we structure collectives of knowers in order to deepen our understanding of the social world?

Pragmatists argue that scientists or knowers should form a community, and that the more democratic this community is, the more empowered each individual member of the community is, the better the understandings of the social world it will produce. If we understand community in the thin sense of referring to agreement on some shared norms or principles of communication, then scientific collectives can be thought to constitute communities of a sort.

Attending to the way this scientific community is riven by power, as feminists suggest, should strengthen the pragmatist account and make it more useful to feminists. Scientific collectives will not be able to capitalize on the benefits offered by marginalized standpoints if scholars have no opportunity to develop these standpoints in the first place, or if scholars ignore marginalized standpoints and continue to work with unrevised versions of dominant frameworks and methods. In order for standpoints to provide the greatest *epistemological* benefit, then, scientific communities must take measures to counter internal exclusion.

A methodology of inclusion

Democratic and feminist political theorists suggest a number of measures for making democratic systems more inclusive of such groups. Inclusive political communication requires a spirit of openness, where all parties both genuinely listen to others and genuinely seek to advance others' understanding of their positions and perspectives. Inequalities in distribution of resources needed for effective participation must be redressed. In addition, non-distributive measures such as descriptive representation, self-organization of marginalized groups, and decision rules that provide greater influence for minority groups are three major mechanisms for countering exclusion of marginalized groups. Decision rules that empower minority groups include rules that set high thresholds for agreement (for example, supermajorities or unanimous consent), while also institutionalizing dissent. I explain these ideas a bit more below, and suggest examples of how they might be instantiated in scholarly practice.

Redistributive measures

In some cases, inequalities among social groups in terms of material resources actually restrict access to deliberations. In terms of scholarship, we ought to make sure that scholarships and grants and other material resources are equally available for those working with marginalized standpoints as they are for those working solely within dominant frameworks. The Committee on the Status of Women in the Profession (2001) makes a similar recommendation in its report on women in political science.

Inclusive decision rules

In conditions of social inequality and difference, truly open deliberations are likely to be characterized by conflict. In such a context, institutionalizing dissent is important for ensuring that a search for agreement does not result in silencing weaker parties. In the absence of such procedures, the assumption of homogeneity of points of view tends to reinforce dominant group positions in discussions and makes it more difficult for marginalized groups to assert disagreement (Mansbridge 1980; Young 1990a; 2000; Williams 1998; Sylvester 1996b).

On the other hand, without any commitment to a common project, it is easy for dominant groups to ignore marginalized groups and pursue their own interests, claiming that they have agreed to disagree. For this reason, it is important to retain some degree of agreement as a goal. So that deliberations can be made more inclusive when consensus-building is undertaken as an ongoing process in relation to specific questions or contexts, disagreement (even fundamental disagreement) is an expected part of the process (Young 2000: 44).

Such rules could be instantiated in IR and in political science more generally by establishing a counter-address to a presidential address that adopted a marginalized standpoint. Journal editors should work to ensure publication of pieces articulating marginalized standpoints, and could solicit critiques of influential articles for symposia that focus on how attending to marginalized standpoints furthers our understandings of the discipline. Editors might make a practice of sending every article to scholars working from marginalized standpoints to ensure that every piece is critically reviewed from a perspective other than the dominant perspective (Women's Caucus for International Studies 1998).

Marginalized standpoints could be more fully incorporated into the discipline by giving scholars adopting these standpoints greater power in disciplinary deliberations. Editorial boards, disciplinary councils, and awards committees, for example, might adopt more stringent decision rules (supermajoritarian or unanimity rules) in order to empower those adopting marginalized standpoints. In addition, extra panel slots could be provided for the sections focusing on marginalized gender, class, race, ethnicity, or sexuality standpoints to ensure that such scholars have a platform at disciplinary conferences. We might also allot extra panels to those sections whose members attend panels organized by scholars incorporating marginalized standpoints. The point is to try to use the structure, the rules, and norms of the discipline to motivate those working within dominant frameworks to listen and incorporate subordinate frameworks (Women's Caucus for International Studies 1998).

Self-organization

In order to ensure that marginalized subgroups or "internal minorities" have the opportunity to develop and voice their distinctive perspectives, they must have the opportunity for self-organization. Feminist theorists have stressed the importance of autonomous organization by women, that is, organization under conditions where women have the opportunity to set the agenda and rules of engagement (Elman 1996; Molyneux 1998; Weldon 2002). Democratic theorists have argued that when dominated groups form a "counter-public" or separate discussion among themselves, they are better able to counter their marginalization in the broader public sphere (N. Fraser 1992; 1995; Young 2000). Such counter-publics function as "bases and training grounds for agitational activities," and provide a mechanism whereby marginalized groups can develop and disseminate new concepts and ideas to the dominant public sphere (N. Fraser 1992: 123–124).

In political science and international relations, feminist scholars have accomplished a significant degree of self-organization (Women's Caucus for International Studies 1998). Other marginalized viewpoints, however, including marginalized subgroups of women, may require more organization (Committee 2001).

Descriptive representation

Without descriptive representation (the physical presence of members of marginalized groups), there are no members of the group who can self-organize. In addition, descriptive representation can enhance the articulation of minority-group perspectives. When marginalized group members are able to speak for themselves they are better able to represent their views. Their presence also confers legitimacy on the proceedings. So efforts to ensure descriptive representation, or the bodily presence of members of marginalized groups, help to ensure that the final product reflects the perspective of the marginalized group (Williams 1998; Young 2000; Mansbridge 1999).

In order to overcome mistrust and include marginalized groups in discussions, descriptive representation must not be mere tokenism; members of marginalized groups must be present in such numbers and contexts that they can discuss issues among themselves, set an independent agenda, and present a perspective that is critical of the dominant group if necessary. Such measures can build trust and improve communication in the context of severe social inequality.

Applied to scholarly communities, these arguments suggest that such communities should take measures to ensure that marginalized groups are physically represented in substantial numbers. Moreover, this representation must not be concentrated in positions of little power or influence (Women's Caucus for International Studies 1998). Marginalized groups must be present in sufficient numbers that self-organization is a possibility, and scholarly communities should take steps to encourage and support such efforts at self-organization. In critical decisions for the scholarly community, rules should be adopted that ensure that marginalized group standpoints are voiced and heard.

Many of these recommendations are not new: as noted, some have been proposed by committees studying the status of women in the profession, others by feminist scholars advocating greater inclusiveness in the discipline (Women's Caucus for International Studies 1998; Committee 2001). But measures to reform the discipline in the ways I have outlined above are not usually thought of as methodological or epistemological issues. Both Zalewski (this volume) and Sylvester (1996b) refer to the status of feminist work in the field (in journals, in the International Studies Association) in responding to questions about what makes research feminist, but neither frames this discussion as a discussion of collective method. Indeed, Zalewski (this volume) explicitly rejects efforts to define or identify feminist methodology.

Alternatively, the measures proposed here have been thought to bring epistemological benefits mainly to those who seek to understand gender inequality. Tickner (1997), for example, claims that gender analyses are "not irrelevant" for understanding the canonical questions of international relations related to states, sovereignty, markets, and anarchy. But she argues that "feminists claim that the gendered foundations of states and markets must be exposed and challenged before adequate understandings of, and prescriptions for, women's (and certain men's) security broadly defined can be formulated" (131).[12] The argument that

---

[12] In more recent work Tickner (this volume, ch. 2) clarifies her meaning in the 1997 passage I cite here (see also Tickner 2001). In this passage, it seems, Tickner intended to emphasize the importance of feminist issues that would likely be seen as irrelevant, or

these analyses are "not irrelevant" to core questions of IR is not a particularly strong claim, especially given that the piece in question is intended (among other things) to motivate mainstream International Relations scholars to read feminist work. Moreover, in spite of the fact that Tickner presents arguments illustrating how feminist scholarship forces revision of dominant conceptual schemas, she closes by emphasizing how these accounts improve our understanding of *women's* and *certain* men's lives. This implicitly suggests that feminist work has little or less relevance to most men's lives, and suggests that the prevalent understanding of men's lives and of core questions of international relations need not be revised in light of feminist work. Certainly this is not the intended effect of the argument, but the implication is there nonetheless.[13]

Similarly, the Committee on the Status of Women explicitly enumerates the benefits of including women in political science: "First, it opens the profession to the very best political scientists without regard to gender; second, it enables the profession to take account of the contributions of women to politics and so keeps the profession on the cutting edge of new gender-related research" (2001: 319). Although this committee is discussing the inclusion of women, rather than feminist research, it is clear that the committee makes a connection between greater numbers of women and the likelihood of more feminist research. One might expect that integrating women and feminist research more effectively would bring different perspectives to bear, not only on gender politics, but also on how the discipline is constituted more broadly. Indeed, as many IR feminist scholars have argued, the absence of

not core questions, of IR. However, in this chapter I am arguing that the feminist claim on mainstream scholars (as it is articulated by Tickner elsewhere) is more extensive than merely claiming space for feminist scholarship in IR. It is to force *transformation* of mainstream paradigms as they confront (for example) the different security needs of women and some men, so that the *limits* of these paradigms, *even as they apply to questions of interest to mainstream scholars*, become clear. (As is no doubt evident from the rest of this chapter, I think Enloe 1996; Tickner 2001; and Locher and Prügl 2001 are excellent examples of how adopting feminist and other oppressed standpoints forces a reconsideration of our understanding of power in international relations.)

[13] Clearly, this is not the intended effect (see the discussion in n. 12 above). Still, I think it is vital to point out that in an important argument aimed at mainstream scholars, put forth by one of the most articulate and distinguished feminist IR scholars, the claims made for potential feminist contributions to the field seem rather weak, and seem to leave unchallenged the dominant paradigm's claims to greater objectivity and rigor. In more recent work, Tickner (2005) acknowledges the need for a mode of constructing knowledge that "acknowledges differences but allows claims that can be generalized to be made." Still, she expresses concern about the positivist associations of projects seeking objectivity and universality.

women is a telling symptom of broader problems in a discipline (e.g. Sylvester 1992b; 2002; Zalewski and Kronsell, this volume).

I am arguing for greater inclusiveness in scholarly deliberations on the basis of an elaborated standpoint epistemology, as opposed to arguments about fairness to women. I suggest that inclusiveness is a question of *methodology*. As I noted above, methodology is often thought of as constituting questions about how individuals construct their research programs. The above discussion suggests that methodology should be thought of more broadly, and should include collective aspects of research that are necessary for individual researchers' work. Harding notes that the US National Academy of Sciences has urged a broader understanding of methodology, expanding the concept to include "the judgments scientists make about interpretation or reliability of data . . . the decisions scientists make about which problems to pursue or when to conclude an investigation . . . the ways scientists work with each other and exchange information" (US National Academy of Sciences, in Harding 1998: 134). Thus, this call for a broader understanding of methodology is hardly an isolated one (Harding 1993; 1998).

Theorizing the structure of the collective required by standpoint epistemology highlights the importance of aspects of methodology that have received little attention. It also provides epistemological grounds for arguing that mainstream theorists should try to understand feminist and other marginalized standpoints in order to deepen their understanding of international relations; confronting such perspectives will show them new ways in which their accounts are limited and partial. As scholars committed to objectivity, they should seek the stronger objectivity that results from engaging these standpoints. But more broadly, it suggests that many important decisions about methodology are not made by individuals, but are collective, or, in the case of feminist IR, disciplinary. A disciplinary decision to treat scholarship from marginalized and dominant standpoints as if it were on an equal playing field in fact reinforces the marginality of standpoints already disadvantaged by power relations in the discipline. This is a more important reason for the marginalization of feminist perspectives than is sheer difference between men and women, feminist and mainstream IR discourse.[14]

The most compelling arguments exhorting mainstream scholars to attend to feminist work focus on how studying the experiences and perspectives of people at the margins, or on the bottom of the power

---

[14] It is worth noting that in other sub-fields, such as comparative politics, where feminist work has not been as widely characterized by a distinctive epistemological approach, feminist work is equally marginalized and ignored (Mazur 2003).

hierarchy, provides a *better*, fuller picture of social reality. As Enloe (1996) puts it: "It is only by delving deeper into any political system, listening more attentively at its margins, that one can *accurately* estimate the powers it has taken to provide the state with the apparent stability that has permitted its elite to presume to speak on behalf of a coherent whole" (emphasis added). Similarly, Tickner (this volume) argues that "constructing knowledge from the standpoint of the outsider provides us not only with a wider perspective but also with a unique perspective on knowledge about insiders. Since it offers us a *more complete picture of reality*, it has the potential to enrich and transform the discipline in ways that are beneficial for *everyone*" (41, emphasis added).[15]

Attending to gender *improves* our understanding of social reality in general. Feminist IR scholars do not merely aim to generate scholarship on gender, but rather seek to transform dominant paradigms, to change the broader discipline. "Its [feminism's] goal is nothing less than to transform [mainstream] disciplinary frameworks and the knowledge to which they contribute" (Tickner, this volume, 21). That is why feminist scholars object when mainstream scholars do not cite or refer to feminist theoretical and empirical work (Sylvester 1996b; Tickner 1997; Whitworth 1997). Specifying the important place that the standpoints of marginalized groups should occupy in a discipline oriented towards understanding social reality provides an epistemological and methodological basis for these demands that mainstream scholars attend to eminist work.

It is important to emphasize that the argument here is *not* just that a greater diversity of viewpoints results in better discussions (that too might ground more openness on the part of dominant viewpoints, but would still hold that all viewpoints are equally valuable) (Tickner 2001). Marginalized viewpoints are *especially* valuable for seeing the limits of dominant conceptual schemes because they offer a perspective on social reality that is invisible from the perspective of the dominant group (again, not necessarily for individuals from that group). These perspectives and experiences have generally been devalued as possible starting points for thinking about scientific problems (Harding 1993). Although all perspectives are limited, some are more limited than others *in terms of*

---

[15] Sylvester (1996b) criticizes this tendency to refer to "women" as a group and to social reality as inadvertently recreating an authoritarian, exclusionary epistemology. Her argument here is reminiscent of Butler's (1995) critique of Critical Theory in *Feminist Contentions*. In response to Butler, Nancy Fraser argues that it is perfectly coherent to maintain a critical perspective on modernist metanarratives while simultaneously engaging in corrective historiography. I follow Fraser (1995) in this essay.

offering a critical perspective on existing concepts and theories. (They are not better in an *absolute* sense.) If we wish to see the limits of the conceptual systems and perspectives that define the field, we are most likely to find these in the standpoints of marginalized groups. The payoff of taking a marginalized standpoint will be inversely related to the degree to which a dominant group is hegemonic. Thus, this approach does *not* argue that every standpoint is equally valid, and that we cannot adjudicate between and among them (Harding 1993; 1998; Locher and Prügl 2001).[16]

The criteria for preferring marginalized standpoints, then, are not timeless or placeless, nor is the preference for such standpoints absolute. Rather, the preference for marginalized standpoints is a response to the political reality that some scholarly views are disadvantaged because of their constituencies, the people they are "of" and "for." Marginalized standpoints are to be preferred for a specific purpose, that is, their ability to generate an "outsider's" perspective, a critical perspective on assumptions of which dominant groups may not even be aware (Harding 1993; 1998; Tickner, this volume).

More objections: objectivity, positivism, foundationalism

Some scholars are concerned that attending to the political context in which knowledge is generated compromises the scholarly value of *objectivity*. But, as Harding points out, this is true only if objectivity is understood weakly as "the absence of politics" or "the absence of values." But science *cannot* be value-free, especially in those dimensions of research that govern "discovery" (the identification of problems, the formulation of hypotheses, and the elaboration of key concepts) (Harding 1993: 70). Objectivity, Harding argues, is actually a much more complex and valuable concept than the mere elimination of passion or value. Objectivity implies less partiality, less distortion. A community of scientists that merely reflected the views of the dominant group (even if they tried hard to be dispassionate and "value-free") would be less objective than one which took into account a broader set of views, including those of marginalized groups.

On a more robust understanding of objectivity, such as Harding's notion of "strong objectivity," we must explicitly consider how our own personal experiences, loyalties, privileges, and group memberships

---

[16] This last claim, as I discuss later in the chapter, is controversial among feminist IR scholars. I think the idea that oppressed standpoints offer unique epistemological advantages is central to standpoint theory and important for IR theorists to retain, for reasons I explain later in the chapter.

affect our research. This does not mean that we should strive to be value-free. Some values (for example, democratic values) improve our objectivity by ensuring that research findings are widely discussed and criticized (Harding 1993). Rather, strong objectivity requires that we seek out and and take account of those perspectives that are suppressed by current power relations (Harding 1998: 129, 143).[17] These standpoints are likely to provide fundamental challenges to dominant conceptual schemes. This understanding of objectivity can ground efforts to counter those who would use power to define the best scientific outcomes: It helps to counter "might makes right" in evaluating knowledge claims (Harding 1993; 1998).

On the other hand, some feminist scholars have rejected standpoint epistemology's affirmative action for marginalized views, fearing that introducing any criteria for adjudicating between perspectives provides tools for repression and control, and suggests an implicit foundationalism (Sylvester 1994a: 45–49, 53; see also Sylvester 1996b: 257; Zalewski, this volume). But this unwillingness to adjudicate between views leaves us with little ground for arguing that scholars who are *ignoring* feminist work are working with a more limited, less accurate picture of the world than those who *do* attend to such work. Moreover, standpoint epistemology does not require a commitment to positivism or foundationalism more generally.

For example, standpoint approaches do not require the naïve assumption that the researcher is separated from the social reality she investigates (an important positivist tenet) (Harding 1993; Deising 1991). Indeed, Harding emphasizes that it is central to standpoint epistemology that the subject and object of research be placed on the same critical plane. "The fact that subjects of knowledge are embodied and socially located has the consequence that they are not fundamentally different from objects of knowledge. We should assume causal symmetry in the sense that the same kinds of social forces that shape objects of knowledge also shape (but do not determine) knowers and their scientific projects" (Harding 1993: 64).

Nor does standpoint epistemology require foundationalism, the view that "all knowledge and justified belief rest ultimately on a foundation of noninferential knowledge or justified belief" (Fumerton 2000). Standpoints do not give us some raw, infallible basis for knowledge. Rather, as noted, they give us questions, problems, and issues. Moreover, the preference for marginalized standpoints is not based on a closer

---

[17] Harding (1993) calls this *strong reflexivity.*

correspondence between the views of marginalized people and external reality (invoking a correspondence theory of truth). Rather, the grounds for preferring marginalized standpoints are contingent, and relative to the social relations that characterize society and science itself:

> Starting off thought from [marginalized] lives provides fresh and more critical questions about how the social order works than does starting off thought from the unexamined lives of members of dominant groups. Most natural and social scientists (and philosophers!) are themselves members of these dominant groups, whether by birth or through upward mobility into scientific and professional/ managerial careers. Those who are paid to teach and conduct research receive a disproportionate share of the benefits of the very nature and social order that they are trying to explain. Thinking from marginal lives leads one to question the adequacy of the conceptual frameworks that the natural and social sciences have designed to explain (for themselves) themselves and the world around them. This is the sense in which marginal lives ground knowledge for standpoint approaches.   (Harding 1993: 62)

Constructive versus deconstructive strategies

Rather than specify the epistemological advantages of taking a feminist standpoint, as opposed to a mainstream standpoint, some scholars have emphasized a strategy of deconstructing those dominant discourses to create space for oppositional or marginalized standpoints (Sylvester 1994a; Zalewski, this volume). This is a preferred strategy because of the difficulty of defining "women" in the first place, not to mention the difficulty of discovering "a women's standpoint." But as I have already noted above in relation to problems of essentialism, a perspective or standpoint is *not* the view of an individual, and it does not require a shared interest, experience or policy position. So these concerns seem overdrawn to me.

Moreover, a realistic assessment of the impact of such deconstructionist projects must concede that a purely deconstructive, as opposed to constructive, position regarding the structure of the discipline simply permits the current practice of marginalizing feminist work to continue. As Marysia Zalewski noted some years ago:

> The post-modernist intention to challenge the power of dominant discourses in an attempt to lead those discourses into disarray is at first glance appealing, but we have to ask what will the replacement be? If we are to believe that all is contingent and we have no base on which we can ground claims to truth, then "power alone will determine the outcome of competing truth claims."
>
> (in Whitworth 1994: 23)[18]

---

[18] Sylvester more recently (e.g. 1996b) seems to advocate or endorse a constructive project as a legitimate part of the feminist project; Zalewski (this volume) seems to have moved

Failing to specify the political structure of scholarly communities means that the status quo remains largely unchallenged, as alternatives to the current structure of the discipline, and the reasons for advocating them, remain murky. In contrast, the feminist methodology advanced here specifies the structure of scientific communities implied by standpoint epistemology. This specification strengthens feminist scholars' claims on scholars employing dominant paradigms; the demand for inclusion requires not just that feminist IR scholars be given space to do their work, but also that the broader field is forced to confront and grapple with that work (Sylvester 1996b; Tickner, this volume; Enloe 1996; Whitworth 1997). This does not suggest that scholarly collectives are harmonious, characterized by consensus, or conflict-free.[19] Rather, it suggests that the collectives in which we are involved (whether we like it or not) can be structured in ways that further knowledge and understanding, or they can be structured to impede it.[20] Choices about these structures, therefore, are *methodological* choices.

In their Introduction to this volume, Ackerly, Stern, and True define methodology as an intellectual process guiding reflections about the relation between epistemology, ontology, choice of method, and ethics. IR methodology concerns itself with (*inter alia*) the way that power shapes research, with what counts as an IR question, with recognizing and refining research methods. These issues are importantly determined by communities of researchers who decide what work is interesting (publishable or fundable), what counts as a method of research or analytic technique (and what counts as "doing it right"), and who counts as an expert or member of the scholarly community. In other words, it is critical to recognize that issues of methodology are *collective* decisions, for both feminist and non-feminist researchers alike. How should these collective decisions be made?

away from advocating a constructive project to a position that aims solely at destabilization of dominant theories.

[19] Indeed, above I emphasize the importance of recognizing and celebrating dissent in scholarly collectives, including the feminist collective. The implications for the feminist scholarly collective, which I do not have space to explore further here, include ensuring that marginalized groups of women (southern women, lesbians, working-class women) are *particularly* encouraged to voice their distinctive standpoints, including those critical of dominant feminist paradigms.

[20] Zalewski (this volume) declines to speak for feminists, or to take responsibility for feminist scholarship as a body. This makes perfect sense, since no individual can speak for the collective on her own, nor ought she to claim responsibility for their collective products. Still, Zalewski is part of a discussion about feminist international relations. This discussion constitutes the scholarly collective.

Rejecting this question only ensures that the current procedures for structuring our scholarly collective, with all their weaknesses, will continue. On the other hand, requiring that these decisions be made more inclusive provides an alternative model for how our scientific community ought to be structured. This model is a *methodological* approach, a way of improving scientific inquiry and rendering it more objective.

Feminist practice: the global movement against gender violence

Feminist epistemology rejects a privileging of scholarly communities as the only potential source of insight, as the only place to find legitimate ways of knowing.[21] In this case, consideration of other communities of knowers only adds force to the arguments advanced above. Many feminist collectives already adopt practices aimed at greater inclusivity, and the analytic payoffs of greater inclusion in these communities are evident.

The global movement on gender violence illustrates how greater inclusion along the lines sketched above makes analytical sense. Initially, divisions between North and South paralyzed activists in the global movement on gender violence.[22] Movements against "family violence" proceeded separately from movements to address female genital mutilation, *sati*, dowry deaths, and other phenomena identified as problems in "traditional" or "backward" cultures. State terrorism of women was also given a less prominent place in the dominant analysis and discourse about women's rights. Although western feminists proposed that violence against women (sexual assault, intimate violence, sexual harassment, traffic in women) should be seen as a continuum, there was little acknowledgment that the forms of violence against women could vary across cultures and social groups, and that different forms of violence might be salient for different groups of women. In addition, western women tended to see violence against women as an issue of equal rights, and to see it as separate from issues such as poverty or economic inequality. Southern women, on the other hand, argued that the links between violence and poverty had to be recognized. For the first decade, efforts to organize cross-nationally on issues of violence against women were hobbled by internal division (A. S. Fraser 1987; Joachim 1999; 2003; Hosken 1976; Sternbach et al. 1992).

---

[21] Many feminist IR scholars draw on instances of feminist activism as models of theoretical and methodological practice; see, for example, Ackerly 2000 and Sylvester 1994b.

[22] The discussion that follows summarizes the analysis presented in Weldon 2006.

Frustrated with their inability to cooperate, activists sought ways to forge a common agenda. Beginning in the early to mid-1980s, activists began to work to be more inclusive in their organizational efforts and deliberations. Northern women ceded leadership of key meetings to southern women, and southern women's presence at movement events expanded considerably. Southern women formed independent organizations that enabled them to magnify their voice within the transnational women's movement. Southern women were able to discuss issues on their own terms and independently identified violence against women as a priority. But southern women conceptualized such violence quite differently from northern women. As a result of these discussions, southern women began to advance a conceptualization of violence against women that included the "traditional practices" and state violence hitherto conceptualized as different or special problems for Third World women. Female genital mutilation, dowry deaths, state-sponsored violence against women, and the like were framed as part of a continuum of violence against women (Abeyesekera 1995; Tinker 1999; Ferree and Subramaniam 2001; A. S. Fraser 1987).

This broader conceptualization of the issue of "gender violence" emerged from more inclusive deliberations among women. The conceptualization was an analytic advance because it highlighted the connections among forms of violence that were not previously seen as related. This understanding of violence against women has informed, not only analyses of these particular forms of violence, but also the relationship between gender and violence more generally. Focusing on the cultural bases for violence highlighted the role of social norms in perpetuating all violence against women regardless of whether it was immediately the result of actions by men, women, or institutions. It rendered more visible the way that all violence against women enhances social control of women's behavior and maintains hierarchical relations.

Colonial discourse obscured similarities between violence against women in the North and such violence in the South. Violence against women in the South was portrayed as qualitatively different from violence against women in the North. This difference served as evidence of a backward culture or civilization in arguments regarding the civilizing mission of northern powers. In contrast, southern feminists emphasized connections between so-called "harmful traditional practices" (*sati*, dowry deaths, female genital mutilation) and the types of violence more salient in the North (wife-battering, rape). This analytic move revealed how gender was implicated in colonial relations more generally (Ngara 1985; Kishwar and Vanita 1984; Narayan 1997). These connections were not as visible or salient before southern women articulated their perspectives and northern women were motivated to listen and work towards agreement.

This broader conceptualization of violence against women facilitated cooperation among women and permitted the framing of this issue as an issue of women's human rights. These factors contributed to the success of the global movement against gender violence. Thus, greater inclusiveness in women's-movement deliberations advanced understanding of social phenomena and improved the political strength of the movement. This suggests that inclusiveness can be an important methodological as well as a political concern. Moreover, *inclusion* is an important aspect of feminist methodology.

Conclusion

In this chapter I have suggested that feminist theorizing about methodology should include a more worked-out account of what scholarly collectives should look like. This approach provides the conceptual basis on which to argue that mainstream scholarship should, for methodological reasons, attend to and take account of feminist, post-colonial, and other situated standpoints. Taking account of feminist work in international relations will advance our collective understanding of international relations, and will make mainstream work *more objective and less distorted.*

Theorizing what the structure of a scholarly feminist collective *should* look like highlights how the *organization* and *procedural norms* of the discipline pose obstacles to advancing our *understanding* of International Relations. Current feminist epistemology in International Relations emphasizes the situatedness of individual researchers, but the approach advanced here suggests that individual decisions are only part of the story; our disciplinary *structure* cannot be neutral in terms of epistemology. Some feminist epistemological approaches tend to emphasize the benefit of cultivating multiple perspectives, moving away from standpoint epistemology's original emphasis on the superiority of the subjugated standpoint. But this approach provides no political leverage for those who wish to argue that mainstream scholars must attend to feminist work. The "live and let live" approach poses little obligation on mainstream scholars, and does nothing to break down scholarly segregation. In failing to emphasize that some approaches are better than others, it obscures the weaknesses of mainstream approaches and permits mainstream scholars to dismiss feminist work. (Of course, this is not the *fault* of these feminist epistemologies.) To the extent that arguments make any difference, it is important to have grounds for demanding that mainstream scholars attend to feminist work and take it seriously, as opposed to ignoring it. In this chapter I develop the basis for saying that they must do so, not only because ignoring this work is unfair or sexist, but also because doing so blocks them, and the broader discipline, from a *better*, fuller understanding of politics. Attending to feminist perspectives (and the perspectives of other marginalized groups) should force a *transformation* of dominant paradigms and give us *all* a better understanding of international relations. This is an epistemological argument, then, grounded in feminism and pragmatism, for adopting a methodology of inclusion; for ensuring that feminist voices are articulated and heard in scholarly discussions of international relations.

Part 2

Methods for feminist International Relations

In the first part we followed three different explorations into the question of feminist methodology in the field of IR. Building upon this conversation, each author of Part II presents her methodological dilemmas, decision-making processes, and research methods. In this second part, the organizing focus on 'security' enables us to illustrate just how broadly feminists interrogate even one IR concept, and some of the many feminist approaches they have developed for doing so. These approaches are not limited to applications in the area of security studies, but instead offer possible ways of designing and conducting a broad range of feminist studies of global politics. To explore questions of security in sites familiar and unfamiliar to IR disciplinary norms of inquiry, chapters use a variety of research methods, including oral history, ethnography, interviews, archival research, participant observation, and discourse analysis, in the service of different theoretical and epistemological approaches. Centrally, the contributors identify the limitations they faced in posing their feminist research questions within the theoretical frameworks demarcated by IR.

5 Motives and methods: using multi-sited ethnography to study US national security discourses

Carol Cohn

> I needed an approach that didn't require bad guys with bad attitudes
> . . . an approach that would let you look at the nature of the way the
> whole thing was put together. (Hacker 1990)

Follow the metaphor

I embarked on my research on gender and security in the mid-1980s, during the height of the Cold War and the so-called "nuclear arms race" between the USA and the Soviet Union. The manufacture and stockpiling of tens of thousands of nuclear weapons, the quest for more "useable nukes" and more "survivable" weapons delivery systems – all of it seemed so wildly irrational to me that I was consumed by the questions: "*How* can they do this? How can they even *think* this way?"

Initially, those questions were more expressions of moral anguish and political despair than anything I might have ever thought of as "a good research question." However, the intensity of my concern led me to take an opportunity to learn about nuclear weapons from some of the men who made their living thinking about nuclear weaponry and strategy. And that experience, my first close encounter with the discursive universe of national security elites, ultimately led me into an extensive, multi-sited study of the role of gender in shaping US national security paradigms, policies, and practices (Cohn, forthcoming). This chapter is a reflection on the methodological choices I made in the course of that study.

Here is an understatement: in the course of my research, many things shifted.

My questions changed. As I became acculturated into a community of civilian nuclear defense intellectuals, my question changed from "How can *they* think that way about nuclear weapons" to "How can any of us?"

The context within which national security discourse is situated changed, as the Soviet Union split apart and the Cold War ended. The

US military participated in two regional wars and numerous peacekeeping missions. And the military itself was rocked by its own "gender wars" (see Stiehm 1996; Enloe 2000; Herbert 2000).

Thus, the scope of my inquiry changed as well, as I moved from studying nuclear techno-strategic discourse to national security discourse more broadly.

As I engaged in conversation with people in different parts of the national security community, both civilian and military, and as I listened to what they said, my question changed again, from "What is the nature of this discourse?" to "In what ways does gender affect national security paradigms, policies, and practices?"

My subject has been a moving target.

To complicate matters further: national security discourse is a complex cultural phenomenon which is produced and deployed in a wide variety of sites (see, for example, P. J. Katzenstein 1996; Weldes et al. 1999; Evangelista 1999). To study it, I needed a transdisciplinary approach and a composite methodology that combines cultural analysis and qualitative, ethnographic methods. My approach draws upon fieldwork with national security elites and military personnel, as well as upon textual analysis of Department of Defense official reports, military documents, transcripts of Congressional hearings, news media accounts (including print media, radio, and television), and popular film, to explore the ways in which national security policies and practices are deeply shaped, limited, and distorted by gender.

Naming it

In casting about to describe my method, I find myself at an interdisciplinary juncture and quandary. My eclectic background includes a proclivity both for philosophical and cultural studies analyses and for the ethnographic methods of anthropology and sociology; I am never as happy as when I am in there, able to hang out, ask questions, observe, and interview. So, I find myself working in both worlds. Ultimately, my study includes cultural studies interpretation, based in my longstanding engagement in national security issues, where every interpretation both builds on and potentially contradicts every other one. It is also based in the grounded methods of qualitative sociology and ethnographic anthropology. "Blurred genres," indeed (Geertz 1973).

In bringing the two together, I heard voices in my head. First, the objection that any empirical social scientist would have to a cultural studies analysis: "You don't really justify why you chose *these* things to analyze and not others. Since there is an infinite world out there, what's your sampling technique?"

The cultural studies voice responds: "There isn't really an answer. All you can say is, these ones were available to me. My method derives its strength from the juxtaposition and layering of many different windows. Someone else who chose ten different windows might have come up with a very different analysis. I know that. But I think there is a lot of power in the fact that there are ten windows open, and among them, I have found these continuities."

The feminist qualitative researcher chimes in: "Any investigation, and especially one of a field so vast as the production and deployment of national security discourse, is of necessity partial, in a variety of important ways."

One of the most useful ways I found to get the voices to stop talking past each other, and to articulate some aspects of the nature and logic of my approach, comes from anthropologist George Marcus.[1] In his description of multi-sited ethnography, Marcus (1995: 102) figures the mapping of a mobile and multiply situated object of study as occurring on a "fractured, discontinuous plane of movement and discovery among sites"[2] – and that seems to me to be the perfect description of the "chains, paths, threads, conjunctions, [and] juxtapositions of locations" that structure my work. In addition, in Marcus's characterizations of the different modes and techniques through which multi-sited ethnographies define their objects of study, one seemed custom-built to describe the activity that propelled me along my study's fractured, discontinuous path – "Follow the Metaphor" (1995: 108). I have been following gender as metaphor and meaning system through the multi-sited terrain of national security.

Over a decade and a half, my initial interest in ways of thinking about the discourse of nuclear defense intellectuals expanded to an interest in ways of thinking about national security more broadly, at different locations in American society. These included the mass media, Congressional hearings, nuclear weapons laboratories, military bases, and elite military professional education institutions. It is probably a good thing that I undertook my study of gender and national security in stages,

---

[1] At this point I should add something that will be obvious to many readers: this study shares many characteristics with what is known as feminist methodology. For those unfamiliar with this term, a useful overview can be found in DeVault 1999. Two works that have been particularly influential in feminist sociology are Cook and Fonow 1986; Reinharz 1992.

[2] For additional discussions of ethnographic methods when the object of analysis does not have clear boundaries, see also Appadurai 1996; Gupta and Ferguson 1997. For a description of the multi-sited critic as drawn from many feminist sources see Ackerly 2000.

adding on pieces as they became salient, rather than starting with the direct question of how to study the thinking that shapes national security practices, paradigms, and policies – for obviously, the question has no simple or single answer. National security discourse and policies are created by the workings of many complex social organizations, including universities and think-tanks, legislative and executive branches of government, the military, corporations that contract with the military, technological research and development labs, and the mass media. And the discourses used to articulate purposes and policies are not uniform throughout these different locations.

My selection of sites to investigate was both "pre-planned" and "opportunistic," very much shaped by both the nation's history and my own. When I first went to spend two weeks in a summer program run by nuclear defense intellectuals, I did not expect to become so involved in the process of thinking about their thinking. But I was almost instantly intrigued and morbidly fascinated by their world, so, given the opportunity to stay for a year, I jumped at it. Once caught up in the elaborate linguistic and conceptual systems of nuclear strategic analysis, I began to dig deeper into its premises, and started to see their ramifications far outside the specialized world of nuclear strategy (see Gusterson 1996). As the Cold War ended and nuclear weapons began to recede from the front-and-center position in public consciousness (although not from US arsenals or strategic doctrines), a series of other national security events and institutions came into the news, including the Gulf War and the military sex-and-gender controversies. As each heated up, it seemed to me an ideal site to explore the discourses through which national security is constructed and represented. In writing up my research, I sought to "bring these sites into the same frame of study" and "to make connections through translations and tracings among distinctive discourses from site to site" (Marcus 1995: 100–101).

Doing it

In addition to the choice of sites, another inevitable source of partiality comes from the practices I used to investigate my chosen sites. As Marcus describes multi-sited ethnography, "not all sites are treated by a uniform set of fieldwork practices of the same intensity. Multi-sited ethnographies inevitably are the product of knowledge bases of varying intensities and qualities" (Marcus 1995: 100). Inevitably, I could not do in-depth research at each of the kinds of sites where national security discourse is produced and deployed, and there are gaps in my knowledge, as the research had no obvious, inherent situational boundaries.

In my research I engaged in a variety of research practices. Participant observation was central to my investigation. My participant observation started with a year at each of two different institutions where nuclear defense intellectuals work and are trained (1984–5 and 1987–8). I also, throughout a decade and a half, engaged in more discontinuous, sporadic participant observation in the world of defense intellectuals through regular attendance at lectures, seminars, and conferences, both short and long, where defense intellectuals (and, occasionally, their critics) articulated their own framings of national security, and contested each other's. At these events I wrote detailed notes about what people said in their presentations, as well as how they framed their casual asides and conversations.

In addition to maintaining that participation in the civilian theoretician's world, I spent short periods, typically about a week at a time, at various military sites, including two sites where young military officers are trained (military academies) and two where more senior officers receive advanced education (war colleges); three Army bases; four Air Force bases; and four specialized military installations. My research at these sites clusters roughly into one period at the height of the Cold War (1984–9), when my interest was principally in the military variations of civilian national security discourse, and a second in the post-Cold War, post-Gulf War era (1996–9), when I had added a focus on military gender integration to my investigative agenda. In one instance, I was able to spend a week at the same site, a war college, in each of these two very different periods, and to witness both the discontinuities, and the far greater number of continuities, in the professional discourses and practices. As in the civilian part of this study, I also, throughout the entire period, attended conferences and meetings where members of the military speak to each other, as well as six conferences specifically designed to enable academics and military personnel to learn from each other. And again, I took extensive fieldnotes.

Much of the material on which my study is based came from my observations at these sites, as well as the conversations I witnessed and in which I participated. Many of the ones I "participated in" involved my asking endless questions, getting people to explain how and why they understand the world in the ways that they do. When people suggested readings to me, or when I heard readings being referred to, those, too, became part of the material I analyzed.

Aside from my endless informal interrogations, my methods also included more formal, in-depth interviews. I did eight in my earlier research with civilian defense intellectuals, one with a nuclear weapons designer, and eighty-three with members of the military, all but seven of the latter taking place between 1997 and 1999. In addition, I conducted twelve interviews with "wives" – wives of nuclear weapons designers, of military officers, of Citadel graduates, of defense intellectuals. These interviews often lent invaluable perspectives that changed my interpretations of what I was seeing and hearing (cf. Enloe 1989; Sylvester 2002a).

My interviews ran from forty-five minutes to six hours. All but twenty-one were taped and transcribed, and the rest contemporaneously documented with extensive notes. The average interview lasted between an hour and an hour and a half. Most were done in person, although I also did seven over the phone, as a way of gathering background about the gender issues at specific locales prior to my arrival. All those cases but two were followed up with second, face-to-face interviews. In nine cases I conducted a series of several follow-up interviews with the same individual over days or months, and in five cases, these interviewees have become people I consider friends, people I am in touch with about military matters on a regular basis. All but four of the interviews were one on one; each of those four included two or three people at the same time. The taped interviews were all transcribed, and read over and over again. In four cases, I was able to do follow-up interviews after studying the transcripts.

When I broadened out my research to include, not only the national security discourses used by civilian and military professionals, but also an examination of the role of gender discourse in more public, popular debates about national security issues, I drew on different kinds of source materials. For my analyses of the Gulf War, the debate on gays in the military, and *Courage Under Fire* and *GI Jane*, I continued to do interviews, but also relied far more heavily on written and visual texts (see also Youngs, Lisle, and Zalewski 1999). Since my interest in the Gulf War and the debate on gays in the military was in their public representation, I watched C-SPAN religiously, read two daily newspapers, and did online searches for newspaper stories and radio and television transcripts. In addition, for the gay debate, I relied on the Congressional record. My choice of the particular two films I analyzed was purely a result of having been asked to give a guest lecture about them at a military academy.

Asking it

But the description of the interviews in the section above is, of course, far too cut and dried. There was an "I" who asked the questions, and inevitably, who I am shaped not only what I noticed and was able to hear, but also what people what would say *to* me and *in front of* me. At the time I started, in the mid-1980s, being a young woman in the entirely white male world of nuclear defense intellectuals, or in the nearly equally white male world of military officers, was probably a help. As a woman in a male domain, at a time when feminist critique had not really reached it, I was unthreatening. My asking questions did not change that – questions about what people think and why they think that way tend be heard as naïve questions, and naïveté has always been acceptable for a young woman, in a way it is usually not for a man. As long as I made some attempt to frame my queries in the terms of the professional discourse, I could ask questions without evoking the dismissal or contempt that might devolve on a male questioner who appeared so ignorant. Instead, it tended to evoke a straightforward, pedagogical response, or a courtly paternalism, with considerable time taken to explain things to me. In the military, I sometimes found that officers misheard my questions, not expecting the kind of question I was asking to come out of my mouth – and then, the misreadings were fascinating.

I also found that my questions were not likely to be experienced as challenging, since no one expected me truly to understand what they did, and since issues of masculine competition were not evoked by my interactions. I became aware of this during a part of the project when I was working with a distinguished white male psychiatrist, perhaps twenty years my senior. In the interviews he conducted with powerful nuclear decision-makers, he said he often found that he became competitive with them, and vice versa – alpha males from different domains scrambling for dominance in the interviews. Further, when it happened, he said that it became personally difficult for him to ask questions perceived as "naïve" – it was too hard in the competitive environment to give up the mantle of expertise. I, on the other hand, given my age and gender, was perceived as neither an authority in a different domain nor a competitor. And I suspect that being seen as ignorant was an experience that gender, age, and status made far easier for me to deal with than it did him. In short, I think it was very easy for civilian defense intellectuals to talk in front of me without self-consciousness, and they tended to be very generous and forthcoming in responding to my questions.[3]

By the time I started asking questions about gender in the military, both the political context and some of my own identity markers had changed. The context was one of heightened sensitivity around gender issues; the military was not only undergoing continuing conflict about

---

[3] For an interesting discussion of viewing the self "as resource rather than contaminant" see Krieger 1991.

such issues as whether women should be in combat roles, or whether gender integration had "feminized" the military, but was also still dealing with the fallout from highly visible sexual harassment and assault scandals of the 1990s (see M. F. Katzenstein 1998). There was the clear perception among many military men that it might no longer be advisable to voice certain thoughts and opinions about women in the military, unless among friends. I, in the meantime, was still a white middle-class woman, but now in the categories of "middle-aged" and "mother." My motherhood probably served to normalize me to many military men.[4] In contrast, my status as "college professor," which had normalized me to academic civilian defense intellectuals, did not have such a positive effect in the military.

At the risk of stating the obvious, I came to the military officers as an outsider. Not only did they have no particular reason to trust me, but also many probably felt they had reasons not to. In a military context, as quickly became evident, the salient features of my identity were that I was a white woman, a civilian, and a college professor. None of these was a plus. Military alienation from civilian society is a problem that many see as greatly exacerbated in recent years. In military culture at present, there is a general belief that civilians just don't understand the military, as well as an increasing antipathy toward what they perceive as a dissolute, immoral, and undisciplined civilian culture.[5] In addition, considerable resentment is evoked by the perception that civilians are simultaneously attempting to make the military into a social laboratory (for example, through demanding completely equal treatment for women, or attempting to end the homosexual exclusion policy) disregarding and disrespecting its true mission, and, at the same time, deeply cutting the military budget and asking them to do more with less. As to college professors, I must admit that I was taken by surprise by the degree of suspicion and animosity toward college professors evidenced by a large number of officers. That animosity is based on the perception that college professors cluster at the left-liberal to flaming radical end of the political spectrum, and have little regard for truth, fairness, and objectivity because they are so dedicated to so-called "political correctness." Although (not surprisingly) no one stated this directly to me in an

---

[4] Dana Isaacoff, who in 1993 was a US Army captain and an assistant professor of political science at the United States Military Academy, when she spoke about becoming pregnant while on the USMA faculty, said that it made it much easier for many men on the faculty to deal with her. Comments at the Workshop on Institutional Change and the US Military: The Changing Role of Women, Cornell University, Ithaca, NY, November 13–14, 1993.

[5] For an influential account of this divide, see Ricks 1997.

interview, I became painfully aware of this fact when I attended a lecture by a conservative journalist at one of the war colleges. When he made a disparaging remark about Harvard having more Marxists than Russia does, the normally quiet audience of several hundred senior officers roared its assent. I was sitting with a few officers whom I had got to know fairly well, and at the break, I broke my characteristic reserve and vented my anger at the remark, having spent quite a bit of time at Harvard without meeting any Marxists. They seemed interested and surprised (very much as some of my academic colleagues are when I speak about intelligent, thoughtful military officers), and we then got into a discussion in which they offered counter-examples, which they had heard or read about, of egregious discrimination by liberal professors against conservative students.

My status as a civilian professor was exacerbated, of course, by being a white woman, since when you put those together it translates to liberal white woman, which in turn translates to "anti-male" and pro-women's equality in the military. All this before I opened my mouth. In addition, I initially introduced myself as a researcher interested in gender integration in the military, who taught sociology and women's studies at a liberal arts college. But "women's studies" is instantly equated with "feminist," and for many male officers, there was no space between that term and "feminazi" – making the possibility that I would be viewed as a researcher genuinely interested in their perspectives recede yet further into the distance. In later interviews, I introduced myself as a sociologist interested in gender, an only slightly less inflammatory label. As a civilian white woman academic asking questions about gender integration, I was most often assumed to be in favor of it, and against men who resisted it, unless proven otherwise. A further wrinkle in the fabric of who I was perceived as being came from the fact that I was often asked to send a resumé before I arrived. Usually, I suspect these were just filed. But in two cases, officers went to the library, read some of my writing, and reviewed it for others. This made for some interesting conversations; it did not, to my knowledge, prevent many from happening.

But the vast majority of the people I interviewed had read neither my resumé nor my articles, so "white woman civilian college professor asking about gender" probably sums up the terms in which initial assumptions were made. As I hope is clear, I am pointing to these assumptions because they bear on methodological and epistemological issues, not to disparage these officers for having a series of stereotypes. Everyone makes a series of default assumptions based on gender, race, class, and occupation, to name a few; and it is most unlikely that a group of feminist academics would make any fewer about, or be any less suspicious of, a white male military officer who came to interview them. The point is that the usual issues of gaining some degree of trust that are always part of the process of interviewing are compounded in this instance by a set of assumptions rooted in a deep cultural divide between military and civilian, as well as gender difference.

I had some, limited, ways of dealing with this. First, at sites where my participant observation would include formal interviews, I tried, whenever possible, to come to military installations in some official capacity *in addition to* that of research interviewer; for instance, to give a lecture (albeit about gender), or to participate in a seminar, or as a "civic leader" on a public affairs tour. This not only gave me some (*very*) small imprimatur of acceptance, but also, more to the point, gave the officers some time and space to get to know me before we actually sat down for an interview. In this way, many discovered that I did not, in fact, fit their worst nightmare stereotypes.

Second, in this kind of situation, "snowball sampling" becomes crucial. I had the most access, and the best possibility of trust, when one particular officer got to know me over a period of time and then buttonholed others, asking them to let me interview them, vouching for "the way I did business." (Here again, being somewhere for several days before interviewing starts makes it much more possible to develop this kind of relationship.) In this situation I would also tell that officer that I was interested in people with a wide range of positions on the matter, from those very supportive of gender integration to those very opposed, and he or she could quickly arrange for me to get a wider range of opinions than I would have been likely to be able to arrange myself.

Third, at the beginning of an interview, in explaining what I wanted to interview them about, I directly stated to the officers that my interest was not in trying to justify or support any particular position on women in the military. Rather, as a researcher, my assumption was that different people had different opinions, that those opinions developed in understandable ways from their own experiences, and that I wanted to understand more about how people thought about the issue, and what experiences and ideas led them to think that way.

Fourth, before starting each formal interview, I discussed the means by which I intended to protect confidentiality and anonymity, and asked each officer to write, directly on the consent form, a phrase I might use to refer to him (or her) that was sufficiently general not to compromise anonymity. If I had come to the post under the auspices of a high-ranking officer, I was also careful to state that I would not report to him anything people said in the interviews. In addition, both verbally and on the consent form, we agreed on the standard disclaimers – that whatever was said would be the opinion of the individual, and that she or he in no way represented the position of the military institution, branch of service, or the US Department of Defense.

What was the result? Varying degrees of openness and willingness to talk. A very high percentage of people seemed extremely open and forthcoming, often revealing things that clearly would cause difficulties for them if exposed, or clearly deviating from "the official line." Others were guarded, but in only one case did I have the clear sense that an informant had decided he was just going to stonewall straight through the interview. Interestingly, he was the officer who had carried "the football" (the case containing nuclear launch codes) for a past president, a fact he obviously took pride in. But one thing is certain – no matter how open men became in the course of our interviews, none of them ever spoke to me in the same ways they would talk to their buddies in the cockpit or over a beer. So it is safe to say that there was not only a fair amount of self-censorship going on, but also conscious choices about how to say things – not only because I remained an outsider, a member of several different classes of people who were not easily respected or trusted, but also because of the more regular ways in which any of us gauge what it is appropriate to reveal, in what language, to different people in different contexts. But it is also safe to say that, in whichever of their ways of framing their experiences and ideas that people chose, many of them were extraordinarily revealing.

"Getting it"

As part of my fieldwork, one of the ways in which I attempted to assess whether or not I've "got it" – that is, the usefulness of my insights and the persuasiveness of my arguments – was through giving public talks, seminars, and briefings to people in the discourse communities I wrote about.[6] Upon the sixteen occasions when I did so, I received feedback in several forms. First, the questions and comments during the event itself were usually lively, intense, and sometimes contentious. I would always stand at the podium or sit at the seminar table with a pad and pen, and try, at breakneck speed, to write everything people said, before

---

[6] The legitimating criteria important to me in my work include understanding rather than validity, persuasiveness, and pragmatic use (in the sense both of insights that can help produce new ways of seeing things and understanding one's situation, and of contributing to processes of social change). This now would be categorized as a "post-foundational approach to validity and textual authority" (Denzin 1995). See also Ackerly and True, this volume.

I responded to their comments. Second, in many cases I was also able to have more extended dialogues with individuals who attended. Sometimes, these were in the form of the ten-minute conversations you have with people who come up to speak after a talk, or the dinner conversations you have with someone who wants to discuss a paper you have just given at a conference. As quickly as possible after each of these, I would again take detailed notes on what was said.

The third form of feedback I got came in formal interviews. In some instances, these had been scheduled ahead of time, as when I went to give a briefing at a military installation. As the interviews progressed, although my questions were not about the topic of talk, people often got round to telling me what they thought about what I'd said, what I'd got right or wrong, or what new way of thinking about an experience my talk had given them. If they did not, in some instances I would ask, saying that, as an outsider looking in, it would be very helpful to me to hear what they thought I was missing. Although I'm sure that the terms in which they answered were often different from those they had used when speaking to the guy next to them in the audience, people were rarely shy about answering. I am grateful for their willingness to "talk back" to my talk, to challenge my discursive framework with their own; I learned a tremendous amount from those interactions.

Some interviews arose out of other contexts, where I had gone to give a talk as a "one-shot" deal. If someone in the audience had had a lot to say during my presentation, I might approach him or her at the end, and ask if he or she would be willing to talk with me further. I would frequently ask the same thing of people who came up to talk when my presentation was over. If they said yes, we would set up a formal, taped interview.

The fact that my research took place over an extended time, and that I published several articles based on it along the way, provided me with another means by which to assess how well I "got it." A cover story in the *Bulletin of Atomic Scientists* generated voluminous mail from defense intellectuals, as well as phone calls and interviews. It has also meant that for years, whenever I have attended a conference or seminar in the civilian defense intellectual community, the line that follows introductions is often, "Are you the Carol Cohn who . . .?" Lively conversations frequently ensue – and I go back to my room and take more notes.

Finally, I was also fortunate to have trusted insiders in the communities I wrote about, who generously agreed to review my work. I asked them to read drafts to make sure that I would do no harm by inadvertently violating anonymity (or by other means), to try to rescue me if I fell into one of my own knowledge gaps, and to let me know if they thought I had "got it."

Studying up and "listening to the material"

Now, here is a differently voiced version of the story of my methodological choices. I started my study of nuclear discourse because I was deeply troubled by it – a feeling undiminished by the intervening years, and the end of the Cold War. I have long felt that US national security policies, both nuclear and conventional, have been terribly wrong-headed. I thought that I might get a better handle on how to change them by "studying up" – Laura Nader's term for doing anthropological research about "those who shape attitudes and actually control institutional structures" (1972: 284).[7]

My first question came from hearing public figures talk about nuclear war. *How*, I wondered, can *they* think this way? When I met and listened to some of these men close-up, the question intensified. But my (temporary) residence in their "discourse community"[8] had effects on how I thought, and my question changed from "How can *they* think this way?" to "How can any of us?" In other words, my focus shifted from trying to think about individuals and their possible motivations, to the power of language and professional discourses in shaping how and what people think.

My approach has its roots in two places: in social constructionist theory, and in the practice of classroom teaching. My starting point is one that is taken for granted in many academic circles, and either foreign to or hotly contested by the people I write about. I understand reality as a social construction. This is not to say that "there's no *there*, there"

---

[7] Nader's decades-old plea for "studying up" is still quite relevant, and worth reproducing: "Anthropologists have a great deal to contribute to our understanding of the processes whereby power and responsibility are exercised in the United States. Moreover, there is a certain urgency to the kind of anthropology that is concerned with power [cf. D. L. Wolf 1969], for the quality of life and our lives themselves may depend upon the extent to which citizens understand those who shape attitudes and actually control institutional structures. The study of man is confronted with an unprecedented situation: never before have so few, by their actions and inactions, had the power of life and death over so many members of the species." There is now a small emergent literature of anthropologists "studying up," and investigating powerful institutions. Important examples include Gusterson 1996; Kunda 1992; Marcus 1992; Zonabend 1993; and Traweek 1988. For more recent, sociological articulation of the importance of studying the "relations of ruling," see D. E. Smith 1987; 1990a; 1990b; Mohanty 1991a; 1991b. For an example in feminist IR see Prügl 1999.

[8] The term is Clifford Geertz's (Geertz 1973).

(Gertrude Stein's unkind remark about Philadelphia), but that the "there" is accessible to us only through language and other forms of representation. And in our speaking about and representing the world to, with, and for each other, we construct it.[9]

The practice of teaching has also focused my attention on language. In conversations in the classroom, I am repeatedly struck by George Orwell's point that clear thinking is not possible without clear language – and that true democratic politics is not possible without both. Orwell has been my longtime grounding and orienting influence. In many ways, his whole journey might be traced back to his essay "Politics and the English Language"(Orwell 1954) (although rereading it is always a painful reminder of one's own limitations as a writer).

Listening

My study of national security discourse is the product of combining my political concerns with my intellectual interests in how people think, and the role of language in not only constructing and reflecting meaning, but also in shaping systems of thought. Although what impelled me into this research was a political critique, in the actual doing of the work I have had to try to put that aside. This is not because I hold a positivist notion of objectivity, but for several reasons. First, because my goal is to learn, to find out what's out there, without imposing preconceptions about what people are like, what the issues are, or what form of analysis or theoretical framework is most appropriate to engage. I was not trying to prove a point or test a hypothesis, but to see what was there and think about it. I am not as hopelessly naïve as that may sound. Inevitably, everything about who I am – how I am embodied, what my life and intellectual history have been, and so on – shapes what I do and do not notice as significant, and how I interpret it.[10] Other people, with diverse past experiences, political commitments, and favored analytic frameworks would no doubt look at and hear the same things that I heard, and inevitably notice different things and come to different conclusions. But within and despite an awareness of those limits, my thinking about research is in part reflected in the way that Barbara McClintock spoke

---

[9] This is not the place for a detailed exposition of social constructionism. Texts influential in forming my understanding of it include Berger and Luckmann 1966; Foucault 1972; 1980; Latour and Woolgar 1979; Lyotard 1984.

[10] Numerous authors emphasize that the social position of the knower shapes the knowledge he or she produces. Among them I have been especially influenced by Collins 1986; 1989; 1990; Cook and Fonow 1986; Haraway 1988; Harding 1986; Hartsock 1983; [1983] 2003; D. E. Smith 1987); 1990b.

about her work in corn genetics. She emphasized the importance of trying imaginatively to get down there in the kernel of corn, to "listen to the material and let the experiment tell you what to do" (Keller 1985: 162). I think that the material can sometimes even point you towards the tools you need to understand it; not because there is only one, true, accurate understanding to which any one of us has privileged access, but precisely because "nature [and social life] is characterized by an a priori complexity that vastly exceeds the capacities of the human imagination."[11] Each of us will bring different insights to understanding and interpreting that complexity, if we "listen to the material." More than twenty years ago, my sister-in-law came to this country from Japan. Shortly afterwards, when I asked her how New York compared to what she expected, she shook her head, and explained, "Before I came here, I made my mind a blank sheet of paper." Postmodern epistemologies tell us to forget about that possibility. But we can still try to take as many as possible of the sheets that are written all over, and put them aside for a while.

My other reasons for always trying to set aside my politics, opinions, and analyses were much more personal. And since I believe that our research agendas and methodological preferences are shaped not only by intellectual commitment, but also by personal, emotional predilection, I want to note them. First, temperamentally, I am a listener. In a conversation, give me the choice between telling people what I think about something, or finding out how they think about it, and I will almost always choose the latter. After all, I already *know* what I think. I have always loved traveling and talking with people in very different places, getting glimpses into, and trying to imagine, lives very different from my own.

Second, I find it excruciatingly painful to have direct confrontations with very powerful people who are doing (or have done, or will do) what I consider to be terrible things, or things with terrible effects. And I do not see the point in it. All evidence suggests that if I were to argue with them, trying to get them to see their decisions differently, it would have no effect. And it is very painful to be so powerless to stop actions I see as morally reprehensible.

Finally, and maybe most significantly, I find it both personally and professionally untenable to talk with people without being able to be honest about what I want to know, and why I am talking with them. To do that, I have to let my genuine interest in how the world looks to them, and why it does so, be what I and my research are about.

---

[11] Keller describing McClintock's worldview (Keller 1985: 162).

Putting genuine intellectual curiosity – the desire to understand – at the center of who I am when doing research is not difficult. But some of the situations in which I have practiced that centering have made me feel that my head would explode. I will never forget sitting and having lunch with former Secretary of Defense Robert McNamara. For the preceding twenty-five years, he had been to me an icon of arrogant immorality, a man with the blood of hundreds of thousands of innocent people on his hands. It is hard for me adequately to describe the intensity of my feelings about him, especially during the height of the Vietnam War. And now here I was, sitting next to him – we placed our cloth napkins in our laps, were served by uniformed waiters, sipped our wine, and chatted, all as in any other upscale luncheon – except that I have always thought of him as a war criminal. I put that thought aside, and recentered myself in my interest in how he thinks about nuclear weapons now, and why. (This was when he was still holding his long public silence on Vietnam – I knew that it could not be a subject of my questions.) I asked what were for me genuine questions about what he had said, why he believed it, and why he did not take some other position. I was impressed by his thoughtfulness and his intelligence. I remembered the blood. I returned to the connection and respect I felt for him in the moment. It happened several more times before the meal was over. I have never been able to sort out the morality of that particular interaction to my own satisfaction.

Although, in the midst of the incident I have just described, I kept putting them aside, I have, throughout my research, tried to pay attention to feelings. That includes both those of the people I have observed and talked with, and my own. In participant observation and interviews, I've listened for differences in emotional tone and intensity that accompany different utterances, and the focus on both the apparent presence and apparent absence of emotion has been part of what guides my attention to issues that merit further analytic curiosity. I've also found that paying attention to my own feelings has at times been key to my understandings. In my first experience of participant observation among nuclear defense intellectuals, I took the feelings I had while being enculturated, learning techno-strategic discourse, and asked what they could reveal about the discourse and the process of professionalization. I was fascinated to find, after my reflections were published in the *Bulletin of the Atomic Scientists*, that several defense intellectuals told me variations on the same theme – "Yeah, I had those feelings, too, but didn't think they were something to *think* about." It is precisely because techno-strategic discourse rests on the radical separation of thought from feeling, on the assumed necessity of excluding emotions from rational thought (or rather, excluding anything *recognized* as emotions), that acknowledging the integration of thought and feeling is so important to me here. Noticing, and thinking about, feelings has consistently pushed my thinking further – and not only in learning about techno-strategic discourse. The fact that I have liked, and in a variety of ways respected, so many people whose choices and actions I not only "disagree" with but am sometimes enraged by and despairing about, has consistently led me to realize the limits of my understandings, and that I had to go further.

Ending

My method derives its strength from the juxtaposition and layering of what I found in different sites, in different contexts, with different constituencies. I chose what I think of as several different windows through which to look at national security discourses. I know that someone else would have chosen other windows, and, even looking through the same windows, would have been likely to come up with a different analysis. I know that had I listened at a different think-tank, interviewed at a different base, watched C-SPAN on different days, or read different newspapers, I would have heard different things, and might conceivably have come up with a different analysis myself. Nonetheless, it is significant that over fifteen years, as I looked through a variety of windows, and listened to multiple local discourses and contextual permutations of national security discourses, I heard things in common, threads that could be pulled through; whether talking to generals or enlisted men, liberal strategists or a Secretary of Defense, certain continuities could be found. I am very aware of the disjunctures as well as the resonances across the domains I have been privileged to enter, and understand that the discontinuities are also tremendously important, and that, for the sake of my argument, I have probably leaned on the continuities more than on the discontinuities. However, I believe that the continuities across sites are telling, and significant. To study them, I used a variety of methods, and participated in different locations in varied ways. The persuasiveness of my study derives from and must rest upon the very multiplicity of spaces within which I trace metaphoric gendered themes and their variations in the production of national security paradigms, policies, and practices.

6 Methods for studying silences: gender analysis in institutions of hegemonic masculinity

Annica Kronsell

Introduction

Institutions such as the military and state defense organization are central to the field of international relations. Simultaneously, they represent and reify specific gender relations. This chapter centers on methodological issues for feminist researchers interested in these institutions. They are institutions of hegemonic masculinity because male bodies dominate in them, and have done so historically, and a particular form of masculinity has become the norm (Connell 1995: 77). Although many institutions of importance to international relations can be categorized as institutions of hegemonic masculinity, the defense and military organizations have a particularly strong standing. The basis for my methodological reflections is a research puzzle aimed at mapping out and making sense of the gendered practices of the Swedish military and defense organization. Examples are given throughout from the study of military and defense institutions in Sweden. My approach starts from post-structural feminism and gives weight to structural components of gender relations, reproduced when individuals perform within institutions. It follows that I see institutions in general as important for understanding gender relations, but I have a particular interest in institutions of hegemonic masculinity. Apart from feminist IR work I have found much help in organizational studies dealing with gender and sexuality (Hearn and Parkin 2001; Wahl et al. 2001; Alvesson and Billing 1997; Hearn et al. 1989). Here I suggest that gender dynamics

I am indebted to the Swedish Emergency Management Agency for funding my research during the work on this chapter. Many examples given in this chapter are taken from the project "Masculinities, femininities, and the changing Swedish security politics," financed by the Swedish Research Council and conducted together with Erika Svedberg, Örebro University, 1999–2003.

of these institutions be studied through analysis of documents, places and narratives. One way, then, is through the deconstruction of the texts and discourses emerging from these institutions, sometimes "reading" what is not written, or what is "between the lines," or what is expressed as symbols and in procedures. Institutions both organize and materialize gender discourses in historically dynamic ways, while simultaneously enabling and restricting the individual involved in institutional activities. Institutions have a part in forming subjects. At the same time, institutions are actively reproduced as well as changed through practice. Hence, change is not a simple or straightforward process. However, I argue that when institutions of hegemonic masculinity open up to "others" and, for example, no longer rely on strict gender segregation, there is a particular potential for institutional change and development, and hence also of changing gender relations. A method suggested here is listening to the stories of women engaged in such institutions. Through their experience they generate important knowledge that can help explore institutional silences on gender. Interviewing is an obvious method, yet not problem-free as Stern, D'Costa, and Jacoby (in this volume) also point out. I suggest a method for how to work around the problems interviews pose, by also considering narratives formulated in other contexts (such as "internal" newsletters).

Deconstructing the "silence" of gender relations

I became interested in what Hearn and Parker (2001: xii) call "the silent unspoken, not necessarily easily observable, but fundamentally material reality" of institutions. Silence on gender is a determining characteristic of institutions of hegemonic masculinity and this is a key point. It indicates a normality and simply "how things are." Men are the standards of normality, equated with what it is to be human, while this is not spelled out (Connell 1995: 212). Hegemonic masculinity "naturalizes the everyday practices of gendered identities" (Peterson and True 1998: 21). This has led to the rather perplexing situation in which "men are 'persons' and there is no gender but the feminine" (Butler 1990: 19). Hence, masculinity is not a gender; it is the norm. It should be noted that in the Swedish context, this masculinity norm derives from a standard associated with white, heterosexual, male bodies.[1]

---

[1] In our project we mainly focused on the silence around women but suspected that homosexuality and ethnicity were also silenced issues. From some follow-up research I can conclude that this has been the case, basically until 1999.

What I focus on is the normality, reproduced within organizations, and how that can be approached methodologically. The goal is to problematize masculinities and the hegemony of men (cf. Zalewski 1998a: 1). This is a risky enterprise because masculine norms, when hegemonic, are never really a topic of discussion. They remain hidden – silenced – yet continue to be affirmed in the daily practice of the institutions. Kathy Ferguson (1993: 8), for one, suggests we challenge that which is widely acceptable, unified, and natural, and instead perceive it as being in need of explanation. Breaking the silence is to question what seems self-explanatory and turn it into a research puzzle, in a sense, by making the familiar strange. It means giving the self-explanatory a history and a context. Cynthia Enloe (2004; 1993) encourages feminists to use curiosity to ask challenging questions about what appear as normal, everyday banalities in order to try to understand and make visible, for example, as she does, the gender of international relations (IR) both as theory and as practice. The first step is to question even the most banal or taken-as-given of everyday practices of world politics. In her study on women's collective political organizing in Sweden, Maud Eduards (2002: 157) writes that "the most forbidden act" in terms of gender relations is to name men as a political category, which transfers men from a universal nothing to a specific something. If this is so, how can we actually study such silences? What are the methods by which we can transcend this silence on gender?

Deconstructing silences

Since the early 1990s, feminist IR researchers have used deconstruction to highlight how mainstream IR literature is laced with gender dichotomies, stereotypes, and practices, while, at the same time, it is completely oblivious to gender. Ann Tickner is one of the first to deconstruct IR theory, with a reformulation of Morgenthau's principles (1988). She continues along this path in her 1992 book on *Gender in International Relations* by "bringing to light" what she believes are "the masculine underpinnings of the field" (Tickner 1992: xi). Deconstruction makes gender relations visible by overturning the oppositional logic that mystifies categories like woman/man, domestic/international and peace/war. It requires a form of double reading that exposes historically derived norms underlying concepts. Jean Bethke Elshtain's well-known work *Women and War*, from 1987, uses deconstruction as a method to locate the binary gendered categories upon which discourses of war and peace are based (see also Molloy 1995; Elshtain 1988). Christine Sylvester (1994a) deconstructed three IR debates and seriously questioned the epistemological and ontological underpinnings of IR theories that have left "women" and "gender" outside or, at best, in the very margins of the discipline. The activities associated with men and masculinity constitute IR's main story (Peterson and True 1998: 20). Yet, until feminist IR arrived, men, women, and gender were not topics for the discipline. I became inspired by this deconstruction of IR theory that made visible the academic discipline's gendered norms.

There are, however, differences between the academic institutions of IR on the one hand, and military and defense institutions on the other. Yet the connections between them are highly relevant. Craig Murphy (1998: 94) argues that it is the link between the military and men, and the exclusion of women from military activity and combat, that are at the very core of IR. Realism, for example, is a form of embodiment of hegemonic masculinity wherein "the perspective of elite white men and the ideal of the glorified male warrior has been projected onto the behavior of states" (Hooper 1998: 42). Quite obviously also, IR's practice – the diplomatic corps, the defense security, and military organizations – are institutions of hegemonic masculinity where gender has been silenced; and this is where we turn next.

Hegemonic masculinity

Military, defense, and security related institutions have historically been "owned" by men and occupied by men's bodies. This has influenced these institutions' agendas, politics, and policies. In using the concept "institutions of hegemonic masculinity," we denote a particular interest in the norms associated with the institutions. However, there appears to be a strong material dimension to such norms, since, it is argued, they are often associated with male bodies. Robert Connell (1998: 5) says: "Men's bodies do not determine the patterns of masculinity, but they are still of great importance in masculinity." Hegemonic masculinity cannot, therefore, be completely disentangled from male bodies. In some instances the hegemonic masculinity of these institutions directly corresponds to male bodies, as women are completely excluded through legislative acts from the military and defense institutions in a majority of countries.[2] As we shall discuss in some depth later on, women's bodies present a very tangible challenge to institutions of hegemonic

---

[2] This is not the case in Sweden. In 1980, women were admitted to military training if they aspired to become officers. In 1995, conscription on a voluntary basis became an option for women.

masculinity, against this normality of male bodies. The continuity of the domination of hegemonic masculinity, I argue, depends on the maintenance of separate spaces for men's bodies, and hence, women are a clear threat to this order.[3] The hegemonic masculinity associated with military and defense institutions does not necessarily mean that it should reflect the most common form of masculinity in society (Connell 1998: 5). As a matter of fact, Joshua Goldstein's research (2001) shows that in comparison to other institutions in society, defense and military institutions have been associated with specific gender stereotypes, consistent across both cultures and time, which do not always correspond with norms of masculinity expressed in society at large.[4] Furthermore, hegemonic masculinity does not preclude the fact that diverse masculinities can be expressed. On the contrary, some studies point to the necessity of diverse masculinities for the hierarchical structure of the institution to function (Miller 2001; Hearn and Parkin 2001). Although I am interested in exploring this in future research, here I shall not differentiate between possible masculinities.

Let us now turn to an example, where I attempt to show more specifically what we found to be a silence in the Swedish military organization, namely conscription and how we subsequently analyzed this.

The "silence" of Swedish conscription

In the initial stages of the research process it was clear to us that an extremely important and highly institutionalized practice, conscription, was evidently gendered; yet little was said about this fact. There was minimal documentation on gender and conscription within the Armed Forces and related associations, on the political arena, and among societal actors and feminist scholars. The military manpower of Sweden has historically been generated through conscription; hence, it involved a majority of the Swedish male population at one point in their lives. As an

---

[3] A more intangible challenge to hegemonic masculinity – less inscribed in the body – is homosexuality, which will be discussed further on in relationship to the "manly woman." Another challenge to whiteness could be ethnicity. It will not be discussed here. The Swedish Armed Forces seem to be more homogenously ethnic Swedish than the society at large, but no data are available on this.

[4] Since the 1970s we have found examples of different voices – conscripts, politicians, and the public – criticizing the specific masculinity associated with and perpetuated by the Swedish Armed Forces. In a study regarding the situation of homosexuals within the Swedish Armed Forces, Krister Fahlstedt (2000) argues that the view on sexuality is conservative, and corresponds more to the general Swedish view of sexuality twenty years ago, as described in the governmental commission report (SOU 1984: 63).

example: during the Cold War around 90 per cent of the total male cohort was conscripted. "Universal conscription" –*Allmän värnplikt*– is the name used for this activity. "Universal" implies that it involves everyone; it is universal, or, in Swedish, *allmän*. That only half the population has been obliged to serve the country's military, simply because of their sex, has been taken as a given, a "natural" circumstance. In our research, we later came to argue that the institution of conscription was tremendously important for the defense organization (Kronsell and Svedberg 2001a). More importantly, we saw how "universal conscription" was a crucial aspect of building the Swedish nation and for connecting conscripted citizens to state institutions expressed through the concept *folkförankring* (cf. Tilly 1990; Mjöset and van Holde 2002: xiii). Conscription, we concluded, was highly implicated in the construction of gendered Swedish subjects and citizens as well as the nation (Kronsell and Svedberg 2006).

Because the practice is taken for granted, very little has been said to justify the conscription of men only.[5] To research conscription from a gender perspective meant that we had to study what is not said. It was a methodological challenge and created practical problems, mainly because it involved researching a vast amount of official documentation, while basically discovering nothing. It meant finding no material discussing why only men, not women, were expected to defend and die for the country.[6] Indeed, there was no document explicitly saying why men were the ones conscripted. Searching through the material, we actually found very few references to boys or men. Instead, words like 'conscript' or 'officer' were used. What comes across is that conscription and the military profession is for men, and this is so self-evident that it never has to be argued or justified, just confirmed. In our project we concluded that the complete silence was an indication of the norms of hegemonic masculinity embedded in the military institution and the related polity. Hegemonic masculinity does not need any special politics or thematization; it is simply reproduced through daily activities (Connell 1995: 212). Thus, there is no need to talk about it.

---

[5] This is backed up by a law on conscription and an exception made to gender equality in the Swedish bill of rights. Despite radical cutbacks of Swedish defense in the last few years, and the resulting decline of conscripted numbers, conscription remains the way to "man" the forces. In practice only around 20–30 per cent of the male cohort will be asked to go through basic training.

[6] For example, in various official reports on conscription commissioned by the government (SOU 1965: 68; 1984: 71; 1992: 139; 2000: 21) as well as parliamentary debates and motions, the conscripts' magazine, and the Army's magazine.

Because of conscription's importance to the construction of the Swedish nation, both externally towards the world and internally towards the people, our deconstruction of the silence revealed that the male citizen is considered the citizen *a priori*, while the female citizen is expected to perform different duties toward the state. Accordingly, men's "natural and given" role toward the nation-state is that of protectors and soldiers (Kronsell and Svedberg 2001a). *Allmän värnplikt* means "universal conscription," but it is not universal; it is for men only.

In the research process we found ample documentation arguing the relevance of conscription to the defense and military organization as well as to the nation as a whole, and this was very useful in gaining an understanding of the meaning of conscription to the nation-building project.[7] Perhaps even more abundant were the sources stressing the democratic values of conscription. According to this argumentation, through conscription the conscripts become socialized into democracy. Until 2000, virtually all the political parties endorsed this view. We were perplexed at these "democratic" arguments, since it was so obvious that half the population was excluded from this "democratic" activity.

Conscription was represented as an excellent way for the nation's young citizens to become directly involved in, gain important knowledge about, and personally become engaged in the nation's defense and security.[8] It was thus considered an important tool for increasing "democracy." Again, we found no trace of material addressing why women's understanding of the security and defense of the nation was less important or perhaps not important at all. Socialization into democratic citizens and nation-building is, in the texts, discussed only in relationship to what it does for the conscripted, namely, men. Neither do we find attempts to compensate for the resulting lack of understanding of the security and defense of the nation among the female population. Despite the many governmental reports, political debates, and popular articles that we studied, what we found was silence.

The importance of knowledge about the security and defense of the state did, however, arise as an important issue again in 2000, when conscription levels had been reduced and in practice limited to a smaller proportion of the young male cohort. Because of defense cuts, there has been a gradual decline in the proportion of the cohort conscripted, ranging from 90 per cent in 1986 to 30 per cent in 2004 (statistics

---

[7] This was also completely new to me, and it represented a whole new area of Swedish politics to which I had no prior relation, either personally or academically.

[8] For example, in various official reports on conscription commissioned by the government (SOU 1965: 68; 1984: 71; 1992: 139; 2000: 21).

available at <http://www.pliktverket.se>). In the governmental commission report on conscription from 2000, the "information problem" is again addressed (SOU 2000: 21, 173–200). In this report there is a sense of urgency for the need to include the people in the nation's security and defense. In view of the decline in conscription numbers, various information strategies were suggested. What is interesting here is that the "information problem" we noted was never presented as a problem in the past, when 50 per cent of the population, namely women, were excluded from the defense sector. Only when the numbers of males conscripted out of the cohort were drastically reduced did it surface as a relevant issue to care about, and only then were strategies formulated to deal with this "information problem." This led us to conclude that conscription and the military organization in general assign men a specific citizen status. First, as the defender of the nation the man becomes the "real" citizen. Secondly, he is the one entrusted with the knowledge about security and defense matters of the nation. Since, in the texts, we found no trace of worry or concern that women would not be informed about the security and defense of the nation, we suspected that what this did not say straight out, but meant, was that the male citizen was also perceived in terms of head of the household. It was assumed that information on the nation's security and defense would, through him, somehow trickle down to other citizens, such as women (Kronsell and Svedberg 2006: 149). This confirmed how a specific gender order of hegemonic masculinity was institutionalized in the Swedish Armed Forces through the institution of conscription, and how this institutional practice constituted specific national subjects.

In sum, studying "silence" means in practice that the researcher has to rely on methods of deconstruction, to study what is not contained within the text, what is "written between the lines." It is tricky, and time-consuming, because one has to make sure one has not missed any information or documentation. Hence, it requires thorough and broad document searches and meticulous reading of the texts. It can be a methodological challenge because it may mean that we study what is not there, what is hidden in the text. Even so, deconstruction is an absolutely crucial aspect of feminist research work. It often requires a double reading against a critical material that can provide insights and comparisons. Since there was virtually no feminist work on the military in the Scandinavian context, we used studies mainly from feminist IR scholars working on the military in the United States, Canada, and Britain to help us in this double reading. Asking the obvious or common-sense questions, such as "Why do men have to defend the nation?", may present a way to start naming men as men, rather than in what at first may appear to be neutral terms: soldier or citizen. This may also be a first step in questioning and challenging institutions of hegemonic masculinity.[9]

Another silence that we were less successful in getting at when looking at the various sources of documentation coming from defense institutions was in connection with heterosexuality. This was a surprise, not least because of the heated debate on homosexuality in the US Armed Forces (cf. Osburn and Benecke 1997); in the Swedish context there was no debate at all. In reading various kinds of narratives we became aware of a tension around the "manly woman" discussed later in this chapter. Although we sensed a connection to issues of sexuality, we found no documentation on this. Indeed, we had read and heard much about the way sexuality was used in basic training, among conscripts and against women in forms of sexual harassment. However, these stories were expressed[10] more as anecdotes, as stories told among friends and overheard, and hence a quite different type of source. Adding to the difficulty in addressing the issue of sexuality may be the fact that it is often something considered private and something that should be and is kept outside institutional life. Yet Gutek (1989: 67) argues that sexual behavior is a characteristic phenomenon of any working environment and should be researched as such. Moreover, sexuality and power are interconnected and therefore fundamental in the reproduction of gender relations (Hearn and Parkin 2001: 13–14). Hence, issues as intangible as sexuality require perhaps other methods in order to try to understand silence.[11]

---

[9] In the case of Sweden and conscription, the silence was broken in 2000 with a governmental commission on conscription that initiated a public debate (SOU 2000: 21). Today, a majority of the political parties support "truly" universal conscription. This does not mean that universal conscription for both men and women will become the norm in the near future; other arguments speak against it.

[10] Excluding sexual harassment, which, by the late 1990s, had been addressed in most defense and political institutions as well as by the media.

[11] I have done some additional research on the discussion on homosexuality within the Swedish Armed Forces. Until 1944, homosexuality was a criminal act. In 1979 it was no longer considered an illness. Prior to 1979, homosexual conscripts were automatically excluded because they were considered not fit in the admission procedures. Things started to happen in 1999 with the law forbidding discrimination against sexuality in the workplace and the establishment of a Homosexual Ombudsman (HomO). In 2001, an organization for LGBT military personnel was set up. In 2003, a new law criminalized all types of discrimination, including outside the workplace. During 2003, the first comprehensive survey of the working conditions of homosexuals and bisexuals was initiated by the government (n=20 000). One survey result was that male-dominated workplaces showed more intolerance toward homosexuals (Arbetslivsinstitutets rapport 2004: 16).

Learning about gendered practices through symbols and procedures

For our project we found much value in visits to the field, when conscripts participated in military exercise, or were tested, as well as visits to the Armed Forces headquarters, the Swedish National Defense College and to the voluntary defense organizations' meeting places. As anyone who has conducted fieldwork knows, important "knowledge" is attached to the place of study and can be sensed through keen observation. For example, the way we were perceived and treated during our "visits to the field" surely indicated that two middle-aged university women[12] visiting an Army field exercise were indeed a curiosity and out of place in relation to the regular practices and maneuvers of the Army. The reactions we met, of courtesy and curiosity, yet slight incredulity and suspicion, provided us with a sense of what it might feel like to be a female soldier in this setting. Field observations experienced in connection with our presence as civilian women researchers in the military field together gave us a kind of situational knowledge that helped contextualize interviews and narratives.

Apart from texts, we may turn to symbols and procedures in institutional practice to look for clues to how gender relations are played out. Norms of organizations, like norms of hegemonic masculinity, are embedded in institutions as rituals, procedures, routines, and symbols (Gherardi 1995; Alvesson and Billing 1997). An example in the work of Anders Berggren and Sophia Ivarsson at the Defense College can illustrate this. They analyze sexual harassment statistics in relationship to the gendered nature of the Swedish Armed Forces and show how sexual harassment is exemplified symbolically with the different signs on the men and women's lavatory doors of the Defense College. The bathroom doors were labeled according to two different types of planes used in the Air Force, *Jakten* and *Attacken*. Within the cultural context of the Air Force, the symbols took on a specific gendered and sexualized meaning based on the fact that *Jakten* planes are the ones actively pursuing the enemy – and placed on the men's lavatory – while *Attacken* planes are simply the enemy planes under attack and subdued by *Jakten* (discussed in Berggren and Ivarsson 2002). In a different study, Berggren (2002: 156–160) observes the spatial arrangements of a room in the Defense College. He shows gendered practices exhibited through the

---

[12] Here I am referring to myself and my collegue and project collaborator Erika Svedberg, of Örebro University.

bodily movements and seating arrangements in the circumstances around the viewing of a film and a strip-show, a common pastime activity in the military. Although we also made some similar extra-textual observations, our approach did not allow for the kind of intimacy with and closeness to the organizational environment experienced by Berggren and Ivarsson at the Defense College.

Photographic representations found on web pages and in various documents were also very helpful in contextualizing the institution and its activities. It was particularly useful to get a sensation of the femininities (and the limitations on femininity) associated with being a female conscript or officer. Having suggested that one way to study silences in institutions of hegemonic masculinity is by deconstructing both texts and extra-textual sources, in the following section I turn to another important source of knowledge: women's own voices. I argue that women's voices in institutions of hegemonic masculinity are of specific relevance (see also Kronsell 2005). It is a discussion that only briefly touches upon epistemological and methodological issues, because the main emphasis here is on method or how we can actually conduct such research. Interviewing is one obvious method, but, as we shall see, not always easy to carry out in practice. Narratives presented in other contexts, such as newspapers, newsletters, and websites, might provide additional stories on which to build research. The research question from which I will give some illustrations in the following section looked at how femininity was constructed within the Armed Forces of Sweden.

Women's presence makes norms of hegemonic masculinity visible

Observing the everyday practices of women within the Swedish Armed Forces is a rich starting point for deconstructing the male as norm typical of that institution. The hegemonic masculine character of the Swedish Armed Forces is most aptly conveyed through a woman's description of her experience of being on the margins within that institution. Women often have an acute sense of being different. Navy officer Helena Almqvist encapsulates the experience: "When we joined they made a big deal about us being different. Sometimes you felt like a UFO that happened to land on the wrong planet" (Försvarsdepartmentet 1995: 12). The segregation of women's and men's bodies into separate spheres, so important to institutions of hegemonic masculinity, is no longer perfect when women step into the jobs, functions, and roles traditionally associated with masculinity (cf. Hirdman 2001; 1990). The confrontation with difference that comes from a woman's presence can be a crucial source of information for understanding the gender dynamics of institutions of hegemonic masculinity. The experience of women in institutions of hegemonic masculinity has often been ignored and seen as irrelevant because they are so few. These women tend to be perceived as either coopted by the institutions or insufficiently representative of women's knowledge, standpoint, or interest to be significant for feminist research (Kanter 1977; Dahlerup 1988, cf. Peterson and Runyan 1998: 69–111).

I want to challenge the notion that a woman in institutions of hegemonic masculinity is "a male in disguise" or "a mere token" and thereby unable to contribute any valuable knowledge and experience. My somewhat contradictory, and perhaps controversial, view is that the inclusion of even a small percentage of women makes all the difference in the world. This suggestion is related to the character of institutions of hegemonic masculinity. A woman's presence can make gender and masculine norms visible, "break the silence," and completely alter the way institutions are perceived and understood. Thus it has powerful transformative potential. In institutional settings of hegemonic masculinity, women are not represented *en masse* but have a minority position. The knowledge gained in such institutional settings has previously not been considered relevant to feminist epistemological debates. My argument is that women in minority positions within institutions of hegemonic masculinity should not be brushed off as irrelevant for feminist knowledge production, and I suggest this may have applicability beyond the defense organization. During the last few decades, women's engagement in public life has increased considerably but has not sufficiently influenced feminist work. Much attention has been given to grassroots activism and mobilization around women's issues, to protest, and to articulation of critical and alternative politics outside institutions. As the public increasingly adopts the values carried by feminist and other social movements and puts them on institutional agendas, there is a need to study such institutions.

I also learned about hegemonic masculinity within the Swedish military institution when it became visible and shown to be highly complex through the narratives of women confronted with the military institution. Women were gradually included as officers from 1980, and in 1995 they were brought within conscription practice. Although women's presence as officers and later as conscripts remains minimal, when they engaged in the everyday activities taking place within the military institutions its gendered norms were verbalized and made apparent. A woman's mere presence in the work previously done solely by men made the various shapes and forms of gender constructions within that organization appear. An example follows.

The Armed Forces have often spoken with pride about the changes taking place when a woman or a few women join as conscripts. When a woman was included in a group of men at a garrison, it often resulted in a "shaping up" both of the language used among conscripts and in the less overt use of pin-up and pornographic pictures in the bunks. The frequent use of sexualized language and pornography in the military is widely known and an embarrassment to the Armed Forces. Thus the "shaping up" of the language is viewed as an important and positive contribution of women's engagement within the Armed Forces. The abusive language commonly used within the military is sexualized, and the association between sexuality, aggression, and violence is significant (Meola 1997; Jacobsson 1998; Berggren and Ivarsson 2002). It indicates that military institutions and military practice build on a particular understanding of violence and sexuality – a relationship that is, according to Hearn and Parkin (2001: 15) "a fundamental aspect of the reproduction" of institutions of hegemonic masculinity.

That pornographic pictures were removed from the soldiers' quarters when women entered, either as a gesture from the soldiers themselves or on the command of a superior, was considered positive by the officers as well as by conscripts. What this shows us is that the masculine norms in the military are entangled with notions of women as objects of sexual desire and as "others" outside the realm of military activities. When the object of desire – represented by the pin-up girl – stands beside con- scripted man, as a woman at arms, the norms become visible through the ensuing awkwardness resulting from the encounter. The woman who signs up and becomes a conscript in the Armed Forces or goes into officers' training (where 97 per cent are men) challenges and tests the norms of the entire military. Our argument was that the contradic- tion between the "woman at arms" and the norms of "man-protector- soldier" embedded in military ideology becomes evident only when it is challenged by the female soldier or officer (Kronsell and Svedberg 2001a).

Women's knowledge in institutions of hegemonic masculinity

Does this mean that women in institutions of hegemonic masculinity have a privileged position in seeing the male as norm? This has been an argument in feminist standpoint theory (Hartsock 1998; 1983; D. E. Smith 1987; Flax 1990; Harding 2004; 1991; Haraway 1991; Hennessy

1993), but only in relation to women in marginal positions. The stand-point claim that knowledge is socially situated is, as I see it, indisputable. The production of knowledge is deeply embedded in the gendered power structures of society and has excluded large segments of society from participating in the articulation of experiences as knowledge. That is clear. The women I purport to speak about are mainly part of the white elite or middle class. Obviously, it is not their knowledge as classed, gendered, ethnicized, or sexed beings that interests me. Rather, it is the knowledge generated when they engage in the activities of an institution of hegemonic masculinity, which is in focus here. By women's very interaction with the institutional practices, the gendered norms of such institutions become visible, and hegemonic masculinity becomes "real." It may be useful to think in terms of knowledge as being generated through struggle (Hartsock 1983: 231–251), because what these women often do is struggle with the norms of hegemonic masculinity in the institutional setting of which they are a part (see Weldon, this volume). Knowledge about social relations is acquired through performing social acts (cf. Butler 1990: 25), and women seem to "discover" gendered practices through experience as they struggle with it in their daily lives (cf. M. F. Katzenstein 1998). I want to suggest that the notion of struggle within feminist standpoint theory may be a useful way to look at the knowledge achieved by women coping with norms of hegemonic masculinity. The type of knowledge gained from the experience of women in these circumstances is, I argue, valuable to feminist politics. To talk to these women about their experience thus seems highly relevant as a method.

Working with interviews and narratives

Interviews are an important source of information because they can provide an in-depth, detailed account of how gendered practices are actually carried out within institutions as well as of how gendered identities are constructed and contested. We used semi-structured and open-ended interviews as one technique for gathering information and, at the start of the project, we expected it to become our main method of collecting material. Despite this intention, we ended up relying on interviews to a lesser extent than originally anticipated. We encountered some problems. One was related to the specific nature of the Armed Forces and another had to do with the marginal position of women. Since the Armed Forces are rather hierarchically governed, once we received the approval of a senior officer we had basically free access to conscripts. Although we always insisted on the voluntary status of the interviews, I am not convinced that the conscripts always perceived it this way. The problem was to get access to the Armed Forces without compromising our independent research. When, having pursued the research for about a year, we were asked to send in our research questions to the military headquarters for approval in order to continue to have access, we decided against it and discontinued our interviews with conscripts in the field.

Another problem interfered with our ambition to talk with and interview female officers and conscripts active within the Armed Forces. Rather soon it became clear that, apart from a few officers, most females really wanted to be left alone. They either flatly refused to participate or showed signs of being uncomfortable with the situation. It seemed as if all the attention given to female officers and conscripts in the media, because of the uniqueness of the phenomenon and because of the alleged cases of sexual harassment in the military, was a heavy burden on the women. When a journalist or researcher arrives in the garrison and asks to speak with a female conscript or officer, she is singled out. The difference between her and her male colleagues is accentuated and noted by all. It is understandable that for her this is undesirable, since throughout her daily tasks she is working to not be different but to become a soldier or officer just like everyone else. Hence, we learned that to research gender identities with the help of interviews in a context where women are in a minority position is not without complication. Since a woman challenges the hegemonic masculinity of the institutions by her mere appearance, the interview setting can accentuate that challenge further. So we had to look for narratives elsewhere.

Fortunately, the headquarters of the Armed Forces had commissioned reports on female soldiers' status and on sexual harassment, which were carried out by the Defense College.[13] These reports are based on extensive survey and interview material with female officers and conscripts with "inside" access to the personnel. These reports turned out to be a useful alternative source for our work. Another complementary and useful source of information for our purposes has been articles in various newsletters, web pages, and newspapers. An example was the conscripts' own newsletter, *Värnpliktsnytt*. It has been published bimonthly since the early 1970s[14] and gives a picture of the life of a conscript with many of its problems, benefits, and joys. Here one finds articles expressing the

---

[13] For example, Carlstedt 2003; Försvarshögskolan 2002; Ivarsson 2002; Ivarsson and Berggren 2001; Weibull 2001.

[14] It is a newsletter run by the conscripts themselves, who take on the role of journalists etc. This becomes part of their training.

difficulties related to being simultaneously a conscript and a father, or to being a woman or a homosexual and coping with military life. In *Värn-pliktsnytt* we found stories based on interviews with women in the Armed Forces, stories about their experience of military life. It gave us import-ant information about the attitude among conscripts towards women. From these accounts in narrative form, together with the studies from the Defense College and our interviews, we have been able to say something about how women adjust to life and work in institutions of hegemonic masculinity and, through this information, we have gained an insight into the gender dynamics within the Swedish Armed Forces. The following section will briefly outline some these findings.[15]

The woman at arms challenges hegemonic masculinity

When women try to adapt to the Armed Forces they take on or assume different feminine identities. This becomes a struggle, because there are no notions of femininity in the military institution for female soldiers to relate to or tap into. Institutional norms give meaning to the practices and procedures that individuals are to perform through daily tasks in institutions (March and Olsen 1989: 40–52). Hence, women's identities in the military are constantly negotiated, always in relation to the norms of hegemonic masculinity (cf. Kvande 1999: 306; Davis 1997: 185). When women enter this workplace of hegemonic masculinity, institu-tional norms "appear" and mark them as different from men, who, according to these norms, are the "real" soldiers. With respect to femi-ninity, the Armed Forces virtually lacked norms. From the perspective of formal legal norms, women were to be treated as equal, that is, as soldiers, and were not to be subject to differentiating treatment.[16] We chose to characterize the process of identity formation that followed as a delicate balancing act in reaction to institutionalized masculinity norms in the Armed Forces. The narratives accounting for this "identity struggle" were of use to our analysis.

Women, as well as other "norm-deviant" individuals, pose a direct challenge to norms of hegemonic masculinity that mark the soldier as the heterosexual male. However, masculinity is meaningless without a com-plementary construction of femininity. For example, any type of militar-ization demands that men are willing to die for their country, while it simultaneously requires that women will not sacrifice their lives for the

---

[15] Also documented in Kronsell and Svedberg 2001b.

[16] This was the policy of the government from the very beginning, in 1980, when women were first accepted into military training (SOU 1977: 26).

nation but are willing to be the protected ones. Masculinity is constructed and defined as non-femininity (Enloe 1993: 17–20). This suggests that, even if we are looking at an institution of hegemonic masculinity, femininity is there as the backdrop against which masculinity can be constructed and defined. In the narratives, interestingly enough, feminine identities were also often described in negative terms, that is, by reference to what is not feminine.

From other feminist work we know that women have their given and specific roles in the military situation associated with femininity. Women are expected to serve, nurture, and nurse the citizen-soldier, to reproduce new soldier-citizens, and perhaps to take over the soldier's civil work in wartime while returning to the traditional role in peacetime (Reardon 1985; Kaplan 1994). Such identity can be associated with the civil employees of the Armed Forces who have been present in the military kitchens, laundries, snack bars, and offices since way back.

The pin-up pictures in the barracks, discussed earlier in the chapter, represent one feminine subject – the "bimbo" – against which military masculinity is defined. It was quite clear from the narratives that the "bimbo" femininity was an undesirable identification, both to the male and to the female soldiers. The "bimbo" may disrupt and disturb the troops. Suddenly, the sex object, otherwise limited to pornography and pin-up pictures, is standing among the men. Heterosexuality is no longer contained when the men's attention is diverted to her and the competition over "the bimbo" begins. Ruth Lister (1997: 70) writes that it "is the very identification of women with the body, nature and sexuality" that is "feared as a threat to the political order." Sexuality must be controlled and kept outside the organization; only women and homosexuals are sexual beings and thereby represent sexuality (Hearn et al. 1989). Heterosexuality has to be controlled in order for the homo-social relations of military comradeship to fully flourish (Lipman-Blumen 1976). Sexualized femininities are threats to the military order. Thus it is important for women soldiers to not be associated with "the bimbo" femininity. It was pointed out in an interview with a female captain that one of the essential survival skills for women is to be very modest: to de-sexualize themselves in both behavior and clothing and, for example, never to dress in a short skirt and high heels when in civil clothing.

Femininity turned out to be a very important yet tricky and always fluid concept, and the female soldier constantly has to manage her femininity. Femininity was often associated with attributes and looks, but also with attitudes and behavior. Eva, a conscripted soldier says, "It is possible to retain your femininity in the Armed Forces, you don't have to turn into a tomboy, but you definitely cannot be girlish"

(*Värnpliktsnytt*, December 1989). There is a fear that a girl will have to be treated differently and that the soldiers will have to treat her in a special way; carry her backpack, help her through tough exercises, and so on. In this way, she would also violate the norm that all soldiers are equal. We noted that women soldiers often express concern that they might become too masculine in the military training. If the women are not feminine enough, they can pose a threat to the men (cf. Gutek 1989: 65). Yet, "the girls who do voluntary conscription are far from any womanly stereotypical ideals. They are tougher," say two male conscripts (*Värnspliktsnytt*, December 1989). Thus, within the military institution, the female soldier has to perform a balancing act. She has to be prepared for the physical challenge and the rougher masculine comradeship, while not being perceived as masculine. At the same time, and particularly through interviews, it has become clear that bodily strength, endurance, and physical achievement are necessary for a woman to fulfill her soldier image, a necessary feature of an acceptable "woman at arms" identity, while at the same time her strength may not be over-exaggerated in its bodily or behavioral expression. An extreme in either direction leads to problems. It is not surprising, then, to hear that it is very common for the same female officer to be viewed as "both too feminine and not feminine enough," as Blomgren and Lind (1997: 18) concluded in their study of the officer training.

The "manly woman" is widely known as a highly problematic identity by recruitment officials, conscripts, and women themselves. Female officers talk about the dread of being like "Female Russian Shot Putters" (Nilsson 1990: 11). Russian women shot-putters evoke the image of an androgynous woman, big, strong, hairy, and unattractive. There is something wrong with her hormones (cf. Dowling 2000: 198ff.). Not unlike the image of the "Female Russian Shot Putter," the "manly woman" has taken on too many traits of the masculine world. While the "Female Russian Shot Putter" is about the looks and the bodily expression of an undesirable femininity, the "manly woman" also relates to undesirable behavior. It is an image that has to do with inappropriate behavior when engaged in by women, such as drinking excessively, being rough, and swearing (*Värnspliktsnytt* November 1995: 18; February 1998: 13). It may seem logical that the "manly woman" would be most suited to serve the military, since she would pass the physical challenge of the military, an ability so often evoked as lacking among women when arguments against women's suitability to become soldiers have been aired (cf. van Creveld 2001). This is, however, not so in our case, as the "manly woman" is clearly the most undesirable identity associated with a woman at arms. She would thereby compete in strength, toughness, and roughness with men, and her unfeminine, almost masculine appearance blurs the strict borderline between masculinity and femininity (Kronsell and Svedberg 2001b). More important, I suggest, is the fact that the "manly woman" challenges the norms of heterosexuality associated with hegemonic masculinity. Heterosexuality needs to be preserved; homosexuality, including lesbianism, disrupts and threatens an order that tacitly relies on homo-sociability. Homo-sociability, the glue that holds the military organization together, is possible only between heterosexuals (men).

Another possible and far more tolerated femininity is the "mother" identity, suggested by stories about women who make the military a more human place with a nicer atmosphere. Claims are also made that women are more psychologically stable and mature. One female recruit says: "If we are out on an exercise and I see that a guy is tired, I will give him a part of my chocolate. It is some kind of mother instinct and I don't think a guy would do that" (*Värnspliktsnytt* November 1995: 16). Elshtain has pointed out that there are indeed similarities between the soldier and the mother. They are both concerned with, and are anguished and traumatized by, whether they have done enough – for the country as soldiers, or for the children or family as mothers. While the roles of soldier or mother are constraining in their demands of complete loyalty, they are also enabling in that they create clear and defined role expectations and establish identities (Elshtain 1987: 222–225; see also Sylvester 1994a: 329). Finding a feminine identity as mother might provide a safer haven, as it is also a more de-sexualized identity.

Our study has shown us that female officers and conscripts, in the search for an appropriate identity as a woman at arms, struggle with the question of what femininity to adopt. Viewing this struggle, we have found it possible to say something about the norms of hegemonic masculinity at the same time, as it is evident how the institutions form subjects in specific ways. The woman at arms cannot be, within in an institution of hegemonic masculinity like the Swedish Armed Forces.

The contribution of the IR researcher

To my surprise and that of my colleague, we often felt a sense of recognition when we visited various sites of the Swedish defense and security organization. We were often struck by the similarities between the way military women described their realities and the way we interpreted our own experiences as women in the university. It was also very useful when we analyzed our findings and when trying to make sense of them. This might point to a commonality in our experience and the experience of other women who enter traditional male institutions and thereby challenge their norms. The role of feminists in academic institutions, such as within the field of IR, can be an important starting point for making comparisons, since, in a way, we have been subject to similar experiences. We have "learned" many things from this, but perhaps the most important is to see how "the personal is the international," or how women's lives are intertwined with global patterns and world politics. This is where feminist researchers have a special, important task ahead of them. While the women in the military might, through experience, realize how gender structures work in their particular lives, they might not want, or be able, to connect those experiences to general power practices in society. To do so is our task. We can help interpret the discursive and material power structures that inform daily practice (O'Leary 1997: 47). As feminist theorists we can make the normal strange, as, through feminist analysis, we explicitly connect what is done in everyday life with the gender structures of society, local, national, and global.

The ways in which the experience of one particular woman is part of a wider set of gendered power-relations can be understood if we contextualize individual experiences and isolated events, putting them in a larger context of societal relations so that the gendered practices may become more apparent. This may be done through a perspective that takes into account "the relations between socioeconomic and political institutions, on the one hand, and everyday signifying practices, on the other" (Weeks 1998: 129). Here I see the important role for the feminist IR researcher as being that of "mediator" between the knowledge from experiences in the everyday life of women and the knowledge of global gender relations (cf. Welton 1997: 14–15). Even though feminist knowledge is produced out of experience, it is always constituted by the theorist, who reflects on that experience (Hekman 1997: 352). Such reflections may connect the experience in the Swedish Armed Forces with general patterns of silence on gender related to differentiated expectations on female and male citizens, and thereby also to processes of nation-building or to other types of institutions of hegemonic masculinity. Furthermore, the theorist may connect the narratives to general discussions of militarism and its link with sexuality and masculinity. Valuable comparisons can be made across cases and in relation to previous feminist IR research.

Concluding thoughts

It has been my ambition to suggest that, beginning by questioning the simple observation that "men have the duty to protect the nation," we can start to untangle the relationship between military, gender, and nation-building, which have previously been contained as one "natural" and "taken for granted" practice of the armed forces in Sweden. Asking "obvious" or "common-sense" questions is one way to do so. By seriously questioning and investigating the common-sensical, we are showing something strikingly and intriguingly unusual and different. The method suggested for this endeavor was deconstruction of texts. A visit to the "field" to analyze symbols, procedures, and performances can be an important complement to textual interpretation. Finally, it was suggested that a focus on the experience and knowledge generated by the few women struggling in institutions of hegemonic masculinity is an extremely important source of knowledge. Interviews are suggested as a method for collecting information about experiences. However, interviews often have to be supplemented by narratives from other sources. This, it is argued, is because of the particular position of women in institutions of hegemonic masculinity, as marginalized and different. In sum, the chapter argues that the knowledge generated from the experience of a few women in institutions of hegemonic masculinity has a transformative potential that ought to be taken seriously and considered part of a feminist project. This is particularly relevant knowledge, as we see how feminist struggle is moving to political and institutional arenas and is no longer solely restricted to grassroots activism and the traditional women's movement.

7 Marginalized identity: new frontiers of research for IR?

Bina D'Costa

This chapter explores the methodological implications of putting otherwise marginalized research subjects at the center of IR inquiry. Centering the marginalized subject – namely the survivors of gender-based violence during and after the Independence War of Bangladesh – requires asking ethical and substantive questions that impact not only the research design but, more fundamentally, the research question itself. I began my methodological journey by asking questions about a gendered silence – the rape of of women during this war – and ended up exploring the story of nation-building. The subjects of my study were written out of that history, but that history was drafted on and with their bodies and families. Placing their stories as the focal point of my study, I demonstrate that centering the marginalized yields otherwise inaccessible theoretical insights to the question of nation-building, a central theme in mainstream IR.

IR, with its primary interest in state power, is now increasingly paying attention to normative frameworks of analysis. In addition, violence in Rwanda, Bosnia, Kosovo, and Haiti demonstrated that an unresolved past has the power to ferociously destabilize the present. A new generation of IR scholars[1] is gradually daring to pursue unconventional projects that bring in people's voices and deploy them within the boundaries of the discipline. This is what feminist IR scholars,[2] working on areas that have been traditionally overlooked by IR, such as gender, race, and class, have been doing for years. Although the theoretical contribution of feminist IR scholars is no longer frowned upon or ignored, major scholars still do not incorporate gender and women's concerns in their primary research agenda. Action-oriented research in marginalized areas has the potential to demonstrate, with empirical evidence, how gender

---

[1] A brief glance at the recent abstracts or papers in the ISA conventions in the USA, the British International Studies Association in the UK, the Australian Political Science Association, and the first Oceanic IR Conference in Australia will substantiate this claim.

[2] Tickner 2001 provides an excellent account of feminism's encounter with IR.

exclusion creates some fundamental flaws in IR academic work, and therefore shapes inadequate policy and governance measures.

Following the wave of violence at the end of the twentieth century, recent research into the history of genocide (Gellately and Kiernan 2003) and the genocidal intent of mass rape (MacKinnon 1993; Askin 1998) has contributed to the area of human rights and of peace and conflict studies. Likewise, active involvement in human rights movements and mobilization around human rights issues intensified, focusing on struggles of ordinary people generating demands for truth and justice, and acknowledgment of war crimes.[3] Humanitarian involvement in post-conflict societies has increased significantly because of this research and activism. IR as a discipline has been broadly engaged with these issues. However, IR scholars have been less interested in the insights of survivors and survivors of geopolitically marginal conflicts.

IR always has been, and remains, an elite and exclusive discipline, where poverty, hunger, and war all happen to the disadvantaged but are analyzed by refined researchers in the North and the South. The rhetoric of scholars and northern expatriates working in the South is so sophisticated that it is hard to challenge it from various positions that do not share the IR nomenclature and conceptual frameworks. One purpose of this chapter, therefore, is to demonstrate that extensive field research with marginalized groups can contribute to understanding, and perhaps even policy prescriptions for, some of the dark realities that IR faces at the moment.

Marginalization is a much-contested concept and is often associated with economic and political weakness or powerlessness. It is a social status which is linked to particular identities or social groups. To give an example, women and children remain socially, politically, and economically marginal in traditional and patriarchal societies because of their gender or age. Refugees, illegal immigrants and religious minorities in developed states are marginalized because of their nationality, ethnicity, lack of knowledge of the dominant languages, and religious affiliations. Identities associated with caste, class, geographic origins, or location in poor, rural areas also result in marginalization. Such marginalization is manifest in South Asia, and in Bangladesh even more so.

Marginalization is also linked to two other practices: exclusion and discrimination. It is the most dominant form of exclusionary practice by states or social groups over which marginalized groups have little or no control. Because of this exclusion, several forms of discrimination occur,

[3] For example, the People's Tribunal in December 2000, in Japan.

such as limited access to government services or high-profile political roles, discriminatory access to higher-education institutions such as medical and engineering schools, and limited access to resources such as agricultural products and social welfare. In his explanation on social marginality,[4] Peter Leonard describes the marginalized as outside "the major arena of capitalist productive and reproductive activity" (Leonard 1984: 181). In addition to Leonard's understanding of marginalization, I point out three separate yet related forms of marginalization. First, gender, ethnicity, class, and race are now accepted as important areas to look at, but doing so is often left to the scholars who work in those fields primarily. Secondly, under-researched locations receive scant attention from major scholars in the field of IR, or are left to area specialists. Bangladesh remains largely marginalized because it does not have significant strategic importance to global politics. Other parts of South Asia are not so marginalized. The issue of nuclear rivalry between India and Pakistan dominates South Asian international politics. Conversations on Kashmir, Maoist guerrillas in Nepal, or the Sri Lankan conflict appear in international headlines when tensions reach extreme points. Thirdly, people and communities who are under-researched may have concerns, knowledge, and experience which are theoretically important. Because Bangladesh is a poverty-stricken country that is heavily dependent on foreign aid, and a country where the NGO sector is a substantial part of GDP, it has been researched by development practitioners and scholars. However, the war of 1971 remains one of the most under-researched conflicts in the world, and the traumatic experiences of the civilians after the war remain virtually unknown despite growing interest in nationalism and ethnic violence.

However, inattention to the civilian experience of Bangladeshis is not an oversight, but rather the result of the exercise of power. The power of dominant groups to define and address the concerns and interests of marginalized groups makes it impossible for those groups to put their own needs on the public agenda. For example, in post-conflict Bangladesh, survivors of genocidal mass rape were considered sacrificial victims for the nation. As such, their sexuality, motherhood, and identity had been defined in state-sponsored welfare programs

---

[4] Leonard (1984) characterizes social marginality as "being outside the mainstream of productive activity and/or social reproductive activity" (180). According to him, there are two kinds of marginality. One group is voluntarily marginal, such as communes or artists. The second group experiences "involuntary subordinate marginality" (181). He emphasizes direct material experiences involved in this kind of marginality, such as poverty and the absence of wage labor (187). In this chapter, I refer to what Leonard calls involuntary marginality.

by social workers, medical personnel, government officials, religious groups, and others, but not by the women themselves. Despite all these groups' intentions to help the women reintegrate into the society, the rape survivors remained marginalized, because their needs, as understood through the eyes of dominant groups, were not their own.[5] As such, the rehabilitation strategies for the women – the large-scale abortion and adoption programs or the government's "marry them off" campaign – did not change their subordinate position. The situation became much more complicated because a large number of the women came from poverty-stricken rural areas. Pathologizing the helplessness, frustration, and anger of rape survivors diverted attention not only from the deprivation of equal access to resources or the gendered subordination they faced every day,[6] but also from demanding justice and from having the perpetrators punished for the war crimes they had committed.

What kind of insight can case studies of marginalized groups, such as the women described above, offer IR? If marginalization and social marginality are to be considered seriously in IR, fieldwork with those marginalized is essential for bringing the knowledge of those marginalized into scholarly discussions.[7] Field research is one of the most effective ways to evaluate the impact on the lives of people of policies and decisions made in the upper echelon of the society. Often the highly sophisticated language of rebuilding peace and restoring law and order in post-conflict societies is not in touch with reality on the ground. Further, the rhetoric of gender justice that gets deployed references an "imagined" group of women and men, not the women and men who are actually suffering. Scholarly works in IR are still heavily reliant upon reports and excellent research conducted by practitioners in NGOs and other community groups who are directly informed by local experience. However, such research relies on these intermediaries who may (or may not) have their own biases in impact assessment, program design, and conceptualizations that mirror government biases. Scholars intending to make a difference in people's lives need first to set off to their field location and listen and witness themselves. In my own research project, such preliminary fieldwork led to other inquiries.

---

[5] Elsewhere (D'Costa 2003) I detail this problem.
[6] For an excellent account of the ideological context of marginality see Leonard 1984: 187–201.
[7] Please note that my contention is not about "giving voice to the voiceless." Although they may remain powerless, people are not voiceless under any circumstances.

After listening to the war stories of women, my initial questions about the silencing of rape in war broadened into questions about nation-building. How do the nation state's political elites maneuver its history in order to shape a singular dominant national identity? What is the policy impact on women, especially in the aftermath of a violent conflict, of this practice of nation-building through the construction of a national identity? Why is it important to discuss issues of truth, justice, and reconciliation within the disciplinary boundaries of IR? I attempt to answer these questions by exploring what implications the experiences of the *Birangona* in Bangladesh might have for nation-building and the study of security in IR. *Birangona* ("war heroine") was the term introduced by the first prime minister, Sheikh Mujibur Rahman, to acknowledge the sacrifice of women who were subjected to rape and sexual violence during the war. The Prime Minister's intention was good, but, rather than doing justice to the women or granting them special status, the term, a homonym of the word for "prostitute", labeled them as fallen women. It isolated their experience from the mainstream narratives of the heroic tales of the war (D'Costa 2004: 229–30).

"Telling the truth" is considered a necessary step for peace-building, promoting democracy, striving for social justice, and transforming society more broadly. But whose truth is being told? What kind of reconciliation is being assured by this telling? Is justice being compromised in the name of fostering peace in a post-conflict society? The formal and officially sanctioned mechanisms to "speak the truth" are often subjected to manipulation by the elite. Without investigating the historical truth claims and retrieving historical documentation, it is impossible to establish democratic development and respect for human rights in a war-torn society. Nowhere is it more evident than in Bangladesh, which now has infamous war criminals serving as ministers in the country, running major newspapers, and owning important businesses. The power of anti-liberation forces which actively collaborated with the Pakistani Army and participated in gross human rights violations has penetrated deep into the written history over the years since the war. This manipulation occurred through the government's authorship of textbooks and the media's selective memory, both of which result in a public historical account of independence that is inconsistent with the lived experience of the war. None of the ruling regimes showed commitment to seeking justice after 1971, and their tacit support for installing war criminals in powerful positions seriously undermined human rights and democracy in the country.

In this context, marginalized groups such as women, freedom fighters[8] and poverty-stricken minority Hindu communities[9] bore the burden of the experience of 1971. Although for various reasons they were the main targets of the Army brutality, their demands for justice have been continually ignored by the post-conflict governments. One of the primary motivations for this research was to explore the possibilities, for these marginalized groups in Bangladesh, of demanding a tribunal[10] or a Truth Commission[11] to render a public account of the historical injustices that occurred in 1971.

The complicated interactions of marginalization, "truth" politics, and IR inform this chapter. I explore the methodological challenges I faced in relation to these while researching in the field. In the first section I briefly provide the background of the research project in general and of the conflict in Bangladesh, where truth politics marginalized experiences of women who were already socially marginalized. In the second section, I describe my methodology and methods generally. In the third, I discuss some unresolved conceptual challenges that I looked at before entering the field, and some challenges experienced in the field that had to be dealt with on a case-by-case basis. In the final section, I detail my use of the oral history method bound by the methodological and conceptual challenges laid out in the preceding two sections.

While the research I describe was based on two case studies, one being the Partition of India in 1947 and the other the creation of Bangladesh in 1971, I will focus on the 1971 case here.[12] Interviews with *Birangona* and those who worked in the reconstruction form my primary sources. I also looked at archival sources, including diaries, memoirs, letters, newspaper reports, official documents, reports of inquiry commissions, and

---

[8] In Bengali this term translates to Mukti Jodhya, mainly to indicate Bengali men and sometimes women who fought the guerrilla war against the Pakistani Army.

[9] Due to the British policy of playing one community against the other, Hindu and Muslim nationalism divided the two communities with a strong wall of antagonism in the Indian subcontinent (Prasad 2001). This played a significant role in post-conflict Bangladesh and the attitude of the governments toward the Hindu minority community.

[10] I suggest that a gender-sensitive People's Tribunal for Bangladesh would provide an important step toward addressing past atrocities (D'Costa 2004).

[11] Formal mechanisms that establish accountability for wartime abuses, such as war-crimes tribunals (punitive justice) or truth commissions (restorative justice), are important peace-building components. Recent literature on post-conflict peace-building that emphasizes issues of memory, justice, truth-telling and truth-seeking identifies war-crimes tribunals and truth commissions as necessary mechanisms for achieving reconciliation. For details see Hayner 1994; 2001; Minow 1998; and Robertson 1999.

[12] Although I interviewed social workers in India to shed light on the 1971 case, for the 1947 case study I used primarily secondary sources as my research material.

books, both fiction and non-fiction. From these I have reconstructed many different narrative accounts of the war and of the national identity politics in which my presence as an analyst is quite visible. In the process of working on 1971, I have become like every other researcher who gets involved: passionate about this work and intending to make a difference.

Background

Following the anti-colonial nationalist movement, when the British Raj finally decided to leave India, political leaders divided the country on the basis of religious identities. In August 1947, Pakistan emerged as the homeland for Muslims, and India as the nation rightfully belonging to Hindus. Both of the states ignored the other minority communities within their borders. Bengal, where Bengali Muslims and Hindus lived as neighbors, was partitioned, with East Bengal becoming East Pakistan, and West Bengal remaining with India.

A civil war broke out in 1971 between West and East Pakistan, in which Muslims slaughtered their fellow Muslims, dispelling the previous notion that religion alone was sufficient to hold Pakistan together. The conflict was, however, "sold to West Pakistanis not as a fratricidal war but as a *jihad*, or a holy war against the infidel" (Sobhan 1994: 71). Bangladesh became a sovereign, independent state after nine months of guerrilla warfare, and, at the very end (December 3–16, 1971), with Indian armed intervention. The main reasons for the emergence of Bangladesh were the lack of Bengali political participation in the decision-making processes of the Pakistani government, and the colonial style of economic exploitation of East Pakistan by the central government, which was situated in West Pakistan (D'Costa 2003). Ironically, the Bangla-speaking population constituted the majority segment of the citizenry of the former Pakistan.

The Pakistani soldiers especially targeted women and bragged that "they would 'convert' East Pakistan through engendering true Muslims" (Sobhan 1994: 71). Sultana Kamal, a social worker,[13] wrote:

In January, 1972, while I was working with the rehabilitation projects for the women affected by war, I came across a number of women who were captured by the Pakistani army and were subjected to systematic torture, rape and sexual slavery. There were some women who were forcibly made pregnant. In the

[13] Currently, she is the Executive Director of Ain-O-Shalish Kendro, a major human rights organization in Bangladesh.

interview with me these women said that while raping them the army would say that the (traitor) Bengali women must produce "pure Muslim breeds". "They must carry loyal 'Pakistani' offsprings instead of bootlickers of India or the Hindus in their wombs." (Kamal 1998: 272)

There was a strategic motive to rape the Bengali women to alter an *impure* Bengali identity to a Muslim one that was imagined by the Pakistani political elite. Unfortunately, little public evidence exists on the Pakistani military strategies about targeting women. Pakistan categorically denied such strategies. However, a letter by one Major M. Afzal Khan Saqib (who was in Hyderabad, West Pakistan) to another major, Muhammad Ikram Khan (Jessore, East Pakistan) on August 21, 1971, would indicate the mentality and planning of Pakistani soldiers. He stated: "I was not surprised about the news of Bengali tigresses (*women*) being tamed by Rashid. It is a must to change their next generation . . . In the meantime you also plan carefully to tame some wild bitches there" (Rahman 1984: 762). The strategic use of rape as a genocide tactic makes the 1971 war between East and West Pakistan a case in which rape was a war crime (Brownmiller 1975; Copelon 1995; Manchanda 2001; D'Costa 2004). During the conflict an estimated 200,000 Bengali women were raped by soldiers (Copelon 1995: 197; Manchanda 2001: 30), with an estimated 25,000 forcefully impregnated (Brownmiller 1975: 84; D'Costa 2004).

However, neither scholars in Bangladesh, nor scholars working elsewhere, conducted detailed research on the use of rape and forced impregnation as a strategy used by the Pakistani Army and their collaborators in Bangladesh. I argue that the 1971 rapes not only violated women's rights, but also became an intrinsic part of the state's nation-building. I further suggest that a silence in research about what happened to the women not only silenced the women themselves but also marginalized the whole issue of violence and mass rape in the 1971 war of Bangladesh and in world politics.

An exploration of these marginal states and their domestic politics provides significant insight into the issues of peace and justice. The persistent importance of the past is evident in domestic politics such as during election campaigning. For example, in the last few elections, the two major parties in Bangladesh, the Awami League and the Bangladeshi Nationalist Party (hereafter BNP), both made rhetorical use of their so-called heroic leading role during the war. Likewise, in order to access power, both parties are partnered with known collaborators with the Pakistani Army, including infamous war criminals and the Islamic nationalist party Jama'at-I-Islami (which opposed the liberation of Bangladesh and whose members have been implicated in mass killings and rapes).

Centering the margins: a methodological journey

Not unproblematically, the cornerstone of my research design was the oral history method. However, I chose this method in a context of methodological reflection on the role of situated knowledge in IR scholarship, as discussed above, and of methodological reflection required by the use of that method itself, as discussed in this section. Consequently, before engaging in a detailed discussion of the oral history method, I lay out the larger methodological framework of which it is a part and focus on a few methodological concerns and unresolved conceptual issues I had in the process of developing the research design. These issues became more visible as I proceeded with the different aspects of my fieldwork. Consequently, it is particularly challenging to give an account of my fieldwork because the significance of certain parts of the process became evident only when I could reflect on them afterwards. Thus, as my respondents constructed their narratives of their lives, so I, too, am constructing a narrative of my field research in order to present a comprehensible account of what was actually a dynamic, non-linear, and interpretive research process. Before I delve more deeply into this narrative, I shall first map out some of the methodological puzzles which shaped my work.

Who is the Other? Whom do the women represent? Who speaks? Who has the experience?

Post-colonial theory criticizes the process of production of knowledge about the Other. I found that many of the questions raised in this literature were important to ask in relation to my study, even though they could not be satisfactorily answered. The major criticism put forward is that colonial discourses ignore the production of knowledge by the Other (Williams and Chrisman 1993). However, post-colonial theorists articulate the knowledge by the Other and of the Other. Yet, as Said asked, how and who can know and respect the Other (Said 1978)? Tensions between western feminism and the Other around this question are articulated in works by post-colonial feminists (Spivak 1988; Mohanty 1988; hooks 1989; Minh-ha 1989; Suleri 1992).

The first conceptual challenge to my project derived from these tensions. I experienced an analytical trap here because I needed to analyze not only western feminist scholarship but also the authenticity and position of Southern feminists. With a few exceptions, most southern feminists emerge from privileged backgrounds in their own location.[14] This privilege may vary according to class, religion, ethnicity, or education. Often, they are able to speak and interact in the language of the West, which is predominantly English. Many southern feminists are trained in western institutions and also located there. In my experience, I have seen respondents being more comfortable speaking with women researchers from locations other than their own.[15] The power inequality between the respondents[16] and the southern researchers is quite visible in some cases. The "complicated interplay between sameness and difference" (Stephens 1989: 100) reveals that, by virtue of being researchers, all feminist researchers should address the orientalist problematic.

I avoided this "trap" as follows. In order to explore the overwhelming silence of women whom feminist researchers intend to represent, one needs to build a triangular passage of interaction that connects western feminists to marginalized women to southern feminists. We, as feminist IR scholars, can no longer afford the time to argue about who has the right to represent, or whose representation is more "authentic." We should discard our self-protective stand on who is best able to represent the marginalized and become more forthright with our research commitment. We should be able to say what we have to say while being aware of the politics of location.

Another related challenge I encountered came from the feminist discourse of fieldwork which often insists on recording the direct experiences of "real" women. For example, discussing feminist writings on India, Julie Stephens comments that women who are in the field location receive special recognition as the "real" women, as opposed to other women. Stephens is critical of feminist researchers who make deliberate attempts to bypass theoretical frameworks in favor of "direct experience" (Stephens 1989: 93). Their arguments are based entirely on little-known materials documenting the direct experiences of women

---

[14] I also am part of this privileged class.

[15] In 1993, Brooke Ackerly and I conducted research on micro-credit organizations in Bangladesh as part of her PhD project. I remember how the respondents reacted positively to Brooke. While a researcher's attitude and personality contribute to the kind of response she receives, I am suggesting that the respondents also have a preconceived notion about whom they could trust and to whom they could open up more.

[16] Here I am referring to women respondents, many of whom are interviewed for development, population, or women's rights policies. Therefore, most of the respondents belong to marginalized categories, such as the poorest of the poor, the lower-caste women, or minority groups.

from the field, which is in most cases the Third World (Stephens 1989: 93–94). As a harsh critic of this type of feminist research, Stephens claims that this is a certain kind of "image-making," and that the effectiveness of the "I was there so it must be true" position rests on an assumed, unfiltered identity between fieldwork (as presented in feminist texts) and reality. She condemns the view that "women as women" have a special drive for liberation by feminist researchers, and writes: "What are considered questionable research methods are replaced by the unchallengeable 'we were simply women talking together'" (Stephens 1989: 95).[17] By contrast, Nordstrom (1995: 139) writes: "On entering the field, we enter the domain of lived experience." The question is not only "What exactly can be regarded as experience?" and "Which experiences can be included in the feminist research agenda?" but also "What are the politics of methodological choice?"

In the context of research on women in the South, especially in development discourses (such as WID or GAD), the category of experience has not been critically analyzed and the prestige of direct experience in the field often remains unquestioned. However, in conflict studies or peace research and in the analysis of "different kinds of war stories," what Nordstrom talks about (the simplicity of experience) is not a simple construct. The different experiences and contexts of the subject, the interviewer, and the anticipated reader (Stephens 1989: 111–114) mean that representation is an intricate process. For example, one *Birangona* who did not wish to be interviewed was barred from fetching water from the communal tubewell in her village after her community realized she was labeled a *Birangona*. This particular story received special attention from me, the researcher, not because of her experience of exclusion but rather because of what this exclusion signified for my research. Whether I understand this story as an illustration of her oppression or as a story about her strength in adversity, her hardship will determine and be determined by my project.

Even though fieldwork itself cannot bestow legitimacy on data, some feminist research emphasizes the immediacy and directness of the researcher's experience. As I did, many feminist field researchers prefer conversational modes to the structured interview, and use little or no formal questionnaire (D. L. Wolf 1996; Stack 1996; Nielsen 1990). For these feminists, "the deliberate non-structured approach is a way of marking a text as knowledge" rather than as a source of information. However, though I used the unstructured interview method, in my

---

[17] Stephens here is quoting from Huston 1979: 12.

methodology I treat the narratives obtained as sources of data whose meaning I interpret (see also Cohn, Jacoby, and Stern, this volume).

Birangona and their very raw experience of violence have not been present in the studies of war or violence in South Asia. Most theories and debates about violence against women in wars in South Asia have distanced themselves from the actual experience felt by the bodies of women. Rape, being an unsettling topic, raised questions about ethics, responsibility, and respect within the nationalist discourse. However, the fact that I interviewed these women does not mean that I have captured the "truth" of their experience. Recognizing the unfixed character of these data, I recognize my analysis as what Ackerly and True call in this volume a "deliberative moment," and seek to analyze it as I understand it at this moment in their narrative and in my research (see also Stern, this volume).

How should I write about the women? As victims or as survivors?

I discussed both of these categories, victims and survivors, with my colleagues and friends, and realized that we all have quite different ideas about whom we would consider as a survivor and whom a victim. I asked this question randomly and in an abstract manner. The responses indicated that, more than being defined, these terms need to be contextualized. When I consider these terms, I immediately think of Hiroshima survivors or rape survivors, who have also been victims of particular kinds of violence; whereas for others the contexts might vary and might not be so straightforwardly interchangeable. For example, one friend thought of someone being lost in desert for a few days and then being rescued. He regarded his hypothetical subject as a survivor but not as a victim.

In representing *Birangona* women, I used both of these terms. A *Birangona* is a survivor who has the power to control her destiny within the limitations of her context, and also a victim of a traumatic event and the limitations of that context. However, neither "victim" nor "survivor" is a simple construct when the women do not think of themselves as survivors and do not see their own agency, but instead remain within the limitations of their context. While the term "survivor" has an empowering meaning attached to it, a survivor might remain captive to her past. Her past might haunt her and re-victimize her in the present. One example of this is Duljan Nesa,[18] who was raped by two

---

[18] Duljan's story is published as part of Ain-O-Shalish Kendro's Liberation Oral History Project (ASK 2001).

Pakistani soldiers in front of her husband. She was asked to provide testimony at the People's Tribunal[19] in Dhaka, the capital of Bangladesh, with two other rape survivors in 1992. The tribunal proceedings were not successful, but the three women were photographed for the press and their stories published without their consent (Akhter et al. n.d.: 80–104). The press reports led to cruel consequences for them, and Duljan Nesa and her family were banished from their community.

These methodological puzzles placed in high relief the remaining conceptual problem of how to relate a rigorous structural analysis of women's positions as agents of history through their struggles and survival. Why and where are the political shifts taking place? Merely making women visible (as was implied in my original intention of bringing to the fore the silencing of the act of rape) is an insufficient step towards intellectually and politically satisfying explanations of the subordination of women's interests to the nation-state. Bearing this in mind, the guiding force in my research project was the life stories of women and their survival initiatives. The possibilities for social change can be found in analyses that locate and link the political margin (that is, the voices of the *Birangona*) with the political center in diverse social theories and political practices. Feminist methodology makes such research possible. In light of these insights, I will now return to my story of the unfolding of my research process.

Fieldwork methodology and methods: in search of silent/silenced history?

I began my journey in the field location in 1999 and then revisited it in 2001.[20] Although my point of entry at both times was "Where do women situate themselves in the state-sponsored discourse of nationalism?" there was a significant shift in the analysis and theoretical framework after my fieldwork. I embarked on this project expecting to examine the issue of silence and silenced narratives in Bangladesh through interviews with women who suffered sexual violence during the war. I realized how difficult it was to find survivors willing to speak. Moreover, serious ethical issues arose relating to the safety of the women who did speak to

---

[19] I have written elsewhere about the politics of the People's Tribunal (D'Costa 2004).
[20] The third phase of field research began in 2005. For this part of the project I designed a workshop method through which scholars and activists interested in justice issues and the trial of war criminals would be able to brainstorm about strategies. Rape survivors interviewed earlier, who wanted to speak about their experiences, would be asked specific questions about their ideas for and expectations of the research outcome.

me. However, most importantly, the silent/silenced voices of these women reveals that the construction of a nation-state's identity relies on controlling women's agency (Feldman 1999; Menon 1999; Menon and Bhasin 1998); that same construction poses additional methodological challenges to the researcher, which I detail below. Wrestling with these issues, I demonstrate that the control of women's agency is essential to the construction of a coherent national identity, the one created through privileged voices, mainly of the national elites. The ruling political elite consists of the Awami League, the BNP and the Jatiyo Party; the Army personnel (many of whom were trained in Pakistan and came to serve the Bangladesh Army after the country became an independent state, and were particularly sensitive to Pakistani propaganda about making true Muslims out of Bengalis) and the religious-political leaders (many of whom, such as Golam Azam and Abbas Ali Khan from the Jama'at-I-Islami were against the creation of a state based on Bengali ethnic identity).[21] The other two privileged voices, those of the pro-liberation[22] cultural elites and of the social workers assisting the women, had a somewhat ambiguous identity. While their politics also helped in subsuming women's agency for the national identity, my research suggests that they genuinely wanted to help the women although their decisions were products of the patriarchal society of which they have long been a part. In particular, the social workers interpreted the *Birangona* as victims rather than as survivors of difficult moral choices.

Since a major focus of my research was the construction of women's identity through political processes after 1971, I was interested in the successive regimes dealing with women's issues. An important question in this regard was "What sort of silence did they create through their policies, which included the reintegration of war criminals into the political ground?" As part of my analysis, I investigated three different types of silence and marginalization in the national narrative. The first

---

[21] Although, because of space limitations in this chapter, it is presented in a very simplistic manner, the national elite identity is, however, much more complex and fluid. A detailed analysis of the political processes of Bangladesh would also reveal why women's bodies were so central to the construction of a Bangladeshi identity which the elites desired to achieve.

[22] In Bangladesh, the question of national identity is divided into various identity questions, such as "Bengalis or Bangladeshis?" However, here I focus on another political question of pro-liberation or anti-liberation identity that has been popularized in the media. Pro-liberation forces are supported by civil society and those segments of the bureaucracy and government that are inspired by the national sentiments of 1971. Anti-liberation forces consist of groups and political elements which actively opposed the creation of Bangladesh and are against any kind of demands for justice.

type was created by successive governments' silencing of the survivors. In the rehabilitation programs coordinated by the Awami League government, which was in power till 1975, women's agency was denied.[23] For example, the rehabilitation programs controlled the violated female body through forced abortions, maternity through war-baby adoption programs, and women's lives through various means including the "marry them off" campaign (Brownmiller 1975: 83) and their reinstatement in traditional jobs such as needlework, paddy-husking, and poultry-farming.

The second type of silence is reinforced by the women themselves. The family and community pressures on the women made it hard for them to speak of their experiences. In a poor country like Bangladesh, where women struggle for basic rights of food and shelter every day, there was no space or time to share their experiences publicly. Moreover, the stigma, shame, and humiliation associated with rape made it doubly hard for women to speak without being ostracized by their communities. They either internalized the cultural scripts of gender roles or chose silence as their negotiated survival strategy. By "negotiated survival" I mean the approach or strategy used by women to maneuver within their highly patriarchal families, communities, and states. That often meant prioritizing their community identity over their personal one and suppressing their memories of both wartime violence and post-conflict state-building, in which they had been stigmatized because of their gender role and the experience of sexual violence.

Over the last three decades, the first and second kinds of silence hardened and created the third and most dangerous kind, which had the power to erase women's experience from Bangladesh's history altogether and to deny the possibility of seeking justice, reconciliation, or reparation. As stated before, along with the state and the women themselves, social workers, activists, and human rights groups who were assisting the women also played part in this silence.[24] Because the aim was to cause the least pain and trauma for the women, emphasis was placed on concealing their stories. I am not denying or ignoring the serious stigma and isolation or the feeling of shame[25] and humiliation

---

[23] In August 1975, the first Prime Minister of the country, Sheikh Mujibur Rahman, was assassinated.

[24] For further discussion, see Das 1995: 55–83. She calls this a "best interest doctrine," where there is an alliance between the state and social work with an abstract concern for justice (75).

[25] In Bangladeshi villages, women who are raped often refer to the violence in the phrase, "Amar nakphool niya gechey" ("I have been robbed of my nose-ring").

rape can create for survivors.[26] Scholars (Burgess 1995; Culbertson 1995; Muran and Digiuseppe 2000; Henseley 2002) have investigated the traumas related to rape, the psychotherapeutic needs of the rape victims (Draucker 1999; Harris 1998), and the consideration of cultural difference to assist the women (Low and Organista 2000; Hansen and Harkins 2002). Yet I suggest that the individual silencing of the first two kinds also creates a collective silence. Burying women's traumas thickens the silence and therefore contributes to the denial of justice. While publicly talking about rape might mean stigmatization for the victim, covering it under shrouds of silence might also mean not documenting, and therefore publicly denying, what happened to her or to women like her. The failure to address women's experiences on a case-by-case basis had the cumulative effect of downplaying the extent and severity of the rapes and sexual violence during 1971 war.

Were the actual or symbolic silences of their memories and lived experiences created through shrewd and calculated political maneuvers? This concern builds upon the complicated politics of the subcontinent, the rise of religious parties in Bangladesh, and the reinstatement of war criminals and collaborators in important government positions. One aim of my research was to assess the impact of the transformation of women's roles after the war in Bangladesh in order to map women's agency in moments of violent social transformation, cultural change, and peacetime. My field research also provides empirical evidence of how the construction of *Birangona* in the immediate aftermath of the war made women double victims of the war.

Methodological solutions to ethical dilemmas

Although interviews with the survivors were an important primary source for this study, a major consideration for the research was to respect the decision of the women who did not wish to have their experiences documented for public viewing. There was also the danger of retraumatization for the survivors. My experiences of interacting with *Birangona* were as much a source of methodological reflection as they were a source of information. Consequently, for the most part, to demonstrate the exclusion of the women's experiences, I used evidence from social workers, religious groups, physicians, and relatives of the women.

---

[26] Similarly, I am also not suggesting that women who do not want to speak about their experiences should be forced to speak. But I indicate that if only a handful of survivors come forward, that will encourage many more to find ways to convey their stories. That is where our task as researchers and activists should be focused.

In addition, I also used my knowledge, based on years of participant observation as a student, social worker, researcher, and human rights activist in Bangladesh.

Finding enthusiastic respondents interested in narrating their war stories was not a difficult assignment. Almost everyone who was born before the war had unique stories to tell. I just had to start with my own family: with my parents and my uncles (who were freedom fighters themselves), or in my own community. By contrast, I could find only a few *Birangona* women who were willing to share their stories with me. This chapter, however, is an analysis not of the interviews but rather of the maneuvering process and the development of my methodology through the difficulties I experienced in transferring the knowledge of the field into my academic writing. Because my research question demanded a unique[27] kind of field technique, I had to create and revise my methods of data collection for each respondent.

I went for fieldwork in Bangladesh and in India at two different stages of my research. During the first phase, from September 1999 until April 2000, I conducted archival research to gain a clearer picture of 1971. In addition I interviewed NGO staff, medical staff, and people whose contact details I received through word of mouth. I also located a few of the women who were willing to speak. I interviewed twelve *Birangona* (none of whom were taped), three social workers directly working with the women, and nearly 100 freedom fighters, journalists, academics, and activists working on 1971-related issues. The second time was from March until May in 2001, when I conducted more archival research, interviewed social workers in Kolkata, India, and shared my research information with Bangladeshi liberation scholars. I went back to Bangladesh once more for personal reasons, during which time I interviewed one *Birangona* who has been very active in seeking justice for the women. I was able to locate one key medical worker in Sydney, Australia, who had coordinated the abortion program after the war; I interviewed this person in 2002.

Basing my work in part on my analysis of the data from the first phase, I developed a theoretical framework of analysis for the second phase of fieldwork. At this critical juncture, I decided to focus more specifically on nationalism and its gendered processes. My question was how the exclusion of certain individual narratives fed into the nation-state's gender-blind approach to constructing a national identity. I was focusing

---

[27] My methods are unconventional but not new, because researchers in other social science fields such as anthropology or sociology have noted the difficulty in discussing sensitive issues with respondents and incorporating them into their theoretical analysis.

on how feminists addressed this by looking at the public and private dichotomy (Pateman 1988; Grant and Newland 1991), nationalist movements and gendered imagery (Elshtain 1987; Tickner 1994), nationalism as boundary marker of difference (Yuval-Davis and Anthias 1989; Pettman 1996; Yuval-Davis 1997), and masculinities in IR (Zalewski and Parpart, 1998). I studied feminist and South Asian post-colonial theory and situated my work in the regional and cultural context (Sangari and Vaid 1990; Radhakrishnan 1992; Chatterjee 1993).

Yet even in the second phase of the research, when my theoretical perspective was well formed, I still did not ask any set questions of the respondents. I found it was too difficult to ask set questions of either the women or the social workers. Often there was a silence, an expectation on the part of the respondents to be guided in a particular direction which they thought I wanted to take in the interviews. On my part, I was unable to guide them because I did not want the women to be the direct object of my gaze. I was more comfortable using open-ended questions. I asked the respondents about what happened to them when they went to the rehabilitation centers and how their communities reacted to them. This helped the women to recall their experiences of rape as well.

Using the responses and the archival research as a basis, I analyzed the state–nation–gender nexus and suggested that the control of women is fundamental to the construction of the nation's identity.[28] This control is closely linked to the processes of state-building, and therefore state-building has fundamentally contributed to the silence/silencing of stories of women and other marginalized groups. In Bangladesh, women's interests are reconstructed to serve nationalist ideology and power. By "reconstruction" I mean that government policies treated all women as similarly willing or docile enough to go through abortions or adoptions of their babies. From the government record we know no stories of resistance or reluctance. However, dispersed stories indicate an underlying violence. One such narration is of a woman whom we know as Tara, who spoke with Nilima Ibrahim, one of the most prominent social workers of that time. Tara's words are reported in Ibrahim's book *Ami Birangona Bolchi*. While discussing her experience after she was rescued from the rape camp, Tara recounts:

A few months later I ended up in the Dhanmondi Rehabilitation Centre . . . after that I started avoiding people . . . In the meantime I had abortion. You have seen

---

[28] For the body of the analysis see D'Costa 2003. Yuval-Davis and Anthias (1989) worked extensively on this.

how many women did not agree to have abortion. They wanted to keep their babies . . . but where will I go with this baby? Do you remember Marjina?[29] That 15-year-old girl who did not want her son to go overseas? She used to scream when she saw you, fearing that you might steal her child.

(Ibrahim 1998: 17–18)

In addition to an unstructured interview, I sought other ways to build a personal relationship with each of the respondents. This required unrestricted time for the interviews. It was very important to have an informal environment in order to make the respondents comfortable. I always started the conversation with an explanation about my own project. During the first phase of the research I was at an early stage with the theoretical framework and was quite honest about this with the respondents. I mentioned that I wanted to learn from them about 1971 and wanted to reflect on *shadharon manush-er kotha*, meaning people's narratives of how they remembered the war. There was no comparative analysis to conduct and each story was intriguing on its own.

Often respondents joked about my enthusiasm and passion, but it always had a positive impact. Even though we talked about the most gruesome violence, the atmosphere was never too grave. Drinking a cup of tea, sitting on a mat next to each other, in moments of remembering pain and sadness, holding hands and comforting each other, all played roles in creating a narrative I wanted to bring back to my analysis.

Menon and Bhasin wrote about ethical and moral implications of the power inequalities that exist between the researcher and respondent, especially when women asked them questions (1998: 14– 15).[30] As they did in their experiences as field researchers, I found it particularly hard to answer when women asked, "Why are you asking this now? No one asked us before! It is too late." Similar questions came from several social workers, who thought it was futile to dig up the past. Although I told social workers that it was important to know about women's stories if Bangladesh wanted to pursue the demand of a tribunal, I did not know how to respond to women's anguish and frustration. I just tried to explain that we needed to address the war crimes committed during 1971 and women's stories were essential to building a case. Women who talked to me after this less than satisfactory answer did so because they wanted to share their experiences, not because they believed I would transform their lives.

---

[29] Ibrahim told me that this was one of the most painful experiences of her life. Marjina was forced to give her son up for adoption to a family in Sweden (personal conversation with Nilima Ibrahim, 2000).

[30] See also Jacoby, this volume.

As Cohn and Stern suggest (this volume), it is always useful to establish a relationship with the respondents. Extremely sensitive information can be shared within familial categories. Often I have been referred to as a daughter or a sister by my respondents. These established relationships hold a very important meaning in Bengali culture. While they signify trust and the comfort of belonging, they also come with certain responsibilities to treat the stories not as material for producing knowledge but rather as a basis for initiating action from that knowledge.

One such responsibility includes continuing the relationship after the interview. This can take the form of activism on behalf of the respondents, or future meetings.[31] I am currently exploring the likelihood of holding a gender-sensitive people's tribunal in Bangladesh, for which I need to revisit some of my respondents. The continuous contact with respondents is very important if the oral history method is to bring significant changes in the lives of the women.

Political or personal?

Speaking with the women, listening to their experiences, and receiving access to their world were very personal experiences, which transgressed my professional boundaries.[32] I was not prepared for the reality and intensity of the field. Conversing with women who were raped, physically or psychologically injured, and humiliated and stigmatized by their communities after the war forced me to come out of the safe shell of an observer. I hoped to capture a glimpse of their lives and struggled to understand and bring back the insights from the field into academic writing. I learned that the enduring reality of war and survival after the war was articulated not only in women's uttered words, but also in those pregnant pauses during the conversations. A new life shaped by a war which they did not initiate was forced on them and enforced by the state at the national and the local level, by their communities, and by their families. In response, they created new identities, with suffering as their hidden narrative, and resistance and survival as their primary narratives. They survived.

---

[31] I volunteer in an expatriate Bangladeshi internet activist group called Drishtipat. One of our campaigns (2003–4) was to assist seven of the rape survivors, in which we successfully raised money for the women. For further details see <http://www.drishtipat.org/1971>. Last accessed May 6, 2004.

[32] This section is inspired by Butalia (1998) and Menon and Bhasin (1998), who reflect on their experiences of interviewing women who survived Partition violence.

Researching and writing about rape and violence in the 1971 war has not been an easy task for me. I was influenced by assumptions, presuppositions, and contradictions. Loyalty and belonging to the nation, admiration for the people who fought and sacrificed their lives to create a homeland for the Bengalis, abhorrence towards the Pakistanis: all that I have learned from childhood shaped the way I planned and carried out my field research. It was a profoundly personal and different process in each interview. However, after the first phase I started asking myself how responsible and how representative my analysis could be. In order to meet this challenge, I analyzed my own personal history and re-thought questions concerning gendered knowledge, culture, and survival. I explored my own location and identity, and had to "unlearn" nationalistic, symbolic, and emotive meanings attached to the history with which I grew up. My sentiments associated with the liberation of 1971 became complicated and less revered as I uncovered the violence by both sides, the unbearable pain and suffering of people, the political appropriation of the nation's narrative to grab power, and the hidden stories of women. While the sacrifice of men and women to realize freedom will always have an important place in history, my project was to demonstrate that new analysis has to address the tensions within history, or rather the asymmetry between what is remembered and what is erased. Some stories are being told, while others are not. In my PhD dissertation (D'Costa 2003) I demonstrated these tensions, and suggested that experiences of violence and a denial of the experiences, especially of women who "bear witness," can offer important understandings about national identity politics.

I consider this method a responsible and responsive one. It embodies a history of intricate experiences and puts into practice a few passions of mine: first, an intense attachment to social justice issues in South Asia; second, a commitment to women's issues that coincides with my own political sympathies as a *brown* woman breathing in a multicultural society and living as a minority at the periphery; and finally, an informed responsibility to reflect on people's voices for the broader IR audience beyond feminist IR scholars or area studies specialists.

Analysis and audience

The final methodological reflection of this chapter is on the audience of this scholarship, and on the methodological implication of the ontological perspective that research with marginalized people such as the *Birangona* is intended to identify practical ways in which international and local communities could be responsive to their needs. I acknowledge that other IR scholars might not share my ontological view of scholarship as intending to change the world and not just study it.[33]Although I have described a methodological process in which analysis and data-gathering are dialogically linked, in this section I detail my technique of analyzing oral history. First, a feminist method sharing my ontological perspective on the purpose of scholarship links the scholar with the activist, and the theorist with the practitioner – so much so that the very research question posed must also become part of an ongoing dialogue with the subjects of the research. Specifically, it aims to create very clear ideas about how to benefit the women by raising their concerns despite the danger of retraumatization. Such a perspective requires, among other things, making the respondents (who are often the previously excluded groups) the primary audiences of the scholarship, not only beneficiaries of the activism associated with the scholarship, which I discussed above as a part of the relationship between the researcher and respondents. In many cases they might not be able to access the written material, read it in the language in which it is published, or read at all. Nevertheless, a feminist oral history method will always work with that "imagined" primary audience in mind. In my project, that audience included the *Birangona* women, their families and communities, and local activist groups.

Consequently, and secondly, the project is also of interest to those IR scholars who are passionate about making a difference, especially those who link the global with the local and whose epistemology assumes that ideas about norms and shared beliefs are better when informed by experiences of marginalized groups. Likewise, feminist IR scholars and South Asia researchers form another kind of audience.

Thirdly, although the IR discipline is not yet so convinced of oral history as one of its research methods, the discipline is increasingly interested in activism and human rights. Therefore, the challenge of this project, as I discussed at the outset, is an action-oriented project to bring marginalized people's voices into theoretical analysis of activism and human rights. To gain recognition of the importance of this work within IR, I needed to link the micronarratives of the *Birangona* with the macronarratives and identity politics of the nation-state. In order to do so, I analyzed the women's narratives in relation to the peace treaties and prisoners-of-war (POW) diplomacy of Bangladesh, India, and Pakistan,[34] and investigated the implications of these and related policy

---

[33] See the discussion of critical theory in Ackerly and True, this volume.

[34] With Bangladesh's support, India and Pakistan signed a treaty in August 1973 to repatriate the POWs (other than 195 prisoners charged with specific war crimes).

decisions in women's lives. I examined the Bangladeshi government's position immediately after the war and its plan to rehabilitate the rape survivors, especially through the abortion and adoption programs. Through interviews with social workers, however, I found that although women (number unknown) were reluctant to go ahead with state decisions, they were forced to comply.

My project provides important evidence for IR that the distance between state decisions and people's lives can create permanent (even if long-buried) tensions and dissatisfaction within the nation-state. The words of the *Birangona* women of my study demonstrate that nation-building policies need to begin with the people, not with the nation, in order that these tensions may be revealed. As Thompson (1998: 22) comments: "Oral history is not necessarily an instrument for change. Nevertheless, oral history can be a means for transforming both the content and the purpose of the history. It can be used to change the focus of history itself, and open up new areas of inquiry." The oral history method in this project opens up the hidden histories of Bangladesh and encourages a rewriting of history which is all-inclusive.

Final reflections: IR, marginal sites, and marginalized people

In this chapter I have reflected on my field research in Bangladesh, which remains a marginal site for IR. Within this marginal site, women, especially the rape survivors of 1971, are the most marginalized of all groups. Their stories, told in their own voice with their own interpretation, have been lost in national history. As such, they are an excluded group which is offered social welfare policies that are inappropriate to their needs and may even be harmful. Deeply embedded patriarchal and traditional values, political manipulation, and women's own choices excluded women's experiences from the national historical narratives. By constructing and deploying these narratives, the state denied these women justice. In the Pakistani context, it is crucial to understand the sexual violence of 1971 because it linked the appropriation of women's bodies to the appropriation of the territory and nation. In the

---

Sheikh Mujibur Rahman, the first Prime Minister, also declared a general amnesty on November 29, 1972, for all the Bangladeshi collaborators detained under the Collaborators Act. With successive government decisions, many of these collaborators were able to assume powerful political positions in the country. It is in their own interests that people who survived violence during the war, especially women, remain quiet. Women's voices have the power to bring the war criminals to justice.

Bangladeshi context, it is imperative to understand the rehabilitation projects for women because the nationalist project of controlling women's sexuality is connected with the neocolonial project of disciplining sexuality.

My research on the historical injustice in Bangladesh required researching women's lives. Throughout this chapter, I have detailed some of the questions that I needed to ask before entering the field, and I have explained my oral history method as part of a feminist methodology attentive to silences and silencing. The feminist methodology my project employs places women's words at the forefront of the IR agenda, and shows how marginalized research subjects have much to teach the field of IR – not only about the lived realities in sites not usually figuring in IR theory, but also about what may constitute relevant and critical research questions.

Like other IR feminists, I aim to change the IR discipline. I imagine a first-year IR class following a compulsory course called "Gender and IR." Students would be required to learn and reflect on the experiences of people whose lives are governed by gender, class, culture, location, sexuality, and religion as they study security, IPE, or foreign policy. I would be delighted to see one of the male superstars of IR giving his key note address on women in a major international conference. The inquiry process in IR would be fundamentally changed if people's interests gained precedence over state interests. In addition, feminist research in IR would benefit greatly from a more extensive empirical analysis examining marginalized women, such as *Birangona*, the rape survivors of Bangladesh.

8   From the trenches: dilemmas of feminist IR fieldwork

Tami Jacoby

Feminist research in the field embodies some of the most significant constraints and opportunities for rethinking the broader conceptions of social science research and its principles of classification, rules, and categories. Long imprisoned within the boundaries of its own realist/ neorealist orthodoxy, the field of International Relations (IR) has yet to grapple seriously with the challenges posed by feminist interventions, which seek to reconfigure the very nature of "knowledge production," that is, the accumulation, classification, interpretation, and (re)presentation of data.[1] Feminists and other critical scholars have sought a basis for knowledge that does not conform to mainstream IR's rational-objective methodology. However, there is little agreement among them about which methods or techniques are more inherently suitable to the process of generating knowledge that is subjective, reflexive, and consenting to the notion of women as knowers.

This chapter uses methods to explore the difficult practice of translating experience into knowledge through fieldwork encounters. Fieldwork involves a series of methodological choices that allow the researcher to enter briefly the lives of those being researched and to generate knowledge by observing behavior, asking questions, and analyzing data. Often, the fieldwork location is far away from home, both figuratively and geographically. Crossing these intellectual, temporal, and spatial divides requires planning, travel, and acclimation to a new milieu. The laboratory for this exploration is fieldwork conducted by the author in Israel/Palestine between 1996 and 2000. The original research question underlying this project was whether women's definition of security is different from that of men in Israel. In mainstream International Relations, security refers to the protection of the territorial boundaries of the nation-state from external military threat. On account of the confluence

---

[1] In this project, "data" refers not to the traditional sense of "number-crunching," but more broadly to concepts, information, or practices that are used qualitatively or quantitatively as a basis for knowledge.

of state power with male authority, the traditional definition of security is androcentric, that is, reflecting men's interests and securing what men perceive as valuable. Since women have traditionally been unarmed and located on the margins of conventional protection systems, it is intuitive to expect that their definition of security would be different from men's. Indeed, answers to this seemingly straightforward question were interesting in themselves. However, the question merely generated more complex epistemological and ontological dilemmas. In order to avoid replacing the "male" concept of security with an alternative "female" concept of security, which does not of course represent the diversity of women's lives, I realized that a definition of security more meaningful to women would undoubtedly ensue from women's *experience* of insecurity. What this new insight meant was that my initial research question was misplaced. While I started out seeking to discover an alternative definition of security more appropriate for women, I ended up researching the concept of identity as it is constituted *through* women's experiences of being insecure in a zone of conflict. In other words, women come to understand themselves, their needs, and their relations with others and the state through their personal experiences of insecurity. But how is insecurity experienced? Do different women experience insecurity differently? Are there other categories (social, political, spiritual) that influence the experience of insecurity? In order to answer these questions, it was necessary to rethink how the women themselves imbue the concept of security with meaning in their own lives.

On account of the highly tense security situation in Israel, female activists are highly politicized. They have a political agenda that they want to present to the world in order to influence public opinion and ultimately the political system. This has a fundamental influence on the ways respondents perceive the field researcher and approach the fieldwork encounter. For this reason, experience may be presented in one way or another as a means for achieving political goals. Therein lies the cyclical quandary of fieldwork. Fieldwork involves dealing with the experience of others. However, experience is a problematic unit of analysis. If experience is something tangible, sensory, and direct, how can it be articulated theoretically? If fieldwork is a site for negotiating meaning rather than a simple means for passing along information from one person to another, can experience be rendered synonymous with truth? In what circumstance is experience politicized? Can experience be written down and represented? How can the experience of one person be interpreted and analyzed by someone who derives from a different culture and context? Is experience at all a useful concept for ethnographic data collection, or can the methodological ingenuity of feminist IR fieldwork be located elsewhere?

The fact that women may experience insecurity differently from men turns out not to be the most fundamental issue. The initial question to be asked is whether women's experience of insecurity can form a unit of analysis to begin with. If experience is represented, interpreted, molded, and used as a conduit for political influence, the onus is more squarely on the researcher to decipher what stands as relevant or valuable knowledge within the context of the research encounter. Increasing the power of the researcher, however, goes against every ethical principle of feminist ethnography to date.

This chapter argues that the feminist standpoint perspective and its concomitant notion of a unified category of "woman" disintegrate when the concept of experience is employed as a unit of analysis in feminist IR fieldwork. Women are active agents in the process of negotiating how their lives are perceived and understood. The experience of being insecure or secure is deeply personal and can mean different things to different women. How that experience is then represented to others is not predetermined by any analytical category. As a result, the concept of *self-presentation* is employed in this chapter to capture both the agency of women (see Stern's discussion of "sites of performance" in this volume) and the element of incommensurability that underlies any researcher–researched relationship in fieldwork. It is the very point of negotiating that relationship in the knowledge process that forms the core objective of this chapter.

Qualitative over quantitative

The use of qualitative methods in feminist ethnography has opened a field of opportunities for researching phenomena that have hitherto been marginalized in traditional social science and mainstream IR, such as feelings, perceptions, fears, and emotions, the real core of human existence. IR has traditionally defined security as the protection of the national boundaries and integrity of the state. Whether in the form of Gross National Product (GNP) and other economic factors, size and scope of the military-industrial complex, or population, indicators of national security could easily be quantified. Once the state-centered approach to security is abandoned (i.e., national security), the theory and practice of security are opened in ways that can capture a variety of different indicators. For example, personal security and sub-national security involve the cross-cultural specificity of actors, their collective affiliations, and the contested nature of their protection systems.

However, abandoning the quantitative means of social science research that has long upheld the field of mainstream IR leaves the researcher without a coherent foundation and facing a new range of challenges that previously did not exist (or at least were considered irrelevant).

New ways of embarking on fieldwork involve redefining the subject matter, renegotiating relations between the researcher and those being researched, reconsidering the meaning, purpose, and role of data, and new approaches to writing, representing, and authoring that data in the post-fieldwork phase. These endeavors demand that the researcher be equipped, not only with the concomitant epistemological questions, but also with the proper methodological tools and techniques of data collection, to ask about, and follow up on, these questions. Quantitative tools are straightforward. Once mastered, they can produce the most sophisticated and highly technological results. But how accurate are these results in relation to what is being studied? Although lacking in bells and whistles, this chapter argues that qualitative tools are better positioned to capture the complex linkages of concepts to the practice, perception, and interpretation of those concepts on the part of those whose lives are under consideration and in recognition of the researcher as an active agent in the research process. The representation of lives through qualitative means is accomplished through meticulous work on the part of the researcher who introduces subjects – ideas, people, and places, and ways of studying them – that have as yet to be considered relevant to IR.

Motivations

The background for this chapter originated in the initial stages of fieldwork toward my doctoral dissertation on women's protest in Israel/Palestine in 1996.[2] My foray into the subject of methods had two mutually constitutive motivations, one personal and the other theoretical. First, I was motivated by the fact that my own academic credentials exposed a complete lack of preparation for the dilemmas and conflicts I would subsequently encounter while on field research. During my field trips, I was faced with the limitations and naiveties of my own proper

---

[2] My doctoral dissertation was based on a case study of two women's protest movements in Israel, the Jerusalem Link and Women in Green. The Jerusalem Link is part of the Israeli women's peace movement and serves as an umbrella organization for two women's centers, an Israeli Center in West Jerusalem and a Palestinian Center in East Jerusalem. Women in Green are situated in the Israeli national religious camp and oppose the peace process.

conduct and protocol, having had little practical training in accumulating data apart from computer programs and statistical techniques. In a zone of conflict, the accumulation of data about people (men or women) is a particularly sensitive matter, as the researcher encounters respondents who are generally involved in difficult and at times life-threatening circumstances. The very "security" of respondents may be at stake while participating in the research project. Therefore, data about their lives must be accumulated and represented in an ethical manner. As well, identities in a zone of conflict are often expressed in antagonistic and extremist ways on account of the highly politicized atmosphere.

While unprepared for my initiation into fieldwork, I was nevertheless, and by necessity, *already* involved in the field. My own personal history is intricately woven through the politics of the Middle Eastern region, since I have lived, worked, and studied there for many years, not to mention the familial and collegial connections that I continue to hold dear. This recognition of the centrality of my own subject position was an essential methodological mechanism for negotiating my relations with those I researched. Although this project began officially in 1994, when I commenced doctoral studies, my deeper connections to the region were formed much earlier. My familial lineage was profoundly influenced by the course of Jewish history, as my grandparents survived the concentration camps of the Second World War and immigrated to Israel after the establishment of the state in 1948. This ancestry, along with my residency in Canada, defines me simultaneously as a second-generation Holocaust survivor, a descendant of Israeli *yordim* (literally "to descend" and derogatorily referring to Israelis who emigrate), and a Diaspora Jew (a Jew living outside Israel).[3] I can in no way claim objective status in relation to my subject of inquiry. My fieldwork forced me, then, to reflect upon my own social location as a partially observant, Canadian Jewish woman and new Israeli immigrant. This was the root of my deep passion for the region as well as an embodiment of all the restrictions, complicities, and privileges of the broader affiliations to which I belong. These elements form the prism through which I perceived the subjects of my research and through which they perceived me.

The second motivation for this discussion of methods derives from the state of IR theory. The lack of methodological critique in IR may have

---

[3] I visited Israel for the very first time in 1980 as a young child. Since then, the journey that is my subject position has evolved over a time span of twenty years. From 1987, I studied at the Hebrew University of Jerusalem and worked in the Israeli Ministry of Immigrant Absorption. In 1991, I immigrated and took Israeli citizenship. Since then, I have developed intricate social and familial bonds through my marriage to an Israeli citizen and the birth of my first child in Jerusalem in 1994.

resulted from numerous contemporary trends. For one, the backlash against realist/neorealist quantitative research methods in general, which have been implicated in a history of post-colonial ethnographies of mapping and representing others, may have led critical scholars in IR to shy away from the thorny dilemmas of method. As well, the postmodern turn, while useful in problematizing questions of representation, may also have contributed to the trend toward highly textual analysis. However, an escape into the realm of metatheory is neither useful nor desirable for those interested in continuing the fascinating, albeit problematic, engagement with actual, living people in cross-cultural contexts. For this reason, the concepts proposed here lie somewhere between the postmodern call to deconstruct theoretical unities and to pay attention to the intervening impact of language (Foucault 1972) and the feminist post-colonial commitment to continue politics based on the lived differences of, and "discontinuous locations" inhabited by, real women (Mohanty 1991: 3).

A growing, albeit loose, collection of works outside mainstream IR, which ties together such diverse strands as Marxism, historical materialism, feminism, and postmodern theory, has begun to challenge the dominance of realist/neorealist IR and its rationalist/objective perspective on knowledge. These so-called critical IR scholars have insisted upon the need to discuss the "conditions for knowledge production," a move that coincides with growing concern in critical IR journals and scholarly debates with issues of epistemology and ontology since the late 1980s (Wendt 1991; Carlsnaes 1992; Lapid 1989; Neufeld 1993). Despite the welcome contribution to discussions about knowledge these developments in the field have entailed, little effort has been invested in translating these discussions into methodological practice and in terms of suggesting different research methods and techniques of data collection and analysis in the field. It is unduly problematic that critical IR fails to face fieldwork dilemmas at the very moment at which the call to eradicate residual ethnocentrism by going out into the field and embarking upon local, detailed, cross-cultural, and contextually based studies of other societies has been made. Studying the very problematic and controversial "other" cannot be merely textual. It is *precisely* during time spent "in the trenches," so to speak, that researchers must inevitably dirty their hands and face political, methodological, and epistemological dilemmas. Otherwise, there is no trace of proper tools for ethical conduct or critical introspection while navigating the intricate shoals of fieldwork and reflecting back upon those tools in the post-fieldwork phase.

This weak link in the chain between epistemology and methodology in critical IR leaves a difficult legacy for those, like me, who grapple with practical dilemmas in fieldwork, particularly in conflict zones. Methods shed light on some of the thorniest conceptual dilemmas of representation in social science research, that is, ways of knowing about others. While critical IR scholars have noted these dilemmas *in theory*, there has been little effort to develop tangible grounds for a research *praxis* that would apply the lessons of the epistemological debates (see also Ackerly and True, this volume). In other words, for critical IR scholars, there is little indication of how to *do* our theoretical assumptions.

Feminist IR has yet to document specific methods and their use, despite the fact that they have long been a staple of feminist discussions in other disciplines such as sociology (Cook and Fonow 1986; Daniels 1975; Srinivas, Shah, and Ramaswamy 1979; Farrell 1992; D. E. Smith 1987), anthropology (Asad 1973; Bell, Kaplan, and Karim 1993; Gluck 1977; Golde 1970; Huizer and Manheim 1979), and psychology (Chodorow 1989; Dutton-Douglas and Walker 1988; Seu and Heenan 1998). Feminist researchers in these fields have developed practical tools such as ethnography and psychotherapy for dealing with the challenges, contradictions, and limitations in the process of researching and representing others in concrete, direct, and therapeutic settings. These fields have long asked the following questions. How does one grapple with dilemmas of difference, authority, and identification? What constitutes a reflexive or critical relationship between the researcher and the researched? How does one overcome axes of power in fieldwork encounters? What are appropriate and ethical ways of gaining access to and information about others? And what is the role of the researcher in the political agendas of the researched?

Sociologist Diane L. Wolf has suggested that these dilemmas of knowledge and representation are *so* complex that one may ask: "Should we do fieldwork at all?" Nevertheless, she contends that fieldwork is a useful and important process that opens vistas to other societies and alliances that would not otherwise be available. Therefore, "confronting and understanding the multiple and often irreconcilable contradictions" in fieldwork is a necessary step if we are to "refocus our gaze beyond ourselves" (D. L. Wolf 1996: 3–4).

As noted in the Introduction to this volume, the distinction between feminist methods, methodology, and epistemology represents the mutually reinforcing nature of theory and practice, or of research and subjectivity in any social scientific endeavor. Prior to embarking on fieldwork, it is essential for scholars to work through the implications of their epistemological perspectives, levels of analysis, political commitments, and practical procedures (Code 1995: 43). Yet, for anyone familiar with the practical dilemmas of fieldwork, difficulties inevitably arise when employing these tools in the researcher–researched relationship. In the following section, I use my own encounters in Israel/Palestine as a laboratory for exploring concretely the complex methodological dilemmas of fieldwork on the subject of women and security.

Fieldwork encounters in Israel/Palestine

My doctoral dissertation on the politics of women's protest in Israel/ Palestine posed many methodological dilemmas and involved situations in which the tendency to make decisions, determine the questions, affect the environment, and influence the process was fully in my hands. In addition, unlike other feminist academics involved in fieldwork, I chose to study women situated on opposite ends of the political spectrum. This diversity of women as subject matter disqualified the type of "passionate scholarship" (Dubois 1983) that many feminist scholars have used to join their methodology with their political orientation. As opposed to feminist scholars who write in accordance with their own political sympathies, I did not sympathize with some, or even *all*, of the political commitments of the various research subjects I interviewed. This aspect of my project is politically ambiguous and unpalatable for researchers who seek to "give voice" only to politics that they support. The assumption of shared politics with the research subject may be equally problematic because it may incline the researcher to miss differences between himself or herself and those being researched, and to project affirmations that do not exist. Nevertheless, the tension within my work between my politics and the politics of my research subjects made me aware of the many choices involved in doing fieldwork and gave me cause to question continuously the motivations for my research.

The interview

The first methodological choice in my fieldwork was the interview as my principal method of data collection.[4] Although my project is also based

---

[4] My fieldwork consisted of a series of interviews of women (and men) activists in English and Hebrew, approximately eighty in total. My access to the activists was generally facilitated through a contact in the movement whom I approached initially by telephone and who introduced me to others. I also approached activists at public demonstrations. In either case, the relationship commenced by my initiative. There was neither institutional affiliation nor previous association to provide me with right of entry into these relationships. The length of the interviews ranged between one and three hours, during which time I took handwritten notes. On several occasions, at the behest of the interviewee, I sent the notes back for approval.

on archival research and secondary literature, contact with individuals significantly enhanced my understanding of their politics and perspectives on security. Choosing the interview requires taking experience seriously as an element of knowledge, something that quantitative aggregated data does not encompass. The interview allowed me to incorporate the feelings, fears and hopes of the participants in terms of how they feel larger structures and discourses such as war and peace in their daily lives. In this sense, speaking directly with the women I interviewed was a more tangible method of data collection, as my contact was direct and "in the flesh."

Numerous feminist scholars have applauded the benefits of interviewing. Shulamit Reinharz, for example, argues that feminist interview research is particularly suited to capturing the differences *among* people because of its use of non-standardized information. Interviewing provides access to people's ideas, thoughts, and memories in their own words rather than in the words of the researcher (see also D'Costa, this volume; Reinharz 1992). This technique of proceeding from the subjects' own words rather than from the theoretical framework of the researcher seeks to destabilize the subject/object dichotomy in fieldwork, while addressing a history of social science research that has treated women either as invisible or as objects of masculine scientific knowledge.

The possibility and implications of the use of experience in fieldwork required reconsideration in my project. When transcribed from the interview, experience is a problematic unit of analysis, particularly when it forms the basis for knowledge. Experience is generally defined as the knowledge gained from what one has observed, encountered, or undergone. It is important to remember that knowledge does not merely exist, but is *interpreted* and *represented* in a myriad of ways. This process occurs first within the self as one comes to terms with one's own identity or subject position. Then, one's identity is translated through the field of social interactions as individuals represent themselves to others. By acknowledging that experience is a source of legitimate knowledge, one encounters a series of methodological difficulties. The most difficult dilemma is the tendency to equate the validation of experience with truth. The current trend in many areas of feminist research is to represent those being researched "in their own words." This concept of writing using direct quotations or reproducing oral history accounts is intended to take the researcher out of the text in order not to downplay the voices of those being represented. This method is certainly commendable for its celebration of the individual and the diffusion of authority that the micronarrative entails.

However, the problem with this method is that it cannot overcome the various discrepancies and even misunderstandings that occur in the process of inserting fieldwork data into the broader text. Indeed, with any independent analysis, what the researcher understands may not necessarily be synonymous with the original intention of the statement. In my case, cultural factors and other differences intervened in the translation of experience from researched (Israeli women) to researcher (Canadian academic). Some researchers suggest that an element of cross-cultural incommensurability pervades the process of interviewing, and sustains a residue of meaning that is not reached in cross-cultural endeavors. The epistemological problem with using direct quotations transcribed from an interview is that it implicitly equates experience with knowledge. My own sense of collecting data on fieldwork is that experience should be understood, not as truth, but simply as a telling of one's story, a narrative that represents the choices and priorities of the particular individual or group. There are many ways to tell a story, many purposes for telling the story, and many ways to interpret the stories of others (see Cohn and Stern, this volume). It is useful to provide space within the research context, not only for informants to reveal their intersubjectivities, but also to interpret what that means to the research and to their lives. By bringing in a range of critical perspectives, the interpretive process can allow for a less dichotomous process of inquiry (Ackerly 2000).

In order to come to terms with these dilemmas, I found the concept of *self-presentation* to be more meaningful than experience. Self-presentation denotes the ways in which agents form their own subjectivities (Stern in this volume) and actively present their lives to others. The concept of self-presentation implies that those being researched do not merely respond to the agenda and questions of the researcher, but are actively engaged in shaping their own agenda of how they *want* to be represented. For example, respondents tend to want to legitimize their actions or the actions of their constituencies, and not to be seen as violent or extreme. In response, the researcher cannot simply disappear from the text, but must actively assess the relation between the subjectivity (experience) and self-presentation of a respondent. The way a respondent perceives himself or herself may differ from the way he or she wishes to be perceived. An element of ambiguity may be inevitable in all research encounters, particularly in cross-cultural dialogue. In other words, genuine understanding may never be fully attainable. However, by weeding through contradictions, silences, self-doubts, and changes in opinion in the content of the respondent's words, a researcher may, at the very least, discern how subjects assert their agency, imbue their actions with meaning, frame their own representations, and determine how these data are accumulated, classified, stored, and interpreted accordingly.

An additional obstacle in using experience as a basis for knowledge is that in a zone of conflict, respondents are generally more cautious about revealing personal information, particularly when they are active in dissenting or extremist movements that may be targeted by the state. Informants of this nature may worry about making statements that are critical of established authority and that may prejudice either their security or the security of their families. As a result, what they say may be motivated more by fear or caution than by a desire to tell the researcher what they really feel.

One of the ways I sought to establish a more relaxing interview atmosphere had to do with place and timing. I generally conducted the interview either in the home of the respondent on a day off work or at the weekend, or in a neutral place such as a public demonstration or coffee shop. Fieldwork encounters in the home facilitated the expression of personal feelings, thoughts, worries, and fears as photo albums were brought out and an individual's life circumstances were displayed in his or her belongings. In fact, a few women shed tears during the interview because the discussion raised difficult memories for them, of a son or husband who died or was injured in war, or fears about their own insecurity or the insecurity of their family.[5] These expressions allowed me greater insight in to the person's life and provided background that would not have been captured in survey research or opinion polls.

At first, the interviews were based on questions about "security" I prepared in advance; for example: "What is your definition of security?" Although a seemingly straightforward question, it created very complex epistemological and ontological dilemmas. Although all respondents were concerned with the general context of insecurity in Israel/Palestine, questions about security prompted varying perceptions of threat and strategies for promoting a political agenda. Recognizing this dilemma, I moved early on to an open-ended framework for dialogue in the interviews rather than use predetermined questions and definitions in order to allow the respondent to set the agenda and talk without interruption about what he or she thought relevant. For example, I asked such open-ended questions as "What motivates your political activism?" or "Can you explain your choice of political perspective?" in order not to preclude any meaningful information about their

---

[5] I gave subjects the choice of anonymity so that statements would not be attached to them in future publications.

definition of "security." These questions helped to capture the complexity of women's perceptions and politics in a zone of conflict and provided space for respondents to articulate themselves in ways they most wanted to be represented.

All respondents claimed to reject violence in principle, although most did not define themselves as "pacifist," that is, non-violent or non-resistant to aggression, when it came to particular goals and actions. Feminists have pointed out that in the context of a war society, the luxury of being anti-militaristic is often unavailable for those who strive for the right to fight for their cause and promote change (Yuval-Davis 1997). This perspective differs greatly from my own experiences, since I lived most of my life in a society (Canada) in which the need to fight, at least in my generation, has not been an issue. Considering this cross-cultural difference, I made every effort not to judge the respondents on the issue of violence.

Instead of defining security in a straightforward way, such as "freedom from violence" or "national self-determination," respondents evoked a range of justificatory strategies for legitimizing the violence of "their side" and blaming the other side for provoking a response. In zones of conflict, groups often point out the "dispositional motives to aggression of the other side" while explaining the "violence on their side" in situational terms (Liebes and Ribak 1994: 108). In this sense, the violence of the "other" is universalized and presented as predispositional, as a part of "their character." On the other hand, the violence on "our side" is explained rationally in terms of the imposition of external factors and the need to respond defensively to them, but not as a part of the internal traits of the group. For example, during the interviews, women from the national-religious camp in Israel defined Palestinian violence as aggressive, while defining Israeli violence as "entirely self-defensive."[6] The contestation over "who commits violence" was an interesting methodological issue in the interviews. Most of the women respondents felt that their collective affiliation engaged in the "legitimate" right to fight, in relation to which they compared the violence of others as "illegitimate." Indeed, in a zone of conflict, groups tend to feel more threatened than threatening, regardless of the reality of power, on account of the overriding concern about one's own security. However, regardless of the real degree of insecurity in their lives, feelings such as insecurity, fear, and victimization are felt subjectively rather than objectively. This idea of defining violence subjectively captures

---

[6] Member of Women in Green, in interview with Jacoby, November 26, 1997 (English).

the different interpretations and frames of references for "security" as expressed by different groups. It also helps to explain how violence figures in the ideas and understandings individuals have of their own identities and the characteristics they most associate with themselves as political agents and human beings, versus the characteristics they associate with those they view as "other" or outside the boundaries of their group.

By engaging in processes of legitimization, respondents imbued the concept of security with their worldview and political orientation. For example, women of the national religious camp defined "security" as part of a broader politico-theology based on a belief in the divine and spiritual destiny attributed to Jews (the referent object of security), who, they believe, were chosen by God to fulfill transcendental imperatives. For them, the Arab–Israeli conflict is but a contemporary manifestation of a century-long metaphysical struggle of the Jewish nation to exist against the enmities of a hostile world. As a result of the infusion of security with religious meaning, respondents insisted that their security rested on the survival of the Jewish people, which in turn depended upon the settlement of biblical land and the holy, incontestable, and thus inalienable right to that land.[7]

National religious women conceived their own individual security, that of their families, and the security of the state of Israel to be targets of existential threats. Therefore, despite the superior military capacity of Israel in relation to its adversaries in the Middle Eastern region, these women felt personally insecure. They believed that their security would ultimately derive, not from the state of Israel, but from the transcendental directives given by God. For this reason, national religious women used the interview as a context to promote political goals such as Jewish settlement in the biblical "Land of Israel" and rejection of any territorial concessions. The language used by these women was highly politicized[8] with reference to concepts such as victim, threat, enemy, fault, and vanquish. The constant use of scripture and biblical analogies imbued those concepts with an ultimately theological and even messianic content.

By way of contrast, Israeli women peace activists expressed alternative perspectives on security through very different legitimizing strategies and language. For example, Israeli peace activists equated the term "insecurity" with Israeli settler violence against Palestinians and Israeli military

---

[7] For background on the Israeli national religious camp and the settler movement, see Schnall 1979.

[8] See Stern's discussion of "political rhetoric and personal experience" in this volume.

occupation of Palestinian territory. This more self-critical definition of security derives from a different metaphysical understanding of the existence of the state of Israel and the Jewish nation. Women peace activists defined security as connection with, and understanding of, the Palestinian cause. As a result of engaging in years of cross-national partnership and struggling for the rights of the other, Israeli women peace activists used the interview as a means for denouncing policies perpetrated by the Israeli government against Palestinians, such as home demolitions and land confiscation, checkpoints, and human rights violations. These perspectives on security were expressed in secular and humanist language such as sacrifice, responsibility, social justice, peace, coexistence, and partnership. This contestation over the meaning of security, as captured through self-presentation by the different parties to the conflict, led me to reexamine the process through which I accumulated data about the term "security" in fieldwork. It also led me to rethink the researcher–researched relationship and realize that my questions about security were actually questions about identity, agency, and politics. When seen from the perspective of particular individuals and groups the concept seeks to represent, security becomes a relative concept, one that – although not unrelated to material circumstances – is in essence a matter of perception, a result of experience that is variable, subject to emotions in place and time, and never predetermined (see also Stern, this volume).

Reciprocity, transparency, and involvement

Feminist researchers have proposed a variety of methods to facilitate the researcher–researched relationship and to overcome the power dynamics inherent in social science research. In particular, they have suggested the importance of reciprocity, transparency, and involvement.

First, the principle of reciprocity is an attempt to create a more open and interactive relationship during research encounters (Acker, Barry, and Esseveld [1983] 1991: 141). In practice, reciprocity can be established on the part of the researcher by offering to share personal information and allow those being researched to ask questions themselves. It is useful for those being researched to know why the research is being done, what motivated the research design, where they fit in the research project, how they are classified in relation to theoretical concepts and theories, and how their words will be used (whether in direct quotations, paraphrases, or references in general). Respondents will generally want to know if they are described as "mainstream" or "radical" agents in the political spectrum, and whether their political perspective is articulated as "progressive" or "regressive." Access to this type of information can mitigate the power relations inherent in fieldwork encounters by allowing respondents to choose whether or not they want to take part in this type of research and, if they do, to have some control over the way in which their contribution will be used (see also D'Costa, this volume).

Power dynamics were not as visible in my fieldwork as they would be in cases where a western researcher does work with women such as sex-trade workers or victims of domestic abuse. However, my own personal connection to the region as an Israeli Jewish woman did create dilemmas for some of the women I interviewed and potentially for myself as well. As a result, there were certain cases in which reciprocity was difficult to attain. I began each interview by encouraging the respondent to ask questions about me. With this information out in the open, not all the respondents I interviewed felt comfortable about the fact that I was an Israeli immigrant who worked to absorb Russian Jewry in Israel (a policy that many Palestinians see as detrimental to Arab demographic representation in Israel), or that I am married to a former officer in Israeli Army intelligence. These roles were particularly sensitive for Palestinian respondents and created ethical dilemmas in fieldwork.

Feminist ethnographers have raised questions about issues of deception during field research. Intuitively, the best research environment would be one in which both the researcher and the researched feel sufficiently comfortable with one another to leave the research encounter feeling empowered or at least satisfied with having contributed to the research. No ethical researcher would intentionally exploit, humiliate, or endanger the life of his or her subjects. So it would seem that every effort should be invested to make the research encounter a positive experience for all. However, is a positive experience necessary for good research? The interview is not a completely controlled environment as in a laboratory experiment. There are many extraneous variables that may compromise the best intentions of those involved. For example, if the researcher holds views or affiliations that conflict with those of the researched, full disclosure up front may cause discomfort or caution on the part of the research subject. Full disclosure at the end of an interview may cause regret and even anger.

During an interview, should the researcher openly disagree or even argue with respondents when touching upon contentious issues? Or should the researcher remain silent and even put on a "poker face" when opposing views are voiced? If the respondent is aware of the researcher's perspective, this may cause him or her to withhold information, articulate views differently, or even choose to leave. Is full transparency necessary for a good interview? How much personal information must be made available? There are no clear answers to these questions. The trade-off between honesty and disclosure versus a good research opportunity must be considered in all research encounters. Often, full disclosure can close doors that would otherwise yield important information. In order to prevent these dilemmas, researchers can limit their research to subjects they fully identify with. However, while this type of research may be enjoyable, it is in some respects an extravagant form of navel-gazing, celebrating the "self" and duplicating the "same" through the medium of social science. Is this what research is all about?

My research has to do with difference and diversity. Interviewing respondents with views different from mine caused much discomfort in the research encounter. There were periods of tension and frustration. At times I even felt antipathy on account of views being expressed with which I did not empathize. My choice to avoid full transparency in some cases allowed me to access much-needed information, but created dilemmas that haunted me throughout the project. I intend to work in this area for many years to come. The possibility of maintaining ties with my research subjects would ultimately be problematized by the divulgence of my identity in future publications. Elusiveness, then, while sometimes a useful tool for access to information, carries with it the risk of deception.

One example of deception came about during an interview I conducted at a Palestinian women's organization in the West Bank in 1998. The details of my marriage came up late in the conversation, when the respondent noticed my wedding ring and asked about my husband. The question would have otherwise fitted well in the interview, as we had been discussing personal status law and family relations in Palestinian society. However, by disclosing that I was married to an Israeli man, I caused alarm on the part of the respondent after she made political statements against the Israeli occupation, statements she would not have made had she known about my subject position. The respondent had assumed I was "neutral" on the issue of the Israeli–Palestinian conflict and the context of the interview did nothing to signal to her otherwise. The interview turned decidedly negative at the point at which she figured I was an activist in my own right. Although I had no intention of endangering this woman, greater initial transparency about my subject position would have precluded any such apprehensions on her part and I would not have felt that I had deceived her. However, full disclosure may have closed off the research opportunity to begin with.

Despite efforts to create an evenly balanced rapport between researcher and researched, there is a tendency for built-in asymmetries in fieldwork to arise and interfere with that relationship. Asymmetry may result from the fact that researchers are sufficiently far from home that their research subjects do not encounter their family members or friends, whereas respondents are usually surrounded by kin and friends and "cannot similarly withdraw, hide and alter aspects of their identity" (D. L. Wolf, 1996: 11). I did not set out intentionally to deceive my respondents. However, on occasion I did not feel comfortable with exposing my Jewishness to some women I met throughout my travels if they rejected normalization with Israel or were involved in militant movements such as Hamas (The Islamic Resistance Movement) or the Islamic Jihad.

During interviews with women who committed acts of violence against Israeli citizens, I found myself implicitly hiding behind my Anglo-Saxon appearance (pale skin, blond hair, blue eyes), so that respondents assumed I was "uninvolved" in the conflict. This issue came up during an interview I conducted of a woman who had been affiliated with the Islamic Jihad and was sentenced to life for her role in the kidnapping and murder of an Israeli soldier. She received amnesty as part of the Oslo Agreements (1993) and connected with me through the organization of Women for Female Political Prisoners.[9]

During the interview, the issue of my surname came up. "Jacoby" is an anglicized version of "Yaacoby," the name I took upon marriage to my husband, whose family is of Israeli Kurdish origin. The respondent asked if the name was German, and instead of elaborating, I answered, "I don't know," and we completed the interview without incident. I doubt that any negative consequence would have resulted, but in the context of fieldwork in a zone of conflict, the security of the researcher may be threatened. Uncertainty on the part of the researcher concerning issues of threat and safety can be a powerful motivating factor against full disclosure.

The issue of intimacy with subjects during fieldwork is another research dilemma raised in feminist methodology. While many feminist ethnographers favor a friendship-like rapport with their subjects, there are problems associated with this type of research relationship. Diane Wolf argues that most friendships cultivated during fieldwork are short-lived and could end up being more manipulative than traditional positivist methods, in which there is no guise of solidarity, empathy, or friendship (D. L. Wolf 1996: 20). Particularly in a zone of conflict, research is accumulated on the basis of crises, which occur to those

---

[9] Women for Female Political Prisoners is an Israeli Palestinian organization that supports female Palestinian political prisoners in Israeli prisons with basic necessities, legal representation, and help with reintegration into society upon release.

being researched. No matter how much the researcher participates in advocacy for the research subjects or attains a close relationship, there is ultimately the issue of promoting one's professional career. Even with the best of intentions, there are possibilities for exploiting the research subjects, either explicitly or implicitly, that need to be taken into consideration (D'Costa and Stern, this volume). Further, the researcher always retains that privileged ability to leave the field that may not be available for those being researched. Therefore, friendships may be fundamentally gratifying, albeit problematic, relations to navigate during fieldwork.

The issue of reciprocity came about when I was asked to join respondents at political rallies or politically motivated programs. Feminist researchers have noted the rewards of helping those in need, as respondents often feel they are not duly compensated for the time and effort they invest in someone else's research. Most often, the researcher rather than the researched is ultimately rewarded with the glory of publishing and public speaking. Indeed, in order for the researcher to obtain information, hours of an activist's time may be sacrificed that could otherwise have been invested in the cause. For those researchers who are not already involved with the politics of the researched, volunteering to work for their organization during fieldwork is often a way to mitigate the asymmetrical benefits of research.

However, I encountered dilemmas with respect to volunteering on account of my leftist political perspective in Israeli politics. I was prepared to work for one of the two organizations that formed my case study, but not the other. While I volunteered my time to work in the office of the Jerusalem Link, an organization in the Israeli women's peace movement, answering phones and writing reports, I was not prepared to do the same for the Women in Green, an organization of national religious women in Israel. This created certain asymmetries in the relationship with my respondents. For example, there were occasions when I refused to attend rallies of the national religious camp because being another body in attendance inadvertently contributed to their campaign. However, sometimes it is necessary to partake in activities in order to collect information. For example, I joined a tour of the West Bank organized by the Women in Green, which was designed to express support for Jewish settlement in disputed territory, a goal with which I do not sympathize.

Feminists have debated whether researchers must identify with all their subjects. Complete identification may well be gratifying but it can problematize the capacity for critical analysis. For example, the researcher may downplay certain unpalatable aspects or may be blinded to the contradictions or negative implications of the politics and worldviews of those being researched. I wondered about the degree to which my volunteer work would alter my critical edge towards one organization over the other. I admit I may have been less critical of the Jerusalem Link in the initial stages of writing, as a result of consorting with them more comprehensively. These dilemmas of fieldwork represent the complex and arduous process of negotiating the relationship between the researcher and those being researched with a range of qualitative methods that are not always adequate to the difficult demands of actual fieldwork encounters.

Concluding remarks

This chapter highlights some of the basic methodological dilemmas posed by fieldwork encounters in a zone of conflict. Feminist IR fieldwork challenges the methods long employed by mainstream IR, which yield a particular type of knowledge based on the assumption of subject/object dichotomy. In feminist IR fieldwork, both the researcher and the researched are subjects with agency. The research encounter is an intersubjective process through which subject positions are negotiated and politics of the broader context are played out in microform. The negotiation of the fieldwork encounter is itself a basis for creating knowledge, which depends to a large extent on *how* that knowledge is accumulated, stored, employed, and authored for research purposes. Methods and their use are an important consideration when evaluating the product of any research encounter. Whether that encounter was amicable or antagonistic, it is the role of the researcher actively to interpret, to the best of his or her ability, the intentions of those whose words are transcribed and the ultimate meaning those words represent in the worldview of the researcher. The transition of data from researched to researcher is a mutually constitutive process that must be managed with the use of effective and ethical research methods.

However, while it is important to strive for ethical conduct during fieldwork, many of the prescriptions for proper research, such as reciprocity, transparency, and friendship, are highly normative and difficult to obtain in actual research encounters. Fieldwork involves limitations in terms of emotional concerns, time constraints, political context, financial and other resources that may not accommodate the ideal epistemology of ethical research. It may be impossible to create a research process that completely erases the contradictions in the relation between researcher and researched on account of the necessities of writing, authoring, and ultimately publishing data. Important is an awareness of the role that methods play in power relations and possibilities for exploitation (see D'Costa and Stern, this volume). Once the researcher's gaze is squarely on the methods, only then is it possible to seek to reduce the possible negative implications, and ultimately to acknowledge the limitations of field research. Coming to know the methodological and epistemological boundaries within which knowledge is accumulated is an important aspect of learning, writing, authoring, and becoming part of the field.

Different approaches to security and diverse interpretations in the process of threat perception suggest that an ethnographer must enter the field with an open mind about what "security" means to different subjects. One group or individual may designate a referent object as security which does not figure in any known or established paradigm. During my fieldwork, the definition of security ranged anywhere from a theological imperative to a cultural partnership. What security means "in the last instance" depends on the point of view and authority of the person who defines the term. Interviewing respondents and asking them to articulate their *own* perspectives on security help to imbue the concept with concrete meaning.

Understanding research as an ongoing negotiating process between subjects with agency involves continual revision of initial questions and hypotheses. My initial question regarding whether women have definitions of security different from or similar to those of men changed when I realized the extent to which my own categories did not fit the research context. First, I discovered that to capture a woman's definition of security requires understanding her experience of insecurity. However, although women may experience insecurity in specific ways "as women," those experiences are mitigated and presented through a variety of categories (political, social, spiritual) not always or explicitly related to gender. This rendered experience a difficult category to work with. Thus, not only did I focus attention away from my own framework of analysis (security); I faced the complexities of the actual process through which knowledge was generated by the fieldwork encounter. In the end, I realized that information communicated to the researcher is not in the form of a prepackaged category (experience), but is actively presented through the encounter itself, which means that the knowledge process is not simply a reflection of "reality" but a purposeful tool for legitimizing political views and influencing the political process.

These insights from the practices of feminist IR fieldwork touch upon the broader questions of social science research, but in relatively new and particular ways. Traditional social science seeks to overcome the dilemmas of our times by imposing order and achieving certainty. The development of classifications and rules is intended to assure us that society is progressing towards a definitive resolution of the time-honored questions posed by the political sphere in a way that is rational and under our control. By contrast, critical social science celebrates the uncertainty of the political sphere by virtue of its boundless nature and thus its possibilities for change. It points to all that is excluded or marginalized from dominant classificatory systems and thereby opens the field to new understandings. Feminist IR fieldwork demonstrates that social science is not the equivalent of an Archimedean truth, but simply a snapshot of life, one that captures the vicarious nature of research encounters that are at once partial and yet deeply personal. While a snapshot may be limited in its definitive capacity, it – along with many others of its kind – builds knowledge by being potentially meaningful for broader groups and affiliations, which identify with phenomena that exceed the specificities of place and time. Violence, danger, and fear are intercontextual relations and feelings insofar as people throughout the world experience them in their own circumstances and at varying degrees of intensity. Out of encounters between researchers and subjects, knowledge about security and insecurity in different places and contexts is forged, negotiated, and interpreted, continuously and in some respects unendingly as we go on to learn from our experiences and the experiences of others, as we change and imbue our memories and introspections with new meanings. As opposed to the disciplinary boundaries of traditional social scientific inquiry, meaning in feminist IR fieldwork is not a linear process of confirming hypotheses but rather a set of positionings through which researcher and researcher negotiate with each other and, in so doing, establish their subjectivities. Together, they move in a cyclical conjecture from theory to practice and back again. The fieldwork encounter provides space for respondents to frame their subjectivities, thereby mitigating the power relations inherent in social science research. However, fieldwork ultimately calls for the researcher to interpret the self-presentations of the subjects through his or her own understandings. As a result, it may be that definitive representations of others will always be left with a measure of incommensurability. However, regardless of the tensions that this process may involve, a lot can be learned from the trenches, so to speak. Awareness of the mutually constitutive relationship of experience, interpretation, and representation in fieldwork is necessary for *doing* feminist IR and framing future narratives for security and insecurity that IR scholars have yet to consider as relevant to the field.

Racism, sexism, classism, and much more:
     reading security-identity in marginalized sites

Maria Stern

> We are women, poor, indigenous; we are . . . triply discriminated
> against.
> 'Onelia'

> The [Civil Patrols] always threaten the women. [They ask,] "Why don't
> you have husbands, where do you get these bad ideas?" [Once] the
> chief of the patrols said: "Now we are going to put all the patrollers
> together and all the widows together . . . These women need husbands,
> because now they are not doing anything, that is why they are organiz-
> ing . . . take two or three for each of you". . . Several days ago [someone
> told me] that they raped four women.
> 'Carmen'

> My consciousness was born [after fleeing from the army and hiding in
> the jungle]. It is not correct when they tell us today that we are not
> worth anything, that we don't have any participation in the society, in
> the development of Guatemala . . . The same situation that I have
> experienced since I was a child up until today has made me have this
> consciousness to rise up as women to guard our heritage, to guard
> our sacrifices . . . Always the female elders said that . . . when the
> Spanish came here to Guatemala, when they came to invade, our
> grandparents . . . were tortured, burned alive. All the books where they
> had their scriptures were burned . . . In this sense I understood . . . the
> situation that they talked about when I had to live it. So, I came to
> appreciate the elders because it is they who know more of the culture,
> how we have been for 500 years . . . For me it is painful that we have
> not [only] been suffering for ten, fifteen years, but we have resisted
> for 500 years.
> 'Andrea'

Introduction

The above testimonies reflect the experiences of many politically active
Mayan women in Guatemala in 1995. These words were spoken on the

I would like to thank my co-editors and Maria Eriksson-Baaz for their helpful comments on
this chapter. This chapter reconsiders the methodology I used in writing my PhD dissertation (M. Stern 2001). Some of the text presented in this chapter can also be found in M.
Stern 2005.

"eve" of a peace agreement that would officially end over thirty years of violent conflict and promise substantial inclusion of the Mayan peoples in the Guatemalan nation- state project.[1] Among other things, these testimonies raise questions about security. How do people like "Onelia," "Carmen," and "Andrea" speak about their experiences of insecurity and their struggles for security? And what might their words imply for rethinking security and insecurity in the field of International Relations (IR)? Inspired by these questions, I set out to research security from the perspective of Mayan women.

Mayan women's experience of insecurity was drastically different from insecurity as it was conceived by the security elite in Guatemala, as well as by most theorists of security in IR. Researching Mayan women's insecurity within the framework of security studies in IR therefore proved to be problematic.

In this chapter, I retrace the methodological journey my research took in the hope that my experiences might shed light on possible ways of studying security for people like Mayan women. However, in addition to offering insight for security studies, my intention is to make explicit the challenges I faced in engaging in a study informed by feminist theorizing with the theoretical and methodological tools of a discipline that has paid little attention to questions of gender. By making visible the types of difficulties I encountered, as well as the ways I chose to "resolve" them, my methodological journey may be useful for others designing and

---

[1] Roughly, the Guatemalan population includes indigenous peoples, ladinos (of mixed Spanish and indigenous descent), and about 2 per cent "Spanish." Most estimate that the indigenous population (mostly "Mayan") comprised 55–70 per cent of Guatemala's entire population in the 1990s, although this is a highly politically charged question. The dividing lines between ladinos and Mayans are porous and blurry; they therefore became even more politicized in attempts both to homogenize the population on the part of the army or state, and to make political claims based on cultural identity, on the part of the Mayan *pueblo*.

Guatemala's recent history features a "ladino state," where an insidious and violently overt racism pervaded society. Between the years 1960 and 1996, an insurgency–counter-insurgency "civil" war officially took place in Guatemala. The ruling elite of the Guatemalan state defined the indigenous population as inherently threatening to the nation because of its role as a popular base for the guerrillas – and because their identification with their "ethnic" group challenged national unity, if not militarily, then symbolically. This period, at the final stages of the peace negotiations, offered a unique moment in Guatemala's history, when there was a definite change in the political climate – a "democratic opening." Those who had suffered the heritage of over thirty years of armed conflict, counter-insurgency tactics, and unjust distributions of resources saw the prospect of peace and perhaps substantial social transformation as a real possibility. Hence, people whose voices of resistance, which had been (almost) successfully silenced during the bloodiest period of the civil war, began to reformulate their demands and to tell their stories in light of their visions of a better future.

conducting feminist IR studies of other concepts and practices central to
the understanding of global politics.

Who are the Mayan women of my study?

In 1995, I conducted life-history interviews with leaders of different
organizations within the popular or Mayan movement in Guatemala in
order to gain a better understanding of what security meant to them. The
people I interviewed had endured violent experiences at the confluence
of several injurious relations of power: racism, sexism, and classism.
Furthermore, their experiences of insecurity were distinct in the very
different yet related contexts that made up their lives, such as their
families, their "ethnic" group and their organizations, as well as the racist
Guatemalan nation-state. In one context, for example, Mayan men posed
threats to their well-being; in another, Mayan men were their greatest
allies against the threat posed by the army or the racist ladino society.

The multiple insecurities experienced by Mayan women cannot be
understood separately from their claims to political identity; what they
considered threats and envisioned as promising safety and security
depended upon *who they were*. They did not identify themselves with
the particular articulation of Guatemalan national identity that prevailed
at the time; instead, they identified themselves, in part, in opposition to
the homogenizing claims of Guatemalan nationalism, stating that their
culture and identity (*being Mayan*) were placed at risk by this violent
national project. They identified themselves as Mayan *women* whose
femininity was defined in part by their roles as guardians and transmit-
ters of the Mayan culture. As women, however, they were particularly
vulnerable both to the harms of sexism within their communities (and
households) and to the sexualized violence of military tactics. They also
identified themselves as poor peasants (*campesinas*) whose connection
and therewith access to cultivatable land was vital for their cultural and
physical survival. In this regard, poverty related to the neoliberal economic policies of an export economy, and consequent national land
distribution was a great threat to their security. In sum, Mayan women's
insecurity was multiple, contingent, and defined in terms of their identity. Furthermore, it was clear that their "security" transgressed many of
the subdivisions of IR, such as IPE and identity studies.

The subject of security

The field of IR – and indeed everyday global politics – is understand-
ably preoccupied with security, or perceived threats to security. This

preoccupation has traditionally revolved around the nation- state: the state has been cast as both the agent and the referent object of security; other states have acted as the source of possible threat (as well as temporary allies). Yet the insecurity experienced by many does not neatly *fit* into the prevailing security discourses. On the whole, women and members of marginalized ethnic groups (such as Mayan women) – although seemingly assumed to be included as members of the state – have not been considered valid subjects of security in their own right, at least in terms of the dominant theories and practices of IR.[2] Furthermore, feminist political theory has shown how the seemingly gender neutral basic grammar of "modern" political imaginaries masks the gendered workings of power which cast the masculine as the norm (Flax 1987; Pateman 1988; Brown 1988; Elshtain 1987; Okin 1989; Spelman 1988; Tickner, this volume). Similarly, feminist scholarship has revealed how the very exclusion of the feminine has been necessary to construct modern political community (see Pin-Fat 2000; Pin-Fat and Stern 2005; and Zalewski in this volume for a discussion of the feminine as the "constitutive outside"). Scholars sensitive to the workings of gender have called for studies designed to explore the insecurity of marginalized women in a manner that redresses their marginalization from IR and global politics more generally.[3]

Nonetheless, the meaning of security and insecurity ([in]security)[4] has been fiercely contested within IR, especially in light of the changing nature of threat posed by the globalization of terrorism. Clearly, the state-centric view has loosened its stronghold; the concept and practice of security have been transformed to reflect both the changing practice of global politics and alternative conceptualizations of political communities, actors, and identities. There have also been considerable advances in questioning what security may signify and *do* as a discursive practice (further explained below). Nonetheless, despite these developments, studies that seriously engage with the contextual and specific meanings

---

[2] For a further discussion of the notion of different meanings of marginality and marginalization in terms of IR scholarship, see D'Costa, this volume.

[3] See for example, Cohn 1993; Elshtain 1987; Enloe 1989; 1993; 2000; Moon 1997; Peterson and Runyan 1991; Peterson 1992a; Pettman 1996; Reardon 1985; 1993; Sylvester 1994a; 2002; Tickner 1993; 2001; Youngs 1999; Zawelski 1998a; among others.

[4] Central to an understanding of security is the intimate and "indissoluble relation" of security with insecurity. "The not-secure of security is the radical excess of security that continuously contours security" (Dillon 1996: 127). Mayan women's struggles for security can be seen as inseparable from their experiences of danger and threat. Hence the term (in)security.

of (in)security in sites other than those privileged by the grammar of state sovereignty are markedly absent.

Security studies within IR therefore does not provide an adequate ontological, theoretical, or methodological base for the study of marginalized women in multiply precarious positions, such as Mayan women in Guatemala. Hence, when I set out to research the meaning of (in)security in terms of Mayan women – people who understood themselves to be marginalized by the many different power relations that informed their lives, and whose political identities were constructed at the intersection of, and in resistance to, these different relations – I found myself without a methodological guidebook.

My initial research aim was to understand security from the perspective of peoples who are "most" marginalized in a society in order to challenge the dominant IR scripts of security. My choice to focus on the experiences of Mayan women in Guatemala reflected my attempt to reveal the gendered, state-centric biases in security studies by juxtaposing traditional understandings of (in)security with marginalized subaltern ones. This intention was further motivated by the particular context in Guatemala, where, instead of exercising its official protector role, the Army posed the main direct threat to the Guatemalan population, especially to the Mayan *pueblo*[5] and Mayan women.

My research was guided by the following overriding research question: "What does (in)security mean from the perspective of Mayan women?" More specifically, I intended to learn from the fear, threat, danger, and harm that Mayan woman articulated in their struggles to create a desirable and sustainable peace. My hope was that such a study would contribute to rethinking (in)security in a post-Cold War, post-colonial, globalized world. Hence, the focus of the research question entailed that I look at "security" *starting from* the political site and perspective of Mayan women.

Finding a theoretical/methodological framework

In doing research of any kind, and, in particular, research *on* others, the epistemological question of "where" to begin is arguably crucial. Much feminist literature has emphasized the importance of theorizing from women's lives, of not fitting women or other marginalized groups and their experiences into the already formed molds of IR theory

---

[5] The term *pueblo* in Spanish means people, nation, or even village. In this context it connotes a strong sense of cultural and political belonging.

(cf. Tickner, this volume). One can learn surprising things, and disrupt existing theories that purport to explain "reality," from grounding an inquiry in "empirical" material that is otherwise silenced or excluded from the authorized subjects of research (cf. Enloe 1989; 1993; 2000; Sylvester 1994a). If nothing else, such research prompts the recognition that alternative accounts may exist and that dominant discourses require hard work to sustain a semblance of naturalness.[6]

It is perhaps obvious to any feminist scholar of security that the dominant teachings on security, which focus on the military security of the state, would not offer adequate guidelines in terms of designing a study on Mayan women's insecurity. The simple facts that the state itself was perceived as the "problem," and the referent object of security was a select group of marginalized people, made a conventional study of security (e.g. using a positivist research method to map weapon capabilities and military threat assessments) a contrary endeavor (cf. the Introduction to this volume; Terriff et al. 1999). With its inclusion of referent objects besides the state, alternative security studies offered more diverse possibilities for research of other "subjects of security" (e.g. Booth 1998; Buzan, 1991; Terriff et al. 1999). Could, for instance, Mayan women's experiences of threat and danger be addressed through a conceptual apparatus that divided security into sectors (environmental, societal, economic, etc.) or located security at different levels (e.g. the individual, ethnic group, state, region, globe) (Buzan 1991)? How might Mayan women's security fit into these categories? And would fitting their experiences into these discursive frameworks allow for a serious rethinking of security as I had intended?

One possible approach would be to address Mayan women's (in)security as "individual" or "human security." A notion of "individual" security rests on an idea of the Enlightenment subject – a particular, gendered notion of being human that is universalizing, yet hardly universal.[7] A shift in focus to "human security" reflects an attempt to emphasize people as the referents of security, instead of the individual

---

[6] Enloe, for example, explains how militarization rests on a notion of the citizen-soldier as a (violent) masculine figure. This notion requires much discursive work (e.g. reproducing men and masculinity as warring, and women and femininity as peaceful) to maintain its stronghold (Enloe 1993; 2000).

[7] A further discussion on these points can be found in Brown 1988; K. E. Ferguson 1993; Grant 1991; Jabri and O'Gorman 1999; Peterson 1992b; Tickner 1993; 2001. Another example of the universalization of the "universal" can be found in feminist accounts of the discourse of human rights. The notion of human rights rests on a notion of the "human" that masquerades as universal, yet which is built on a particular picture of humanity (A. S. Fraser 1999; Peterson 1990; Pin-Fat 2000).

as member of a state (UNDP 1994; King and Murray 2002; *Security Dialogue*, 2004: vol. 35, 3). However, this shift, although arguably important, does not significantly alter the underpinning ontology. Much feminist scholarship has asked the question "Which individuals (or humans), in which contexts?" and has disclosed security as a gendered construct that disregards many women's experiences (cf. Peterson 1992b; Tickner 1992; 2001). Furthermore, both the category "individual" and the category "human" become increasingly unstable when one begins to ask questions around identity and embodiment (Hansen 2000). As noted above, Mayan women's experiences of insecurity were multiple and integrally related to who they were, to their specifically gendered and racialized identities. Reducing and reifying it to respond to "basic human needs" could not reflect its contingency or dynamism, or make sense of its seeming contradictions. Attempting to address Mayan women's (in)security through the grammar implied by "individual" or even "human" security therefore became highly problematic.

A feminist standpoint of security?

Because my intention was to arrive at a different, marginalized, silenced notion of security, I rejected the conceptual apparatus of the dominant discourses which would inevitably hinder a substantially different voice from emerging. Could I theorize security from the *starting point* of Mayan women's lives instead of imposing a preconceived notion of security as a way of categorizing their experiences? Would a study informed by a feminist standpoint epistemology unearth Mayan women's (in)security and thereby offer a truer, purer, or even more "strongly objective" model for understanding security more generally (cf. Jacoby and Weldon, this volume)?

   In the course of conducting several pilot interviews with leaders of different organizations, I employed a qualitative interview method whereby I asked the people I was interviewing how they conceived of their security, as well as what they thought was threatening and dangerous. Their responses seemed to be particularly coded within an already established discourse. For example, in response to a question about her experience of threats, one person responded, "No, I have not received any death threats this month." I did not sense that I was "getting at" the multiplicity or the depth of what security and insecurity meant for Mayan women in terms of the interrelated power relations and the different contexts that circumscribed their lives, fears, and hopes. It was also increasingly clear that their political identities *as (self-defined)*

Mayan women informed how they expressed their insecurities; that is, their naming of particular dangers could not be separated from their representation of their (political) identities. Tami Jacoby incisively points out how experiences of insecurity, when conveyed to the researcher, must be read as self-presentations (this volume). However, since I was interested in understanding their security as integral to the multiple ways the narrators identified themselves, I found that my research question required a way of inquiring into the *coproduction* of security (and identity). A "feminist standpoint" epistemology, although tempting in its politics, fell short in reflecting the relationship between the discursive practice of security and the construction of identities.

Security as a discursive practice?

A growing body of literature within post-structuralist IR theory emphasizes the centrality of identity and discourse in articulations of security and insecurity (see also Jacoby, this volume).[8] Discourse, in this sense, connotes the production and re-presentation of meaning, which delimit the realm of understanding, action, and imagination within a certain framework (Eriksson Baaz 2004; Foucault 1980; Hall and duGay 1996.) Security, according to this line of thinking, is meaningful as a "speech act"; it does not have an essential, fixed, reified meaning outside of discourse (Wæver 1995). I therefore could not understand Mayan women's security as somehow "real," outside, separate from their speaking about it.

Scholars such as Campbell (1992) and Dillon (1990–1; 1996) have explored the notion of (in)security as a discursive practice and have carefully shown how sovereign power constructs itself through the workings of discourses of danger and insecurity in various contexts. Attempts to secure a subject rely upon the myth of the subject as already existing and in need of security. However, instead of the subject of security being separate and existing prior to the act of "speaking" or writing security, it is through the very naming of threat and danger that the "subject of security" is formed. This "subject" is evoked in a temporal narrative with a clear beginning and origin (the past), middle (now), and the promise of a happy ending (security realized in the future).

---

[8] E.g. Buzan et al. 1998; Campbell 1992; Connolly 1991; Der Derian and Shapiro 1989; Dillon 1990–1; 1996; George 1994; Hansen 2000; Krause and Williams 1997; Sylvester 1994a; Wæver 1995; R. B. J. Walker 1993; Weldes et al. 1999.

The need for addressing subjectivity became particularly salient in a study of Mayan women's (in)security, since many Mayan women articulated their security needs in terms of their political identities: *as* Mayan, women, and poor (cf. Edkins et al. 1999; Jabri and O'Gorman 1999: 2). Political identification can be seen as a process of constant reconstructions, which depends on the establishment of both a Self and an Other partially through "discourses of danger" (Campbell 1992; Connolly 1991; Dillon 1996). Many scholars of ethnic, national, and gender identity have focused on the importance of boundaries and markers of difference between groups or individuals: we know who and where *we* are in contrast to who and where *they* are (cf. Barth 1969; Connolly 1991; Eriksen 1993; Hall and duGay 1996; Yuval-Davis 1997). The politicization of identity connotes a temporary fixing of a subject position within discourse in order for an individual or group to create a stable basis from which to make political claims. Hence, understanding Mayan women's (in)security would involve analyzing how security as a discursive *practice* informs their identities, as well as how the workings of inclusion and exclusion in their identity formation (and politicization) inform the naming of threat and danger.

A textual treatment of (in)security therefore seemed to be an appropriate way to address my research question. However, in looking for guidance from the leading texts within post-structural and critical security studies on *how* to do such work, I found excellent examples of analysis of discourses of danger written by state security elites (Campbell 1992; Weldes et al. 1999), yet little work in "marginalized" sites upon which to model my research design (cf. D'Costa, this volume; Milliken 1999). I was faced with a number of difficulties. First, scholars like Wæver understand security as a "speech act" executed only by the security elites in naming threats which jeopardize the ultimate existential security of the state (Wæver 1995). If security is used to connote other "things," he argues, it becomes reified to mean "all that is good" and becomes so broad that it loses its relevance as a concept or practice in IR (1995: 47; Buzan et al. 1998; Guzzini and Jung 2003). If I accept that security is indeed a speech act (or a discursive move), how then can one study security in marginalized and silenced sites without falling into the trap of "infinitely expanding the concept," thus rendering Mayan women's (in)security irrelevant for IR (Wæver 1995)?

Secondly, the subjects of my study had not written particular security documents, which I could read and analyze. Those documents that were produced by the Mayan movements did not necessarily represent the voices of the people whose articulations of security I wished to study. As scholars of gender and ethnicity/nationalism have so aptly pointed out, the mechanisms of identity politics often cast women in the role of symbolic marker of difference, and not as active participant in negotiating the meaning of that difference in terms of identifying threats or making political claims (cf. Yuval-Davis 1997; McClintock 1993; Kandiyoti 1991). Furthermore, many of the people whose (in)security I aimed to study could neither read nor write.

Life-history narratives

The narrative as text

Because I found little guidance within IR in terms of how to study marginalized (and not written) discourses, I consequently turned to other fields of social science. The method of "life history" presented me with a possibility for constructing a base "narrative," or "text," which could offer a representation of Mayan women's voices and which I could read as a security discourse.[9]

I decided to conduct partial life history interviews in which I asked the people whom I interviewed to tell me about their "struggles as Mayan women," to tell me their partial life story around this theme.[10] In total, I conducted life history interviews with eighteen different narrators, some of whom I interviewed twice. The narratives they recounted were about their processes of politicization, their coming-into-being as political subjects. The stories about (in)security they conveyed to me were embedded in their representation of themselves as political subjects.

What is a text?

How one views, and therewith analyzes, a text or a testimonial narrative depends upon one's ontology as well as one's epistemology. Is a text a description of, or a producer of, "reality"? The answer to this question bears with it a host of implications, including, for example, how one views the insecurities and threats articulated in such a text. However, instead of delving into a detailed discussion on the different ways of

---

[9] Cf. Arias 2001; Behar 1993; Clifford and Marcus 1986; Gluck and Patai 1991; Fonow and Cook 1991a; Langness and Frank 1981; Ochberg and Rosenwald 1992; Sommer 1991.

[10] All of the participants were active in organizations and made explicit political claims as "Mayan women." This was their primary political self-definition and served as one of the criteria I used to select the participants.

viewing a text, I will briefly explain how I perceive the security narratives upon which I base my work.[11]

Like all narratives, life story narratives must be seen as meaning-constructing activities, instead of meaning-preserving ones. When one constructs a story, events become meaningful through the act of narrating. Events certainly meant certain things when they were experienced; however, the process of making connections, of developing a plot (or many plots) in a narrative of one's life fashions new meanings to these events and to the representation of the self in these stories. The spoken story must also therefore be seen as inscribing, not only the narrative, but also the self/subject as character in the narrative, and the narrator. Furthermore, the act of narrating occurs in a particular political moment which crucially informs the story told (see also D'Costa and Jacoby, this volume).[12]

Life history narratives necessarily rely on memory. In relaying a memory to another person, the narrator places the memory into a narrative schema, a framework for meaning that can make sense to the listener, as well as to oneself (D. Stern 2004). The form of narrative surely influences not only the structure of the memory, but also what is remembered. Memory therefore is in effect constructed not only in the moment of remembering, but also in the telling of the memory. So memory can be seen as part of the present and the past, as well as shaped by expectations for the future.[13] Memories can also be embodied – both in the individual body, which experienced pain, and in the body politic (Green 1999; D. M. Nelson 1999; Scarry 1985; Zur 1998). Understanding Mayan women's remembered stories therefore entailed studying the political moment in the particular interview situation, as well as in the larger context of peace negotiations after about thirty years of armed violence in Guatemala.

Given the above discussion, it would have been impossible for me to be able to understand the subjectivity of the person I was talking to as she lived her experiences. I was privy only to the interpretations, the meaning-giving narratives, of these experiences and feelings that

[11] Cf. Arias 2001; Clifford 1986; Gluck and Patai 1991; as well as Derrida 1981; Foucault 1980; Hall and duGay 1996.

[12] Literature on narratives (e.g. Whitebrook 2001), resistance literature, and testimonial literature (e.g. Arias 2001; Gugelberger 1996) address the political and historically specific moment of telling as integral to both the story being told and the construction of the identity of narrator/narrated.

[13] For further discussions on the memory see Bruner 1990; D. Stern 2004; for the politics of memory, Edkins 2004; Passerini 1992; and for identity and memory in narrative, Disch 2003; Whitebrook 2001.

she shared with me: in Jacoby's words, her "self-presentation" (Jacoby, this volume). The prevalence of this "discursive filter" may explain my initial frustration at somehow not *getting at* the narrators' sense of (in)security, and instead hearing experience informed by "political rhetoric." However, upon further reflection I understood experience to be always mediated through discourse; a narrative recalling a memory is the closest one can come to being privy to another's experience. A memory may not be "reality," but it can be considered a verisimilitude (Bruner 1990; D. Stern 2004).

However, a focus on the discursive, constructed character of stories, or lives, does not deny that people *really* live, and experience threat and harm, or safety and well-being. We act, experience, and live, but the *meaning* we give to our actions is continually constructed within a web of different discourses. Similarly, we as subjects are continually reconstructed or reinscribed through narrative and representation. The naming of security and insecurity *can be seen as a crucial discursive move in this process*. Importantly, however, a textual treatment of (in)security is not intended to preclude attention to, or to call into question, the very real terror and danger that Mayan women experience; instead, it is intended as a means by which to claim those experiences as also valid subjects for IR.

Co-authorship

Not only are there many "subjects" in the texts of life histories, but there are also many co-authors of this text (Gluck and Patai 1991; Behar 1993; Clifford and Marcus 1986). I cannot just assume that I was a passive, objective recipient of Mayan women's stories (cf. Cohn and Jacoby, this volume). Nor can I assume that the story the narrator told is the same story that I heard, the same story that she would have told in another situation to another person, or that the main character in the story is the same subject as the person with whom I conversed. Moreover, who I am and how I acted surely played an integral role in the construction of her narrative, and of the subject positions (Mayan women) produced in the narrative (cf. Jacoby, this volume). What they included and excluded, as well as the structure of the narrative, was decided (in part) by *who* they thought I was, what they wanted *me* to know, what they wanted me to tell *other people*, and who these other people are, as well as what they *did not* want me to know (Behar 1993; D. M. Nelson 1999; Ochberg 1992). Additionally, security concerns, personal trust, and political aims were all significant factors in the construction of their stories. As I provided each of the narrators with the opportunity to censor their texts, they explicitly reflected over how they wanted to represent their stories.[14]

A statement made by one of the narrators provides rich insight into the dynamics of co-construction of a text. When I expressed my concern that many people might not want to talk with me about their personal experiences, given who I am and what I may represent to them, as well as the need for safety precautions and for considering the needs of their organizations, she replied, "Maria, they are not going to tell you anything they do not want you to know, so do not worry." Hence, unlike the objective form of evidence that is demanded by conventional IR, the narratives that made up the base of my study were both relational and co-authored.

Method: conducting discourse analysis

Creating a text

In preparing for the fieldwork, I conducted research on the popular movement in general and the women's and Mayan movement in particular, during several initial trips to Guatemala. With this knowledge, I was then able to select key organizations which represented the immediate positions and interests of the Mayan women acting politically in the Guatemala civil society (excluding party politics) in Guatemala City.

The common denominator in all of the interviews was that the narrators explicitly identified themselves, and acted politically as, "Mayan women." I attempted to include members of the most widely known and influential organizations on the national scene. These organizations were not comprehensively representative of all the interests of Mayan women, or even politically active Mayan women. Faced with what Ackerly and True call a "deliberative moment" (this volume), I chose to focus on those organizations that represented the main interests articulated in the "official" discourse of the Mayan popular movement. People who worked within the popular movement *explicitly* related their struggles in some way to the ramifications of the violence of the civil war, thus indicating that they would also address some of the issues "traditionally" considered by security studies in IR (thereby also enabling a comparison and challenge to conventional wisdom.) This choice was clearly problematic, as it involved inevitable exclusions; nonetheless,

---

[14] One narrator even asked me not to cite or refer to her text after she had read its transcription, out of fear of the repercussions for herself and her family.

because my study does not pretend to be representative, I hope that making visible the choices I made and why mitigates its limitations.

All of the persons I interviewed were leaders. Each of the organizations had a base of some sort, even if the extent of the base varied greatly. Initially I had planned to interview two women from each organization: one from the base and one leader but, after becoming more acquainted with the context, I realized that the differences between the two were enormous. My language limitations (most rural indigenous speak their local languages) made communication difficult. The women from the base were also much less explicitly politicized than those women in leadership positions, who were in a more fruitful position to represent the most prevalent discourses of the Mayan women working in the Mayan popular movement. Furthermore, the research process itself (see below) demanded that those participants whom I interviewed twice could read the transcription of the first interview. Rarely could women from the base of the organizations read and write down their comments or corrections. This provided yet another limitation on the selection process, and certainly bears mentioning, given my discussions on the silent voices unable to "speak security."[15]

As this study was not intended to be representative of the organizations' work, my focus was on the narratives of the people whom I interviewed, not on the organization itself. Of course, because I contacted them through their capacity as leaders in an organization, and made it clear that I was interested in their struggles as Mayan women, much of their personal testimony was informed by their political involvement and their relationship to their organization, as well as circumscribed by my question. The collusion of political rhetoric with personal experiences became the subject matter of the narratives and the "material" upon which my work rested.

The first interview

Once I had established contact, I met with the participants to explain to them in more detail what my project was about and what the interview process would involve. I gave each participant a brief written (in Spanish) project description and explanation of the research process. I then explained orally in more depth, also attempting to communicate

---

[15] I also talked with women from the "base" of the organizations, who greatly helped me to understand better the situations from which the leaders came and the context of their daily work.

who I was, where I came from, and what I was planning to do with the interviews.[16] I addressed any questions, doubts, or fears, assuring the narrators that they would have the right of complete veto over their words.

I began each interview by asking the participant to tell me about her experiences and struggles as a Mayan woman. Usually a brief restating of the goal was enough encouragement to get the interview started. Sometimes I made introductory requests such as "Please tell me anything you can to let me get to know you a bit." In most cases, the participant steered the narrative herself; my interjections (I tried to make as few as possible) were often requests for clarification. In some cases, however, I asked further questions, trying to open space for a more in-depth explanation. Sometimes, I introduced new topics based on insights gained from other interviews.

The first interview lasted between one to three hours. After the interview, I wrote down my reflections and noted the interview setting and context. I then had the tape(s) transcribed by a trustworthy person, whose work I checked by comparing the recorded words with the transcription. I gave a copy of the document to the participant. I then worked with the document in order to arrive at an appropriate strategy for the second phase of the interview process.

Because my intention was to gain a better understanding of the multiplicity of Mayan women's insecurity, I decided to address the different insecurities they evoked in relation to the different spheres and moments that structured their narratives. *I therefore read the narrative in terms of its main organizing spatio-temporal contexts*, such as the home and family, the Mayan community, the ladino society, their organizations, the political economy, and the Guatemalan nation-state. I also noted the different power relations (mechanisms of inclusion and exclusion) which were articulated in the narratives (e.g. racism, nationalism, classism, sexism) in the different contexts, as well as how they seemed to interrelate. My intention was to lay the groundwork for comprehending how the narrators articulated (in)security in relation to different contexts, as well as in relation to different relations of power.

I also read the narratives in terms of their nodule points (Doty 1996), identifying organizing oppositional relations that I found in the

---

[16] This is extremely important in a context where trust was difficult to earn and psychological warfare promoted a culture of fear, where people were afraid to confide in most others. There have also been incidents when information "collected" by anthropologists and other researchers was then used to discredit or persecute the informants.

narratives, such as education–ignorance, sickness–health, childhood–adulthood. I made note of the themes that I considered in need of elaboration or explanation.

The second interview

After explaining my intentions for the second interview,[17] I asked the narrator if the contexts I identified were accurate or if others were more or equally important. We read the document together and I raised questions. I often asked the narrators to evaluate an interpretation of mine, to elaborate, or to talk about a particular theme that may not have arisen. Frequently, I asked her to tell me a little more about the contexts in her text, namely things that harmed or hurt her and things that made her feel good or gave her a sense of well-being.[18] Sometimes, I asked specific questions around these contexts, such as "Can you tell me a little more about what life was like inside your family?"

Finally, I asked her how she felt on reading the testimony, and how the things she talked about had influenced who she was at the time of the interview as well as her struggles. I concluded by asking if there was anything she would like to add and about restrictions on use of the document, the change of name and of places, and so on, and what she thought of the research process. The narrators received a copy of the transcribed second interview when possible. Thereafter I treated the text as if it were any other citable document. I did not consult the contributors in my citing (or translation) of their words.

Ethics: doing research in a post-colonial context

Can I suppose that my very intention of conducting feminist research immunizes me from exploiting my research subjects? Does doing research in a marginalized site give my research "authenticity" or authority at their expense? Many "post-colonial" scholars address central questions about power in their writings about colonialism and its implications for the construction of both the West and "the rest."[19] In particular, feminist post-colonial scholars have aided in bringing to the

---

[17] I conducted second interviews with only half of the participants, for a variety of reasons ranging from the limitations of logistics to the narrator's level of literacy.

[18] These questions were guided by my "working modality" of security, which I discuss below.

[19] There is a large and nuanced discussion within post-colonial studies which addresses issues relating to the "imperialist/colonizing gaze and the politics of 'Writing Back'" (e.g. Bhabha 1994; Chow 1993; Min-ha 1989; Mudimbé 1988; 1994; Said 1993; 1994; Spivak 1988).

theoretical fore relations of power imbued in the representations of "Third World women" and the exoticised, native, Other in western/ northern discourses, even supposedly emancipatory ones (e.g. many feminisms).[20] Often even well-meaning representations of the "South" repeat the power relations of colonialism through different, "modern," yet insidious modes of violence and exploitation. Many attempts to "give voice" to the oppressed of the world thus represent the South as mere (inferior) reflections of the North and turn it into not much more than another self-reflective, narcissistic look in the mirror.[21]

In research geared towards "giving voice" to marginalized groups or even exploring marginalized discourses, the benefits of providing a space for people who are not able to "speak for themselves" has often been mistaken for paying sufficient attention to power differences.[22] In the edited volume *Women's Words* (Gluck and Pattai 1991), the authors raise crucial questions around whether ethical research is possible at all when northern academics research "Third World women," questioning who gets to do research on whom, and critically discussing the implications of the very existence of privilege that allows the research to be undertaken. Yet perhaps, in paying attention to power relations, we (researchers) overestimate our power. The people with whom we converse also wield power over *what, whether,* and *how* they choose to narrate. They are not only victims, but also agents in the forming of their own subjectivity (Olsen and Shopes, in Gluck and Pattai 1991).

During the process of conducting my research, these ethical considerations have informed both my methodology and my methods. For example, I shared the transcribed texts of the interviews with the narrators, and honored their requests for editorial changes and restrictions of usage or dissemination. I have thus tried to respect their authority over their words. However, I have not consulted them over the use of certain quotations cited from their already authorized text. Nor will I restrict the dissemination of my work. This is inherently problematic and attests to the congenital exploitation of this type of research. Attention to these problematics – although uncomfortable and unsatisfactory in terms of

---

[20] For further discussion see D'Costa, this volume. See also Chow 1993; Marchand and Parpart 1995; Min-ha 1989; Mohanty et al. 1991; Parker et al. 1992.

[21] The fields of anthropology and ethnography have been particularly aware of many of the politics of the development of their "disciplines" and the discourses that define them. For example, Clifford challenges us to take power seriously, not just in the process of interpreting, writing about, and disseminating others' words, but also in the relations that authorize certain people to research and write about others (Clifford and Marcus 1986: 13).

[22] For a critique of this, see Spivak 1988.

the difficulty of resolving them – is nevertheless crucial, I believe, to any responsible scholarship, feminist or otherwise.

Analyzing marginal security narratives: rethinking IR

Mayan women's narratives as security discourses?

What *was* the text that I (co)created? In what sense could I conceive of the life histories of eighteen Mayan women as security discourses valid for IR scholarship?

The narrators told me stories of the development of their political consciousness, how they made sense of their past, and how they had come to be who they were at the time of the interview.[23] Learning from Hall, Butler, and others working on the notion of subjectivity as created within discourse, one can read the narrators' texts as reproductions of discourses through which the subject position, "Mayan woman," was created (Hall and duGay 1996: 11). In part, these accounts reflected how this subject position was "hailed into place" ("interpellated") by dominant discourses (such as those at work in the triple oppression they struggled to resist) (Hall and duGay 1996: 11). Nonetheless, Mayan women's narratives were not only reactions to, or subversions of, the relations of power enacted by dominant discourses. They also reflected the narrators' individual attempts to invest in the subject position, "Mayan women," to imbue this political identity with new meaning and agency.[24] The narratives that were inscribed in the interview process were therefore sites of "performance" *as well as* of negotiation and resistance (Butler 1990; 1993). In my analysis of their texts, I focused on the ways (in)security was invoked in the production of the subject position, "Mayan woman."

Problems of definition: identifying "(in)security" in the texts?

How to determine when the narratives were relevant in terms of security, especially since the narrators did not talk about security *per se*, except in a very narrow sense, proved problematic. I was wary of employing a fixed

---

[23] The narratives consist of about forty to sixty pages of text. The interviews were conducted in Spanish; I bear full responsibility for all translations from Spanish to English.

[24] "The notion that an effective suturing of the subject to a subject-position requires, not only that the subject is 'hailed,' but that the subject invests in the position, means that suturing has to be thought of as an articulation, rather than a one-sided process, and that in turn places identification, if not identities, firmly on the theoretical agenda" (Hall, in Hall and duGay 1996: 6).

or essentialized definition of (in)security and of thereby inhibiting other understandings to emerge from the texts.[25] I addressed this dilemma by relying on an open-ended definition of security for the purposes of my analysis, but by resisting the tendency to reify either identities or insecurities. When looking at other security discourses (i.e. the dominant and alternative ones in IR), one can discern that insecurity has to do with danger, threat, harm, and the peril involved with change and openness. The security of someone or something refers to its safety and its well-being as well as to its limitation, its stability in order to assure its safety. I accepted this broad definition of security as a working modality, because these were also organizing terms or principles in the Mayan women's text.[26]

By adopting this modality of security, I did not intend to create a new and improved model or definition that could be used universally. I rejected the supposition that the referent objects, the sources, and the specific content of (in)security exist outside of specific discourses. For instance, many of the narrators talked of discrimination in the different contexts of their lives. I read their identification of discrimination as also a naming of threats and of danger or harm – as a source of insecurity. I thus depended upon the "security modality" loosely defined above, with which to identify discourses of danger. For example, one narrator, Onelia, explained how different systems of discrimination converged to create different "enemies" and a generalized climate of what I read as (in)security that had reproduced itself since colonialism:

The people began to work in the plantations . . . In our history it is said that the woman was considered to be less. She is paid less than the man, although the work is the same . . . So in this sense, women began to suffer discrimination . . . The woman works from the morning until the night without gaining a cent . . . This was cultivated in the minds of people until [our] own *compañeros*, [our] own Mayan man began to see his *compañera* in the same way as the Spanish does, so *machismo* began to be created. [We] continue suffering from *machismo*. The Mayan woman does not only suffer discrimination from the owners of the plantations, from exploitation, from the Army . . . She also suffers from her husband . . . Already as children, girls are seen as less than boys.

As evidenced in this example, one must understand the particular context of sexism, racism, classicism, and violent nationalism that

---

[25] The texts have gone through several translations: from spoken to written language; from Spanish to English, etc. Given my own language limitations, I could not rely solely on my assessment of the precision of language as the exacting tools of a "speech act."

[26] This broad working definition arises out of reflection inspired by numerous texts on the concept of security, e.g. Buzan 1991; Booth 1998; Johansen 1982; Krause and Williams 1997; Lipschutz 1995; Stephenson 1988; Terriff et al. 1999.

inform Onelia's words in order to grasp how she might view her security needs. (Indeed, her notions of threat criss-cross the dividing lines of IR-appropriate areas of inquiry, such as security and IPE.) I have therefore defined (in)security in the broadest terms and left the assignment of referent objects, agents, recipients, and so on to be determined by the texts, to be formed within Mayan women's discourse.[27]

Reading and analyzing the texts

When reading the narratives in preparation for writing, I organized them in terms of the common spatio-temporal contexts noted above. Explorations of (in)security within these contexts later became the distinct chapters in my book (M. Stern 2005). The nodule points I identified served as organizing themes throughout these chapters. Specifically, I focused on the following general questions in each context:

1. In what ways are definitions of (in)security tied to identities in the text? Who or what connotes safety or danger, and who or what needs safeguarding? How are the self and other relations articulated, and difference addressed?
2. How and where do the narrators name and locate their (in)security? How do processes of interpellation and articulation of their identities converge with the naming of (in)security (through discourses of danger and safety)?

To exemplify how I analyzed the texts, I will return to Andrea's citation at the beginning of this chapter and show how I analyzed her (and others') narratives around some themes raised in the context of ladino–Mayan relations (excerpted from M. Stern 2005).

The narrators explained that the culture lay buried somehow in the soul or roots of the Mayan *pueblo*, and, through rediscovering and revaluing their identity, the Mayans would revive their ancient and majestic culture. Culture became essential, tangible, yet still out of reach; it lay in waiting. In this sense, the culture remained a *thing* of the past that could be repossessed. The clarity with which the narrators connected themselves to a certain past also distinguished Mayans from ladinos. A clear distinction between Us and Them resonated with the

---

[27] In reading the narratives in the above manner, I adopt the position of deciding when and where in the text the textualized subjects experience "(in)security" – of giving meaning to their words. Throughout the research process I remained aware of these problems and have striven to be open to whether or not my working definition resonates with what I read in their texts.

locating of threat and danger: "*We* have been hurt by *Them* for 500 years" (Andrea). The nature of the threat had remained essentially the same, as had the struggle.

As was shown in Andrea's citation, a recounting of their histories provided the narrators with a discursive strategy to resist and subvert the harmful stereotypes which inscribed their subjugated positions *vis-à-vis* the ladino world. They placed the themes of discrimination and marginalization into the context of the struggle of their *pueblo*, in myths of 500 years of suffering and resistance. They thus made sense of their own personal struggles and joined their sufferings with those of their ancestors. For instance, Andrea talked about her process of politicization as a turning point, a gaining of "clarity," and a connecting of her experiences to those of the collective. Andrea described in detail the injustices against Mayan women, as well as the reasons why Mayan women should be revindicated, drawing upon the history of the Mayan *pueblo*. She reinterpreted her experiences and placed them in the context of Mayan women throughout history, as ever sacrificing and resisting. In so doing, she also defined who she was in relation to those who threatened her at the time of the interview, such as the military, the state, and men, as well as her enemies of the past, the Spanish (who were discursively interchanged with their descendants, the ladinos). Andrea thus established her political identity, placed it in the context of her past and fixed it as a timeless given, thereby creating a stable base for resistance that rested upon the heritage of over 500 years. A "we" of the past was created, and it resurfaced in the present.

Nonetheless, the narrators' need to maintain cohesion in the face of external threat led to circumscribing the identity categories upon which claims for change were being made. Security and safety involved cautiously defining and limiting who they were, as well as carefully weaving a direct lifeline to a certain and linear history to which they belonged. The narratives reinforced the belief that the safety of political identity required a stable subject that could be identified throughout history, the present, and even the future. If so, then the stability of this subject demanded specific safeguarding. Andrea also claimed at another point in her text, for example, that Mayan women must reclaim the identity of the past (M. Stern 2005). Hence, rescuing the culture entailed ensuring the meaning of identity and culture, as well as the borders that determine it from the Other. Mayan women played a particular role in such archeology and "excavation" of identity demarcation. Resistance, for them, meant preservation, revindication, reproduction, and reconstruction.

Implications for IR

In revisiting my original aim, I find myself resisting the question "What has my research on Mayan women's (in)security narratives brought to the study of IR?" This question seems to concede that focusing on Mayan women's (in)security must be somehow justified as a valid subject for research relevant to understanding security and global politics (see Zalewski, this volume). However, as Zalewski implies, resisting the move to justify or legitimate the boundaries of the discipline need not entail refusing to engage with it at all; instead, it may mean both disturbing and destabilizing its dominant stories. One way of doing this is by taking seriously Mayan women's narratives as valid texts on security – texts which transform the knowledge of the discipline, and reveal its scaffolding as constructions that need not take the form they do. My research does this in at least four ways.

First, it is clear that the Mayan women I interviewed are indeed valid political subjects whose (in)security is not located outside of global politics. Those processes traditionally considered relevant to security studies also constitute their lives and struggles, thereby revealing how global politics are already gendered and, in many instances, include subaltern women by their very exclusion and silencing (cf. Pin-Fat and Stern 2005).

Secondly, reading Mayan women's narratives also exposes the limitations of the accepted understandings and practices of security; their (in)securities cannot be reduced to a location, level, or category ultimately determined by the logic of state sovereignty. For instance, their narratives disrupt the familiar relationships between domestic and foreign, inside and outside, Us and Them, protector and protected, citizen and enemy, that provide many of the building blocks for our understandings and practice of politics, political community, identification, and conceptions of (in)security. Indeed, the very attempt to reduce their (in)security to the familiar category of, for example, "individual in state" can be read as complicit in the violence that has so greatly punctuated their lives.

Thirdly, and perhaps most significantly, the intricate and inseparable relationship between (in)security and identity explored in post-structural security studies is cast in a different light when one pays attention to marginalized security discourses. The identities articulated in Mayan women's security narratives – as well as the (in)securities that were co-constructed along with these identity positions – were multiple and complementary; they informed each other, and at times even implied contradictions. Mayan women's (in)security narratives underscore the complexity, hybridity, and contingency of security (as an ontological condition of identity) and draws attention to the often violent conflict and marginalization that occur at the intersection of identities and in attempts at securing identity positions.

Fourthly, discourses of danger and the mechanisms of inclusion and exclusion that foster violence in conflicts over national securities and identities also resound in security discourses in marginalized sites (such as was expressed in the need for cohesion in the Mayan *pueblo* in the face of its enemies). Exploring how these potentially violent mechanisms work in these sites also discloses openings for possible resistance, such as the way certain narrators resisted the pinning down and circumscribing of who they were and for what they struggle. For example, when speaking of her identity, one narrator, Manuela, said: "How are we going to construct something on the basis of exclusions and auto-exclusions, if on one side you exclude, and on the other you try to homogenize? It's a big contradiction . . . My work implies a permanent revision, a permanent study of myself and what I am doing." These lessons are relevant not only for marginalized subjects of security, but also for how to conceive of security and its concomitant subject positions more generally – even in terms of the traditional subject of the state.

In sum, my intention has been to challenge the limitations of political imaginaries that exclude from IR the articulations of insecurity of the Mayan women I interviewed because they represent impossible political subjects in their capacities to write IR-valid (in)security discourses. I hope to have brought to the fore some subjects of security that do not comfortably reside in the homes of IR. Although their "subjugated" knowledges may not provide better or more objective solutions to critical questions of politics, they might be able to help those working in these fields to begin reformulating their imaginaries, and to be open to the possibilities of conceiving of (in)security differently.

Concluding comments

I have attempted to make visible *how* I conducted my research of Mayan women's (in)security so that my study can be useful for other scholars attempting to address "feminist" questions in the field of IR, or any other field of study whose theoretical assumptions and methodological tools appear awkward and counterproductive in addressing research questions informed by feminist theorizing.

I would like to conclude by raising the question "Why is my method feminist?" My answer is simple: it is not necessarily feminist. However, the research question I asked (what does security mean for marginalized women?) came into being because of a frustration with theories about global politics that are based on a view of the world and the relevant actors in it that excludes women and the feminine from the picture (yet implicitly locates them in veiled sites that legitimate their absence). As I noted in the introduction to this chapter, experiences of (in)security like those articulated by Mayan women do not make up the body of empirical "data" upon which security is theorized and policy is formulated. Feminist theorizing around processes of identity formation which takes into account not only the workings of particular discourses but, importantly, a collusion of distinct relations of power (such as sexism, racism, classism) led me to look for articulations of (in)security in (for IR) unlikely and often silenced sites. These sites (such as the ones where Mayan women dwell and struggle for both agency and security) occupy the realm of the feminine in the gendered codings of the dominant readings of both IR and the praxis of global politics.

My research question, then – informed by feminist theories' attention to the workings of gender discourses – implied that the methodology of security studies in IR could not adequately serve to address the question I set out to explore. The ontology underpinning the assumptions in how security is conceived reflected a notion of politics that necessarily ignores attention to gender and to the multiple violence implicated in this conception. Therefore, in order to address my question, I began a research process that resulted in the methodology and method outlined above. Hence, although my method may not be specific to feminism, feminism (in all of its unlimited diversity) has provided many of the guideposts for my methodological journey – a journey that, in its own way, challenges the authority of those who purport to know what security means for all peoples in all contexts, without ever asking many of them.

Part 3

Methodologies for feminist International Relations

How can feminist IR scholarship expand its already rich and varied array of methodologies? Taken together, the chapters in Part III invite the reader to appreciate the range of ways that feminists provoke themselves and one another to think beyond the boundaries of the IR discipline. They call for further movement in the development of innovative feminist IR methodologies which can attend to the ever-emerging questions, puzzles, and issues in global politics.

10 Bringing art/museums to feminist International Relations

Christine Sylvester

It is commonplace for theorists, practitioners, and observers of international politics to speak about the art of politics, the art of diplomacy, even the art of war. A terrorist bombing is said to produce "surreal" effects, Surrealism having been a prominent school of visual and literary arts in the interwar years. This or that election is called a "farce," as though referring to a light dramatic work in which highly improbable plot situations, exaggerated characters, and often slapstick elements feature. UN Security Council members "dance" around each other on the issue of war with Iraq. There are "dramas" in the Pacific as asylum seekers are shunted from one would-be haven to another.

Fine-arts references to international relations are meant to be gestural and expressive. They do not signal a formal relationship between visual, literary, and performing arts and such phenomena as terrorism, war, elections, immigration, or politics in general. Yet the throwaway metaphors should tell us that there is art (hidden) within international relations – or at least there is the suspicion that the typical methodologies employed by the field of International Relations (IR) are not creative and imaginative enough to grasp the world it studies. Missing from IR (discouraged, in fact) and present in art is the non-rational realm of bodily sense. We may read an IR piece and think the author shows a "feel" for the topic, that he sees the issues well – but always within the confines of rational analysis, as demonstrated by a clear problem statement, robust evidence, interpretive consistency, and logical argumentation.[1] By contrast, art historian James Elkins (2004: x) alludes to a

A happy thanks to colleagues who have helped me to think through these issues: Brigitte Holzner, Henriette Riegler, and the editors of this volume.
[1] Louiza Odysseos (2001) finds IR unable to incorporate the comedic in its epistemological toolbox. Costas Constantinou (2001) finds it woefully lacking in a sense of the mythic. Vivienne Jabri (2003) looks to playwright Harold Pinter for an enactment of politics lacking in IR. Erin Manning (2003) dances the tango as a way of getting at neglected touch and other sensory deprivations of IR. The missing tools of the field are too numerous to elaborate here.

methodology one slips into when viewing paintings, a methodology that relocates the mind as it "slides in and out of awareness, that seems to work upward toward the head from somewhere down below: a way that changes the temperature of your thinking instead of altering what you say . . . [and] can tunnel into your thoughts and bring tears to your eyes." And more than tears to the eyes; the type of response Elkins notes is hardly the enemy of clear thinking, as his book on *Painting and Tears* amply demonstrates.

IR has not achieved a level of methodological comfort with the feel, sight, and sense of art-based investigations of international relations, even though it does have some "sense" literacy. Thanks to the third discipline-defining "debate," some branches of IR have developed skills to hear the voices of the subaltern, the subjugated, the oppressed, and the marginalized in international relations. Postmodernism in all forms has many of us reading texts more carefully now, taking into account absences as well as the material presented. Other creative ways of seeing, however, remain under-utilized or ignored as IR methodologies. Social science guardhouses face away from the "irrational" senses, convinced that these are unreliable knowledge sources. But then IR is forced into the adjectival admission that an attack was surreal, the election was a farce, and many aspects of politics seem more artful than rational.

There is subterranean art in feminist IR too, and again it is usually not named as such. Cynthia Enloe (1989) made sense of Carmen Miranda's colorful, fruit-laden hat in the international political economy of bananas by emphasizing the gender politics of the hat rather than its art politics. Jean Elshtain (1987) filled out gendered war narratives in history partly through reference to films rather than through film analysis *per se*. Feminists working in the postmodern tradition today probe much further into the art-and-IR gap by regarding elements of popular culture as international politics (e.g. Molloy 1997; Weber 2001). They regard those arts more to the point than the fine arts, largely because popular arts are of and for "the people" relative to arts once geared to the same elite audiences that ran states. Any rush to one side of the art picture, however, risks overlooking power angles of international relations that lodge in portraits, still lifes, abstractions, and global museum coalitions. Those who do look into issues of fine art, gender, and international relations (e.g., Brocklehurst 1999; Sylvester 2002; 2001) find that doing so opens doors for better viewing of the state, international actors, and "the people." It also provides a set of acuities that work hand in glove with postmodern efforts to reveal multiple sites of meaning, authority, and political process within international relations.

The concern in this chapter is to elaborate two ways of employing the fine arts to advance feminist international relations. One is "the gaze," recuperated from a bad reputation in art history to help feminists learn something about international relations from looking at artworks. Art gazing promotes a form of seeing and feeling that relies on spending time with art as a research-relevant experience. The second way entails adding an overlooked institution of international relations to our data-collecting sites: the art museum. Museums can be rich with insights into the power dynamics of historical international relations, contemporary development issues, and hidden coalitions that are forging power relations in the post-Cold War era. The art gaze and the art site are best probed by illustrating their applications to IR rather than by defining them in the usual style of social science.

Gazing

Red Square, USSR, turns into a red square painted on a small canvas (Kasimir Malevich). Cold War America pictures its masculinity in Abstract Expressionist art (Sylvester 1996). Social metamorphoses of war turn up in Salvador Dali's paintings – some brimming with fruit and some leaning on "crutches." Louise Bourgeois's caged installations of double cones and blue water ruminate on women confined to repetitive jobs that keep global waters running (Sylvester 2001). It does not matter what the artwork is, which century it comes from, or whether it presents naturalistic or abstract images – or sights and sounds, perhaps. The point is to engage the work and engage our responses to it as professionals in the field of IR. The feminist gaze is one way of doing so.

A viewer confronts a work of art and lingers over it, absorbing the lines, the scene (if there is one), the colors, the ambiance of the piece. She might feel an impulse to order her thoughts about the work or figure it out or force it into a relevant learning mode for international relations. Patience in looking enables the viewer to loose herself from the sense that an artwork comprises "data" that she must array, interpret, and know correctly in order to apply it to IR. Elkins's (2004: 7–8, 17) experience in the Rothko chapel in Houston provides important clues to gazing:

I kept walking from one painting to the next, playing at seeing rainclouds or afterimages. I spent an hour making a little sketch map of all the pictures, noting their quirks and half-hidden forms so I could remember them. I had in mind to master the chapel by getting to know each painting, so I could say I had really seen it. It seemed like a good idea – like reporters, historians are trained to take notes – but I began to feel unsure of what I was doing. It dawned on me that I was trying too hard, being too systematic . . . something clever, perhaps, but also something misguided . . . The visitors' books attest that the really hard part about looking at Rothko is just looking: looking, and resisting, as long as possible, the temptation to say what is missing.

The "experience of looking, can be, should be, hard to manage," says Elkins (2004: 54), and there is nothing formulaic in it. With reference to international relations, gazing is about the experience of seeing how an artwork "works," and interacting with it using several dimensions of ourselves, beyond the dimensions we usually bring to IR. That type of looking enables shifts and slides into positions I have described elsewhere as world-traveling, where we enter a situation or knowledge that differs from our usual context for thinking about international relations, and, instead of refusing its relevance to that area, engage with its difference (Sylvester 2002). In this case, we face art and gaze with feminist IR eyes.

There is nothing necessarily neutral about the gaze. It certainly has a wicked reputation in feminist art histories and analyses of visual culture (e.g., Broude and Garrard 1992; Mulvey 1989; Kleinfelder 1993; Pollock 1992). There "the gaze" refers to the longstanding art practice of transferring masculine outlooks, interests, and social privileges to painting and sculpture. The most evident case is the female nude. The human figure is one of the most enduring forms and subjects of western painting and sculpture, but there are clear differences between female and male figures portrayed in artworks. Men often have active roles: they battle, they execute each other, they work in fields, they paint in their ateliers, they eat and drink, they tend horses, they shoot little arrows at pretty girls. Commonly, the men wear clothes for these activities, although not always. Women just as often appear inactive or in socially secluded poses without clothes. We see adult women sleeping or bathing naked, as insouciantly as children, and, of course, the artist does not let them alone. His ingénues are often about to be disturbed, menaced by men who mean them no good. Old men spy rapaciously on young women at bath. Sabines rape women. Satyrs surprise them. The male gazers have grabby eyes.

It is also a common modernist trope to show a naked reclining woman confronting the art viewer with a seductive look. She is the menacer of sorts, the one before whom a heterosexual male stands titillated, as though she were giving herself to him or could be taken by him. Henri Matisse's odalisques – women reclining languidly in tropical settings, their arms thrown above their heads, nothing apparently to occupy them except posing seductively – stand as one case in point. Men can be painted in seductive poses for the enjoyment of other men, too – Caravaggio's "Young Bacchus" springs to mind; but they are less the norm across art eras. The serious art aficionado – and certainly the "real" art historian, whom Elkins (2003) accuses of eliminating "feel" from a field's repertoire of analytic tools – has traditionally trained in ways that overlook salacious female (and male) nudity. The art's the thing, after all. But over-looking legitimizes the male gaze and robs "her" of the fuller autobiography that paintings by men of other men often celebrate. And, of course, "she" has not been taken seriously historically as an artist herself.

In recent years, a preoccupation with male gaze has diminished in feminist art history, neutralized to some degree by male artists who either refuse older traditions of masculinity or actually mock them in their work. The British team of the Chapman Brothers exemplifies the trend. In many of their pieces, "men" appear more as brutal butchers or goofy characters than as privileged beings. A series of dioramas recently exhibited at the Saatchi Gallery in London depicts scene after scene of war battles enacted by scores of tiny plastic toy soldiers. These "men" drip blood as they disembowel, decapitate, or impale one another in the vulgar ways that war permits. The Chapmans also take a series of original Goya etchings and systematically replace the heads of mostly male figures with cartoon heads. That dethroning of masculinity is stunningly direct. Bill Viola, by considerable contrast, depicts the strongest human emotions of fear, joy, mourning, and despair in ultra-slow motion video works. He is after believable portrayals of compassion that show "the strong empathetic connection we have to other human beings" (Viola, in Belting and Viola 2003: 201); thus Viola's men often cry. Both sets of artists implicate the viewer in the emotions and actions of their work, but neither does so in ways that covertly or overtly celebrate masculinity.

In a Viola work called "Catherine," the artist strives to depict "the sense of privacy and inner strength in the image of a woman alone in a room" (Belting and Viola: 211); a great many of his works feature women who in no way could be called either inactive or sexualized for viewers. His men sob in profound sorrow or silently bellow their pain and despair in excruciating detail. In the face of this artistic gaze, it would sound old-fashioned to bear down now as hard as feminist art historian Carol Duncan (1990: 207) could in 1990, when she accused her field of not taking gender seriously. She said then that efforts were under way to redeem the art-historical "greats" "by fitting them out with new, androgynous psyches or secret female identities or by applying to their work new, postmodern 'readings.' " A scant decade later some fine-arts works (increasingly a difficult category to delineate) feel unself-consciously feminist. They "work" as feminist pieces whether that is the intent of their creators or not. The gaze has equalized.

There is another fascinating aspect of the male gaze. The audience for art galleries and museums these days may be ill equipped to get "it." The intended audience has changed entirely. Steve Garlick (2004) finds a consistent pattern over the past forty years of women predominating over men as museum visitors. From that basis, he argues that engaging with works of art is an activity that western men just do not do any longer. He attributes the flight of men from art to "the popular notion that the experience of art is an *emotional* and *passive* one (thus representing a moment of *weakness*), [which] effectively locates the notion of art on the side of the feminine" (2004: 121, emphasis original). Quite an irony: we tend to think of art geniuses as men, yet men now look away and women are looking with democratized eyes. That does not mean that women will suddenly stop gazing with male-aware eyes at women in art, in films, and on the street (Mulvey 1989). Rather, a change in the museum audience for art counters the older supposition that the male viewer and male gaze compose defining features of much art production and reception.

Audience is terribly important, as Garlick (2004: 123, emphasis original) tells us. Art

requires not merely a creator but also an audience who will receive the work, and who will thereby allow it *to work*. The work of art is an inherently social happening. Hence, it is not sufficient merely to concentrate on who is producing it, or on what is "in" it. Instead, we must consider whether the work of art can still be received today, and to ask questions concerning those who are at present unable to allow art to work . . . pre-eminently, *men*. It follows that in contemporary Western societies, insofar as they are dominated by implicitly masculine ways of thinking and being, and insofar as men are constituted in part by notions of masculinity, there will be little space for the work of art to take place.

If art no longer works in the social ways once assumed or intended, we must ask how art does work today for its contemporary audience of women. We are in the museum looking at the art and looking at ourselves and at other women looking. We are where the gazing men are supposed to be but where we are instead, as is often the case in other locations of international relations (Sylvester 2004). Because we are in the museum, and because some art there "works" differently today from how it might once have worked – and us with it – the challenge is to graft the insight of a differing acuity to what we see and feel. Such constitutes a feminist eye graft. As long as we know that "the relation between what we see and what we know is never settled," as John Berger (1972: 7) told us decades ago, we can begin to gaze with *our* eyes.

Clues from portraiture

Consider two paintings from the National Gallery of London's exhibition, "Encounters: New Art from Old" (2000).

One is a portrait of Jacques Marquet, Baron de Montbreton de Norvins, painted by Jean-Auguste-Dominique Ingres in 1811 and reworked by him after 1814. Marquet is an international bureaucrat of his time – Chief of Police for the Roman States conquered by Napoleon. Determined to celebrate himself and the empire he is installed to safeguard at its margins, he commissions a well-known French artist to do him up in grand portraiture. There he sits; he is shifty-eyed and insecure and has a faint sneer on an unaristocratic face. His neck tucks into a fluffy white shirt collar, his torso into well-tailored clothes. Rich red satin drapes behind him suggest royalty and opulence, and, like the master who will serve for only a short time longer, his left hand rests inside his jacket.

The second painting is by David Hockney. Titled "Twelve Portraits after Ingres in a Uniform Style" (1999–2000), it is meant to interpret the portrait of Marquet through contemporary eyes, awareness, and painterly skills. Knowing Hockney's popish portrayals of Los Angeles life, we might imagine him giving us a police chief diving into a cool blue swimming pool in some tropical British colony. Instead, he offers us a series of ordinary National Gallery of London security guards – women and men – sitting on their ordinary chairs in the drab, mock police uniforms we associate with "security." The two portraits link around the location in international relations of their sitters: at the edges of empires. Marquet is on the margins of the erstwhile Napoleonic empire – and he is about to fall. The security guards sit at the edges of a flourishing, ongoing international art empire. In both places, the task masters work to keep the goods or people in and the barbarians out. At both margins, it is likely that supremos install and then forget their security agents, unless a transgression occurs – a painting is stolen on their watch or a rebellion breaks out in the provinces. There is power at those out-of-the-way margins, though, and it is the type of power that governs, restricts, and orders the lives and viewing possibilities of people who are not themselves necessarily making the world of imperial power. There is also weakness at the margins. Events can occur in the centres over which one has no control at the margins. Marquet is in-secured against his will.

The art guards stifle yawns – securing the empire is dull work – or hand back our coats and bags with shy smiles when we recognize "the woman in the painting." Marquet, who very much wanted to be a celebrity of his time, just sneers at us. His position in art is secured but he himself is a historically marginal man. We know that he wanted the bust of Napoleon's son, the so-called King of Rome, painted out of the portrait in 1814. It used to be behind him to the left and now hides in the folds of those red satin curtains. If we look closely we can actually see that bust showing through, haunting Marquet's history. Nothing else in the portrait changes in the fall. Marquet wants us to see that he has no intention of going down gracefully. Yet what we see is that imperial power relies less on flashy and transient forms of security than on the steady, unglamorous, and reliable securers. These are the ones who should be in the picture of international security.

Feminists and postmodernists have often said that the angles we usually take on international relations provide only partial views into complex phenomena. Suppose we make the two "encounter" paintings into one picture, by putting a transparency of the National Gallery guards over the Marquet portrait. Would this technique enlarge the view and enable variegations of security to show that usually get lost in IR's parsimony? No and yes. Placing Marquet's portrait over that of the gallery security guards yields a collage of sorts. A collage harbors different assumptions about materials, time, space, and composition than does a portrait. It puts incongruous elements together in ways that are foreign to each but evocative of what could be (unexpectedly) similar about them or about us gazing at them. If there is a storyline to the collage, "it" is one we must provide for it. Juxtaposed art security guards of 2000 and a provincial imperial dignitary of 1814 summon multiple narrative angles and questions. What memories of Napoleonic Empire are being secured by the guards at the National Gallery of London? Is Marquet similarly securing the empire they guard today by securing the security guards? What is the political economy of this collaged security picture? How are the fruits of empire distributed between different types of guards and securing missions?

These are questions of history, society, economics, and relations international. Alexander Wendt's *Social Theory of International Politics* (1999) promised pathways into neglected social aspects of international relations, but ended up with a too-narrow range of international actors and agency and an oddly unjuxtapositional constructivism. We are thrown back on to materials, peoples, histories, and narratives that still need gluing on to IR, and IR on to them. Those are the collages yet to be made.

Clues from still lifes

There is another way to illustrate the points about margins and centers and the rewriting required when they are combined. In 1633 Francisco de Zurbaran painted "Still Life with Basket of Oranges." Conventional art history considers the still life a minor or marginal form of artistic expression. Still life draws our attention not to heroic events and people, as could portraiture of the time, but to the inanimate wares and trivial objects used and consumed by wealthy members of society. The artist composes a scene carefully, giving the appearance of a reality one just happens upon. The composition classically induces desire for what we see – those oranges and lemons, that teacup with a flower on the saucer. Think of sumptuous shellfish, toppled wine goblets, and sparkling grapes in a Dutch still life of the Golden Age. The still life is the good life.

Art historian Margit Rowell (1997: 16) talks about still lifes as cultural signifiers full of strategic symbols about "the priorities and desires of a given society at a given time." In Zurbaran's time, the still life reflected desire for the pleasures of food and flowers, and for the implied after-maths of a good time at table. Those who prepared the food and set the tables – the women, children, servants – were never pictured. Indeed, all bodies are absent from still lifes, except, of course, for the body mark of the painter man, who leaves his signature at the corner of the work.[2] Along with the missing bodies are colonial sagas that rendered the production of luxury foodstuffs available in Europe. All of this is strategically missing in a classic still life of desire; but a feminist gaze can restore them and lead us to interesting research questions about the life and times of gender in a certain era of international relations.

If we show a woman's hands placing the teacup on the table and the flower on the saucer of the Zurbaran painting, what happens? Again, a collage effect juxtaposes unexpected elements, thereby changing the priorities in the painting and their signification. The painting can no longer be a still life, nor does it become a portrait or domestic landscape as conventionally understood. It might come closest to a Surrealist painting of a dream, where an odd object enters from beyond the frame and throws off the narrative, thereby jolting the eye and the order of thought. From an imagined set of amendments to any still life, a round

---

[2] It would be inaccurate to argue that all women still-life artists were invisible in the genre. One who was especially esteemed and made wealthy by her floral paintings was Rachel Ruysch (1664–1750).

of stories springs to mind beyond the pristine one an artist leaves for us. We realize the sacrifices in meaning that accompany our efforts to cut out excess and strive for the parsimonious, made-to-look-uncluttered painterly processes. We can thereby characterize the invisibles, whether these are missing handmaids (Sylvester 1998) or elements of colonial production.

Change the time, region, and point of entrée to still life, gender, and international relations. A chapter of an IR textbook, *Global Politics in a Changing World: A Reader*, edited by Richard Mansbach and Edward Rhodes, has a chapter entitled "Failed States." It reads, in part:

> A potent combination of ethnic hatred manipulated by unscrupulous leaders, intense poverty, population growth, and environmental catastrophe has made a number of African states virtually ungovernable and unable to satisfy even their citizens' most fundamental needs for security and survival. Indeed, during the 1980s and 1990s, many African states actually suffered a decline in living standards as measured by per capita gross national product, in some cases to below pre-independence levels. Those countries whose institutions of statehood have melted away and whose inhabitants depend on outsiders for the essentials of survival are *failed* states.
>
> (Mansbach and Rhodes 2000: 93, emphasis original)

There is a still life for you: still and failed! The litany of development catastrophes and intense horrors leads to a stultified outcome. While not denying troubles across Africa, not least in the country of longstanding interest to me, Zimbabwe, I cannot help but notice that signs of failure are not usually painted into contemporary Zimbabwean arts. From the continent globalization forgot (N. Smith 1997), I see Crispen Matekenya's wooden sculptures of animated people at table and of baboons waiting, tails in the air. No stillness there. Sue McCormick presents a more still "Vase with Swit," except that the swit, a slash down one side of it, keeps moving our eye about. Berry Bickle shows cryptic writing pounded on to and running off sheets of scavenged aluminium, as if there were no end to the words and the aluminium. A defiant Zimbabwean art carries on in a "failed state" of international relations; meanwhile, Mansbach and Rhodes lament "an odd disconnect between many international relations textbooks and the reality of what was happening 'out there'" (1997: xi).

Learning to see from painted and written still lifes has to do with locating excesses that a certain visualization, characterization, or measurement tries to control or keep out. It is not a matter of peeling away layers of lemon skin hermeneutically, to get a deeper and truer pip. It is about deeply looking at the lemons we see, and their surrounds, and asking the clichéd question: "What's missing from this picture?" From that methodologically inductive spot our research task is to recognize and theorize how the colors, lines, compositions, and implied narratives would have to change – do change – with various additions to the painting. Colors and conditions of hands, different sizes of them attached to various bodies and locales and storylines – the fictions multiply, pry apart the frames, and open up the phenomenon under investigation for new insights.

Clues from abstractions

I have pondered the relevance of art abstractions to the study of international relations, focusing lately on correspondences between modern scientific abstractions, abstractions of the modern art world, and the stilted and limited abstract designs of IR (Sylvester 2001). Abstract works come without inbuilt narratives. One must gaze and feel, intuit and decipher, go forwards and backwards around the painting and make our own sense of it.

Jackson Pollock's *Blue Poles* contains an emotional and factual history of the US Cold War effort to project a hunky, masculine image abroad, all sweep and danger swirling around power poles. Australia purchases the painting and makes it the signature piece in the international collection of the Australian National Gallery. One narrative would have it that to own a Pollock, or other example of the New York School of Abstract Expressionism, is to display good taste and good bipolar politics. Yet, as happens at such moments of triumph, other storylines etch the painting – an Australian line and a gender line. The Australian line goes like this. Australia paid an unusually high price for *Blue Poles*, and, when questioned on this, the then Prime Minister, Gough Whitlam, guffawed that the purchase was a form of overseas aid to the United States. America was "facing defeat in its war in Vietnam, beset by inflation, and under pressure from the rival economies of Japan and West Germany, which it had previously done so much to rebuild. That was the great irony of 'Blue Poles' in Australia" (Barrett 2001: 3). Another art joke, surely – or is it, in fact, a way into the international relations of the western alliance in the mid-1970s? The gender line shows Pollock's wife, the artist Lee Krasner, retreating from prominence while her husband rises. This was an omnipresent theme of those times in the West. An echelon of US men rose to power and influence during the Cold War, while their wives made the household still lifes that gave the era an early image of domesticity and plenty. A feminist eye grafted on to *Blue Poles* sees the power and the dangers of that particular time as gendered international relations.

Change the abstraction. Multiple storylines encircle sculptures of vaguely Asian looking men with cheerful eyes and animated mien. Engaged in what can look like sparkling conversations, these men are set around museums in groups devised by the late Spanish sculptor, Juan Muñoz. The figures are abstractions. They contain some recognizable human elements, but are smaller than most humans, and have footless legs that disappear into the floor. All the heads are shaved and all the figures have identical faces and clothing, down to the same oversized grey coats that hide elements of the body. Still, we can see them as some version of us. A vast number of these *Conversation Pieces* greeted the (mostly women?) visitors to the Chicago Art Institute in September 2002. Bent toward us as we entered, they smiled and smiled. We smiled back at them . . . and then felt peculiar. Were they the art or were we the art? It was momentarily difficult to say, because those who gaze at others can also be gazed upon. The confusion over who was looking at whom was the power the figures communicated at the cusp of naturalism and abstraction (see Benezra 2001: 42).

We have seen that power before, less felicitously, in the elongated, indented steel figures of Alberto Giacometti, striding solitarily, repetitively, toward some destiny etched tragically into their abstract faces. Muñoz's "men" stand still and have the gaze of jocular sociality. But, like Narcissus made multiple, the "men" do not actually connect smiles or see into one another's – or our – eyes. They seem to be attentive only because of the placement of their bodies. Polite sociality is merely mimed. Conversation eludes. No one sees anyone else. So is it with us, too? The cross-cultural encounters seem to work, but not quite? Think of international diplomacy, where talking is ubiquitous but nothing is really being said. Can we see ourselves seeing and talking to others in such unconnected ways? Or, consider this gender gem: my male companion regards Muñoz's "men" at the museum entrance, and others set about with round bottoms anchoring them to the floor, and whispers, "They're trapped in their masculinity." That's one alternative narrative. Imagine the others as this art works on us.

Welcome to the museum

Behold the art museum in a postmodern moment of international relations. Ostensibly an institution that houses collections of various fine-art pieces, increasingly it is something far in excess of that. It is a site of powerful but invisible international relations that encompass transnational pilgrimages of people and pieces to ever more difficult locations. Think of the new art cathedrals that thrust unexpected places and politics into prominence. The mammoth Tate Modern in London and the newly designed MOMA in New York are where they are supposed to be, in art capitals of the world, with historical and contemporary tales of international relations to tell. But very local spaces, such as provincial cities, villages, and even hotels, can have international art ambitions. International coalitions are also forming around private, public, and philanthropic art actors. These are dynamics that IR, and feminists within it, neglect to see as the sites and data sources of international relations.

The Guggenheim phenomenon

Look at the Bilbao Guggenheim and the two new Guggenheims in Las Vegas. One museum is in a European city scarred by intractable separatist conflict – a city of bombs, sirens, and considerable post-industrial decay. The other two sit in separate, purpose-built additions to the Venetian Hotel and Resort, home of thousands of jingling gambling machines in Sin City USA. Each is a come-hither kind of building designed by the coolest of international contemporary architects using the latest materials and design techniques. In the case of Bilbao, California-based architect Frank Gehry conceives a shimmering centerpiece of titanium and limestone for a regional redevelopment effort. The museum's unusual angles owe something to the CATIA computer programme developed by the Dassault aerospace firm to create Mirage fighter planes; that programme digitally translates and rearranges design elements to create structural options. In Las Vegas, the winning architect is Dutch – Rem Koolhaas – and his designs feature rusted Korten steel for the Guggenheim Hermitage space, and glass, steel, and concrete woven around a lime green staircase for the larger Guggenheim Las Vegas museum. Inside the rusted one are paintings from the famed Hermitage in St. Petersburg, a partner with Guggenheim in the venture. Inside the glass space, since closed, was a soaring exhibition on "The Art of the Motorcycle"; like someone at the margins of another place and time, Marlon Brando sneered gigantically at us from one wall.[3]

It is almost too much to see: in tinny Las Vegas, the Russian Hermitage, desperately short of cash in the post-Cold War era, shares the till with a New York-based art giant that is also a bit short on cash these days. A sister Guggenheim brings motorcycles to "the people" (beckoning men to the museum?) as a form of art. Meanwhile, the

---

[3] The Guggenheim Las Vegas claimed to be "temporarily" closing in January 2003, while it sought a backer for its next show. The downturn in the US economy has taken its toll on the Guggenheim's global ambitions.

Guggenheim Bilbao attracts people from all over, and in the process single-handedly changes the image and the economics of a troubled city. To take the long view, buildings designed by celebrity architects, financed largely by a private hotel or by a local government-to-international coalition, connect to the global Guggenheim empire in ways that help redevelop the Hermitage in Russia and the Basque region, while keeping the international art empire pumped up. There is a world of under-researched international relations in the Guggenheim spectacles, a world we might call the art of the global museum. Have we catalogued all this for IR?

A gender world is also there. From soaring architectures to the lowly motorcycle, from Mirage to titanium to rusted steel, the images show muscular ambition. Yet look closer. The Bilbao Guggenheim would not exist but for the vision of a Basque Administration redirecting regional identity from guns and bombs to culture, the soft side of political economy. The museum wears extravagant and gently curving attire. It dominates central Bilbao and yet gives the appearance of always having been prettily there. One analyst thinks "the curvilinear shapes of the 'flower,' Gehry's interpretation of the traditional museum dome, evoke the flora of the lush Basque countryside" (Newhouse 1998: 245). And then, of course, there is Jeff Koons's gigantic flower puppy greeting visitors at the entrance. Lest it all be too tender, for the opening in 1997, Jennie Holzer's abstract LED word artistry ran wild up folded contours of the sculpture gallery.

Switch to Las Vegas. Known for showy women, gambling, and graft, the city is now associated as well with the gentleness of impressionist and post-impressionist works in the Guggenheim Hermitage space. The 130 motorcycles once parked around the corner in the second Guggenheim presented a roaring "American guy" image that was juxtapositioned hilariously with the pinks and blues of Monet, the evening desert sunshine on the surrounding mountains, and the gaudy neon and painted ladies of the Strip. Viva collage! One can get drawn into the details of this international relations of culture, complete with its Van Goghs, fake resort canals, and soaring buildings that refuse the modernist box. The point, however, is that if IR has been slow to come to the museum for viewing lessons from the art it shows, it has been even slower to recognize the art museum as a prime location and exemplar of globalization and its relations of development.[4] Along with employing art as a

---

[4] In 2001, the Bilbao Guggenheim earned $147 million for the city of Bilbao, despite the downturn in global tourism following September 11 (*Art Newspaper*, 2002).

methodological tool for seeing some things we have not seen quite before, the locations and institutions where art is exhibited now need to enter IR.

Power marbles

On December 8, 2002, an NGO that nearly no one in IR will have heard of issued a statement of some international import. The International Group of Organisers of Large-scale Exhibitions (also known as the Bizot Group), a powerful forum of the forty leading museum directors in the world, declared that "museums serve not just the citizens of one nation but the people of every nation" (*Art Newspaper* 2003a: 1). The immediate impetus for declaring universal museums valuable came from international relations. The British Museum was under considerable pressure to repatriate the Parthenon sculptures, which it has held since 1816, in time for the 2004 Greek Olympics.

Most art restitution claims result from the colonial or war practices of international relations. Napoleon seized Dutch national collections as war booty. Numerous paintings were stolen from Jewish owners during the Nazi sweep through Europe. In the case of the Dutch art losses, the Director of the Rijksmuseum argues that, rather than seeking restitution, "we see this as history and are not going to claim them back from the Louvre" (*Art Newspaper* 2003a: 6). The Greeks, and many of their sympathizers worldwide, have not seen things that way. They have insisted on their rights to the marble works against British Museum claims that the sculptures would not exist today had they not been "saved" from vandalism and environmental degradation, and despite the argument that Greece *per se* did not exist at the time the sculptures were made. Classicist Mary Beard (2004) tells us that over a 200-year period, the international relations of the Parthenon removals and display in London have attracted as much attention, if not more, than the sculptures themselves. Meanwhile, IR – feminist or otherwise – looks at other things, not at international museum pieces or their international politics.

The caretaking universalism of the Bizot Group strikes a colonial note, and a rather naïve one at that; clearly, the museums have not been taking on board feminist postmodernist and postcolonial messages about difference. Once again, however, the art of international relations is not straightforward in its messages. In late 2000, the former South African president, Nelson Mandela, spoke at the British Museum. His message stood outside a text that is often critical of large western museums for becoming the vestibules for stolen art worldwide. He said: "This great museum may have begun as the beneficiary of British imperial power, but it has become a truly international institution supported by global donors and attracting scholars and tourists from across the world to its unique collection of artistic treasures in which every continent is represented" (*Art Newspaper* 2003b: 2). One may accept Mandela's angle or not. The point is that the culture of fine arts lends itself to myriad power/knowledge/viewing combinations. It therefore enables us to resist, as some post-colonial scholars (e.g., Chakrabarty 2000) ask us to, any too-easy equation of the West with an unreconstituted, self-centered stealth that overwhelms all interpenetrations of power and knowledge.

Gender questions are not as visibly interwoven with the Parthenon–Bizot debates, but they are there to be seen. The Bizot Group argues that universal, encyclopedic museums engage in an ongoing process of developing international culture rather than exhibiting static pasts. But feminists would ask a series of questions about the claims of these "universal" museums. Which and whose historical cultures are on show? Who determines culture and "its" standard-bearers versus its castaways? Importantly, who owns whose cultural artifacts, and who resists that ownership? Olu Oguibe (1994: 51) makes the point that there is no "clear and shared understanding of what we mean by internationalism," which suggests that the international culture declared by large, established museums is both museum-serving and partial. Those of us wedged into pockets of development studies know these issues well and also know that they beg for responses that are not too simple in their statements of imperialist oppression or too forgiving of it. This is an area where visual acuity of the type nurtured by feminist art analytics provides a useful entry point for examining the "saved" art of international relations and the international politics of art-saving museums.

Twin towers of international relations

The World Trade Center (WTC) did not start out as a museum, so ostensibly its towers fall outside this discussion. Nonetheless, in their absence from September 11, 2001, on, the twin towers have been memorialized as the negative imprint on lower Manhattan's skyline. "It" – the buildings, their occupants, and the land they occupied – has been museumified as "an" artifact now lost but resistant to being forgotten. This new, multifaceted phenomenon links the international relations of "terrorism" and "fundamentalist" backlashes to the "soft" and power-marbly political economy of the West.

One angle in is through a notion of the twin towers' architectures as power-monumentalizing structures in and of themselves and, simultaneously, as frames supporting daily international relations. Among many things that can be said about the WTC is that it stood as a Cold War power monument or architecture of persuasive American power, to expand a term coined in Robert Venturi et al., *Learning from Las Vegas* (1972). Although its towers were dedicated in 1973 and not completed until 1978, their idea originated in the 1940s and then took off during John F. Kennedy's time, when the USA became serious about projecting wealth, confidence, and ambition overseas through monumental Abstract Expressionist art, monumental land-based intercontinental ballistic missiles, and monumental capitalist statuary. The Rockefeller family was in on all this from its beginnings, just as it was a persuasive force in promoting American modern art abroad (Sylvester 1996a). In 1958, David Rockefeller anticipated an increase in postwar transatlantic trade and commissioned an architectural firm to plan an international business center in lower Manhattan. At the time, US international trade accounted for less than 3.8 per cent of Gross National Product, with 80 per cent of that handled by multinational corporations having no interest in a world trade center.

Is there gender here? Yes, and in odd places. The New York/New Jersey Port Authority had domain over the land in the proposed area of the center and it had muscle as a US agency. Angus Gillespie, author of a biography of the World Trade Center, describes the agency in a way now familiar to students of feminist IR:

> [The Port Authority] unabashedly took a masculine outlook on the world . . . Its bridges and tunnels were all business . . . It favored male recruits with backgrounds in engineering or law. Though it was never made explicit, a tour of duty in the military – especially the US Navy – helped to place a newcomer on the fast track to promotion. Engineers especially found the Port Authority to be a place that was a manly environment rewarding the brave and the courageous . . . who could turn in not only engineering successes but financial successes as well . . . Pride ultimately fueled the ambition to build the world's tallest building.
>
> (Gillespie 1999: 20)

At the completion of that virile pride, the double icon of power started a tour of duty that was awe-inspiring. Yet, like the Vietnam War that had just ended, like the Abstract Expressionist art of the Cold War, the twin towers were scorned at home. Chilly, with their closely packed steel beams lacking ornamentation, they received no architectural awards. The sense that the buildings were big and dead only deepened after the 1993 bombing, when many high-end firms moved out. The architect was also a relatively unknown and uncelebrated Japanese American – Minoru Yamasaki – operating in a world of WASP architectural practice. And then Malaysia beat the tall towers in height before the American ones could be completed. Nevertheless, this support structure for a colossal international political economy affixed itself to the land, unloved at home and certainly unloved by super-toughs who made the towers Humpty Dumpty one September morning. And then how we loved those towers.

Ostensibly they are gone. But viewers sketch towers into the New York landscape when gazing at Manhattan from the Whitestone Bridge or flying over the city. Those architectures were not art when they were "alive." Now they are a museum of the mind, full of treasures and tragedies. And more than that. The competition to rebuild on the ruins of the WTC gave us Daniel Libeskind's designs for a cluster of buildings combining business and leisure with commemorative areas dedicated to the old towers and the humans lost within them. Quickly and abruptly the politics of New York and its landlords modified Libeskind's plans and, in effect, internationalized the architect pool of talent for the site. There is considerable commotion at Ground Zero these days; however, it cannot overshadow the international relations of the WTC.

A new landscape will emerge in Lower Manhattan and become like so many other altered cityscapes in all ways except one. The new WTC area will compose a picture of the fear, the fragility, the can-do spirit, the colossus, the charm and the installations of violence that make up this moment of international relations. At a complicated nexus point, the feminist gaze couples well with museum awareness. We know to ask how the memories and artifacts will work. Will the genius of violent men travel with or against the genius of survivors, many of whom are women and children thrust unexpectedly and painfully into the hard core of international relations? What of the many looking on, the ones who gaze from a distance, the ones who visit the "museum"? The audience for art matters. The institutions matter. The gazes matter. Which angles of international relations will be in the shadows and which ones on display in this new museum of international relations?

Filling in the sketches

From art and its museums I have learned to see things I had not seen in more than twenty years of professional observations of international relations. The method of feminist gazing – seemingly simple and yet so hard to train the eye to do (it is often said that average visitors to an art museum spend less than thirty seconds looking at any one piece of art) – helps identify the vanities, fictions, and power potentials lying just inside and outside what we usually see. We learn juxtapositions and collage techniques that visually open up unexpected sights of analysis. We visit the Bilbao Guggenheim and get a lesson on regional development that involves a different set of donors, transnational tourists, and NGOs from those one typically comes across in the development studies wing of IR. We enter art museums and enter the world, which makes that institution a good place around which to debate international culture, gender, ethics, security, and memorialization in a globalized era of international relations.

All this jigsaws on to patches of international politics that we feel as much as we see. Can we do feminist theorizing from those senses? Theory-building has not been one of feminist IR's strong suits relative to its talents in critique, discovery, and description. Here, though, art methodologies dovetail well with the empathetic cooperative and world-traveling theoretical positions we have established (Sylvester 1994; 2002). The methodology-to-theory link is this: the gaze features some of our professional registers flowing around an artwork and returning altered by the "feel" (the "temperature") of the experience as much as by the work of seeing something there. Slippage occurs when we go between the Marquet portrait and Hockney's new art from old, a bit of travel that stretches us and the canvases on which IR traditionally painted its Marquets of international relations. Once an artwork begins to work through our travel to it and its travels to us, those who do the artwork of international relations become part of what IR should study. A visit to the art museum as field research site thereby joins up with art encounters of the gaze. We find there, as Hockney so cleverly helped us to see, that the art of international relations is more than some ghostly point at which rationalistic methodologies fail and we fill the holes with little phrases on the art of politics. Art can offer, in fact, a way into the ellipses of IR.

Art methodologies are not for everyone and they are not necessarily easy to use, even for the "women" who have long been assigned the realm of the "decorative" and are now assigned "museum visitation." Many will not be moved by fine arts at all, and those of us who are might not feel anything while gazing at certain artworks. Equally, we may abhor crowded, commercialized, and trendy museums and seek to flee them for the hard terrain of old international relations. We must also bear in mind that art is not the only route to improved feminist theorizing. It offers inductive research tools and substantive areas of research, but we must be careful: feelings can mislead, sight can deceive, and truth comes in multiples. Nonetheless, art helps IR to realize that there are many ways into a puzzle. Some gazers will learn by crying in front of Viola's weeping "portraits," the way many cried looking at the lost World

Trade Center. Some will flinch at the Chapmans' war dioramas *and* carry away with them a theory-relevant sense of international relations as the realm of violent claustrophobia.

Apropos of any such senseful thought, I close with a resonant museum moment. It is not a moment directly taken from my own experience, nor is it even a feminist citational moment *per se*, at least judged by the predominant genders gazing and being gazed at. And, as a final blow, it is not even "about" international relations, is it? It is an indicative feminist art moment, though, that puts art, the art viewer, and the methodologist into a larger picture, evoking a relevant sense:

Vincent Van Gogh's Irises called – crowd pleaser, postcard surface belying the pain of intense vision within. I stood with the crowd, all shapes and sizes, in several languages, spanning most of the 20th century. I almost lost it again – I can't go into the museum anymore to come face to face with all this innocence – raw beings, especially the older ones. A man gave the camera to his wife to take a picture of him standing next to Vincent's Irises. There he was – white jacket unzipped over his cotton plaid shirt, khaki trousers, an uncertain, panicked look spreading across his face as he realized that once he turned his back to the painting, the people were all looking at him and Vincent both, side by side, one on one.   (Viola 2003: 207–208)

11 Methods of feminist normative theory: a political ethic of care for International Relations

Fiona Robinson

> All forms of feminist theorizing are normative, in the sense that they help us to question certain meanings and interpretations in IR theory, because many are concerned, says Jane Flax (1987: 62) with "gender relations . . . how we think or do not think . . . about them" (or avoid thinking about gender).
>
> (Sylvester 2002: 248)

Introduction

Feminist approaches have always occupied a marginal position within International Relations; this is also the case within feminist ethics and normative theorizing in the discipline. It could be argued, of course, that feminist scholarly activity – driven as it must undeniably be by the goals of bringing to the fore marginalized feminine and feminist perspectives, and of reducing asymmetries in power between men and women – is always, at least implicitly, normative. Indeed, it is often the case that feminists working within IPE or security studies are, implicitly, relying on many of the same, ethical, methodological and epistemological claims that have been explicitly articulated within feminist ethics. Thus, we could say that the opening quotation by Christine Sylvester is both illuminating and confounding. It is illuminating because it clearly reminds us that "the normative" – questions and issues of value, including ethical questions – must be seen as intrinsic to the feminist enterprise more generally. The quotation is also somewhat confounding, however; if all forms of feminist theorizing are normative, what, then, is feminist normative theory? Indeed, can there be such a thing – a distinct form of feminist theorizing that, in some way, specifically and directly addresses normative issues? If so, *how* would one undertake such theory? In particular, what kind of methods would one use to address ethical questions from a distinctly feminist perspective? In addition, one might ask whether the study of ethics in IR should entail only theoretical inquiry.

What might it mean to study ethics, in the "practice" of IR, and how might one go about it?

In this chapter, I argue that methods of feminist normative theorizing in IR differ substantively from those of non-feminist normative IR. Methodology in most normative IR is drawn from canonical "western" ethics, which focuses exclusively on "pure moral reflection," abstracted from time, place, and context. Feminist normative analysis, by contrast, bears a far greater "descriptive and empirical burden," in pursing details of actual moral arrangements (Sylvester 2002: 13). Thus, feminists interested in the ethical dimensions of international relations must be prepared first to undertake careful ethnographic, sociological, or economic research, which may involve detailed case studies of, for example, the distribution of paid and unpaid labor within a household, or the changing nature of women's employment as a result of the globalization of production. From here, however, feminist normative analysis must reflect critically on the consequences of such arrangements, using a particularly feminist moral framework, such as a feminist political ethic of care. A framework of care starts from the position that the giving and receiving of care is a vital part of all human lives, and that it must therefore be a normative guide in the creation of decent societies. Such a framework may then be used as a basis for discursive analysis – of policy documents, for example – as well as a critical tool for the philosophical critique of actual human social arrangements, and, ultimately, the creation of transformative policy.

In making this argument, I will suggest that feminist normative theory is characterized by a commitment to what I call "relationality." Relationality in feminist ethics is manifest in at least two ways: first, in the relational ontology which understands human existence in the context of social and personal relations, and the related view that morality is grounded in those relations; and secondly, in the idea that ethics is not above or distinct from politics or social life in general, but rather intrinsically related to and indeed embedded in asymmetrical power relations. Here, then, is a view of ethics which is fundamentally different from what Margaret Urban Walker has called the "theoretical-juridical" model of ethics; this model prevailed as the template for "serious" or "important" moral theorizing in ethics in the twentieth century, as well as, I would argue, most normative theory in International Relations (M. U. Walker 1998: 7). The theoretical-juridical model prescribes the representation of morality as a compact set of "law-like propositions that 'explain' the moral behavior of a well-formed moral agent." Walker contrasts this with her "expressive-collaborative model," which sees morality as "culturally-situated and socially sustained practices of responsibility that are taught and defended as 'how to live'" (1998: 7, 201). Her model is representative of feminist ethics more generally, which is culturally and socially situated, practical, and interpersonal. It relies on moral concepts such as responsibility and care, attentiveness, responsiveness, trust, and patience – concepts which make sense only in the context of the interconnected lives of mutually dependent, real people.

This chapter is divided into three sections. In the first, I examine the nature of feminist ethical thinking in the context of international relations. This section explores the notion of "relationality" in the context of ontology, and in the relationship between ethics, politics, and power. In the second section, I address the implications of this view of ethics for questions of method and methodology. Here, I rely on the work of Margaret Urban Walker. Specifically, I borrow, and seek to flesh out, two of her conceptions of *how* to study morality: first, *critical moral ethnography*, and second, *geographies of responsibility* (M. U. Walker 1998: 211, 99). Finally, in the third section, I briefly describe two examples of these methods in the context of social policy, citizenship, and, more broadly, global political economy. These examples are taken from the work of Selma Sevenhuijsen, whose research stands apart from other "care" theorists in its commitment to understanding care as both a concrete activity and a moral orientation – as a set of values that can guide human agency in a variety of social and political fields (Sevenhuijsen 2000: 6).

Relationality in feminist ethics and International Relations

Ontology: personal and social relations

While the field of "feminist ethics" by no means constitutes a singular, unified body of theory or set of principles, it is possible to isolate some broadly shared characteristics. One of the most important premises of feminist ethics is that, like much gender analysis in general, its analytical starting point is relational; more specifically, feminist ethics begins from a relational ontology, regarding individuals as existing in, and morality as arising out of, personal and social relations. Genealogies of feminist ethics usually begin with the object relations theory of Nancy Chodorow, whose influential work *The Reproduction of Mothering* argued that male children need to differentiate themselves from their mothers and create a separate, oppositional entity. This early childhood psychology was said to account for the fact that the basic feminine sense of self is one of relatedness or connection to the world, while the basic masculine sense of self denies relation, or is "separate" (Chodorow 1978: 169). It was this book which was to have the greatest influence on the work of Carol Gilligan, whose 1982 book *In a Different Voice* is now regularly cited as *the* pivotal work in the development of one prominent branch of feminist ethics now widely known as the "ethics of care." Gilligan's empirical investigations of women's responses to a series of moral dilemmas led her to argue that women define themselves "in a context of human relationship" and judge themselves according to their ability to care (Gilligan 1982: 8).

Feminists working in ethics, political theory, and legal theory have taken these initial ideas on ethics and psychology and have sought to apply them to the social and political realms. In particular, they have emphasized the importance of relationships, thus rejecting the more orthodox view in these fields that objects are isolated and individuals are separate. For example, Martha Minow (1990: 194) has argued that many feminists find relational insights crucial to any effort to recover women's experiences. These insights have been used by feminist legal theorists, including Minow, in order to rethink "rights" as a legal, political, and moral concept. Minow and Mary Lyndon Shanley, for example, advocate a renewed conception of "relational rights,"which draw attention to the claims that arise out of relationships of human interdependence. On this view, rights comprise not only individual freedoms, but also "rights to enter into and sustain intimate associations consistent with the responsibilities those associations entail, underscoring connection between families and intimates and the larger community" (Minow and Shanley 1997: 102–103).

Similarly, Jennifer Nedelsky has argued that human beings are *both* essentially individual and essentially social creatures. Liberal theory, she claims, has emphasized only the "individualistic" side, overlooking the ways in which our essential humanity is neither possible nor comprehensible without the network of relationships of which it is a part. It is not, Nedelsky points out, just a matter of the rather banal and obvious observation that people live in groups and have to interact with each other; rather, it involves a recognition that we are "literally constituted by the relationships of which we are a part." Thus, in the context of rights, this translates into the recognition that rights construct relationships – of power, of responsibility, of trust, of obligation. Nedelsky proposes that this reality of relationship in rights becomes the central focus of the concept itself, thus leading rights analysis to focus on the kind of relationships that we actually want to foster and how different concepts and institutions will best contribute to that fostering (Nedelsky 1993).

Focusing on ontology in this way is crucial in that it allows feminists to overcome a number of obstacles that are normally associated with feminist ethics. At first glance, feminist ethics is often regarded, by its critics, as an ethic articulated *by* women, that is relevant only *for* women and *their* lives. Indeed, even feminists worry that feminist ethics is likely to reify and valorize "feminine" values such as passivity and dependence, rather than the qualities associated with rights-based or contractualist ethics such as rationality, autonomy, and independence.

Certainly, this is a legitimate concern that threatens to undermine the validity of feminist ethics. But the focus on ontology by a number of theorists enables these feminists to avoid the epistemological problem of having to advocate and valorize any virtues, "feminine" or otherwise, over any others. Rather, they are simply making a claim about the way the world is, while, at the same time, pointing out that this is a "way" that has been overlooked, or has remained invisible, within most male-centered analysis. As Joan Tronto (1995: 142) neatly puts it, "care may be ubiquitous in human life, but it has remained hidden from the conceptual lenses of social and political thought."

This point is made explicit by Kimberly Hutchings, who seeks to make apparent, not just the general relational or social nature of human existence, but specifically the pervasiveness of care and caring practices which arise out of particular relationships. Moreover, what Hutchings's argument highlights, in spite of its emphasis on the "moral ontology of relations of recognition and responsibility," is that such claims about ontology necessarily lead to claims about epistemology. In particular, Hutchings argues that feminist ethics must avoid any attempt to advocate values associated with the private sphere as in some way "better" than the values of rights or justice. The reason for this is not associated with familiar arguments about stereotyping and essentializing the "feminine"; rather, it is based on an *epistemological* argument – in particular, a desire to avoid the kind of totalizing, prescriptive ethical arguments which feminists were engaged in criticizing. Thus, in terms of feminist ethics, she argues in favor of the more modest claim that the "moral ontology of relations of recognition and responsibility which is identified within the private sphere is the key to understanding 'moral substance' as such." Thus, a feminist approach to ethics is fundamentally about ontology – what exists – and the related claim that this ontology provides both a background and a set of conceptual and analytical tools for making sense of ethics, even in the global context (Hutchings 2000: 122–123). The prescriptions following from this view of feminist ethics will vary depending on context; theorists must, she argues, "take responsibility for articulating the conditions within which any prescriptions made are meaningful and therefore the kind of world they imply. Indeed, there is only one prescription that would be common to the practice of feminist ethics: *always be skeptical of any kind of moral essentialism or claims to ethical necessity*" (Hutchings 2000: 122–123).

Thus, on Hutchings' view, what characterizes feminist ethics primarily is not advocating a particular set of substantive values or virtues associated with care and care-giving; rather, feminist ethics is about taking a particular epistemological stance with respect to "ethics" and "the ethical" which allows one to examine and interrogate the gendered nature of what might be called "moral ontologies." Because these ontologies are themselves varied and dependent upon the cultural dimensions of particular contexts, feminist ethics does not lead to the construction and application of generalizable moral principles. Certainly, part of feminist ethical analysis involves the recognition of the importance and nature of care and caring practices within different social and cultural contexts; it also, importantly, involves recognizing how these practices involve, or give rise to, patterns of inequality or oppression, both within and across gender lines.

Politics: the ethics/power relationship

Traditional approaches to ethics – including analytical philosophy in general, and rights-based and Kantian ethics in particular – have generally regarded morality as distinct from the empirical world, the sphere of politics and power. What has been distinctive about much feminist theorizing, by contrast, is its recognition of the intrinsic and inextricable relationship between ethics and politics/power; this, I would argue, must be a central and defining feature of a feminist approach to normative IR theory.

Feminist moral theorist Margaret Urban Walker describes feminist ethics as pursuing transparency by making visible gendered arrangements which underlie existing moral understandings, and the gendered structures of authority that produce and circulate these understandings (M. U. Walker 1998: 73). Furthermore, she claims that moral inquiry must analyze the discursive spaces that different moral views create, and explore the positions of agency and distributions of responsibility that these views foreground or eclipse. She also insists, however, that we have to look at where moral views are socially sited and what relations of authority and power hold them in place (1998: 75). For Walker, moral philosophy must involve both empirical analysis and description – supplied by documentary, historical, psychological, ethnographic, and sociological researches, and critical reflection/political analysis – testing whether moral understandings are internally coherent, and whether social arrangements are sustained by mutual respect and trust, or by coercive power, duplicity, or manipulation (1998: 11–13). This could involve discursive analysis – of the moral language used in local legal, religious, customary, or policy documents, and the implications of that language for distributions of power and responsibility, and the existence or lack of consensus, participation, and trust of all actors involved.[1] It could also consist of empirical and then critical analysis of, for example, the distribution of work – both paid and unpaid – and the distribution of wealth within households in a particular community.

Walker's naturalized epistemology eschews the use of universal authoritative standards in forming our judgments of how others live. Instead she argues that we can and must use actual human moralities as proper standards of judgment, regardless of how flawed or bad they are. Even the worst social-moral systems, like US slavery or – less explicitly but perhaps, I would add, more insidiously, the gendered global political economy – are made up of human interactions based in trust and responsibility. Walker reminds us that as long as human beings are ongoing participants in a social order, and not simply objects of direct violence and slaughter, *there is a moral order there*. It is precisely the job of moral criticism, then, to examine human social arrangements, to find what Walker calls their "moral floors." Part of this involves seeing how participants are unable to see the perversity of their order, or even what parts of an order have as their purpose or effect that this is not to be seen (1998: 211).

For example, while we may denounce the inequalities of the neo-liberal global political economy, we must recognize that it is not simply a socio-economic order, but also a complex *moral* order which works to uphold and vindicate particular patterns of power. This resonates in Walker's prescriptions for the direction of ethical inquiry:

> We know that powers of several types (coercive, manipulative, and productive) in various linked dimensions (economic, political, social, discursive and cultural) can allow some people to rig both the arrangements and the perceptions of them, and so to obscure what's really happening to whom and why. It is this fund of knowledge that needs to be enlarged and theoretically articulated in general accounts of specific studies of different relative moral positions in differentiated social lives. (M. U. Walker 1998: 219)

Like Walker, Kimberly Hutchings has stressed the extent to which the moral practices recognized by women are not isolated, but situated

---

[1] In an interesting discursive analysis of global financial architecture, Jacqueline Best (2003) argues that the use of universalist moral discourse in proposals for global financial reform ultimately serves to obscure the political consequences of, as well as the possible alternatives to, such reform.

within relations of power. She argues that such relations, especially *gendered* relations of power, are a crucial facet of the reality in which relations and moral practices such as care are embedded. In particular, she claims that "Feminist ethicists find ethical significance in those gendered aspects of international ethical reality which, in being presented as necessary, are either not 'seen' at all or are seen as unquestionable" (Hutchings 2000: 123).

This recognition of the fundamental relationship between ethics and power links feminist approaches to other critical approaches to normative IR theory, including, and perhaps especially, to post-structuralist ethics (see Campbell and Shapiro 1999). When combined with the relational ontology described in the previous section, however, feminist normative approaches to IR theory offer a distinct moral perspective which is gender-focused, but not exclusively "women-centered." For example, feminist ethics focuses on how responsibilities for care and caring work are assigned in various societies, and the ways in which this creates and sustains different patterns of power distribution. As Selma Sevenhuijsen points out,

there is a need to analyse the gendered dynamics of access to and exit from caring arrangements and the corresponding patterns of access and exit in the spheres of paid labour and political decision-making. These patterns should not only be assessed in terms of the rights to be guaranteed by the state, but also in terms of the policies that enable citizens to fulfil their responsibilities in several spheres of life.   (Sevenhuijsen 2000: 24)

In focusing on constructions of gender identity and relations, critical feminist perspectives on IPE have focused, like feminist normative theorists, on relationality, and have built on the still often narrowly materialist analyses of "new" and critical approaches to IPE. Because gender is a relational notion, meanings about gender (which are crucial to our understanding of the structures and processes of the global political economy) are maintained and contested through the practices and struggles of actors engaged in relationships with each other and the institutions in which they are involved. As Sandra Whitworth points out (1994: 121), uncovering the content of these relations of gender would involve looking at the activities of "real, living human beings operating within real historical circumstances." Moreover, feminists have argued that, even in its more sophisticated forms, IPE has been unable to raise analyses of gender because of its exclusive emphasis on questions of production, work, exchange, and distribution. Even critical approaches, Whitworth argues, have paid insufficient attention to the realm of ideas and ideology; for example, while Cox stresses the importance of ideas in his theoretical work, he "falls back to more straightforward class analyses in his empirical work" (Whitworth 1994: 125–126). But this largely materialist analysis cannot be sustained when gender is brought into the picture. Social practices and self-understandings, as well as material inequalities, are central in any account of gender. As Whitworth clearly states, "gender does not exist simply at the material level but at the level of ideas and institutions as well" (1994: 126).

These ideas, I would argue, include ethical ideas. Analysis which is located at the nexus of feminist normative theory and feminist IPE would not recognize the global political economy as a set of "apolitical" forces; rather, it is a set of complex social relations which can be regarded as, to use Walker's terminology, a "social-moral system" which, even in its current form, possesses a "moral floor." This, in turn, demands that the moral bases of the global economy be examined, as well as the recognition that strategies of resistance will not be wholly economic in nature, but will involve a shift in values and moral beliefs. This approach also recognizes the multiple sites and various manifestations of power, thus opening up space for analysis of both material and discursive power, emerging not only from class but also from race and, importantly, gender.

In their 2000 book *Gender and Global Restructuring*, Marianne Marchand and Anne Sisson Runyan make use of the concept of "relational thinking" as a framework for understanding and interpreting global restructuring and social reality more generally. This kind of thinking, they argue, involves a recognition of the relationships between "how we think," "who we are," and the world "out there" as "interacting dimensions of social reality" (Peterson, quoted in Marchand and Sisson Runyan 2000: 9). This view mirrors many of the ideas developed above, especially with respect to analyses of the global political economy. Specifically, Marchand and Runyan are concerned to eschew abstract discussion about processes, structures, markets, and states, advocating, by contrast, the introduction of subjects and subjectivity into the analysis. Moreover, they also argue that relational thinking reveals the gendered power dimensions of global restructuring, forcing us to ask, "How and to what extent is global restructuring embedded in and exacerbating unequal power relations? How are processes of inclusion and exclusion being mediated through gender, race, ethnicity and class?" (Marchand and Sisson Runyan 2000: 9).

Moreover, the focus on the embeddedness of social relations in real contexts is crucial to feminist normative theory. While studies of "cosmopolitan" citizenship and democracy dominate the normative literature in international relations theory, feminist approaches to ethics remind us that people's lives remain heavily embedded in the particular contexts of real places.[2] In spite of, and perhaps also because of, globalization, the struggles that occur at the local level are of great significance for most of the world's peoples.

That said, however, it is crucial that not only do we reflect and act upon our responsibilities to particular others which arise out of our relations with them, but also that we are aware of how social structures and institutions give rise to relations and practices of responsibility which privilege some groups over others and which may make caring difficult or unlikely between members of groups (Jaggar 1995: 196–197). Thus, its goal is not just person-to-person caring, as in some traditional versions of feminist ethics, but also to try to refine understanding, extend consensus, and eliminate conflict within a society. This is obviously made difficult through imperfect understandings, conflicting judgments, and incomprehension; however, these potential roadblocks can also be seen as opportunities to rethink understandings or to search for mediating ideas or reconciling procedures within or between communities. They can, as Walker claims, "disturb the superficiality, complacency, or parochialism of moral views" (M. U. Walker 1998: 64, 71).

Clearly, these feminist approaches to IPE differ significantly from much of the literature in normative IR theory, which rehearses tired debates between cosmopolitans and communitarians over the scope of rights and duties, with very little reference to the actual structures and processes of the global political and economic life. Feminist research on IPE, by contrast, offers a contextualized, if often implicit, understanding of morality, concentrating both on the needs of real people in particular and local situations, and on the way that patterns of responsibility are situated within globally shared social-moral systems.[3] As such, it has much to contribute to research into the normative dimensions of world politics from a feminist perspective.

Methods of feminist moral inquiry

In the sections above, I have set out a feminist approach to ethics in IR which is built around the concept of "relationality"; this notion can be

---

[2] On cosmopolitanism see especially Held 1995; Linklater 1998. For an important feminist argument on the importance of the "concrete" as opposed to the "generalized" other, see Benhabib 1992; 1996.
[3] See Marchand and Sisson Runyan 1994; Bakker 1994; Gabriel and Macdonald 1994; chapters by Anne Sisson Runyan, Gillian Youngs, and Eleanore Kofman in Kofman and Youngs 1996.

seen as integral to its ontology, its epistemology, and the very nature of morality itself. While I have touched on questions of methodology, the questions remain: how, exactly, might one use this understanding of ethics to study its place or role in the context of world politics from a feminist perspective? What actual methods would one use to design and carry out a research project on feminist international ethics? In most non-feminist normative theory in IR, methods have traditionally been those of canonical western moral philosophy – philosophical reflection on moral problems, supported by the work of other moral philosophers. Often, the research questions themselves have been metatheoretical – in other words, they have been questions about the nature of moral theory/ philosophy itself. The aim, then, has been to produce new or better grand moral *theories* – either for their own sake, or for the purpose of applying them to questions or issues in international relations, such as war, intervention, or development (O'Neill 1992; 1994; Beitz 1979; Frost 1996).

The understanding of feminist ethics that I have outlined above, however, rejects these orthodox notions of ethics as "moral theory" in favor of a view of morality as socially situated. Thus, Walker has argued that in order to understand what morality is, we must understand how it is seated and reproduced in actual human societies (M. U. Walker 1998: 211). This involves "insistent, empirically steeped examination" of the arrangements that actually obtain when people interact with each other (1998: 221). To the extent that moral criticism is possible, it must begin with "finding out precisely how relations of trust and responsibility" are created, maintained and, often, manipulated and deformed (1998: 211). Thus, the task of moral inquiry is not the construction of universal, generalizable, and often abstract moral principles; for example, Frankfurt school critical IR theory relies on the universalism of Kant, Marx, and Habermas in an effort to create "cosmopolitan citizens who aspire to make progress together towards the ethical ideal of a universal communication community" (Linklater 1998: 211). By contrast, feminists seek to understand, reflect on, and possibly transform the patterns of moral relations as they exist in a variety of everyday contexts. As Michelle Moody-Adams (1997: 189) argues:

Some of the most important moral inquiry . . . takes place in the difficult contexts of everyday life. Understanding the contexts of moral inquiry – within as well as across cultures, and in familiar as well as unfamiliar contexts of everyday life – requires careful articulation of the attitudes, assumptions and standards of argument at work in those contexts. It requires, that is, a kind of moral ethnography. More precisely, it demands thick descriptions of the contexts in and through which moral intention, expectation, and meaningful action take shape.

Clearly, this is an ambitious task; one could be forgiven for thinking that this approach to moral inquiry sounds unwieldy, amorphous, and virtually impossible. Especially in the context of international relations, how could one possibly uncover and know the details and nature of all social relations – including gender relations – in all social and cultural contexts? Clearly, this *would* be an impossible task; what *is* possible, however, is a commitment to moral inquiry which focuses on, rather than overlooks, the everyday lives, the permanent background, of real, embodied people. While the study of ethics in international relations has tended to focus on "big" or macro events, such as the Gulf War or "9/11," feminist moral inquiry reminds us that, in between and amid these events, moral experience and action are ongoing (see Enloe 1993; 2000).

Critical moral ethnography, then, as a feminist method for ethics in IR, would require a number of different things. First, it would demand an awareness of, and exploration into, the socio-political and cultural context in which moral contestation is taking place. No doubt the word "culture" suggests, to many IR scholars, a kind of anthropological journey into the unfamiliar; while that may, at times, be necessary, it is important to remember that "we" in the North and West also have a culture in which our understandings of morality are deeply immersed. For example, no research on human rights should take place without a thorough examination of the history and political culture which surrounds that concept, including its highly gendered nature (see Robinson 2003: 161–180). "Rights" should not be discussed without asking who is making use of the idea of rights, and for what purpose. Despite their ostensibly "universal" nature, rights are understood differently by the President of the United States, the World Bank official, and the poor Guatemalan woman. This cultural exploration may include a detailed analysis of the history of western political thought in order to understand the historical and philosophical development of rights concepts; it may involve a discursive analysis of the use of the concept of rights and rights language by major international institutions, corporations, and NGOs; finally, it may require fieldwork on the ground – including interviews with women in grassroots organizations – in a country such as Guatemala, to find out precisely how women are using the concept of rights to articulate their needs and claims (see Blacklock and Macdonald 1998). Such cultural awareness is also necessary in examining the practices of care-giving and care-receiving. As Selma Sevenhuijsen points out, needs for care are "subject to shifting cultural standards about how children should be socialized, how food should be treated and consumed, how birth, sickness and death should be dealt with" (Sevenhuijsen 2001: 13).

If moral ethnography is to be critical, however, it requires more than just "looking"; it also requires looking critically, in the hope of moving towards transformation. While feminist moral epistemology eschews the "view from nowhere" view of moral objectivity, it does not relinquish the idea of moral criticism. This is because of the feminist commitment to understanding ethics, not as apolitical or "socially modular," but as immersed in social relations – including differential relations of power. As Walker points out, we know that many different types of powers (coercive, manipulative, and productive) in various linked dimensions (economic, political, social, discursive, and cultural) can allow some people to rig both the social-moral arrangements and the perceptions of them, and so to obscure what is really happening to whom and why. Knowing this compels feminists to go beyond mere moral and cultural relativism, especially when arrangements are rigged to make women among the most vulnerable and oppressed peoples in a society. While it is never the job of moral inquiry, or of the moral philosopher, to compel or even persuade others to adopt one's own moral point of view, it is possible to be "better or worse justified in our own moral beliefs," and to make "justified judgments on others' moral practices and beliefs" (Walker 1998: 208). As Moody-Adams points out, "Moral inquiry is capable of transcending the boundaries of culture and history because the complexity of moral concepts makes possible complex realignments and reinterpretations of the structure of moral experience" (Moody-Adams 1997: 192).

An excellent example of this kind of work in international relations is Kimberly Hutchings's ethical analysis of war and rights from a feminist perspective (Hutchings 2000). In her discussion of female circumcision – a highly contested case in women's human rights – Hutchings stresses the importance of establishing how this practice is "ethically meaningful within the context of a particular form of ethical life." As she puts it:

Since practices such as female circumcision are invariably linked to accounts of ethical necessity, the second step of a feminist ethics would be to demonstrate that this ethical necessity is not simply given but constructed, and is tied up with a highly complex set of cultural, social, political and economic practices and institutions. (Hutchings 2000: 126)

Similarly, in her analysis of rape as a weapon of war, she argues for the importance of analyzing and deconstructing the background values, practices, and institutions which give the actions of the perpetrators meaning. The possibilities for transformation – which is the focus of feminist ethics – depend on "radically changing the patterns of recognition and responsibility which underpin the identification of women as possessions of men or vessels for the propagation of the race" (Hutchings 2000: 129).

In addition to critical moral ethnography, feminist researchers may approach their inquiry into ethics in world politics as an exercise in mapping "geographies of responsibility" – mapping the structure of standing assumptions that guides the distribution of responsibilities – how they are assigned, negotiated, deflected – in particular forms of moral life. As a theoretical methodology, this idea provides us with a way of conceptualizing morality as something that can be illuminated by looking carefully at the nature of responsibilities within particular social-moral communities (M. U. Walker 1998: 99). It is this methodology that highlights the specifically feminist argument about the substance of moral life being made up of care and caring practices among real people existing in personal relationships and a wide range of social relationships.

If we take relations of responsibility to be the very basis or substance of morality, then our research must be guided towards *foregrounding* these relations. Here we are concerned, not just with responsibility for a particular act or decision – such as who or what is responsible for the genocide in Rwanda – but rather with responsibility understood as ongoing practices and actions of responsiveness and care towards particular others. For feminists, the importance of understanding ethics in this way is its "power to foreground, dramatically and satisfyingly to many women, the ways responsibilities are gendered, and the arbitrary or exploitative fit between social contributions and recognition" (M. U. Walker 1998: 77). Thus, when we are reading the "great texts" of moral and political philosophy, or analyzing the discourse of morality in international institutions, or listening to the struggles of poor women in the South, we need to think about who has been assigned, according to dominant or prevalent norms, responsibility for whom and what. While we must certainly look at states and institutions as agents, even moral agents, in such analysis, feminist methods remind us that we cannot simply see these actors as faceless and genderless institutions. Searching for, and foregrounding, patterns and practices of responsibility – including and especially responsibilities for care – rather than the more familiar rights and obligations, will help us to see more clearly the existence and causes of power differentials in international society, and how these can lead to inequality or oppression.

For example, recent research has indicated that where women have been incorporated into globalization's increasing export manufacturing sector, there has been a continuing erosion of their potential and existing social entitlements (Razavi et al. 2004). Failure to address this can be explained in part by the normative frameworks used by states and the institutions of global governance in the measurement of development and the formulation of macroeconomic policy. In particular, the continued division between the "economic" and the "social" introduces what Elson and Çağatay have called a "male breadwinner bias" that links citizens' entitlements to a model of life-long employment not constrained by the reproductive responsibilities of women in terms of childbearing, childrearing, domestic work, and caring for the sick and the elderly (Elson and Çağatay, quoted in Pearson 2004: 606). A feminist political ethic of care does not ignore or eclipse these responsibilities, but foregrounds them as central to its relational view of morality. Furthermore, because a feminist ethics maintains that morality is not "socially modular," normative analysis and critique can be carried out only in conjunction with social, economic, and political analysis (M. U. Walker 1998: 17).

Methods of feminist normative analysis: two examples

Perhaps more than any other feminist political theorist focusing on "care ethics," Selma Sevenhuijsen has demonstrated a determination to illustrate the ways in which care ethics may be used both as a "lens" to analyze the normative frameworks of social policy, and as a normative basis upon which to reshape existing conceptions of democratic citizenship, and thus to build new accounts of these which take into consideration the vital moral and practical importance of care to the daily lives of all people. While she does not explicitly cite the two methodological approaches described above, or situate her work within the discipline of "International Relations," I would argue that her work illuminates a uniquely feminist methodological approach to the study of norms and ethics in specific socio-economic and political contexts which can inform and enhance feminist international relations.

Critical moral ethnography: the ethic of care and
South African social policy

In a 2001 paper, Selma Sevenhuijsen explores the challenges faced by the South African government in designing new forms of social policy since the fall of the apartheid system. Specifically, she analyzes the 1996 *White Paper for Social Welfare*, using the feminist political ethic of care as a "lens" to trace the report's normative framework and to judge its adequacy for dealing with issues of care and welfare (Sevenhuijsen 2001: 2). She points out that while the language of care is used in the report, it does so in a way which inserts care principally into a "familialist framework, that is not equipped to address current South African social problems and also does not correspond with principles of social justice as endorsed in the same report" (2001: 2).

By contrast, Sevenhuijsen recommends a framework of "justice into care," which allows care to be seen as an issue of citizenship, rather than one pertaining solely to family relations. While such a view of care might be recommended for a number of societies, including affluent western ones, the "justice" part of the framework is particularly important for South Africa. Specifically, she argues that social and political justice – as understood through norms of human rights and equality – are urgently needed to provide citizens with the right of deliberation around legal issues, which was denied them for so long. However, she also argues that it is important to see apartheid, not just as a denial of individual rights, but as a system of brutality and organized negligence which denied an ethic of care in which the concrete relationships and conditions of citizens' lives could be negotiated. She proposes the need to integrate the ethic of care into notions of citizenship by recognizing that the tasks of citizenship cannot be exercised without the existence of care-giving and care-receiving (2001: 2–3). Thus, care does not completely replace justice; rather, the two ethics are integrated and reconceptualized, so that one makes sense only in the context of the other. This is achieved by making care, like justice, a "public" value; thus, where civil and political rights and freedoms are recognized as being owed to all citizens, so too the provision and organization of caregiving become a common concern for all, including those responsible for policy design.

Sevenhuijsen's work here is different from, and instructive for, most non-feminist work on ethics in international relations for at least two reasons. First, it does not examine a "macro" issue or event – such as humanitarian intervention, "poverty," or "exclusion" – and try to come up with a grand moral theory which can be applied across a range of cases. Rather, it looks closely at a particular historical, socio-economic, political, and cultural context with an already existing set of gender relations and a particular set of policy challenges. Second, it applies a particularly feminist methodology by using a political ethic of care as a "lens" through which to undertake a discursive analysis of the White Paper, highlighting the use of particular moral discourses, and unmasking the practical implications, especially in terms of gender relations, of those discourses. She uses discursive analysis to reveal the contradictions inherent within the South African White Paper; while the overarching framework is neoliberal, this sits uncomfortably with an attempt to play up social-democratic values such as needs and basic welfare rights. For example, the paper claims that declining GDP, decreasing *per capita* income, and declining job opportunities have put a strain on the welfare system. The most prominent solution to the poverty resulting from these developments is sought in leading as many people as possible to the organized labor market and to other forms of income generation, so that the degree of economic self-reliance can be enhanced. But the paper also uses the language of social welfare, arguing for necessary provision so that "households can adequately care for their members." While the language of care is used, it is relegated to the private sphere of "households" and "families"; this not only serves to devalue the importance of care-giving and care-receiving in public life, but also glosses over the gendered divisions of labor and the "power constellations" in which these are embededded (2001: 7). Sevenhuijsen argues that what is missing from the discourse is a fully societal model for the provision of care, which would allow these two moral vocabularies – of economic efficiency and self-reliance on one hand, and social democracy, equity, and basic needs on the other – to be more effectively combined.

Thus, while the analysis is explicitly a normative one, it is also one that is critical and feminist in its method. This is evident in Sevenhuijsen's argument:

Gender remains an add-on in the WPSW document, and a "gender consciousness" only shows itself where women can be conceptualized in its language of social groups with "special needs" . . . If an integrated gender approach [had] informed the text of the document, normative concepts and unquestioned sociological statements would have been interrogated. Shifting relationships of care, responsibility and security embedded in kinship systems, communities and state structures would have been taken as the focus of analysis, instead of questionable notions of "the" family. (2001: 12)

Finally, the critical moral ethnography used by Sevenhuijsen is not only focused on description or critique; it also demonstrates a feminist commitment to progressive transformation. Using the four phases of care – attentiveness, responsibility, competence, and responsiveness – Sevenhuijsen demonstrates how integrating the norms and values of an ethic of care into social policy frameworks could lead to important and progressive change, both for women and for the society as a whole.

Welfare organizations should be set up as institutional places for attentive and interactive forms of policy-making, as crucial points in "chains of care" on a social basis: this should in fact be integrated in professional training and professional ethics . . . Welfare related income-generating projects for women can, for example, be useful instruments in enabling them to sustain their lives and those who are dependent on their care. (2001: 14)

Mapping geographies of responsibility: care-giving and care-receiving in the new global economy

In her critique of Anthony Giddens's book *The Third Way*, Selma Sevenhuijsen focuses primarily on British society, comparing it in places with recent policy proposals in the Netherlands. However, like Giddens' book, Sevenhuijsen's work has, as its backdrop, the post-1989 world, and the transformations that have ensued for both global politics and the global political economy. As she states at the outset of the argument, there is a need for a "renewed social democratic policy vision that can grapple with the complexities of globalization and the changing role of the nation-state" (Sevenhuijsen 2000: 7).

In this piece, Sevenhuijsen is engaged in mapping the changing responsibilities for care and caring work in the contemporary era. This is achieved through both her own empirical research and the use of government statistics on, for example, the relocation of care from women to men, from inside the home to outside, and for the need for more and better care, for the aging population and the increasing numbers of chronically ill (see also Sevenhuijsen 2003). These changes are taking place on both a global and a local level; at the level of the nation-state, she uses Dutch and British societies to demonstrate the extent to which caring work is less and less carried out in the home, and increasingly in the intermediate institutions of civil society: neighborhoods, communities, schools, women's centers and self-help groups (Sevenhuijsen 2000: 25).

While this empirical work is not, in itself, normative, it is, as Walker argues, the necessary groundwork for moral analysis. Although Sevenhuijsen does not elaborate on the global level, she does suggest that current transformations of production and distribution on a global scale are influencing relations of care (2000: 15). I would expand on this by arguing that inequality in the global economy should be understood through the lens of gender and care. Despite women's increasing paid labor in global production, women around the world still do almost all of the household work in addition to their wage labor and informal work; they often work between sixteen and eighteen hours a day (Dickinson and Schaeffer 2001: 15). Thus, it is important to analyze a number of issues related to caring work in the global economy: the differing and constantly changing responsibilities for caring work within households and communities; the ways in which these responsibilities are affected by macroeconomic constraints imposed by external and internal organizations; and the ways in which unpaid or low-paid caring work helps to sustain a cycle of exploitation and inequality on a global scale.

The process of mapping these changing "geographies of responsibility" points, she argues, to the need for new normative frameworks to assist in the formulation of social policy. In a world with rapidly shifting sites of power, responsibility, and accountability, equality and justice are, she argues, "limited normative guidelines for (post)modern citizens." Taking the values of the ethics of care (attentiveness, responsibility, competence, and responsiveness) as citizenship values, and thus as guidelines for thinking about democratic social policies, enables forms of policy-making that are better attuned to the needs of persons living in networks of care and responsibility than if we start from the position of citizens as equal rights holders. The areas of policy-making would include not just family politics but also healthcare, education, city planning, and business management (Sevenhuijsen 2000: 28–29).

Rather than asking who or what is morally and politically responsible for some problem or crisis, using the method of mapping responsibilities allows us to interrogate existing patterns of responsibility and ask how changing material and social conditions may be transforming these. This means that the methodology begins, not with the formulation of moral principles that can be applied to a wide variety of moral problems, but rather with the existing and transforming conditions of what Sevenhuijsen calls "achieved" responsibility (2000: 27). The feminist ethic of care, and the values associated with it, then emerges as an appropriate normative framework to address these patterns of responsibility, and to recognize the fact that people can exist as individuals only through caring relationships with others.

Conclusion

The purpose of this chapter has been to explore the nature of feminist ethics in International Relations, and then to ask what this means for questions of method and methodology within this specific field of research. I have argued that feminist ethics should be characterized by a commitment to detailed case studies of the social arrangements – including the nature of gender relations, the distributions of responsibilities, and the valuing (or devaluing) of certain practices or activities – in particular contexts. In addition, however, a feminist political ethic of care may be used as a normative framework from which to carry out critical reflection, discursive analysis, and policy critique and formulation. This framework is characterized by "relationality," which is manifested in at least two distinct areas. First, and perhaps most obviously, relationality is central to feminist moral ontology. This relational ontology – which sees human beings as existing, at a fundamental level, in relation to and in relations with others – contrasts sharply with the traditional ethical and social science ontologies, which see humans and other objects as essentially autonomous, atomistic, and existing only in disinterested, contractual relations with other individuals. Moreover, this relational ontology is itself the source of the feminist ethical commitment to values such as attentiveness, responsiveness, trust, patience, and responsibility, which emerge naturally from it. This is not to say, however, that feminist ethics must necessarily prescribe these virtues as distinctly "feminine" or morally superior; rather, the focus on ontology over epistemology in this sense leads, more simply, to the need for feminists to uncover, and highlight, the varied but always essential role of care and other relational moral practices in the everyday lives of all people in all social settings.

Feminist ethics in IR must also, I then argued, be characterized by a focus on the relationship between ethics and moral practices on one hand, and politics and power relations on the other. Because of the paramount importance of gender subordination to feminist theorizing in general, and to feminist projects for transformation, feminist normative theory in IR must start with an approach to ethics which regards ethics as always infused with, rather than separate from, politics and power. This perspective is especially evident in theories of the ethics of care: "In our present culture there is a great ideological advantage to gain from keeping care from coming into focus. By not noticing how pervasive and central care is to human life, those who are in positions of power and privilege can continue to ignore and to degrade the activity of care and those who give care" (Tronto 1993: 111).

"Critical moral ethnography" and "mapping geographies of responsibility" are two methods of feminist normative inquiry for the study of international relations. When these methods are used in conjunction with an account of morality as relational – as in the feminist ethics of care – the result is socially situated, critical normative inquiry which is sensitive to gender – as well as racial and class – subordination.[4] While this method will not result in grand theories of justice or rights, it may just help intricately connected human beings to engage together in a "search for shareable interpretations of their responsibilities and/or bearable resolutions to their moral binds" (M. U. Walker 1998: 144).

---

[4] Many authors have pointed out the extent to which care is not only gendered, but also "raced" and "classed." See, for example, Narayan 1995; Tronto 1993, esp. 112–116.

12 Studying the struggles and wishes of the age: feminist theoretical methodology and feminist theoretical methods

Brooke A. Ackerly and Jacqui True

Introduction

Global inequality and mass poverty persist in spite of recent attempts by states and international organizations to promote economic growth and development through global integration. Indeed, the phenomenon of globalization has made this injustice within and across states even more apparent. Citizens and activists have mobilized across borders – in international forums, such as the United Nations' world conferences on human rights, population, environment, and women, and the World Social Forums. They have also mobilized on the streets of Seattle, Porto Alegre, Washington, Melbourne, Prague, Genoa, and Mumbai, demanding that multilateral institutions address their lack of democratic accountability and redress global injustice. And these ideas are being heard. For instance, the 2000 United Nations Millennium Declaration established eight development goals and fifteen targets that put the social and economic well-being of peoples on the international political agenda. In 2005, global poverty and inequity were key themes of the elite World Economic Forum meetings in Davos, and spokespeople from citizen movements were speaking inside the forum, not out on the streets. At the United Nations' conference on global poverty held in Monterey, Mexico (March 2002), world leaders acknowledged that globalization has done far less to raise the incomes of the world's poorest people than they had hoped.[1] As a result of the conference,

We thank the Center for International Studies at the University of Southern California for sponsoring a conference on the engagement between critical theory and feminist IR, and the participants for their feedback on an earlier version of this chapter: particularly Andrew Linklater, Richard Devetak, Molly Cochran, Cecilia Lynch, Janice Bially Mattern, Steve Lamy, Hayward Alker, and the engaging students in the USC School of IR. In addition we thank Maria and three anonymous reviewers.
[1] There is considerable debate over whether global inequality and poverty are increasing or declining in the context of global economic integration. London School of Economics

these leaders agreed to a new, expanded role for foreign aid to the developing world.

Mirroring these real world transformations in global politics, the study of International Relations (IR) has also been undergoing significant change. Although in the twentieth century the discipline was largely concerned with questions of interstate power and order, contemporary IR scholars are increasingly concerned with human rights (Risse et al. 2000; Falk 2000; Donnelly 1989), political economy (Cox with Schechter 2003), inequality (Hurrell and Woods 1999; Gill and Mittleman 1997), peacekeeping (Fortna 2004), human security (King and Murray 2002; Weldes et al. 1999; Krause and Williams 1997; Buzan 1997), norms (Onuf 2002; P. J. Katzenstein 1997; Finnemore 1996; Klotz 1995), international law (Goldstein et al. 2001), and non-state actors (Khagram et al. 2002; O'Brien et al. 2000; Florini 2000; Keck and Sikkink 1998). The changes afoot within IR are empirical, ontological, epistemological, and methodological. How have feminists contributed to these changes?

Scholars might consider feminists' greatest contribution to IR to be empirical. Certainly, their empirical contributions have been considerable. Asking questions such as "Where are the women?" or "What is women's experience of this?" is a critical starting point for examining any framework of global politics and transnational justice. As demonstrated in the essays by Stern, D'Costa, and Kronsell in this volume and in the work of many feminists, without asking these questions we

---

development economist Robert Wade (2001; 2002; *Economist* 2001) has argued in *The Economist* among other publications that financial liberalization and technological change have increased both income inequality and absolute poverty worldwide. His arguments are supported by the World Bank study of household income distribution compiled by Branko Milanovic (2002). This study covers 85 per cent of the world population between 1988 and 1993 and is considered the most reliable dataset we currently have. Wade's arguments are further supported by other scholars, notably Harvard economist Dani Rodrik (2001; 1999), whose own work shows that there is no relationship between expanded liberal trade and faster economic growth and eradication of poverty. However, in a recent *Foreign Affairs* article, World Bank economists David Dollar and Aart Kraay (2002) contend that world income inequality has declined over the past twenty to twenty-five years. They reach this finding by calculating the percentage gap between a random individual and the world average income and tracking the gap between these variables over time: the bigger the gap, the more unequal the distribution. However, Dollar and Kraay's standard mean deviation methodology (without country weighting) is biased toward Indian and Chinese individuals. India and China not only have disproportionately large populations; they have also experienced the fastest growth over the past decade. Thus, using this statistical methodology to calculate income distribution masks both the inequality growing in other world regions and within China and India. See the critical responses to Dollar and Kraay in a later issue of *Foreign Affairs* by John K. Galbraith, Joe W. Pitts, and Andrew Wells-Dang (2002) (also Freeman 2002).

underestimate the amount of power required to sustain or change the global system.[2] Certainly, by asking these questions and developing the tools of gender analysis, feminist scholars have made important empirical contributions to IR.

Others might consider the feminist contribution to IR to be onto-logical. The purpose of studying the struggles and wishes of the age is to help relieve them. Certainly, by rethinking key IR concepts such as security, international justice, political economy, the military, the state, and the global order, feminists have made ontological contributions to the field. But these ontological contributions also have an epistemo-logical dimension (Pettman 1996; Peterson 2003). For example, when D'Costa (this volume and 2003) sets out to study rape as a war crime, she intends to study gender insecurity during nationalistic war. Through her research, she discovers that the gendered violence was not confined to rapes during war, but continued in the processes of nation-building in the form of repatriation of women, forced abortions, and forced adoptions. These practices were a result of explicit government policies and international treaties. Ontologically, D'Costa is interested in the struggles and wishes of the women affected by the war and postwar nation-building. But the epistemological implication of this ontological focus and her finding that the *women* experienced other gendered violence led her to reframe the research question. As she discusses in her chapter, this led to a need to change her research methods so as not to rely on the women to retell their stories because this retelling would cause further violence to her research subjects.

While many feminist IR contributions have been empirical, onto-logical, and epistemological, they have also been methodological, as this volume testifies. Following the aim of this book, in this chapter we identify two methodological contributions of feminist IR to the broader field of IR. We draw on methodological inspiration and insights from within feminist IR in contrast to other chapters in this volume which build on methodological scholarship outside feminist IR.

First, we describe a feminist theoretical methodology that takes up the challenge most closely associated with IR critical theory: that is, how to generate a theory of international relations that not merely describes and explains global politics but that contributes to the transformation of global politics through its own theoretical practice. This methodology draws on the work of *some* IR feminists who are studying problems in international political economy and security, particularly those

---

[2] See notably Enloe (1996) on this point, and Weldon's discussion in this volume.

studying activists engaged in articulating their struggles. The theoretical methodology begins with sociological analysis of women's and men's experience and their gendered social contexts, uses this analysis to inform normative theory (also Robinson, this volume), and, in turn, considers current practice as the testing ground of theory. This feminist critical IR methodology is good for IR and essential for IR scholars who claim to be critical theorists. We laud the efforts of Robert Cox, Andrew Linklater, and kindred colleagues to construct a critical theory of IR which could foster a rethinking of core concepts. However, in light of the terrible injustices and inequalities that persist and deepen, especially in the context of heightened globalization, these efforts fall short both on their own theoretical terms and for the purpose of guiding political practice.[3] Critical scholars' neglect of the gender dimensions of injustice in their analysis of injustice is a demonstrable weakness for the practical application of the theory. Moreover, it is one that has important theoretical implications for the IR critical project itself. In our assessment, feminist IR offers a more critical, critical IR theory and practice.

Second, using immanent critique, we make explicit a theoretical method that is implicit in feminist IR scholarship. By observing feminist IR scholars, we identify their shared practices of skeptical scrutiny, inclusionary inquiry, explicitly choosing a deliberative moment, and conceptualizing the field as a collective. Taken together, these four practices constitute a theoretical method of doing feminist IR. Scholars

---

[3] We are not the only feminist scholars to note the limits of critical theorizing in international relations to date. Fiona Robinson (1999) has also concluded that Linklater's critical theory, in particular his Habermasian dialogic model, fails on its own terms to provide an adequate critical epistemology for understanding and transforming unequal and unjust international relations. Molly Cochran (1999) has also noted the failure of normative IR theorists to take up feminists' questions in a systematic way. She attributes this neglect to the dichotomous framework of the communitarian versus cosmopolitan framework in IR theory within which most ethical concerns have been addressed. This framework is based on an assumption of a male subject, and thus is not helpful for thinking through feminist concerns about women's oppression. Since writing this chapter we have become aware of another article, by Mairi Johnson and Bice Maiguashca (1997), that exposes the gaps in critical international relations theory from a feminist perspective. Not only does this article independently verify our own critique of Robert Cox's and Andrew Linklater's scholarship in particular (although it refers to their work before 1996, whereas we develop our critique on the basis of their work produced in and after 1996); it makes this critique even more relevant, since to our knowledge neither Cox nor Linklater has ever responded to the criticisms of their work contained in Johnson and Maiguashca's 1997 article. Clearly, there needs to be more engagement and mutual learning between critical theory and feminist IR scholars. Toward this end, our chapter moves beyond the earlier critiques of Robinson, Cochran, and Johnson and Maiguashca by invoking a wider range of feminist scholarship in order to offer our own reconstruction of critical IR theory through the development of a feminist methodology for transforming the theory and practice of international relations.

practicing this method become self-conscious about the ontological and epistemological choices implicit in their methodology and empirical methods. We offer this theoretical method back to IR and feminist IR particularly, as a methodological contribution to the study of human rights, political economy, inequality, peacekeeping, human security, norms, international law, and non-state actors.

Critical IR and feminist IR

All social scientists risk introducing biases through unexamined assumptions. Within IR, reflection on how best to subject these biases to examination has come primarily from critical scholars, including those who draw on Frankfurt school critical theory, critical international political economy, post-structuralism, and feminism. Critical scholars argue that critical self-reflection on the ontology and epistemology behind the method needs to inform the discipline as a whole. According to critical theorists, critical theory fills that role. Yet, in our view, critical theorists lack a theoretical method that *requires* and *guides* self-reflection. As we show, even a theoretical approach that is ontologically and epistemologically self-reflective requires a theoretical method that necessitates and guides the self-reflective process.

How can IR scholars contribute to clarifying the struggles and wishes of our globalizing age?[4] For critical IR scholars, theorizing international relations with regard to recent transformations and historical developments is the principal challenge facing the discipline (e.g. Linklater 1994: 120). Scholars such as Robert Cox and Andrew Linklater, among others, uncover the ideological bias sustaining the existing world political and economic order in orthodox approaches that claim to give an objective, politically neutral account of international relations. Taking the view that all knowledge is socially constructed on the basis of specific interests and purposes, they offer a theoretical methodology for challenging the prevailing ways of knowing, and advance an explicitly normative social change agenda for IR (see Keohane 1986). But the inadequacy of the critical IR approach is apparent in its failure to offer a theoretical method to guide other scholars in the practice of informing and transforming global politics.

In the same epistemological vein, feminist scholarship can be seen as a collective effort to make theories of IR better able to wrestle with

---

[4] According to Karl Marx, the task of the social critic as scholar joins that of the world: to improve "self-understanding of the age concerning its struggles and wishes" ([1843] 1967: 215).

questions of global justice. IR feminists recognize that the reification of disciplinary and political boundaries limits the possibilities for a truly critical IR theory (see, e.g., Zalewski, this volume). Specifically, but not exclusively, they address the gender-based oppression and injustice suffered by women and men within and across states. Although it is possible to include women within existing IR frameworks, such as constructivism, while leaving these frameworks theoretically intact and empirically strengthened, in their attention to women's experience feminist scholars do not seek merely to add women to theoretical frameworks derived from men's experiences in the world (cf. Keck and Sikkink 1998; Carpenter 2002). Rather, knowledge about the diversity of women's experiences and contexts leads feminists to appreciate the interrelated character of social hierarchies and their influence on oppression and the gendered ontology of the discipline that professes to study global justice (Brown 1988; Elshtain 1981; 1985; 1987; 1998). Consequently, feminists seek to break down, not only the exclusionary boundaries of gender, but also those of race, class, sex, sexuality, ethnicity, caste, religion, country of origin, national identity, aboriginal status, immigration status, regional geography, language, cultural practices, forms of dress, beliefs, ability, health status, family history, age, and education. By focusing on *intersections* rather than *boundaries* as loci of power and oppression, feminist scholars reenvision the way we conceptualize international relations (Crenshaw 1989; 2000).

As theorists and social critics, we understand the measures of justice and equality in our globalizing age, not by absolute standards, but by provisional standards. Justice cannot be determined by fixed *a priori* standards because our notion of justice needs to capture the injustices that we cannot yet see and cannot yet comprehend.[5] Nor can inequality be determined *a priori*, since we understand equality to mean, *not sameness*, but lack of hierarchy, as has been demonstrated in much of women's activism (Ackerly 2001; MacKinnon 1993; Bock and James 1992).

---

[5] Compare with Lyotard's notion of injustice: a wrong is "the harm to which the victim cannot testify" (1993: 144). If the critic cannot see it, and the victim cannot testify to it, is it an injustice? Yes; if concrete or abstract hierarchies have created the conditions of exploitable inequalities, then, even if we cannot see it, we know there is injustice. Vulnerability and insecurity, the direct result of merely the possibility of being exploited, are unjust (cf. Okin 1989). Although not every particular exploitable hierarchical relationship is exploited (for example, most parents do not sell their children into slavery), the fact that a hierarchy is potentially exploitable requires local, national, and global mechanisms to prevent its exploitation by particular individuals (for example, to prevent illegal trafficking and slavery).

Given the contingent basis for criticism and therefore social change within this ontological framework, our theoretical methodology requires a reflexive method as well (cf. Harding 1991). By observing that a diversity of feminist IR approaches are consistent with the theoretical method we present, we lend coherence to feminist work, which has been seen by some as offering no coherent research agenda (Keohane 1998). Feminism offers a well-tested theoretical method that is relevant to the study of all important questions.

We also use this theoretical method as a source for immanent critique of feminist IR and demonstrate its function by referencing the scholarship in this volume. In this emerging field, as in others at their naissance, the theoretical import of certain methodological choices by scholars is often obvious only in retrospect.

A feminist critical methodology for International Relations

In the early 1980s, Robert Cox ([1981] 1996) called for an explicitly *critical* IR theory that would focus not only on how our current form of world order is maintained but also on how it can be transformed. Toward that end, he set out an alternative historical materialist methodology for studying IR, drawing on neo-Gramscian concepts of hegemony, social class, and state/civil society complexes. More recently, in the 1990s, Andrew Linklater (1992; 1998; 2001) has provided a blueprint for how the critical theory of international relations, as advanced by Cox and others, might be further developed by incorporating aspects of a range of theoretical approaches. In the context of the IR discipline's diversity and its many unresolved divisions with respect to epistemology and methodology in particular, he has sought to "reunite international relations under the guidance of critical theory" (1992: 79). In Linklater's view, "there is more to critical theory than normative inquiry, since critical approaches seek to understand how social systems marginalize and exclude certain groups and how actual or potential logics of change might deepen the meaning of human freedom and expand its domain" (1994: 130; cf. Cox 2001a). Normative, sociological, and praxeological analyses are all crucial to the task of developing a critical theory approach to IR. Normative analysis provides a vision and set of values that we might actively defend and work towards. Sociological analysis elucidates the historical forms of inclusion and exclusion that prevent the realization of this vision and set of values at the global level. Finally, praxeological analysis is a form of practical theorizing that suggests the possibilities for advancing social justice and expanding human freedom in our present context.

Within a feminist approach to IR, the *synergy* among these lines of inquiry is most important. Sociological inquiry into women's and men's lives guides normative theorizing about justice and equality, while normative theoretical precepts are continually evaluated in terms of their import in actual struggles against injustice and inequality. However, while IR critical theorists acknowledge the importance of change-oriented theorizing, feminist IR scholars privilege the moment of practice in the process of theorizing and judge theories in terms of the practical possibilities they open up. As a consequence, feminists cannot discuss the sociological dimensions of their subject without making extensive use of women's and men's lived experiences or gender analysis. They cannot discern the normative dimensions of their work without considering their implications for feminist practice and social change. For feminists the connections between sociological, normative, and practical inquiry are methodologically crucial and demanding.

By way of illustration, consider the example of human trafficking. Trafficking now involves a massive global trade in humans for sweatshop, domestic, sex and other labor.[6] Despite the existence of such exploitation on a global scale, trafficking has until recently received scant attention from states or from IR scholars, even critical scholars.[7] One might expect that the feminist contribution would be to analyze the specific problem of sex trafficking and frame it in terms of global gender relations of inequality. But, while critical feminist analysis *may start* by examining the plight of women and children trafficked for sex work, in order to explain and understand their situation more fully, feminist scholars conduct a far broader analysis. An adequate analysis of sex trafficking implores the feminist scholar to investigate human trafficking across borders for sweatshop and domestic labor, all child labor, migrant patterns in the exporting countries, labor conditions and legal wages in the importing countries, the coexistence of transnational organized crime and liberal economics, and the global political economy processes that render human beings mere *factors* of production. In addition, feminist scholars may be interested in what could be learned about the

---

[6] The trade in women and girls for sexual exploitation is a business estimated to be worth US $7 billion (UNDP 1999: 5). Worldwide, approximately 1.2 million women and girls are trafficked for prostitution annually (UNDP 2000: 4). Because of the illegality of the trade, estimates vary widely (Kempadoo and Doezema 1998).

[7] For a discussion of the global rise in all forms of forced labor and slavery, especially among women and children, see the report prepared by the International Labor Organization (2001), debated by its 175 member states in June 2001.

dynamics of the global political economy from comparing the trafficked pattern of Eastern European and South Asian women, for example, or the experiences of those trafficked for sex work versus those trafficked for sweatshop work, for another example.

Understanding the agency, experience, and conditions of trafficked women should lead us to gain a better theoretical understanding of how the global political economy works to reproduce gender, race, class, and other forms of domination *simultaneously*.[8] Further, when we understand the instruments of the successful trafficking operation, such as fraudulent immigration, money laundering, and trafficking in weapons, we will better understand the mechanisms of other international crimes. Thus, beginning with the sociological analysis of trafficking and related crimes, feminist critical IR leads to a better understanding of global social injustice and the threats to national and global security. This feminist methodology has implications for both our theorizing of global social power and our global policy prescriptions. Finally, the methodology suggests a testable hypothesis: a more just and secure world order will result if international security efforts to combat terrorism, the drug trade, the arms trade, human trafficking, and other globalized threats to human security are coordinated to counter *all* those who rely on fraudulent immigration, money-laundering, illegal weapons, and so on, than would result if our remedies were focused on distinct but in fact inseparable kinds of international crime (True 2004). Although further examination of this hypothesis and its theoretical and policy implications is beyond the scope of this chapter, the trafficking example suggests what a feminist critical method could contribute to the theory and practice of IR.

Sociological analysis

Feminist critical theorists examine a wide range of exclusions and inclusions in the global system. In particular, they have contributed to sociological analysis in global politics in two key ways (see Cox 1996; Linklater 1990; 1998). First, they draw our attention to forms of disciplinary and political inclusion and exclusion. Secondly, and most importantly, by suggesting methods that reveal the *agency* of the seemingly excluded, feminists illuminate the *practical* possibilities for a

---

[8] This is only an illustrative example of our broader argument about feminist critical theory; it only suggests and does not provide an empirical analysis of sex trafficking and transnational sex work. For such an analysis see Heinrich Boll Foundation 1996; Global Survival Network 1997; and Kempadoo and Doezema 1998.

transformation of political community. For example, they locate injury in transnational spaces unseen, unappreciated, and untheorized in the familiar study of politics. Returning to the global sex trade example: through the operation of gendered power relations, the sex trade includes many women in the wealth- and foreign-exchange-generating activities of the global political economy, while excluding them from the profits, citizenship rights, and other gains of that economy. But feminists have also highlighted the international significance of marginalized, poor, and vulnerable women's political agency in a range of sites, including in civic and church groups, in networks of sex workers, homeworkers, and mothers, in forms of counter-cultural production, and in global forums such as the United Nations' conferences on environment, human rights, population, and women.[9]

Especially for women and minorities, it is not the exclusionary nature of citizenship in itself which compels them to migrate and be led inadvertently into an illicit, transnational sex trade. Rather, it is the fact that citizenship in a globalizing political economy increasingly comes without any social and economic protection. By assuming that the citizen is a neutral category, and that national citizenship rights have been practically extended to all subjects, critical theorists like Linklater fail to appreciate the deeply gendered and racialized character of citizenship regimes and the struggles of groups without effective citizenship rights. In a world where opportunities are so unevenly distributed across and within states, classes, genders, races and so on, national or cosmopolitan forms of citizenship are not the only or even the most adequate frameworks within which to address injustices. Rather, political solutions must reflect integrated social, economic, and political analysis of exclusion.

Although Robert Cox's critical political economy analysis of the differential impact of globalization on various groups of workers holds promise for the development of a critical sociology of IR, his categories of analysis remain too narrow and generalizing. According to Cox (1995a; 1999a), workers around the world can be categorized as the integrated, the precarious, and the excluded. Cox argues that economic restructuring is creating new forms of marginalization which serve to break up the existing social contract in many western states. While this appears a reasonable contention in light of certain empirical evidence,

---

[9] See Chin (1998); Moon (1997); Pettman (1996); Boris and Prügl (1996); Enloe (1989); Belenky, Bond, and Weinstock (1997); Friedman (1995: 18–35); Kempadoo and Doezema (1998); and Gibson, Law, and McKay (2001). In this volume, see chapters by Jacoby, D'Costa, and Stern.

Cox's three categories do not capture the many ways of being a worker, particularly *an excluded* worker, in the global economy.

A gendered analysis that takes into account the various ways in which women labor and in which labor is gendered serves to extend Cox's categorization and further deepen the argument flowing from it. Women's labor is often devalued relative to men's in the process of global and local restructuring. As the majority of those precarious homeworkers and unpaid laborers in informal household economies, women cushion the deleterious effects of structural economic reform.[10] They also constitute the core laborers in the multibillion-dollar, transnational sex business. For example, in post-socialist countries such as the Ukraine, Poland, and the Czech Republic, there are large numbers of unemployed persons, or, as Cox would say, excluded workers. Women and youth make up the bulk of this group. In such circumstances, migration, even for sex work, has thus become one of very few options open to young women. These young, migrant, women workers are definitely among those excluded workers. But to lump them along with other marginalized groups into one broad category of workers would appear to limit our analysis. In contrast, making explicit use of a gender lens allows us to begin asking a range of fresh questions about the differential impact of globalization and the processes that lead to these different outcomes for differently situated social groups. We see gendered global and local capitalisms together creating a spectrum of forms of economic exploitation and exclusion. In such contexts it is unlikely that privatization, liberal trade, and European citizenship will create economic security for all women and men (True 2003). It is also doubtful that the strengthening of state borders will prevent their migration. Even an integrated political and economic strategy will leave women marginalized within their own states and within the global economy if the reform strategy does not include mechanisms designed to create equal employment and participation opportunities in their local economy and society.

In sum, feminist sociological analysis is complex, reflecting an appreciation of multiple dynamics of exclusion. Feminist inquiry does not explain material exclusion in terms of Marx's logic of capital, gender

---

[10] For instance, while Cox notes that the global integration has resulted in states' being less able to control the impact of economic activity on the well-being of their citizens, he does not observe that one of the main ways states have responded to these external pressures is by cutting public expenditures and shifting the costs of social reproduction to families and households and, by implication, to women. See Bakker 1994; Marchand and Sisson Runyan 2000.

hierarchy, or any other such singular logic.[11] It seeks to make IR theory relevant to *all* the struggles and wishes of the globalizing age.

Normative inquiry

Feminist normative inquiry takes its cues from the sociological analysis of gendered power relations. As critical scholars, we are required to engage, to some extent, with practical efforts to bring about greater justice. We acknowledge that there is a range of perspectives on the appropriate closeness we should have to the so-called real world, or, more specifically, to our object of study. Some feminists are closer than others to concrete political struggles, but most if not all feminists are self-conscious about the critical distance they have from struggles on the ground.[12]

There are two forms that feminist IR normative inquiry can take generally.[13] One is to draw on gendered experience to reveal the normative gender bias inherent in the dominant conceptual frameworks for thinking about international relations (Enloe 1989; Tickner 1992). The other is to use that knowledge to revise core IR concepts such as the nation-state, security, and power in such a way that they might illuminate rather than obscure a range of social relations on a global scale (Cockburn 1998; Moon 1997). This second form is relatively undeveloped within the field. For example, let us consider feminist challenges to and revisions of security (D'Costa, Jacoby, and Stern, this volume). By conceiving of international security in terms of national security, IR scholars ignore other forms of insecurity and their gender dimensions. For example, a range of economic and other gendered insecurities lead young Eastern European women to get caught in an illegal transnational sex trade. These young women face physical insecurity as they are trafficked across borders, and bought and sold on the "free market" as sex slaves. As another example, in their homes many women face physical insecurity from domestic violence (in war *and* peacetime, especially in conflict zones). As another, women confront economic insecurity given the global feminization of flexible forms of

---

[11] Evelyn Reed ([1970] 1984: 170–173) is a possible exception. Even Engels's (with Marx [1884] 1972) analysis was not based exclusively on a critique of capitalism. He attributed "the world historical defeat of the female sex," not only to the advent of private property, but also to the exclusion of women from production as a result of its movement out of the household in the course of the Industrial Revolution.

[12] See Benhabib et al. 1995; Benhabib 1995; Haraway 1988; in this volume, see Stern, Jacoby, and D'Costa.

[13] Here we can only mention the forms of feminist inquiry.

labor and of poverty. And another: women live with the ecological insecurity of communities where water and fuel sources are increasingly scarce or remote (Ackerly and D'Costa 2004).

From a neoliberal perspective, traffickers choose to trade in women and youths as opposed to adult men in order to meet the western demand for sex services. The seemingly endless magnitude of this demand must be understood as intimately related to the accepted gendered norms which inform and regulate the construction of gender and national identities. However, from a feminist perspective, the demand can be met only because women – in economically depressed areas or in gendered labor markets that limit women's potential for economic security – seek economic opportunities. Many feminists are inspired by the insight that, if gender identities and relations are essential to the workings of power, then we can change the way they are constructed to bring about greater security. This constructivist understanding of sex and gender has broad significance for our understanding of how power operates in the global system (Locher and Prügl 2001).

Practical reflection

Critical feminist scholars scrutinize their normative assumptions by evaluating their practical import to women's activism against gender inequality and for greater global justice.[14] These feminists extend critical theorists' concern with the actual possibilities for transformation through practical theorizing.[15] As noted above, their practical theorizing is informed by particular struggles of women and men located in varied social contexts, and, within those contexts, in a myriad intersecting power relations.[16] Women trafficked for sex work from Eastern Europe to the West, for instance, are located in a number of hierarchies, including gender hierarchies *vis-à-vis* their male traffickers, men in Eastern

---

[14] In this volume, D'Costa. See also Ackerly 2001; Whitworth 1994; 2001.

[15] See Aron 1966: 577–579; Linklater 1992: 151, 137; also Cox 1992; 1995a; 1999a.

[16] There are a number of rich, theoretically informed, historical, empirical studies of transnational solidarity among actors in professional scientific communities, peace movements, and environmental movements that have been broadly construed as falling within a "constructivist" paradigm within IR. Like feminist critical scholarship, some of these studies are explicitly normative and designed to enhance our knowledge of the possibilities for transformation in world order; see, for example, Evangelista 1999; Lynch 1999; and Wapner 1996. But much "constructivist" scholarship has not engaged with epistemological debates. As a result, many constructivist scholars have not explicitly challenged mainstream IR's more normative assumptions and their implications for global social change, choosing rather to be located in a "middle ground" between the IR mainstream and its critics. For a discussion of these tensions within the emerging constructivist approach to IR, see Adler 1997; Price and Reus-Smit 1998.

Europe, and those western men who employ their sexual services. But analyzing their historically specific experience of domination and resistance does not merely add another, new group of oppressed subjects ("the trafficked workers") to existing normative frameworks. On the contrary, the knowledge produced through reflection on these experiences helps us to understand other oppressions and the global social forces that create and sustain these oppressions.[17]

Feminists do not assume that critical spaces are immanent within existing social formations (cf. Linklater 1999; Cox [1981] 1996). For example, trafficked women may recognize their conditions and even complain to one another or eventually to immigration and police officials.[18] But the organization of the illegal trade in humans and the credible threats of traffickers may prohibit strategic activism on their own behalf. Differently located women – including women activists, female politicians and foreign ministers, and gender policy entrepreneurs in international organizations, sex worker unionists, and trafficked women themselves – have come together, using their commonalities as women to forge a transnational alliance from which to leverage significant broader political change.[19] Though not without challenges associated with their range of political interests and knowledge, women have created coalitions that have overcome cultural and political differences – differences that in the hands of political elites typically represent insurmountable barriers to such change. Within women's collective practice, therefore, there are resources for building a normative theory about the possibility of a more universal, intercivilizational, or global dialogue (Cox 1999b; 2001b; Linklater 1998) and for determining the form that it could and should take (see, e.g., Ackerly and D'Costa 2004; Ackerly 2003). Such a theory need not rely on fully democratic states.[20]

---

[17] See Agathangelou 2004; Mohanty 1997; 1988; Goetz 1991. On the use of class as a process for an analytical tool, see Gibson et al. 2001. Analysis of the intersections also enables (women and men) consumers to appreciate their complicit role in slave labor and sex work generally. By not being aware of the working conditions under which our consumer items are made, consumers are directly complicit in the conditions of their manufacture and indirectly complicit in the choices women make to go into the sex trade over other forms of production.

[18] D'Costa (this volume) describes silent women, conscious of their lack of agency with regard to government policy and yet practicing a form of agency through their silence.

[19] For discussions of the making of transnational feminist alliances see, for example, True and Mintrom 2001; United Nations News Agency 1999; Clark et al. 2001; Prügl and Meyer 1999; Cockburn 1998; Gabriel and Macdonald 1994; Stienstra 1994; and Mies and Shiva 1993.

[20] Many so-called democracies function below the ideal, often causing significant harm to their citizens (Arat 1991).

A feminist theoretical method for International Relations

Individual scholars, including the contributors to this volume, build critical feminist IR by contributing to its sociological, normative, or practical projects. Taken together, these IR feminists present an important methodological development for IR. However, this theoretical methodology alone cannot make critical IR theory transformative theory. Theorizing is an ongoing process that needs to be guided by a method in order to be true to its stated normative goals. While critical IR scholars have identified key aspects of such a method, here we further refine the critical method. This feminist critical method is essential if critical IR scholars want to make good on their theoretical aspirations. Moreover, though not all feminists practice the method, that *some* practice this method contributes to defining the field of feminist IR, as a field, as a sub-field of IR, and as a sub-field of gender and feminist studies.

The method

Some aspects of the theoretical method we outline here have been identified by critical IR theorists. Important elements of this method are consistent with the methods of the IR feminists writing in this volume.

According to Linklater and Cox, the requirements of a critical IR approach are that the theory should

1. be grounded in observation of human experience, key material developments, and processes of historical change;
2. evaluate current practices and policies from the perspective of how they are constructed;
3. draw out the emancipatory potentials of existing social formations, the processes of social learning of which they are the result, and the implications of both for the transformation of the world order;
4. reflect on the very process of theorizing and role of the intellectual or scholar in society; and
5. be ongoing.

As demonstrated in the range of contributions to this volume, feminist scholarship meets these requirements of critical IR theory. However, in our view, feminism extends this critical theorizing process further, and a range of feminists, not just self-identified "critical IR" feminists, demonstrate the ways in which this theoretical method should be further defined.

A theoretical method enhances a scholar's confidence that her work succeeds in her aspirations to be grounded in human experience, to be attentive to gender and other social constructions, to identify emancipatory potential (and not practice forms of oppression through research), to be self-reflective, and to be cognizant of the ongoing nature of the processes under study and of the research process. As immanent critics, we draw from the work of feminist scholars to make explicit *their own* feminist theoretical method.

For example, with reference to the first critical requirement, the feminist scholar asks: what counts as key historical information (D'Costa)? What human experiences is it important to observe (Jacoby, Stern)? With respect to the second requirement, the feminist scholar interrogates the evaluation techniques she has used to assess the kinds of power that have had a formative effect on the historical structures inherited and the accepted means of evaluating them (Cohn, Kronsell, D'Costa, Jacoby, Stern). With respect to the third requirement, the feminist scholar examines emancipatory social forms; she notes who is set free and who is not by any social formation or form of inquiry; she scrutinizes a society's professed homogeneity regarding social norms; and she seeks to identify internal sources for and against change of established social institutions (Kronsell, D'Costa, Jacoby, Stern). Finally, with reference to the last two requirements, the feminist scholar considers her own theorizing to be ongoing, self-reflective, and, crucially, to be complemented by dialogue with activists and policymakers about the accuracy and relevance of her work (Zalewski, Weldon, D'Costa, Jacoby, Robinson). In the ideal, no aspect of a feminist's conceptual or empirical scholarship is left unexamined (Zalewski, Weldon, Kronsell, D'Costa, Jacoby, Stern, Robinson, Sylvester). In reality, those aspects of theory and empirical research which are for the moment unexamined become important items on the collective research agenda of feminist IR theorists (Weldon, Robinson).

From observing feminist scholars wrestling with these questions, we identify four key theoretical practices of that method: skeptical scrutiny, inclusionary inquiry, choosing a deliberative moment, and conceptualizing the field as a collective. First, these feminist scholars give critical attention to all key elements of their research designs and their contexts. They note the institutions, constructs, systemic conditions, and actors, however powerful or seemingly powerless, aware of those they will include and exclude as relevant or not to their project (Cohn, Kronsell, D'Costa, Stern). They self-consciously examine their own and disciplinary assumptions for their exclusionary potential (Stern). They diligently examine the representative or exclusionary potential of their sources. They critically assess their own research agendas (D'Costa 2003). For example, Elisabeth Prügl (1999: 147–148) is explicitly self-conscious about the epistemological costs of locating her research about home-based workers at the headquarters of the International Labor Organization:

> On the negative side, my geographical research location at the headquarters of an interstate organization removed the analysis from the experiences of individual home-based workers and limited the degree to which I could investigate the interaction of constructions at different levels. The issue carries deeper implications in the context of feminist debates about epistemology

In this way, while setting out a specific research agenda, Prügl calls on herself and other scholars to take up important questions concerning the relationship between local *and* global constructions of gender that she examines within a particular context (see True 2003). In this volume Cohn, D'Costa, and Jacoby reflect on the power relationships between researcher and research informants. The multiple positions of any given research informant and the multiple positions of any given researcher make the terrain of research itself a terrain of power. "Inequality" is an oversimplification of this terrain. Power is not just the subject of feminist IR inquiry from which we can gain critical distance; it is infused in the research process. Consequently, many feminist scholars incorporate their self-critical reflections on the process of doing research as a part of their findings. In this way the community of feminist scholars is continually aware of the limits of our scholarship and what has yet to be done (Marchand and Sisson Runyan 2000; Prügl and Meyer 1999; Peterson 1992). Collectively, feminist scholarship subjects all aspects of empirical inquiry and theoretical conclusions to *skeptical scrutiny* so that individual research designs do not neglect crucial questions (Ackerly 2000; 2003).

Feminist scholars practice their method in a second way: concerned about the exclusionary effects of epistemology – because all epistemology excludes as it includes – feminists endeavor to be *inclusive* in their inquiry and attentive to the marginalized (see also Minow 1990). They often draw broadly on others' empirical work and theoretical insights to complement and provide the context for their own work (Weldon, Robinson, Tickner, D'Costa). In their own empirical research, feminists use creative means for identifying and conducting appropriate research, and for seeking out available, marginalized, and less visible sources and subjects (Stern, Jacoby, D'Costa). Feminists investigate, in addition to the subjects of study in this volume, the particular circumstances of overseas contract workers, home-based workers, domestic workers, sex workers, and international women's movements.[21] Without a feminist

---

[21] Gibson et al. 2001; Enloe 2000; Prügl 1999; Chin 1998; Moon 1997; Stienstra 1994.

theory and method, the importance of learning about these precarious, marginalized, suppressed, and excluded people's experiences for advancing our understanding of IR would not be obvious.

Thirdly, while the theoretical projects of inquiry and improved inclusion are ongoing, feminist critical scholars choose a point of self-conscious inclusion of some subjects and exclusion of others in setting their research agendas. This point is a *deliberative moment*, amid continual change, at which the research question can be adequately investigated. Ideally, the scholar's contribution will promote inclusion and greater understanding, despite conscious omissions of possible points of view that could be illuminated through a broadened line of inquiry. For example, in the research project Carol Cohn describes in this volume, she draws on twenty years of data. At some point, in order to share her findings and have an impact on the field, she had to stop accumulating and analyzing data and start publishing her findings. Yet she does so aware that she is truncating the data artificially. By contrast, rather than constructing a narrative using data from the past twenty years, Maria Stern relies on her informants to construct their own narratives of those years. Stern uses these life stories as her data. Each scholar is aware of the impact of her choice of method on her findings. When she reflects on these, she makes explicit the deliberative moment of her scholarship. In this way, the scholar can pursue a particular research agenda without offering only hypocritical lip-service to the exclusions associated with any such narrowing of inquiry. While circumscribing the field of inquiry for her own purpose, she places her project in a broader context by clarifying an aspect of a larger collective research agenda. In so doing she also reveals the inherent limitations in all scholarship.

Fourthly and finally, while reasonably concerned about the disciplining of feminist IR, particularly from within feminist IR, the feminist method relies not on a unitary but on a *collective conception* of a field of knowledge and its theoretical and its empirical problems. In this volume Tickner opens up the ground of collective feminist engagement. Weldon stakes out a position within it, arguing that the feminist form of collective scholarship makes a distinctive contribution. Zalewski cautions against such confidence. We think that, taken together, these seemingly competing accounts of feminist IR in fact describe a dynamic and developing field whose disciplinary boundaries are porous but whose contribution is to develop the IR field by critiquing it both from within and from the margins.

It may seem odd to suggest that there should be one feminist theoretical method, given the scope of feminist inquiry referred to in this chapter and volume and the range of theoretical affinities of feminist scholars. Certainly, the collective feminist IR research agenda is vast. Consequently, feminist theorists have yet to be understood by the IR field at large as articulating a coherent research agenda either on their own terms or on the terms of the mainstream IR discipline.[22] Ann Tickner (1997) has suggested a possible research agenda that might explore the relationship between traditional gender hierarchies within states and state actions affecting war and peace (see Goldstein 2001; Caprioli 2002). However, such a feminist addition to the democratic peace research agenda is only one of many avenues of inquiry consistent with a feminist theoretical framework. As illustrated by the chapters in this volume, many of the questions emerging from such a research program belie a conventional view of the state as the source of citizens' security and are therefore not consistent with a feminist critical research agenda which asks us to consider *why*, and specifically *how*, the security of women's lives, and indeed human beings' lives, has not been on the agenda of states.[23] Moreover, Tickner is skeptical about the prospects for feminist IR to cohere around such a singular research agenda. Rather, and importantly, feminist investigations have served to disrupt the discipline and its narrow focus on questions of interstate relations, the causes of war, and national security defined in military terms. Thus, the scope of feminist scholars' theoretical interests does not lend an obvious coherence to feminist IR.

Despite its ongoing empirical interest in women and gender, we suggest that *the collective contribution of the range of feminist inquiry to IR theorizing is its theoretical method*, a method that is not specific to any particular question, set of questions, or theory. As feminists, we are appropriately skeptical that "a" feminist method could conceivably be used to discipline the field. In fact, the method we identify *cannot conceivably discipline*; it does, however, offer a critical lens through which

---

[22] Moreover, there is an explicit lack of common ground between some feminist and realist or neo-institutionalist approaches to international relations. See Zalewski 1998; Weber 1994; Tickner 1988; 1997; Sylvester 1994b.

[23] International security policy is no longer exempt from the agenda-setting efforts of women's movements and the United Nations, however. In October 2000, at its 4,213th meeting, the United Nations Security Council for the first time designated a special session for discussing the impact of war and armed conflict on women, violence against women and girls, gender issues in peacekeeping missions, the role of women in rebuilding societies in the post-conflict phase, and women's participation in peace negotiations and decision-making processes. On October 31 they adopted a Security Council Resolution (No. 1325, 2000), which recognizes the importance of a gender perspective on international peace and security, and calls for further efforts to mainstream gender issues in United Nations operations, and for more research and expertise on the gender impact of armed conflict and peace processes.

to assess all scholarship (including feminist IR). No view is excluded; all are critically evaluated. We argue that an ongoing collective self-reflective method, rather than any *specific* tools of gender analysis, is the common tool of feminist IR.

Conclusion: a better IR theory

By drawing on a range of existing frameworks and setting out new ones, feminists offer rich contributions to the study of global politics. Yet sympathetic colleagues often find it difficult to engage with and incorporate feminist analyses (see Keohane 1998). Even critical theorists, whose epistemological starting points and explicit normative concerns with global social justice would make them obvious partners of feminists, have not engaged with feminist scholarship. Their non-engagement persists, even though they find questions relating to gender intriguing and occasionally refer to women's movements, "feminism," and some feminist scholars (Cox 1999a; Linklater 1998).

The practices of skeptical scrutiny, inclusionary inquiry, explicitly choosing a deliberative moment, and conceptualizing the field as a collective define and constitute our feminist theoretical method. Of course, decontextualized, these practices may seem to us the professional tools of all good scholars, and not merely the tools of IR feminists. Here we have identified them through examples from feminist IR scholarship for the benefit of both feminist scholars and the IR field at large. By articulating a feminist critical method, we offer to critical IR theorists a way to practice their own methodology. In addition, we offer to feminist IR scholars a methodological framework for situating their work as contributing to both international relations and feminist scholarship. And we invite all IR scholars, should they wish to address the challenges of global injustice, to employ this feminist theoretical method.

Conclusion

Brooke A. Ackerly, Maria Stern, and Jacqui True

When read together, the distinct and complementary chapters in this volume show how ontology, epistemology, methods, ethics, and their interconnections are vital considerations in the ways we frame our research questions, conduct our work, make sense of our findings, and envision the world. Individually, the chapters in this collection can be seen as exemplars of the theoretical rigor, analytical acuity, ethical consideration, and political work that conducting responsible IR scholarship arguably demands. Taken together, however, they are intended as inspiration to IR scholars reflecting on their own methodological choices, and as examples of how particular scholars resolve specific problems in their own research. Without intending to codify them or to offer a definitive state of the field, we conclude by highlighting several interrelated key insights from these contributions.

First, this volume illustrates how gender matters in what we study, why we study, and how we study contemporary global politics. In different ways, the contributing chapters challenge what we consider as the subjects of IR (e.g. states, security, military institutions). They suggest creative ways for reenvisioning how to study IR (e.g., through gazing at art or recording life histories), which reach far beyond the traditional confines of the discipline in order to take gender – and the interactions of gender and other power relations – seriously.

Secondly, the chapters in this volume offer fresh insights on questions of power and knowledge which have been vital to critically oriented IR scholarship and feminist interdisciplinary inquiry. Their reflections on the crucial question of the multiple and intersecting workings of power invite us to reconsider the production of subjectivities and identities, ethics and responsibilities, and the politics of conducting research in sites familiar to IR scholars and those sites more familiar to feminists in other fields. The chapters in the volume use conceptual and geopolitical margins as fruitful standpoints from which both to disrupt dominant knowledge claims and to produce gender-sensitive knowledge.

Thirdly, when we reflect together through participating in this volume, we recognize the importance of situating our scholarship in relationship to the work of other feminist and non-feminist IR scholars. Feminist IR scholars share common texts from outside of IR (Harding 1987 is the most-cited work in this volume) and from within IR (e.g., Tickner 1992; Peterson 1992). However, feminist IR scholars are often oriented to their sub-field – security studies, political economy, global governance, and so on. With the goal of integrating feminist and mainstream approaches in our sub-field, we may be tempted to make insufficient use of feminist IR scholarship outside of our area. These divisions may be encouraged by the mainstream discipline and supported by publishers who have not generally published methodology chapters in feminist IR monographs. Such methodological accounting would facilitate cross-sub-field exchange. This volume therefore aims to inspire further conversations within and across feminist IR subject areas.

Fourthly, this volume offers readings of the principal debates about feminist methodology. Perhaps the most familiar debate is that between standpoint approaches and approaches which are characterized as post modern or post-structural. Individual chapters generally worked within one approach, but their work is clearly informed by the other. For example, some contributors demonstrate that it is possible – even necessary – to redefine feminist standpoints in light of the attention to the productive power of discourse offered by post-structuralist interventions. Weldon calls for this, and the contributors to Part II each make efforts to do it, though not necessarily in the ways Weldon prompts. The common commitment of the contributors to engaging in the *question* of methodology adds to our methodological conversations in new and exciting ways, which both combine and transgress longstanding categories. Such engagement of epistemological perspectives has informed the creative ways the contributors devised multiple and "triangulated" methods in order to explore their research questions.

In sum, the chapters in this collection have shown a range of theoretical perspectives and normative commitments which defy definition and classification. Yet the very act of placing the chapters presented here under the collective label of "feminist methodologies for international relations" raises some familiar questions about the politics of definition. In concluding this volume, we resist the seduction of definitively foreclosing what feminist methodology *includes*, *is*, or *does* in order to "talk back" to the "center" or mainstream of IR, or to distinguish feminist *IR* methodologies from feminist methodologies in other fields. We leave exposed the many difficult conundrums that inhere, given the politics of demarcating a field that has been considered marginal (and in need of definition) in order to resist the disciplinary tactics of any academic field. Taken as a whole, the volume lays bare the many different ways of identifying and addressing the paradoxes of feminist scholarship, including (on the one hand) defining feminist methodology as distinct and crucial to the study of global politics, and (on the other) resisting totalizing or imperial definitions. This seeming paradox with which we began the volume has not been resolved; neither, we believe, should it be. The paradox itself requires putting these questions on the table and leaving them undecided.

In short, *Feminist Methodologies for International Relations* aims to facilitate mutual learning and inspire greater self-reflection on how we do our work on global politics – and on how feminist work done in the field of IR can be helpful in spurring innovative methods and methodologies in other fields of inquiry. In distinctive ways, each of the chapters raises questions to prompt future research (the bounds of which seem limitless), to offer tools of research, and to explore theoretical methodologies for promoting the ongoing collective, critical self-reflection on the confines and content of the field. The methodologies for IR represented do more than bring marginalized problems, research subjects, and analytical tools into the landscape of IR. They show that global politics cannot be understood without exploring and challenging the conventional frameworks and methodologies of IR – or any other "discipline." In so doing, the contributions of these studies reach beyond the feminist IR community and speak to the politics of International Relations as a discipline and to the conundrums of feminist research and practice more generally.

Bibliography

Abeyesekera, Sunila. 1995. "Consolidating Our Gains at the World Conference on Human Rights (Vienna, 1993) and Dealing with our 'Differences.'" <http://www.lolapress.org/artenglish/abeye4.htm>.

Acker, Joan, Kate Barry, and Joke Esseveld. 1983. "Objectivity and Truth: Problems in Doing Feminist Research." *Women's Studies International Forum* 6, 4: 423–435. Also reprinted in *Beyond Methodology: Feminist Scholarship as Lived Research*, ed. Mary Margaret Fonow and Judith A. Cook. Bloomington: Indiana University Press, 1991.

Ackerly, Brooke. 1995. "Testing the Tools of Development: Credit Programs, Loan Involvement, and Women's Empowerment." *IDS Bulletin* 26, 3: 56–68.

——— 2000. *Political Theory and Feminist Social Criticism*. Cambridge: Cambridge University Press.

——— 2001. "Women's Human Rights Activists as Cross-Cultural Theorists." *International Journal of Feminist Politics* 3, 3: 311–346.

——— 2003a. "Lessons from Deliberative Democratic Theory for Building Global Civil Society." Paper presented at the annual meeting of the American Political Science Association, August 28–31.

——— 2003b. Review of *Fields of Protest: Women's Movements in India*, by Raka Ray; *Feminists Doing Development: A Practical Critique*, ed. Marilyn Porter and Ellen Judd; *Human Development Report 2000: Human Rights and Development*, by United Nations Development Programme; and *Women and Human Development: The Capabilities Approach*, by Martha Nussbaum. Signs 29, 1: 248–254.

Ackerly, Brooke, and D. Bina D'Costa. 2004. "Transnational Feminism and the Human Rights Framework." Paper presented at the annual meeting of the International Studies Association, Montreal, March 17–20.

Adler, Emanuel. 1997. "Seizing the Middle Ground: Constructivism in World Politics." *European Journal of International Relations* 3, 3: 319–363.

Agathangelou, Anna M. 2004. *The Global Political Economy of Sex: Desire, Violence, and Insecurity in the Mediterranean Nation-States*. London and New York: Palgrave.

Ahmed, Ishtiaq. 1996. *State, Nation and Ethnicity in Contemporary Asia*. London: Pinter.

Akhter, Shahin, Suraia Begum, Hameeda Hossain, Sultana Kamal, and Meghna Guhathakurta, eds. N.d. *Narir Ekattur o Judhyo Porobortee Kothyokahini*. Dhaka: Ain-o-Shalish Kendro.

Alker, Hayward. 1996. *Rediscoveries and Reformulations: Humanistic Methodologies for International Studies*. Cambridge: Cambridge University Press.

Alvesson, Mats, and Yvonne Due Billing. 1997. *Understanding Gender and Organizations*. London and Thousand Oaks: Sage Publications.

Andrews, Bruce. 1980. "Poetry as Explanation, Poetry as Praxis." In *The Politics of Poetic Form: Poetry and Public Policy*, ed. Charles Bernstein. New York: Roof Books, 23–43.

An-Na'im, Abdullahi Ahmed. 1992. "Toward a Cross-cultural Approach." In *Human Rights in Cross-cultural Perspectives: A Quest for Consensus*, ed. Abdullahi Ahmed An-Na'im. Philadelphia: University of Pennsylvania Press, 19–43.

Anzaldúa, Gloria, ed. 1990. *Making Face, Making Soul, Haciendo Caras: Creative and Critical Perspectives by Feminists of Color*. San Francisco: Aunt Lute Books.

Apodaca, Clair. 1998. "Measuring Women's Economic and Social Rights Achievement." *Human Rights Quarterly* 20, 1: 139–172.

2000. "The Effects of Foreign Aid on Women's Attainment of their Economic and Social Human Rights." *Journal of Third World Studies* 17, 2: 205–230.

Appadurai, Arjun. 1996. *Modernity at Large: Cultural Dimensions of Globalization*. Minneapolis: University of Minnesota Press.

Arat, Zehra F. 1991. *Democracy and Human Rights in Developing Countries*. Boulder: Lynne Rienner Publishers.

Arbetslivsinstitutets rapport 2004. Homo- och bisexuellas arbetsvillkor. Stockholm: Arbetslivsinstitutet.

Aretxaga, Begona. 1997. *Shattering Silence: Women, Nationalism and Political Subjectivity in Northern Ireland*. Princeton: Princeton University Press.

Arias, Arturo, ed. 2001. *The Rigoberta Menchú Controversy*. Minneapolis: University of Minnesota Press.

Aron, Raymond. 1966. *Peace and War: A Theory of International Relations*. London: Weidenfeld and Nicholson.

Art Newspaper. 2002. "The Year in Review, June 2001–June 2002." 1: 34.

2003a. "We Serve all Cultures, Say the Big, Global Museums." 132: 1–6.

2003b. "Global Values." 132: 2.

Asad, Talal. 1973. *Anthropology and the Colonial Encounter*. London: Ithaca Press.

Ashley, Richard K. 1989. "Living on the Border Lines: Man, Poststructuralism, and War." In *International/Intertextual Relations: Postmodern Readings of World Politics*, eds. James Der Derian, and Michael J. Shapiro. Lexington: Lexington Books.

Ashley, Richard K., and Robert B. J. Walker. 1990. "Reading Dissidence/Writing the Discipline: Crisis and the Question of Sovereignty in International Studies." *International Studies Quarterly* 34, 3.

Askin, Kelly. 1997. *War Crimes Against Women: Prosecution in International War Crimes Tribunal*. The Hague: Kluwer Law International.

Aslanbeigui, Nahid, Steven Pressman, and Gale Summerfield, eds. 1994. *Women in the Age of Economic Transformation*. New York: Routledge.

Atwood, Margaret. 1985. *The Handmaid's Tale*. New York: Fawcett.

Ayoob, Mohammed. 1995. *The Third World Security Predicament: State-making, Regional Conflict, and the International System.* Boulder: Lynne Rienner Publishers.

Baden, Sally, and Anne-Marie Goetz. 1997. "Why Do We Need Sex When We've Got Gender?" *Feminist Review* 56: 3–23.

Baca Zinn, Maxine, Lynn Weber Cannon, Elizabeth Higginbotham, and Bonnie Thornton Dill. 1986. "The Costs of Exclusionary Practices in Women's Studies." *Signs* 11, 2: 290–303.

Bakker, Isabella, ed. 1994. *The Strategic Silence: Gender and Economic Policy.* London: Zed Books.

Bannerji, Himani. 1995. *Thinking Through: Essays on Feminism, Marxism and Anti-Racism.* Toronto: Women's Press.

Barrett, Lindsay. 2001. *The Prime Minister's Christmas Card: "Blue Poles" and Cultural Politics in the Whitlam Era.* Sydney: Power Publications.

Barry, Peter. 2002. *Beginning Theory.* Manchester: Manchester University Press.

Barth, Fredrick. 1969. *The Social Organization of Cultural Difference.* Oslo: Universitetsförlaget.

Basu, Amrita, ed. 1995. *The Challenge of Local Feminisms: Women's Movements in Global Perspective.* Boulder: Westview Press.

Bauer, Janet. 1993. "Ma'ssoum's Tale: The Personal and Political Transformations of a Young Iranian 'Feminist' and her Ethnographer." *Feminist Studies* 19, 3: 519–548.

Baylis, John, and Steve Smith, eds. 2001. *The Globalization of World Politics: An Introduction to International Relations.* Second ed. Oxford: Oxford University Press.

Beard, Mary. 2004. *The Parthenon.* London: Profile Books.

Begum, Suraya. 2001. "Masuda, Elijan, Duljan, Momena: Kushtiar Charjon Grihobodhu." In *Narir Ekattur o Judhyo Porobortee Kothyokahini,* ed. Shahin Akhter, Suraia Begum, Hameeda Hossain, Sultana Kamal, and Meghna Guhathakurta. Dhaka: Ain-o-Shalish Kendro.

Behar, Ruth. 1993. *Translated Woman: Crossing the Border with Esperanza's Story.* Boston: Beacon Press.

Beitz, Charles. 1979. *Political Theory and International Relations.* Princeton: Princeton University Press.

Belenky, Mary Field, Lynne A. Bond, and Jacqueline S. Weinstock. 1997. *A Tradition that Has No Name: Nurturing the Development of People, Families and Communities.* New York: Basic Books.

Bell, Diane, Pat Caplan, and Wazir Jahan Karim. 1993. *Gendered Fields: Women, Men and Ethnography.* London: Routledge.

Belting, Hans, and Bill Viola. 2003. "A Conversation," in John Walsh, ed., *Bill Viola: The Passions.* Los Angeles: Getty Publications, 189–220.

Benería, Lourdes. 2003. *Gender, Development, and Globalization: Economics as if All People Mattered.* New York: Routledge.

Benería, Lourdes, and Shelley Feldman, eds. 1992. *Unequal Burden: Economic Crises, Persistent Poverty, and Women's Work.* Boulder: Westview Press.

Benezra, Neal. 2001. "Sculpture and Paradox," in *Juan Muñoz*, ed. Neal Benezra, Olga M. Viso, Michael Brenson, Paul Schimmel, Washington: Hirshhorn Museum and Sculpture Garden.

Bengtsson, Rikard, Magnus Ericson, Martin Hall, and Annica Kronsell. 2001. *Perspektiv på Världspolitik*. Lund: Studentlitteratur.

Benhabib, Seyla. 1992. *Situating the Self: Gender, Community and Postmodernism in Contemporary Ethics*. New York: Routledge.

1995. "Feminism and Postmodernism: An Uneasy Alliance." In *Feminist Contentions: A Philosophical Exchange*, Seyla Benhabib, Judith Butler, Nancy Fraser, and Drucilla Cornell. Introduction by Linda Nicholson. New York: Routledge, 17–34.

1996. "The Generalized and the Concrete Other." In *Feminism as Critique*, ed. Seyla Benhabib and Drucilla Carnell. Minneapolis: University of Minnesota Press.

Benhabib, Seyla, and Drucilla Cornell, eds. 1996. *Feminism as Critique*. Minneapolis: University of Minnesota Press.

Benhabib, Seyla, Judith Butler, Nancy Fraser, and Drucilla Cornell. 1995. *Feminist Contentions: A Philosophical Exchange*. Introduction by Linda Nicholson. New York: Routledge.

Berger, John. 1972. *Ways of Seeing*. London: Penguin.

Berger, Peter L., and Thomas Luckmann. 1966. *The Social Construction of Reality: A Treatise in the Sociology of Knowledge*. Garden City: Doubleday.

Berggren, Anders. 2002. *Undercover Operations in No-women's Land: The Swedish Armed Forces through a Gender Lens*, PhD dissertation, Department of Psychology, Lund University.

Berggren, Anders W., and Sophia Ivarsson. 2002. *"Jakten sätter på Attacken."* Stockholm: Försvarshögskolan.

Bertaux, Daniel, and Paul Thompson. 1993. *International Yearbook of Oral History and Life Stories: Between Generations*. Oxford: Oxford University Press.

Best, Jacqueline. 2003. "Moralizing Finance: The New Financial Architecture as Ethical Discourse." *Review of International Political Economy*, 10, 3, 579–603.

Bhabha, Homi K., 1993. *The Location of Culture*. New York: Taylor and Francis.

1994. *The Location of Culture*. New York: Routledge.

ed. 1990. *Nation and Narration*. London and New York: Routledge.

Bhabha, Jacqueline. 1998. "'Get Back to Where You Once Belonged': Identity, Citizenship, and Exclusion in Europe." *Human Rights Quarterly* 20, 3: 592–627.

Bhavnani, Kum-Kum. 1993. "Tracing the Contours: Feminist Research and Feminist Objectivity." *Women's Studies International Forum* 16, 2: 95–104.

Billson, Janet Mancini. 1991. "The Progressive Verification Method: Toward a Feminist Methodology for Studying Women Cross-Culturally." *Women's Studies International Forum* 14, 3: 201–215.

Blacklock, Cathy, and Laura Macdonald. 1998. "Human Rights and Citizenship in Guatemala and Mexico: From 'Strategic' to 'New' Universalism?" *Social Politics* 5, 2: 132–157.

Bleiker, Roland. 1997. "Forget IR Theory." *Alternatives* 22: 57–85.

2000a. *Popular Dissent, Human Agency and Global Politics.* Cambridge: Cambridge University Press.

ed. 2000b. "On Authority – Strolling through the Wall: Everyday Poetics of Cold War Politics." *Alternatives: Social Transformation and Human Governance* 25, 3: 391–409.

Blomgren, Ebbe, and Ove Lind. 1997. *Kvinna som man är* . . . LI Serie, T:2, Stockholm: Försvarshögskolan.

Bloom, Leslie Rebecca. 1998. *Under the Sign of Hope: Feminist Methodology and Narrative Interpretation.* Albany: State University of New York Press.

Bock, Gisela, and Susan James, eds. 1992. *Beyond Equality and Difference: Citizenship, Feminist Politics and Female Subjectivity.* New York: Routledge.

Booth, Ken, ed. 1998. *Statecraft and Security: The Cold War and Beyond.* Cambridge: Cambridge University Press.

Booth, Ken, and Steve Smith. 1995. *International Relations Theory Today.* Cambridge: Polity Press.

Boris, Eileen, and Elisabeth Prügl, eds. 1996. *Homeworkers in Global Perspective: Invisible No More.* New York: Routledge.

Boserup, Ester. 1970. *Woman's Role in Economic Development.* New York: St. Martin's Press.

Bouvard, Marguerite Guzman. 1994. *Revolutionizing Motherhood: The Mothers of the Plaza de Mayo.* Wilmington: Scholarly Resources Institute.

Bowles, Gloria, and Renate Duelli-Klein, eds. 1983. *Theories of Women's Studies.* London: Routledge and Kegan Paul.

Brah, Avtar. 1993. "Re-Framing Europe: En-gendered Racisms, Ethnicities and Nationalisms in Contemporary Western Europe." *Feminist Review* 45: 9–30.

Brandes, Lisa. 1994. *Public Opinion, International Security Policy, and Gender: The United States and Great Britain since 1945.* PhD dissertation, Yale University.

Brocklehurst, Helen. 1999. "Painting International Relations." *International Feminist Journal of Politics* 1, 2: 214–223.

Brossard, Nicole. 1980. "Poetic Politics." In *The Politics of Poetic Form: Poetry and Public Policy,* ed. C. Bernstein. New York: Roof Books, 73–86.

Broude, Norma, and Mary Garrard, eds. 1992. *The Expanding Discourse: Feminism and Art History.* New York: IconEditions of HarperCollins.

Brown, Wendy. 1988. *Manhood and Politics: A Feminist Reading in Political Theory.* New Jersey: Rowman and Littlefield.

2001. *Politics Out of History.* Princeton: Princeton University Press.

Brownmiller, Susan. 1975. *Against Our Will: Men, Women and Rape.* New York: Bantam Books.

Bruce, Judith. 1989. "Homes Divided." *World Development.* 17, 7: 979–991.

Bruner, Jerome. 1990. *Acts of Meaning.* Cambridge, MA: Harvard University Press.

2003. *Making Stories: Law, Literature, Life.* Cambridge: Harvard University Press.

Burgess, Annette Wolbert. 1995. "Rape Trauma Syndrome." In *Rape and Society: Readings on the Problem of Sexual Assualt,* eds. Patricia Searles, and Ronald Berger. Boulder: Westview Press, 239–245.

Busia, Abena P. A., 1996. "On Cultures of Communication: Reflections from Beijing." *Signs: Journal of Women in Culture and Society* 22, 1: 204–210.

Butalia, Urvashi. 1995a. "Muslims and Hindus, Men and Women: Communal Stereotypes and the Partition of India." In *Women and Right-wing Movements: Indian Experiences*, ed. Tanika Sarkar, and Urvashi Butalia. London: Zed Books.

1995b. "A Question of Silence: Partition, Women and the State." In *Gender and Catastrophe*, ed. Ronit Lentin. London: Zed Books, 92–109.

1998. *The Other Side of Silence: Voices from the Partition of India*. New Delhi: Penguin Books India.

Butler, Judith. 1990. *Gender Trouble: Feminism and the Subversion of Identity*. New York: Routledge.

1993. *Bodies That Matter: On the Discursive Limits of "Sex."* New York and London: Routledge.

Buzan, Barry. [1983] 1991. *Peoples, States and Fear: An Agenda for International Security Studies in the Post-Cold War Era*. Boulder: Lynne Rienner Publishers.

Buzan, Barry, Ole Wæver, and Jaap de Wilde. 1998. *Security: A New Framework for Analysis*. Boulder: Lynne Rienner Publishers.

Campbell, David. 1996. "Political Prosaics, Transversal Politics, and the Anarchical World." In *Challenging Boundaries: Global Flows, Territorial Identities*, ed. Michael J. Shapiro, and Hayward R. Alker. Minneapolis: University of Minnesota Press.

1992. *Writing Security: United States Foreign Policy and the Politics of Identity*. Minneapolis: University of Minnesota Press.

Campbell, David, and Michael Dillon, eds. 1993. *The Political Subject of Violence*. Manchester: Manchester University Press.

Campbell, David, and Michael J. Shapiro, eds. 1999. *Moral Spaces: Rethinking Ethics and World Politics*. Minneapolis: University of Minnesota Press.

Cancian, Francesca. 1992. "Feminist Science: Methodologies that Challenge Inequality." *Gender and Society* 6, 4: 623–642.

Caprioli, Mary. 2000. "Gendered Conflict." *Journal of Peace Research* 37, 1: 51–68.

2003. "Feminist Phallacies or Scientific Certainties? Examining Feminist Criticisms of Feminist Empiricists and of 'Mainstream' IR." Paper presented at the annual meeting of the International Studies Association, Portland, February 26–March 1.

2004. "Feminist IR Theory and Quantitative Methodology." *International Studies Review* 6, 2: 253–269.

Caprioli, Mary, and Mark Boyer. 2001. "Gender, Violence, and International Crisis." *Journal of Conflict Resolution* 45, 4: 503–518.

Carlsnaes, Walter. 1992. "The Agency-Structure Problem in Foreign Policy Analysis." *International Studies Quarterly* 36, 3: 245–270.

Carlstedt, Berit. 2003. *Vilka kvinnor mönstrar och får uttagning till plikttjänst*, Försvarshögskolan, ILM Serie T:29.

Carment, David, and Patrick James, eds. 1998. *Peace in the Midst of Wars: Preventing and Managing International Ethnic Conflicts*. Columbia: University of South Carolina Press.

Carpenter, R. Charli. 2002. "Gender Theory in World Politics: Contributions of a Nonfeminist Standpoint?" *International Studies Review* 4, 3: 153–166.

2003. "Stirring Gender into the Mainstream: Feminism, Constructivism and the Uses of Theory." *International Studies Review* 5, 2: 287.

Carr, Marilyn. 1991. *Women and Food Security: The Experience of the SADCC Countries*. London: IT Publications.

Carver, Terrell, Molly Cochran, and Judith Squires. 1998. "Gendering Jones." *Review of International Studies* 24, 2: 283–298.

Carver, Terrell, Marysia Zalewski, Helen Kinsella, and R. Charli Carpenter. 2003. "The Forum: Gender and International Relations." *International Studies Review* 5, 2: 287–302.

Chakrabarty, Dipesh. 2000. *Provincializing Europe*. Princeton: Princeton University Press.

Chan-Tiberghien, Jennifer. 2004. "Gender-skepticism or Gender Boom? Poststructural Feminisms, Transnational Feminisms, and the World Conference Against Racism." *International Feminist Journal of Politics* 6, 3: 454–484.

Charlesworth, Hillary. 1994–5. "Feminist Critics of International Law and Their Critics." In *Third World Legal Studies*, special issue, *Women's Rights and Traditional Law: A Conflict?* I, ed. Penelope E. Andrews.

Chatterjee, Partha. 1993. *The Nation and Its Fragments: Colonial and Postcolonial Histories*. Princeton: Princeton University Press.

Checkel, Jeffrey T. 2004. "Social Constructivism in Global and European Politics." *Review of International Studies* 30, 2: 229–244.

Chin, Christine. 1998. *In Service and Servitude: Foreign Female Domestic Workers and the Malaysian "Modernity" Project*. New York: Columbia University Press.

Chodorow, Nancy. 1978. *The Reproduction of Mothering: Psychoanalysis and the Sociology of Gender*. Berkeley: University of California Press.

1989. *Feminism and Psychoanalytic Theory*. New Haven: Yale University Press.

Chow, Rey. 1993. *Writing Diaspora: Tactics of Intervention in Contemporary Cultural Studies*. Bloomington: Indiana University Press.

Clark, Anne Marie, Elisabeth J. Friedman, and Kathryn Hochstetler. 2001. "Latin American NGOs and Governments: Coalition Building at UN Conferences on the Environment, Human Rights, and Women." *Latin American Research Review* 36, 3: 7–35.

1998. "The Sovereign Limits of Global Civil Society: A Comparison of NGO Participation in Global UN Conferences on the Environment, Human Rights, and Women." *World Politics* 51, 1: 1–35.

Clifford, James, and George E. Marcus. 1986. *Writing Culture*. Berkeley: University of California Press.

Cochran, Molly. 1999. *Normative Theory in International Relations: A Pragmatic Approach*. Cambridge: Cambridge University Press.

Cockburn, Cynthia. 1998. *The Space Between Us: Negotiating Gender and National Identity in Conflict Zones*. London: St. Martin's Press.

2004. *The Line: Women, Partition and the Gender Order in Cyprus*. London: Zed Books.

Code, Lorraine. 1991. *What Can She Know? Feminist Theory and the Construction of Knowledge*. Ithaca: Cornell University Press.

1995. "How Do We Know? Questions of Method in Feminist Practice." In *Changing Methods: Feminists Transforming Practice*, ed. Sandra Burt, and Lorraine Code. Peterborough, Ontario: Broadview Press.

Cohn, Carol. 1988. "Sex and Death in the Rational World of Defense Intellectuals." *Signs* 12, 4: 687–718.

1993. "War, Wimps, and Women: Talking Gender and Thinking War." In *Gendering War Talk*, ed. Miriam Cooke, and Angela Woollacott. Princeton: Princeton University Press, 397–409.

Collins, Patricia Hill. 1986. "Learning from the Outsider Within: The Sociological Significance of Black Feminist Thought." *Social Problems* 33, 6: 514–530.

1989. "The Social Construction of Black Feminist Thought." *Signs* 14: 745–773.

1990. *Black Feminist Thought: Knowledge, Consciousness, and the Politics of Empowerment*. Boston: Unwin Hyman.

[1986] 1991. "Learning from the Outsider Within: The Sociological Significance of Black Feminist Thought." In *Beyond Methodology: Feminist Scholarship as Lived Research*, ed. Mary Margaret Fonow, and Judith Cook. Bloomington: Indiana University Press, 35–59.

Committee on Status of Women in the Profession, 2001. "The Status of Women in Political Science: Female Participation in the Professoriate and the Study of Women and Politics in the Discipline." *PS*, June 2001: 319–332.

Connell, Robert W. 1987. *Gender and Power*. Cambridge: Polity Press.

1995. *Masculinities*. London: Polity Press.

1998. "Masculinities and Globalization." *Men and Masculinities* 1, 1: 3–23.

Connolly, William E. 1991. *Identity/Difference*. Ithaca: Cornell University Press.

Constantinou, Costas. 2001. "Hippopolis/Cynopolis." *Millennium: Journal of International Studies* 30, 3: 785–804.

Cook, Judith A., and Mary Margaret Fonow. 1986. "Knowledge and Women's Interests: Issues of Epistemology and Methodology in Feminist Sociological Research." *Sociological Inquiry* 56, 1: 2–29. Reprinted in *Feminist Research Methods*, ed. Joyce McCarl Nielsen. Boulder: Westview Press, 1990, 69–93.

Copelon, Rhonda. 1995. "Gendered War Crimes: Reconceptualizing Rape in Time of War." In *Women's Rights Human Rights: International Feminist Perspectives*, ed. Julie Peters, and Andrea Wolper. New York: Routledge, 197–214.

Corbetta, Piergiorgio. 2003. *Social Research: Theory, Methods, Techniques*. London: Sage Publications.

Cox, Robert W. [1981] 1996. "Social Forces, States and World Orders: Beyond International Relations Theory." In Robert W. Cox, *Approaches to World Order*, with Timothy J. Sinclair. Cambridge: Cambridge University Press, 85–123.

1992. "Multilateralism and World Order." *Review of International Studies* 18, 2: 161–80.

1995a. "Civilisations: Encounters and Transformations." *Studies in Political Economy* 47: 7–32.

1995b. "Critical Political Economy." In *International Political Economy: Under Global Disorder*, ed. Bjorn Hettne. London: Zed Books.

1999a. "Civil Society at the Turn of the Millennium: Prospects for an Alternative World Order." *Review of International Studies* 25, 1: 3–28.

1999b. "Thinking about Civilizations." Lecture to the Annual Meeting of the British International Studies Association, December.

2001a. "The Way Ahead: Toward a New Ontology of World Order." In *Critical Theory and World Politics*, ed. Richard Wyn Jones. Boulder: Westview Press, 45–59.

2001b. "Civilizations and the Twenty-First Century: Some Theoretical Considerations." *International Relations of the Asia-Pacific* 1, 1: 105–130.

Cox, Robert W., and Michael G. Schechter. 2003. *Political Economy of a Plural World: Critical Reflections on Power, Morals and Civilizations*. New York: Routledge/RIPE Studies in Global Political Economy.

Crenshaw, Kimberley. 1989. "Demarginalizing the Intersection of Race and Sex: A Black Feminist Critique of Antidiscrimination Doctrine, Feminist Theory and Antiracist Politics." *The University of Chicago Legal Forum*: 139–167.

2000. "Gender-Related Aspects of Race Discrimination." *Background Paper for the Expert Meeting on Gender-related Aspects of Race Discrimination, November 21–24, 2000, Zagreb, Croatia*. United Nations, Division for the Advancement of Women, Office of the High Commissioner for Human Rights, United Nations Development Fund for Women.

Culbertson, Roberta. 1995. "Embodied Memory, Transcendence, and Telling: Recounting Trauma, Reestablishing the Self." *New Literary History* 26: 169–195.

Dahlerup, Drude. 1988. "From a Small to a Large Minority: Women in Scandinavian Politics." *Scandinavian Political Studies* 4: 275–298.

Daniels, Arlene. 1975. "Feminist Perspectives in Sociological Research." In *Another Voice*, ed. Marcia Millman, and Rosabeth Kanter. New York: Anchor Press/Doubleday, 340–382.

Das, Veena. 1994. "Moral Orientations to Suffering: Legitimation, Power, and Healing." In *Health and Social Change in International Perspective*, ed. Lincoln C. Chen, Arthur Kleinman, and Norma C. Ware. Boston: Harvard School of Public Health.

1995. *Critical Events: An Anthropological Perspective on Contemporary India*. Oxford: Oxford University Press.

Davis, Karen. 1997. "Understanding Women's Exit from the Canadian Forces: Implications for Integration." In *Wives and Warriors*, ed. Laurie Weinstein, and Christie White. London: Bergin and Garvey, 179–198.

D'Costa, D. Bina. 2003. *The Gendered Construction of Nationalism: From Partition to Creation*. PhD dissertation. Canberra: The Australian National University.

Forthcoming. "Coming to Terms with the Past: Forming Feminist Alliances across Borders." In *Feminist Networks, Peoples Movements and Alliances: Learning from the Ground*, vol.1: *Feminist Politics, Activism and Vision: Local and Global Challenges*, ed. Luciana Ricciutelli, Angela Miles and Margaret McFadden. London: Zed Books.

De Lauretis, Teresa. 1990. "Eccentric Subjects: Feminist Theory and Historical Consciousness." *Feminist Studies* 16, 1: 115–150.

De Montigny, Gerald. 1995. *Social Working: An Ethnography of front-line Practice.* Toronto: Toronto University Press.

Deising, Paul. 1991. *How Does Social Science Work? Reflections on Practice. Pitt Series in Policy and Institutional Studies.* Pittsburgh: University of Pittsburgh Press.

Denzin, Norman K., 1995. "Messy Methods for Communication Research." *Journal of Communication* 45, 2 (Spring): 177–184.

Der Derian, James, and Michael J. Shapiro. 1989. *International/Intertextual Relations: Postmodern Readings of World Politics.* Lexington: Lexington Books.

Derrida, Jacques. 1981. *Dissemination.* Trans. Barbara Johnson. Chicago: University of Chicago Press.

——. 1994. *Specters of Marx.* Trans. Peggy Kamuf. New York and London: Routledge.

DeVault, Marjorie L., 1990. "Talking and Listening from Women's Standpoint: Feminist Strategies for Interviewing and Analysis." *Social Problems* 37, 1: 96–116.

——. 1996. "Talking Back to Sociology: Distinctive Contributions of Feminist Methodology." *Annual Review of Sociology* 22: 29–50.

——. 1999. *Liberating Method: Feminism and Social Research.* Philadelphia: Temple University Press.

Devetak, Richard. 2001a. "Critical Theory." In *Theories of International Relations, Second Edition*, ed. Scott Burchill, and Andrew Linklater, with Richard Devetak, Matthew Paterson, and Jacqui True. New York: Palgrave.

——. 2001b. "Postmodernism." In *Theories of International Relations, Second Edition*, ed. Scott Burchill, and Andrew Linklater, with Richard Devetak, Matthew Paterson, and Jacqui True. New York: Palgrave.

Devetak, Richard, and Richard Higgott. 1999. "Justice Unbound?: Globalization, States, and the Transformation of the Social Bond." *International Affairs* 75, 3: 493–509.

Dewey, John. 1939. *Intelligence in the Modern World: John Dewey's Philosophy*, ed. Joseph Ratner. New York: Random House (Modern Library).

Díaz-Polanco, Héctor. 1997. *Indigenous Peoples in Latin America: The Quest for Self-Determination.* Latin American Perspectives Series, 18.

Dickinson, T., and. Schaeffer, R., 2001. *Fast Forward: Work, Gender and Protest in a Changing World.* Lanham: Rowman and Littlefield.

Dillon, Michael. 1990–1. "The Alliance of Security and Subjectivity". *Current Research on Peace and Violence*, Tampere Peace Research Institute, XIII: 3.

——. 1996. *Politics of Security.* London and New York: Routledge.

Disch, Lisa. 2003. "Impartiality, Storytelling, and the Seductions of Narrative: An Essay at an Impasse." *Alternatives* 28: 253–266.

Dollar, David, and Aart Kraay. 2002. "Spreading the Wealth." *Foreign Affairs* 81, 1: 120–133.

Donnelly, Jack. 1989. *Universal Human Rights in Theory and Practice.* Ithaca: Cornell University Press.

Doty, Roxanne L., 1996. *Imperial Encounters: The Politics of Representation in North–South Relations.* Minneapolis: University of Minnesota Press.

Dowd, Siobhan. 1995. "Women and the Word: The Silencing of the Feminine." In *Women's Rights Human Rights*, ed. Julie Peters and Andrea Wolper. New York and London: Routledge, 317–323.

Dowling, Colette. 2000. *The Frailty Myth: Women Approaching Physical Equality*. New York: Random House.

Draucker, Claire Burke. 1999. "The Psychotherapeutic Needs of Women Who Have Been Sexually Assaulted." *Perspectives in Psychiatric Care* 35: 18–29.

Driscoll, Kathleen, and Joan McFarland. 1989. "The Impact of a Feminist Perspective on Research Methologies: Social Sciences." In *The Effects of Feminist Approaches on Research Methodologies*, ed. Winnie Tomm. Waterloo: Wilfred Laurier University Press, 185–203.

Dryzek, John. 1990. *Discursive Democracy*. Oxford: Oxford University Press.

Dubois, Barbara. 1983. "Passionate Scholarship: Notes on Values, Knowing and Method in Feminist Social Science." In *Theories of Women's Studies*, ed. Gloria Bowles, and Renate Duelli Klein. London: Routledge, 105–116.

Duncan, Carol. 1990. "Letters to the Editor." *Art Journal* 49, 2: 207.

Dutton-Douglas, Mary Ann, and Lenore E. A. Walker. 1988. *Feminist Psychotherapies: Integration of Therapeutic and Feminist Systems*. Norwood: Ablex Publishing Corporation.

Edkins, Jenny. 1999. *Post-Structuralism and International Relations: Bringing the Political Back In*. London: Lynne Reinner Publishers.

2004. *Trauma and the Memory of Politics*. Cambridge: Cambridge University Press.

Edkins, Jenny, Véronique Pin-Fat, and Nalini Persam, eds. 1999. *Sovereignty and Subjectivity*. Boulder: Lynne Reinner Publishers.

Eduards, Maud. 2002. *Förbjuden handling: Om kvinnors organisering och feministisk teori*. Malmö: Liber.

Edwards, Rosalind. 1990. "Connecting Method and Epistemology: A White Woman Interviewing Black Women." *Women's Studies International Forum* 13, 5: 477–490.

Ehlers, Tracy Bachrach. 1990. *Silent Looms: Women and Production in a Guatemalan Town*. Boulder: Westview Press.

Ehrenreich, Barbara, Katha Pollit, R. Brian Ferguson, and Jane Jaquette. 1999. "Fukuyama's Follies: So What if Women Ruled the World?" *Foreign Affairs* 78, 1: 118–129.

Eichenberg, Richard. 2003. "Gender Differences in Public Attitudes toward the Use of Force by the United States, 1990–2003." *International Security* 28, 1: 110–141.

Elam, Diane. 1994. *Feminism and Deconstruction*. London: Routledge.

Elias, Juanita. 2004. *Fashioning Inequality*. Aldershot: Ashgate.

Elkins, James. 2004. *Pictures and Tears*. New York: Routledge.

Elman, R. Amy. 1996. *Sexual Subordination and State Intervention: Comparing Sweden and the United States*. Providence, Oxford: Berghahn Books.

Elshtain, Jean Bethke. 1981. *Public Man, Private Woman*. Princeton: Princeton University Press.

1985. "Reflections on War and Political Discourse: Realism, Just War, and Feminism in a Nuclear Age." *Political Theory* 13, 1: 39–57.

1987. *Women and War.* Great Britain: The Harvester Press.

1988. "The Problem with Peace." *Millennium* 17, 3: 441–449.

1989. *Women and War.* New York: Basic Books.

1998. *Political Mothers.* New York: Basic Books.

Elson, Diane, ed. 1991. *Male Bias in the Development Process.* Manchester: Manchester University Press.

Emeagwali, Gloria T., 1995. *Women Pay the Price, Structural Adjustment in Africa and the Caribbean.* Trenton: Africa World Press.

Engels, Friedrich, with Karl Marx. 1972 [1884]. *The Origin of the Family, Private Property, and the State.* New York: International Publishers.

Enloe, Cynthia. 1989. *Bananas, Beaches, and Bases: Making Feminist Sense of International Politics.* London: Pandora.

1993. *The Morning After: Sexual Politics at the End of the Cold War.* Berkeley: University of California Press.

1996. "Margins, Silences, and Bottom-rungs: How to Overcome the Underestimation of Power in the Study of International Relations." In *International Theory: Positivism and Beyond,* ed. Steve Smith, Ken Booth, and Marysia Zalewski. Cambridge: Cambridge University Press, 186–202.

2000. *Maneuvers: The International Politics of Militarizing Women's Lives.* Berkeley: University of California Press.

2001. "Interview with Professor Cynthia Enloe." *Review of International Studies* 27, 4: 649–666.

2004. *The Curious Feminist: searching for Women in a New age of Empire.* Berkeley, Los Angeles, and London: University of California Press.

Eriksen, Thomas Hylland. 1993. *Ethnicity and Nationalism: Anthropological Perspectives.* London: Pluto Press.

Eriksson Baaz, Maria. 2004. *The Paternalism of Partnership: A Postcolonial Reading of Identity in Development Aid.* London: Zed Books.

Eschle, Catherine. 2001. *Global Democracy, Social Movements, and Feminism.* Boulder: Westview Press.

Escobar, Arturo, and Sonia E. Alvarez, eds. 1992. *The Making of Social Movements in Latin America: Identity, Strategy and Democracy.* Boulder: Westview Press.

Evangelista, Matthew. 1999. *Unarmed Forces: The Transnational Movement to End the Cold War.* Ithaca: Cornell University Press.

Fahlstedt, Krister. 2000. "Studie över situationen för homosexuella inom Försvarsmakten", unpublished paper, Stockholm: Försvarshögskolan FHS/MI.

Falk, Richard. 2000. *Human Rights Horizons: The Pursuit of Justice in a Globalizing World.* New York: Routledge.

Farrell, Susan A. 1992. "Feminism and Sociology. Introduction: The Search for a Feminist/Womanist Methodology in Sociology." In *Revolutions in Knowledge: Feminism in the Social Sciences,* ed. Sue Rosenberg Zalk, and Janice Gordon-Kelter. Boulder: Westview Press, 57–62.

Faust, David, and Richa Nagar. 2003. "Third World NGOs and US Academics: Dilemmas and Politics of Collaboration." *Ethics, Place and Environment,* 6, 1: 73–78.

Feldman, Shelley. 1999. "Feminist Interruptions: The Silence of East Bengal in the Story of Partition." *Interventions* 1, 2: 167–182.

Ferguson, Ann. 2002. "On Conceiving Motherhood and Sexuality: A Feminist-Materialist Approach." In *The Socialist Feminist Project: A Contemporary Theory and Politics*, ed. Nancy Holmstrom. New York: Monthly Review Press.

Ferguson, Kathy E., 1993. *The Man Question: Visions of Subjectivity in Feminist Theory*. Berkeley: University of California Press.

Ferree, Myra Marx, and Mangala Subramaniam. 2000. "The International Women's Movement at Century's End." In *Gender Mosaics: Social Perspectives*, ed. Dana Vannoy. Los Angeles: Roxbury, 496–506.

Ferree, Myra Marx, and Mangala Subramaniam. 2001. "The International Women's Movement at Century's End." In *Gender Mosaics: Social Perspectives*, ed. Dana Vannoy. Los Angeles: Roxbury, 496–506.

Finnemore, Martha. 1996. *National Interests in International Society*. Ithaca, NY: Cornell University Press.

Fisher, Berenice. 1984. "What is Feminist Method?" *Feminist Review (New Women's Times)*, May/June.

Flax, Jane. 1987. "Postmodernism and Gender Relations in Feminist Theory." *Signs* 12, 4: 621–643.

1990. *Thinking Fragments: Psychoanalysis, Feminism, and Postmodernism in the Contemporary West*. Berkeley and Los Angeles: University of California Press.

Florini, Ann, ed. 2000. *The Third Force: The Rise of Transnational Civil Society*. Carnegie Endowment for International Peace.

Fonow, Mary Margaret, and Judith A. Cook. 1991a. *Beyond Methodology: Feminist Scholarship as Lived Research*. Bloomington: Indiana University Press.

1991b. "Back to the Future: A Look at the Second Wave of Feminist Epistemology and Methodology." In *Beyond Methodology: Feminist Scholarship as Lived Research*, ed. Mary Margaret Fonow, and Judith A. Cook. Bloomington: Indiana University Press, 1–15.

Försvarsdepartementet. 1995. *Konferens för kvinnliga officerare och aspiranter i Eskilstuna 5–6 April*. Conference proceedings. Stockholm: The Defense Ministry.

Försvarshögskolan. 2002. *Långsamt framåt marsch*. Conference Proceedings of a Nordic Conference on Women's Integration in the Defense.

Fortna, Virginia Page. 2004. "Does Peacekeeping Keep Peace? International Intervention and the Duration of Peace after the Civil War." *International Studies Quarterly* 48, 2: 269–292.

Foucault, Michel. 1972. *The Archeology of Knowledge and the Discourse on Language*. New York: Pantheon.

1980. *Power/Knowledge: Selected Interviews and Other Writings*. Ed. and trans. C. Gordon. New York: Pantheon.

2001. "Power/Knowledge." In *The New Social Theory Reader*, ed. Steven Seidman, and Jeffrey Alexander. London: Routledge, 69–75.

Fraser, Arvonne S., 1987. *The UN Decade for Women: Documents and Dialogue*. Westview Special Studies on Women in Contemporary Society. Boulder and London: Westview.

1999. "Becoming Human: The Origins and Development of Women's Human Rights." *Human Rights Quarterly* 21: 853–906.

Fraser, Nancy. 1992. "Rethinking the Public Sphere: A Contribution to the Critique of Actually Existing Democracy." In *Habermas and the Public Sphere*, ed. Craig Calhoun. Cambridge, MA: MIT Press, 109–42.

——— 1995. "Politics, Culture, and the Public Sphere: Toward a Postmodern Conception." In *Social Postmodernism: Beyond Identity Politics*, ed. Linda Nicholson, and Steven Seidman. Cambridge: Cambridge University Press, 287–312.

——— 1996. "False Antitheses." In *Feminist Contentions: A Philosophical Exchange*, ed. Seyla Benhabib, Judith Butler, Nancy Fraser, and Drucilla Cornell. New York: Routledge, 59–74.

Freeman, Richard B., ed. 2002. *Inequality around the World*. London: Palgrave.

Friedman, Elisabeth J. 1995. "Women's Human Rights: The Emergence of a Movement." In *Women's Rights, Human Rights: International Feminist Perspectives*, ed. Julia Peters, and Andrea Wolper. New York: Routledge, 18–35.

Friedman, Elisabeth Jay, Kathryn Hochstetler, and Ann Marie Clark. 2001. "Sovereign Limits and Regional Opportunities for Global Civil Society in Latin America." *Latin American Research Review* 36, 3:7–35.

Frontiers. 1993. Special issue, "Feminist Dilemmas in Fieldwork." 13, 3: 1–103.

Frost, Mervyn, 1996. *Ethics in International Relations*. Cambridge: Cambridge University Press.

Fukuyama, Francis. 1998. "Women and the Evolution of World Politics." *Foreign Affairs* 77, 5: 24–40.

Fumerton, Richard. "Foundationalist Theories of Epistemic Justification," *The Stanford Encyclopedia of Philosophy (Spring 2000 Edition)*, Edward N. Zalta, ed. <http://plato.stanford.edu/archives/spr2000/entries/justep-foundational>. Accessed January 6, 2005.

Funtowicz, Silvio, and Jerome Ravetz. 1997. "The Poetry of Thermodynamics." *Futures* 29, 9: 791–810.

Gabriel, Christina, and Laura Macdonald. 1994. "Women's Transnational Organizing in the Context of NAFTA: Forging Feminist Internationality." *Millennium* 23, 3: 535–562.

——— "NAFTA and Economic Restructuring: Some Gender and Race Implications." In *Rethinking Restructuring: Gender and Change in Canada*, ed. Isabella Bakker. Toronto: University of Toronto Press, 165–186.

Galbraith, James K., Joe W. Pitt III, and Andrew Wells-Dang. 2002. "Is Inequality Decreasing: Debating the Wealth and Poverty of Nations." *Foreign Affairs* 81, 4: 178–183.

Gallagher, Nancy. 1993. "The Gender Gap in Popular Attitudes Toward the Use of Force." In *Women and the Use of Military Force*, ed. Ruth Howes and Michael Stevenson. Boulder: Lynne Rienner Publishers.

Garlick, Steve. 2004. "Distinctly Feminine: On the Relationship Between Men and Art," *Berkeley Journal of Sociology* 48: 108–125.

Geertz, Clifford. 1973. *The Interpretation of Cultures*. New York: Basic Books.

Geiger, Susan. 1992. "What's So Feminist about Doing Women's Oral History?" In Cheryl Johnson-Odim and Margaret Strobel, eds. *Expanding the Boundaries of Women's History: Essays on Women in the Third World*. Bloomington: Indiana University Press, 305–318.

Gellately, Robert, and Keirnan, Ben. 2003. *The Specter of Genocide: Mass Murder in Historical Perspective.* Cambridge: Cambridge University Press.

George, Jim. 1994. *Discourses of Global Politics: A Critical Re-Introduction to International Relations.* Boulder: Lynne Rienner Publishers.

Geuss, Raymond. 1981. *The Idea of a Critical Theory: Habermas and the Frankfurt School.* Cambridge: Cambridge University Press.

Gherardi, Silvia. 1995. *Gender, Symbolism and Organizational Cultures.* London and Thousand Oaks: Sage Publications.

Gibson, Katherine, Lisa Law, and Deidre McKay. 2001. "Beyond Heroes and Victims: Filipina Contract Migrants, Economic Activism and Class Transformations." *International Feminist Journal of Politics* 3, 3: 365–386.

Gill, Stephen, and James Mittleman, eds. 1997. *Innovation and Transformation in International Studies.* Cambridge: Cambridge University Press.

Gillespie, Angus. 1999. *Twin Towers: The Life of New York City's World Trade Center.* New Brunswick: Rutgers University Press.

Gilligan, Carol. 1982. *In a Different Voice: Psychological Theory and Women's Development.* Cambridge, MA: Harvard University Press.

Global Survival Network. 1997. *Crime and Servitude: An Exposé of the Traffic in Women for Prostitution from the Newly Independent States.* A report in collaboration with the International League for Human Rights, Washington.

Gluck, Sherna B. 1977. "What's So Special About Women? Women's Oral History." *Frontiers* 2, 2: 3–17.

Gluck, Sherna B., and Daphne Patai, eds. 1991. *Women's Words: The Feminist Practice of Oral History.* New York: Routledge.

Goetz, Anne Marie. 1991. "Feminism and the Claim to Know: Contradictions in Approaches to Women in Development." In *Gender and International Relations,* ed. Rebecca Grant, and Kathleen Newland. Bloomington: Indiana University Press, 133–157.

Goetz, Anne Marie, and Rina Sen Gupta. 1996. "Who Takes the Credit? Gender, Power, and Control Over Loan Use in Rural Credit Programmes in Bangladesh." *World Development* 24, 1: 45–63.

Goff, Patricia, and Kevin Dunn, eds. 2004. *Identity and Global Politics.* New York: Palgrave.

Golde, Peggy. 1970. *Women in the Field: Anthropological Experiences.* Berkeley: University of California Press.

Goldstein, Joshua. 1996. *International Relations.* Second ed. New York: Harper-Collins.

2001. *War and Gender.* Cambridge: Cambridge University Press.

Goldstein, Judith, Miles Kahler, Robert O. Keohane, and Anne-Marie Slaughter, eds. 2001. *The Legalization of World Politics.* Cambridge, MA: MIT Press.

Gordon, Avery. 2001. *Ghostly Matters: Haunting and the Sociological Imagination.* Minneapolis: University of Minnesota Press.

Gordon, Deborah A., 1993. "Worlds of Consequences: Feminist Ethnography as Social Action." *Critique of Anthropology* 13, 4: 429–443.

Gorelick, Sherry. 1991. "Contradictions of Feminist Methodology." *Gender and Society* 5, 4: 459–477.

Grant, Rebecca, and Kathleen Newland, eds. 1991. *Gender and International Relations*. Bloomington: Indiana University Press.

Green, Linda. 1999. *Fear as a Way of Life: Mayan Widows in Rural Guatemala*. New York: Columbia University Press.

Grewal, Inderpal, and Caren Kaplan. 1996. *Scattered Hegemonies: Postmodernity and Transnational Feminist Practices*. Minneapolis: University of Minnesota Press.

Gugelberger, Georg M., ed. 1996. *The Real Thing: Testimonial Discourse and Latin America*. Durham: Duke University Press.

Gupta, Akhil, and James Ferguson, eds. 1997. *Anthropological Locations: Boundaries and Grounds of a Field Science*. Berkeley: University of California Press.

Gusterson, Hugh. 1996. *Nuclear Rites: A Weapons Laboratory at the End of the Cold War*. Berkeley: University of California Press.

Gutek, Barbara. 1989. "Sexuality in the Workplace: Key Issues in Social Research and Organizational Practice." In *The Sexuality of Organization*, ed. Jeff Hearn, Deborah Sheppard, Peta Tancred-Sherif, and Gibson Burrell. London: Sage Publications, 56–77.

Guzzini, Stefano, and Dietrich Jung. 2003. *Contemporary Security Analysis and Copenhagen Peace Research*. New International Relations Series. London: Routledge.

Hacker, Sally L. 1990. "Doing It the Hard Way." In *Investigations of Gender and Technology*, ed. Dorothy E. Smith, and Susan M. Turner. Boston: Unwin Hyman, 175–194.

Hall, Stuart, and Paul duGay, eds. 1996. *Questions of Cultural Identity*. London: Sage Publications.

Halliday, Fred. 1988. "Hidden from International Relations: Women and the International Arena." *Millennium* 17, 3: 419–428.

Hansen, L. Sunny, Elizabeth M. P. Gama, and Amy K. Harkins. 2002. "Revisiting Gender Issues in Multicultural Counseling." In *Counseling across Cultures*, ed. Paul B. Pedersen, Juris G. Draguns, Walter. J. Lonner, and Joseph. E. Trimble. Thousand Oaks: Sage, 163–184.

Hansen, Lene. 2000. "The Little Mermaid's Silent Security Dilemma and the Absence of Gender in the Copenhagen School." *Millennium* 29, 2: 285–306.

Hansen, Thomas Blom, and Finn Stepputat, eds. 2001. *States of Imagination: Ethnographic Explorations of the Post-Colonial State*. Durham, NC: Duke University Press.

Haraway, Donna. 1988. "Situated Knowledges: The Science Question in Feminism and the Privilege of Partial Perspective." *Feminist Studies* 14, 3: 575–599.

1991. *Simians, Cyborgs and Women: The Reinvention of Nature*. New York and London: Routledge.

Harding, Sandra. 1986. *The Science Question in Feminism*. Ithaca: Cornell University Press.

ed. 1987a. *Feminism and Methodology: Social Science Issues*. Bloomington: Indiana University Press.

1987b. "Introduction. Is There a Feminist Method?" In *Feminism and Methodology*, ed. Sandra Harding. Bloomington: Indiana University Press, 1–14.

1991. *Whose Science? Whose Knowledge? Thinking from Women's Lives*. Ithaca: Cornell University Press.

1993. "Rethinking Standpoint Epistemology: 'What is Strong Objectivity?'" In *Feminist Epistemologies*, ed. Linda Alcoff, and Elizabeth Potter. London: Routledge: 49–82.

1998. *Is Science Multicultural? Postcolonialism, Feminisms, and Epistemologies*. Bloomington: Indiana University Press.

ed. 2004. *The Feminist Standpoint Theory Reader*. New York and London: Routledge.

Harris, Maxine. 1998. *Trauma Recovery and Empowerment: A Clinician's Guide for Working with Women in Groups*. New York: Free Press.

Hartsock, Nancy C. M. 1983. *Money, Sex, and Power: Toward a Feminist Historical Materialism*. New York: Longman.

1998. *The Feminist Standpoint Revisited and Other Essays*. Boulder: Westview Press.

[1983] 2003. "The Feminist Standpoint: Developing the Ground for a Specifically Feminist Historical Materialism." In *Discovering Reality: Feminist Perspectives on Epistemology, Metaphysics, Methodology, and Philosophy of Science*, second ed., ed. Sandra Harding, and Merrill B. Hintinkka. Boston: Kluwer Academic Publishers.

Hashemi, Syed, Sidney Ruth Schuler, and Ann P. Riley. 1996. "Rural Credit Programs and Women's Empowerment in Bangladesh." *World Development* 24, 4: 635–653.

Hawkesworth, Mary. 1989. "Knowers, Knowing, Known: Feminist Theory and Claims of Truth." *Signs* 14: 533–556.

Hayner, Priscilla B. 1994. "Fifteen Truth Commissions, 1974–1994: A Comparative Perspective." *Human Rights Quarterly* 16: 597–655.

2001. *Unspeakable Truths: Confronting State Terror and Atrocity*. New York: Routledge.

Hearn, Jeff, Deborah L. Sheppard, Peta Tancred-Sheriff, and Gibson Burrell, eds. 1989. *The Sexuality of Organization*. London, Newbury Park, and New Dehli: Sage Publications.

Hearn, Jeff, and Wendy Parkin. 2001. *Gender, Sexuality and Violence in Organizations*. London, Thousand Oaks, and New Dehli: Sage Publications.

Heinrich Boll Foundation. 1996. *Conference Proceedings: Sex Work, Sex Tourism, and Trafficking in Women: A New Reality in Eastern Europe*. Prague.

Hekman, Susan. 1997. "Feminist Standpoint Theory Revisited." *Signs* 22, 2: 341–365.

ed. 1999. *Feminism, Identity, and Difference*. London: Frank Cass.

Held, David. 1995. *Democracy and Global Order: From the Modern State to Cosmopolitan Governance*. Cambridge: Polity Press.

Hennessy, Rosemary. 1993. *Materialist Feminism and the Politics of Discourse*. New York and London: Routledge.

Hensley, Laura G. 2002. "Treatment for Survivors of Rape: Issues and Intervention." *Journal of Mental Health Counseling* 24, 4: 330–348.

Herbert, Melissa. 2000. *Camouflage Isn't Only for Combat: Gender, Sexuality and Women in the Military*. New York: New York University Press.

Hirdman, Yvonne. 1990. "Genussystemet." SOU 1990: 44, *Demokrati och Makt i Sverige*. Stockholm: Fritzes.

———. 2001. *Genus: om det stabilas föränderliga former*. Malmö: Liber.

Hirschmann, Nancy J. 1992. *Rethinking Obligation: A Feminist Method for Political Theory*. Ithaca: Cornell University Press.

———. 1997. "Feminist Standpoint as Postmodern Strategy." *Women and Politics* 18, 3: 73–92.

hooks, bell. 1984. *Feminist Theory: From Margin to Center*. Boston: South End Press.

———. 1989. *Talking Back: Thinking Feminist, Thinking Black*. Toronto: Between the Lines.

Hooper, Charlotte. 1998. "Masculinist Practices and Gender Politics: The Operation of Multiple Masculinities in International Relations." In *The 'Man' Question in International Relations*, ed. Marysia Zalewski and Jane Parpart. Boulder: Westview Press, 28–53.

———. 2001. *Manly States: Masculinities, International Relations, and Gender Politics*. New York: Columbia University Press.

Hosken, Fran. 1976. "Editorial" and "Women and Rape/Women and Violence". *Women's International Network News 1975* 2, 1. Lexington, MA.

Huizer, Gerrit, and Bruce Manheim, eds. 1979. *The Politics of Anthropology: From Colonialism and Sexism Toward a View from Below*. The Hague: Mouton.

Hunt, E. 1990. "Notes for an Oppositional Poetics." In *The Politics of Poetic Form: Poetry and Public Policy*, ed. C. Bernstein. New York: Roof Books, 197–212.

Hurrell, Andrew, and Ngaire Woods. 1999. *Inequality, Globalization, and World Politics*. Oxford: Oxford University Press.

Huston, Perdita. 1979. *Third World Women Speak Out*. New York: Praeger, and Overseas Development Council.

Hutchings, Kimberly. 2000. "Towards a Feminist International Ethics." *Review of International Studies* 26, special issue (December): 111–130.

Hylland Eriksen, Thomas. 1993. *Ethnicity and Nationalism*. London: Pluto Press.

Ibrahim, Nilima. 1998. *Ami Birangana Bolchi*. Dhaka: Jagriti Prokashoni.

Inglehart, Ronald, and Pippa Norris. 2003. *Rising Tide: Gender Equality and Cultural Change*. Cambridge: Cambridge University Press.

International Labor Organization. 2001. *Stopping Forced Labor*. Geneva: ILO.

International Studies Quarterly. 1990. Special issue, "Dissident Voices." 34, 3.

International Studies Review. 2003. Special issue, "The Forum: Gender and International Relations." 5, 2: 287–302.

"Interview with Professor Cynthia Enloe." 2001. *Review of International Studies* 27, 4: 649–666.

"Interview with Ken Waltz." 1998. *Review of International Studies* 24, 3: 371–386.

Irigaray, Luce. 1985. *This Sex Which Is Not One*. New York: Cornell University Press.

Ivarsson, Sophia. 2002. *Diskurser kring kvinnor i uniform*. Försvarshögskolan.

Ivarsson, Sophia, and Anders W. Berggren. 2001. *Avgångsorsaker bland officerare.* Försvarshögskolan, LI Serie T:24.

Jabri, Vivienne. 2003. "Pinter, Radical Critique, and Politics." *Borderlands e-journal* 2, 2. <http://www.borderlandsejournal.adelaide.edu.au>.

Jabri, Vivienne, and Eleanor O'Gorman, eds. 1999. *Women, Culture, and International Relations.* Boulder: Lynne Rienner Publishers.

Jacobsson, Mats. 1998. *Man eller Monster: Kustjägarnas mandomsprov.* Nora: Nya Doxa.

Jaggar, Alison M. 1989. "Love and Knowledge: Emotion in Feminist Epistemology." In *Gender/Body/Knowledge: Feminist Reconstructions of Being and Knowing*, ed. Alison M. Jaggar, and Susan R. Bordo. New Brunswick: Rutgers University Press, 145–171.

———. 1995. "Care as a Feminist Practice of Moral Reason." In *Justice and Care: Essential Readings in Feminist Ethics*, ed. Virginia Held. Boulder: Westview Press, 179–202.

Jaggar, Alison M., and Susan R. Bordo, eds. 1989. *Gender/Body/Knowledge: Feminist Reconstructions of Being and Knowing.* New Brunswick: Rutgers University Press.

Jahan, Rounaq. 1995. *The Elusive Agenda: Mainstreaming Women in Development.* London: Zed Books.

Jameson, Fredric. 2001. "The Political Unconscious." In *The New Social Theory Reader*, ed. Steven Seidman, and Jeffrey Alexander. London: Routledge, 101–107.

Jaquette, Jane S., 1997. "Women in Power: From Tokenism to Critical Mass." *Foreign Policy* 108: 23–38.

Jayaratne, Toby Epstein, and Abigail Stewart. 1991. "Quantitative and Qualitative Methods in the Social Sciences: Current Feminist Issues and Practical Strategies." In *Beyond Methodology: Feminist Scholarship as Lived Research*, ed. Mary Margaret Fonow, and Judith A. Cook. Bloomington: Indiana University Press, 85–106.

Joachim, Jutta. 1999. "Shaping the Human Rights Agenda: The Case of Violence Against Women." In *Gender Politics in Global Governance*, ed. Mary K. Meyer and Elisabeth Prügl. Lanham: Rowman and Littlefield, 142–160.

———. 2003. "Framing Issues and Seizing Opportunities: The UN, NGOs and Women's Rights." *International Studies Quarterly* 47, 2: 247–276.

Johansen, Robert C., 1982. "Toward an Alternative Security System: Moving Beyond the Balance of Power in the Search for World Security," *Alternatives: A Journal of World Policy* 8: 293–350.

Johnson, Mairi, and Bice Maiguashca. 1997. "Praxis and Emancipation: The Lessons of Feminist Theory in International Relations." *Statsvetenskaplig Tidskrift* 100, 1: 27–41.

Jones, Adam. 1996. "Does 'Gender' Make the World Go Around?" *Review of International Studies* 22, 4: 405–429.

Jones, Richard Wyn, ed. 2001. *Critical Theory and World Politics.* Boulder: Westview Press.

Kabeer, Naila, and Ramya Subrahmanian. 1996. *Institutions, Relations and Outcomes: Framework and Tools for Gender-Aware Planning.* IDS Discussion Paper 357. Brighton: Institute of Development Studies.

Kahn, Jospeh. 2002. "Globalization Proves Disappointing." *The New York Times*, March 21: A4.

Kandiyoti, Denise. 1991. "Identity and its Discontents: Women and the Nation." *Millennium* 20, 3: 429–443.

Kanter, Rosabeth M. 1977. *Men and Women of the Corporation.* New York: Basic Books.

Kaplan, Laura Duhan. 1994. "Women as Caretaker: An Archetype that Supports Patriarchal Militarism." *Hypatia* 9, 2: 123–133.

Kasper, Anne. 1994. "A Feminist, Qualitative Methodology: A Study of Women with Breast Cancer." *Qualitative Sociology* 17, 3: 263–281.

Katzenstein, Mary Fainsod. 1998. *Faithful and Fearless: Moving Feminist Protest inside the Church and Military.* Princeton: Princeton University Press.

Katzenstein, Peter J., ed. 1996. *The Culture of National Security: Norms and Identity in World Politics.* New York: Columbia University Press.

Keck, Margaret, and Kathryn Sikkink. 1998. *Activists Beyond Borders: Advocacy Networks in International Politics.* Ithaca: Cornell University Press.

Keller, Evelyn Fox. 1983. *A Feeling for the Organism: The Life and Work of Barbara McClintock.* New York: W. H. Freeman.

1985. *Reflections on Gender and Science.* New Haven: Yale University Press.

1987. "Feminism and Science." In *Sex and Scientific Inquiry*, ed. Sandra Harding, and Jean F. O'Barr. Chicago and London: University of Chicago Press, 233–246.

Kelly, Liz, Sheila Burton, and Linda Regan. 1994. "Researching Women's Lives or Studying Women's Oppression: What Constitutes Feminist Research?" In *Researching Women's Lives from a Feminist Perspective*, ed. Mary Maynard, and June Purvis. London: Taylor and Francis, 27–48.

Kempadoo, Kamala, and Jo Doezema. 1998. *Global Sex Workers: Rights, Resistances, and Redefinitions.* New York: Routledge.

Keohane, Robert. 1988. "International Institutions: Two Approaches." *International Studies Quarterly* 32, 4: 379–396.

1991. "International Relations Theory: Contributions of a Feminist Standpoint." In *Gender and International Relations*, ed. Rebecca Grant, and Kathleen Newland. Bloomington: Indiana University Press, 41–50.

1998. "Beyond Dichotomy: Conversations Between International Relations and Feminist Theory." *International Studies Quarterly* 42, 1: 193–198.

(ed.). 1986. *Neorealism and Its Critics.* New York: Columbia University Press.

Khagram, Sanjeev, James V. Riker, and Kathryn Sikkink, eds. 2002. *Restructuring World Politics: Transnational Social Movements, Networks and Norms.* Minneapolis: University of Minnesota Press.

King, Gary, Robert O. Keohane, and Sidney Verba. 1994. *Designing Social Inquiry: Scientific Inference in Qualitative Research.* Princeton: Princeton University Press.

King, Gary, and Christopher L. Murray. 2002. "Rethinking Human Security." *Political Science Quarterly* 116, 4: 585–610.

Kinsella, Helen. 2003a. *"The Image Before the Weapon": A Genealogy of the "Civilian" in International Law and Politics.* PhD dissertation, University of Minnesota.

2003b. "For a Careful Reading: The Conservatism of Gender Constructivism." *International Studies Review* 5, 2: 294–297.

Kishwar, Madhu, and Ruth Vanita, eds. 1984. *In Search of Answers: Women's Voices from Manushi.* London: Zed Books.

Klein, Renate Duelli. 1983. "How to Do What We Want to Do: Thoughts about Feminist Methodology." In *Theories of Women's Studies,* ed. Gloria Bowles, and Renate Duelli Klein. London: Routledge and Kegan Paul.

Kleinfelder, Karen. 1993. *The Artist, His Model, Her Image, His Gaze.* Chicago: University of Chicago Press.

Klotz, Audie. 1995. *Norms in International Relations: The Struggle Against Apartheid.* Ithaca: Cornell University Press.

Kofman, Eleanore, and Gillian Youngs, eds. 1996. *Globalization: Theory and Practice.* London: Pinter.

Krasner, Stephen. 1996. "The Accomplishments of International Political Economy." In *International Theory: Positivism and Beyond,* ed. Steve Smith, Ken Booth, and Marysia Zalewski. Cambridge: Cambridge University Press, 108–127.

Krause, Keith, and Michael C. Williams, eds. 1997. *Critical Security Studies: Concepts and Cases.* Minneapolis: University of Minnesota Press.

Krieger, S. 1991. *Social Science and the Self: Personal Essays on an Art Form.* New Brunswick: Rutgers University Press.

Kronsell, Annica. 2002. "Homeless in Academia: Homesteading as a Strategy for Change in a World of Hegemonic Masculinity." In *Women in Higher Education: Empowering Change,* ed. JoAnn DiGeorgio-Lutz. Westport: Praeger, 37–56.

Kronsell, Annica 2005. "Gendered Practices in Institutions of Hegemonic Masculinity: Reflections from Feminist Standpoint Theory." *International Feminist Journal of Politics* 7, 2: 280–298.

Kronsell, Annica, and Erika Svedberg. 2001a. "The Duty to Protect: Gender in the Swedish Practice of Conscription." *Cooperation and Conflict* 36, 2: 153–176.

2001b. "Emasculating the Duty to Defend? Gender Identities and Swedish Military Organization." In *Reconstructing the Means of Violence,* ed. Mark Elam. Brussels: European Commission, 88–107.

2003. *Conscription in Sweden: The Making of a Gendered Nation/State.* Paper presented at ISA, Portland, February 26–March 1.

2006. "The Swedish Military Manpower Policy and their Gender Implications." In *The Changing Face of European Conscription,* ed. Pertti Joenniemi. Aldershot: Ashgate.

Kunda, Gideon. 1992. *Engineering Culture: Control and Commitment in a High Tech Corporation.* Philadelphia: Temple University Press, 137–160.

Kvande, Elin. 1999. "In the Belly of the Beast: Constructing Femininities in Engineering Organizations." *European Journal of Women's Studies* 6, 3: 305–328.

Langness, L. L., and Geyla Frank. 1981. *Lives: An Anthropological Approach to Biography*. Novato: Chandler and Sharp.

Lapid, Yosef. 1989. "The Third Debate: On the Prospects of International Theory in a Post-positivist Era." *International Studies Quarterly* 33, 3: 235–254.

Lapid, Yosef, and Friedrich Kratochwil, eds. 1996. *The Return of Culture and Identity in IR Theory*. Boulder: Lynne Rienner Publishers.

Lather, Patti. 2001. "Postbook: Working the Ruins of Feminist Ethnography." *Signs* 27, 1: 199–227.

Latour, Bruno, and Steve Woolgar. 1979. *Laboratory Life: The Social Construction of Scientific Facts*. Beverly Hills: Sage Publications.

Leonard, Peter. 1984. *Personality and Ideology: Towards a Materialistic Understanding of the Individual*. London: Macmillan.

Letherby, Gayle. 2003. *Feminist Research in Theory and Practice*. Milton Keynes: Open University Press.

Liebes, Tamar, and Rivka Ribak. 1994. "In Defense of Negotiated Readings: How Moderates on Each Side of the Conflict Interpret Intifada News." *Journal of Communication* 44, 2: 108–124.

Linklater, Andrew. 1990. "The Problem of Community in International Relations." *Alternatives* 15: 135–153.

1992. "The Question of the Next Stage in International Relations Theory: A Critical-Theoretical Point of View." *Millennium* 21, 1: 77–98.

1994. "Dialogue. Dialectic and Emancipation in International Relations at the End of the Post-war Age." *Millennium* 23, 1: 119–131.

1996. "Citizenship and Sovereignty in the Post-Westphalian State." *European Journal of International Relations* 2: 77–103.

1998. *The Transformation of Political Community*. Columbia: University of South Carolina Press; Cambridge: Polity Press.

1999. "The Evolving Spheres of International Justice." *International Affairs* 75, 3: 473–482.

2000. *Theories of International Relations: Critical Concepts*. New York: Routledge.

2001. "The Changing Contours of Critical International Relations Theory," in R. Wyn Jones, ed., *Critical Theory and World Politics*. Boulder: Lynne Reinner: 23–43.

Linklater, Andrew, and John MacMillan. 1995. *Boundaries in Question: New Directions in International Relations*. London: Continuum.

Lipschutz, Ronnie D., ed. 1995. *On Security*, New York: Columbia University Press.

Lipman-Blumen, Jean. 1976. "Toward a Homosocial Theory of Sex Roles: An Explanation of the Sex Segregation of Social Institutions." *Signs* 1, 3: 15–31.

Lister, Ruth. 1997. *Citizenship: Feminist Perspectives*. London: Macmillan.

Locher, Birgit, and Elisabeth Prügl. 2001. "Feminism and Constructivism: Worlds Apart or Sharing the Middle Ground?" *International Studies Quarterly* 45, 1: 111–129.

Longino, Helen E., 1990. *Science as Social Knowledge.* Princeton: Princeton University Press.

Low, Goergiana, and Kurt C. Organista. 2000. "Latinas and Sexual Assault: Towards Culturally Sensitive Assessment and Intervention." *Journal of Multicultural Social Work* 8: 131–157.

Lowe Benston, Margaret. 1989. "Feminism and System Design: Questions of Control." In *The Effects of Feminist Approaches on Research Methodologies,* ed. Winnie Tomm. Waterloo: Wilfred Laurier Press, 205–223.

Lugones, María C., and Elizabeth V. Spelman. 1983. "Have We Got a Theory For You! Feminist Theory, Cultural Imperialism and the Demand for 'the Woman's Voice.'" *Women's Studies International Forum* 6, 6: 573–581.

Lynch, Cecelia. 1999. *Beyond Appeasement: Interpreting Interwar Peace Movements in World Politics.* Ithaca: Cornell University Press.

Lyotard, Jean-François. 1984. *The Postmodern Condition: A Report on Knowledge.* Trans. Geoff Bennington and Brian Massumi. Minneapolis: University of Minnesota Press.

———. 1993. "The Other's Rights." In S. Shute, and S. Hurley, eds., *On Human Rights: The Oxford Amnesty Lectures.* New York: Basic Books, 135–147.

McClintock, Anne. 1993. "Family Feuds: Gender, Nationalism, and the Family." *Feminist Review* 45: 61–80.

Macdonald, Laura. 1994. "Globalising Civil Society: Interpreting International NGOs in Central America." *Millennium* 23, 2: 267–285.

McDowell, Linda. 1999. *Gender, Identity and Place: Understanding Feminist Geographies.* Minneapolis: University of Minnesota Press.

MacKinnon, Catharine. 1993. "Crimes of War, Crimes of Peace." In *On Human Rights: The Oxford Amnesty Lectures 1993,* ed. Stephen Shute and Susan Hurley. New York: Basic Books, 83–109.

Mclure, Kirstie. 1992. "The Issue of Foundations: Scientized Politics, Politicized Science, and Feminist Critical Practice." In *Feminists Theorize the Political,* ed. Judith Butler, and Joan Scott. London: Routledge, 341–368.

McSweeney, Bill. 1999. *Security, Identity and Interests: A Sociology of International Relations.* Cambridge: Cambridge University Press.

Mama Maquin Organization of Guatemalan Refugee Women. 1994. *From Refugees to Returnees.* Chiapas, Mexico: Mama Maquin-CIAM.

Manchanda, Rita. 2001. "Where are the Women in South Asian Conflicts?" In *Women, War and Peace in South Asia: Beyond Victimhood to Agency,* ed. Rita Manchanda. New Delhi: Sage Publications, 9–41.

Manning, Erin. 2003. "Negotiating Influence: Argentine Tango and a Politics of Touch," *Borderlands e-journal* 2, 1. <http://www.borderlandsejournal. adelaide.edu.au>.

Mansbach, Richard, and Edward Rhodes. 2000. *Global Politics in a Changing World: A Reader.* Boston: Houghton Mifflin.

Mansbridge, Jane. 1980. *Beyond Adversary Democracy.* New York: Basic Books.

1999. "Should Blacks Represent Blacks and Women Represent Women? A Contingent 'Yes.'" *The Journal of Politics* 61, 3: 628–657.

March, James G., and Johan P. Olsen. 1989. *Rediscovering Institutions : The Organizational Basis of Politics*. New York: Free Press.

March, James G., Lee S. Sproull, and Michal Tamuz. 1991. "Learning from Samples of One or Fewer." *Organization Science* 2: 1–13. Also reprinted as Chapter 8 in James G. March, *The Pursuit Of Organizational Intelligence*. Oxford: Blackwell, 1999: 137–155.

Marchand, Marianne H. 1998. "Different Communities/Different Realities/Different Encounters." *International Studies Quarterly* 42, 1: 199–204.

2003. "Challenging Globalization: Towards a Feminist Understanding of Resistance." *Review of International Studies* 29, special issue (December): 145–160.

Marchand, Marianne, and Jane L. Parpart, eds. 1995. *Feminism/Postmodernism/Development*. London: Routledge.

Marchand, Marianne, and Anne Sisson Runyan, eds. 2000. *Gender and Global Restructuring: Sightings, Sites and Resistances*. New York: Routledge.

Marcus, George. 1992. *Lives in Trust: The Fortunes of Dynastic Families in Late Twentieth-century America*. Boulder: Westview Press.

1995. "Ethnography in/of the World System: The Emergence of Multi-sited Ethnography." *Annual Review of Anthropology* 24: 95–117.

Marx, Karl. [1843] 1967. "Letter to A. Ruge, September 1843." In *Writings of the Young Marx on Philosophy and Society*, ed. and trans. Loyd D. Easton, and Kurt H. Guddats. New York: Doubleday Anchor, 211–215.

Maynard, Mary. 1994. "Methods, Practice and Epistemology: The Debate about Feminism and Research." In *Researching Women's Lives from a Feminist Perspective*, ed. Mary Maynard, and June Purvis. London: Taylor and Francis, 10–26.

Maynard, Mary, and June Purvis. 1994. *Researching Women's Lives from a Feminist Perspective*. London: Taylor and Francis.

Mazur, Amy. 2003. *Theorizing Feminist Policy*. Oxford: Oxford University Press.

Menon, Ritu. 1998. "Reproducing the Legitimate Community: Secularity, Sexuality, and the State in Postpartition India." In *Appropriating Gender: Women's Activism and Politicized Religion in South Asia*, ed. Patricia Jeffrey, and Amrita Basu. New York: Routledge.

1999. "Editorial: Cartographies of Nations and Identities: A Post-partition Predicament." *Interventions* 1, 2: 157–166.

Menon, Ritu, and Kamla Bhasin. 1996. "Abducted Women, the State and Questions of Honor: Three Perspectives in the Recovery Operation in Post-partition India." In *Embodied Violence: Communalising Women's Sexuality in South Asia*, ed. Kumari Jayawardena, and Malathi De Alwis. London: Zed Books.

1998. *Borders and Boundaries: Women in India's Partition*. New Delhi: Kali for Women.

Meola, Lynn. 1997. "Sexual Harassment in the Army," in Laurie Weinstein, and Christie C. White, eds., *Wives and Warriors: Women and the Military in the US and Canada*. Westport and London: Bergin and Garvey, 145–149.

Mies, Maria. 1983. "Towards a Methodology for Feminist Research." In *Theories of Women's Studies*, ed. Gloria Bowles, and Renate Duelli Klein. Boston: Routledge and Kegan, 117–139.

1986. *Patriarchy and Accumulation on a World Scale*. London: Zed Books.

1991. "Women's Research or Feminist Research? The Debate Surrounding Feminist Science and Methodology." In *Beyond Methodology: Feminist Scholarship as Lived Research*, ed. Mary Fonow, and Judith A. Cook. Bloomington and Indianapolis: Indiana University Press, 60–84.

Mies, Maria, and Vandana Shiva. 1993. *Ecofeminism*. London: Zed Books.

Milanovic, Branko. 2002. "True World Income Distribution, 1988 and 1993: First Calculation Based on Household Surveys Alone." *Economic Journal* 112 (January): 51–92.

Millennium: Journal of International Studies. 2001. Special issue, "Images and Narratives in World Politics." 30, 3.

Miller, Errol. 2001. "Gender, Power and Politics: An Alternative Perspective." In *Gender, Peace and Conflict*, Inger Skjelsbaek and Dan Smith, eds. London, Thousand Oaks, and New Dehli: Sage Publications, 80–103.

Milliken, Jennifer. 1999. "The Study of Discourse in International Relations: A Critique of Research and Methods," *European Journal of International Relations* 5, 2: 225–254.

Minh-ha, Trinh T. 1989. *Woman Native Other: Writing Postcoloniality and Feminism*. Bloomington: Indiana University Press.

Ministry of Information. 1984. *History of Bangladesh War of Independence Documents*, vol. 7. Dhaka: Ministry of Information, Government of the People's Republic of Bangladesh.

Minow, Martha. 1990. *Making All the Difference: Inclusion, Exclusion, and American Law*. Ithaca: Cornell University Press.

1998. *Between Vengeance and Forgiveness: Facing History after Genocide and Mass Violence*. Boston: Beacon Press.

Minow, Martha, and Mary Lyndon Shanley. 1997. "Revisioning the Family: Relational Rights and Responsibilities." In *Reconstructing Political Theory: Feminist Perspectives*, ed. Mary Lyndon Shanley, and Uma Narayan. Cambridge: Polity Press, 84–108.

Mjøset, Lars, and Stephen Van Holde. 2002. "Killing for the State, Dying for the Nation: An Introductory Essay on the Life Cycle of Conscription into Europe's Armed Forces." *Comparative Social Research*, special issue: *The Comparative Study of Conscription in the Armed Forces* 20: i–94.

Moghadam, Valentine M., ed. 1994. *Identity Politics and Women: Cultural Reassertions and Feminisms in an International Perspective*. Boulder: Westview Press.

Mohanty, Chandra Talpade. 1991a. "Introduction. Cartographies of Struggle: Third World Women and the Politics of Feminism." In *Third World Women and the Politics of Feminism*, ed. Chandra Talpade Mohanty, Ann Russo, and Lourdes Torres. Bloomington and Indianapolis: Indiana University Press, 1–47.

1991b. "Under Western Eyes: Feminist Scholarship and Colonial Discourses." In *Third World Women and the Politics of Feminism*, ed. Chandra

Talpade Mohanty, Ann Russo, and Lourdes Torres. Bloomington: Indiana University Press, 51–80.

1997. "Women Workers and Capitalist Scripts: Ideologies of Domination, Common Interests, and the Politics of Solidarity." In *Feminist Genealogies, Colonial Legacies, Democratic Futures*, ed. Jacqui Alexander, and Chandra Talpade Mohanty. New York: Routledge.

2003. *Feminism Without Borders: Decolonizing Theory, Practicing Solidarity.* Durham, NC: Duke University Press.

Mohanty, Chandra Talpade, Ann Russo, and Lourdes Torres, eds. 1991. *Third World Women and the Politics of Feminism*. Bloomington and Indianapolis: Indiana University Press.

Molloy, Patricia. 1995. "Subversive Strategies or Subverting Strategy? Towards a Feminist Pedagogy for Peace." *Alternatives* 20: 225–242.

1997. "Face to Face with the Dead Man: Ethical Responsibility, State-Sanctioned Killing, and Empathetic Impossibility." *Alternatives* 22, 4: 467–492.

Molyneux, Maxine. 1998. "Analyzing Women's Movements." In *Feminist Visions of Development: Gender Analysis and Policy*, ed. Cecile Jackson, and Ruth Pearson. London and New York: Routledge, 65–88.

Moody-Adams, Michele M. 1997. *Fieldwork in Familiar Places: Morality, Culture and Philosophy*. Cambridge, MA: Harvard University Press, 1997.

Moon, Katherine. 1997. *Sex Among Allies*. New York: Columbia University Press.

Moravcsik, Andrew. 2000. "The Origins of Human Rights Regimes: Democratic Delegation in Post-war Europe." *International Organization* 54, 2: 217–52.

Mudimbé, V. Y. 1988. *The Invention of Africa: Gnosis, Philosophy, and the Order of Knowledge*. Bloomington: Indiana University Press.

1994. *The Idea of Africa*. Bloomington: Indiana University Press.

1998. *Nations, Identities, Cultures*. Durham: Duke University Press.

Mulvey, Laura. 1989. *Visual and Other Pleasures*. Bloomington: Indiana University Press.

Muran, Elizabeth, and Raymond DiGiuseppe. 2000. "Rape Trauma." In *Cognitive Behavioral Strategies in Crisis Intervention*. Second ed., eds. Frank Datiilio, and Arthur Freeman. New York: Guilford, 150–165.

Murphy, Craig. 1998. "Six Masculine Roles in International Relations and Their Interconnection: A Personal Investigation." In *The 'Man' Question in International Relations*, ed. Marysia Zalewski, and Jane Parpart. Boulder: Westview Press, 93–108.

Nader, Laura. 1972. "Up the Anthropologist: Perspectives Gained from Studying Up." In *Reinventing Anthropology*, ed. Dell Hymes. New York: Pantheon.

Nagar, Richa. 2002. "Footloose Researchers, Traveling Theories and the Politics of Transnational Feminist Praxis." *Gender, Place and Culture* 9, 2: 179–186.

Nagar, Richa, Victoria Lawson, Linda McDowell, and Susan Hanson. 2002. "Locating Globalization: Feminist (Re)readings of the Subjects and Spaces of Globalization." *Economic Geography* 78, 3: 257–284.

Nagar, Richa, (in consultation with Farah Ali and the Sangatin Women's Collective). 2003. "Collaboration Across Borders: Moving Beyond Positionality." *Singapore Journal of Tropical Geography* 24, 3: 356–372.

⎯⎯. 1997. "Exploring Methodological Borderlands Through Oral Narratives." In *Thresholds in Feminist Geography*, ed. John Paul Jones III, Heidi J. Nast, and Susan M. Roberts. Lanham: Rowman and Littlefield, 203–224.

Naples, Nancy A. 2003. *Feminism and Method: Ethnography, Discourse Analysis, and Activist Research*. New York and London: Routledge.

Narayan, Uma. 1989. "The Project of Feminist Epistemology: Perspectives from a Nonwestern Feminist." In *Gender/Body/Knowledge: Feminist Reconstructions of Being and Knowing*, ed. Alison M. Jaggar, and Susan R. Bordo. New Brunswick: Rutgers University Press, 256–269.

⎯⎯. 1995. "Colonialism and its Others: Considerations on Rights and Care Discourses." *Hypatia* 10, 2: 133–140.

⎯⎯. 1997. *Dislocating Cultures: Identities, Traditions and Third World Feminism*. New York: Routledge.

Narayan, Deepa, with Raj Patel, Kai Schafft, Anne Rademacher, and Sarah Koch-Schulte. 2000. *Voices of the Poor: Can Anyone Hear Us?* New York: Oxford University Press.

Narayan, Uma, and Sandra Harding, eds. 2000. *Decentering the Center: Philosophy for a Multicultural, Post-colonial, and Feminist World*. Bloomington: Indiana University Press.

Nardin, Terry, ed. 1996. *The Ethics of War and Peace: Religious and Secular Perspectives*. Princeton: Princeton University Press.

Nedelsky, Jennifer. 1993. "Reconceiving Rights as Relationship." *Review of Constitutional Studies* 1, 1: 1–26.

Nelson, Diane M. 1999. *A Finger in the Wound: Body Politics in Quincentennial Guatemala*. Berkeley: University of California Press.

Nelson, Lynn Hankinson. 1993. "Epistemological Communities." In *Feminist Epistemologies*, ed. Linda Alcoff, and Elizabeth Potter. London: Routledge, 121–160.

Neufeld, Mark. 1993. "Reflexivity and International Relations Theory." *Millennium* 22, 1: 53–76.

Neumann, Iver B. 1998. "European Identity, EU Expansion, and the Integration/Exclusion Nexus." *Alternatives* 23: 397–416.

Newhouse, Victoria. 1998. *Towards a New Museum*. New York: Monacelli Press.

Ngara, Abigail Urey. 1985. "Women: African Women Fight Circumcision." Interpress Service. Harare, Zimbabwe, August 15, 1985.

Nielsen, Joyce McCarl, ed. 1990. *Feminist Research Methods: Exemplary Readings in the Social Sciences*. Boulder: Westview Press.

Nilsson, Anne. 1990. *Kvinnan som officer*. Försvar i Nutid 90:2. Stockholm: Centralförbundet Folk och Försvar.

Nordstrom, Carolyn. 1995. "Creativity and Chaos: War on the Frontlines." In *Fieldwork Under Fire: Contemporary Studies of Violence and Survival*, ed. Carolyn Nordstrom and Antonius Robben. Berkeley: University of California Press: 129–154.

1997. *A Different Kind of War Story.* Philadelphia: University of Pennsylvania Press.

Nussbaum, Martha C. 2000. *Women and Human Development: The Capabilities Approach.* Cambridge: Cambridge University Press.

O'Brien, Robert, Anne Marie Goetz, Jan Aart Scholte, and Marc Williams. 2000. *Contesting Global Governance: Multilateral Economic Institutions and Global Social Movements.* Cambridge: Cambridge University Press.

Ochberg, Richard L., and George C. Rosenwald, eds. 1992. *Storied Lives: The Cultural Politics of Self-understanding.* New Haven: Yale University Press.

Oddysseos, Louiza. 2001. "Laughing Matters: Peace, Democracy, and the Challenge of the Comic Narrative." *Millennium* 30, 3: 709–732.

O'Donnell, Patrick. 2000. *Latent Destinies: Cultural Paranoia and Contemporary U.S Narrative.* Durham, NC: Duke University Press.

O'Donohue, John. 2000. *Conamara Blues.* London: Doubleday.

Oguibe, Olu. 1994. "A Brief Note on Internationalism." In *Global Visions Towards a New Internationalism in the Visual Arts*, ed. Jean Fisher. London: Kala Press, 50–59.

O'Leary, Catherine. 1997. "Counteridentification or Counterhegemony? Transforming Feminist Standpoint Theory." *Women and Politics* 18, 3: 45–72.

Olson, Karen, and Linda Shopes. 1991. "Crossing Boundaries, Building Bridges: Doing Oral History among Working-Class Women and Men." In *Women's Words: The Feminist Practice of Oral History*, eds. Herna B. Gluck and Daphne Patai. New York: Routledge: 189–204.

O'Neill, Onora. 1992. "Justice, Gender and International Boundaries." In *The Quality of Life*, ed. Martha Nussbaum, and Amartya Sen. Oxford: Oxford University Press.

1994. "Justice and Boundaries." In *Political Restructuring in Europe: Ethical Perspectives*, ed. Chris Brown London: Routledge.

2000. *Bounds of Justice.* Cambridge: Cambridge University Press.

Okin, Susan Moller. 1989. *Gender, Justice and the Family.* New York: Basic Books.

Onuf, Nicholas. 2002. "Institutions, Intentions and International Relations." *Review of International Studies* 28, 2: 211–228.

Orwell, George. 1954. "Politics and the English Language." In *George Orwell: A Collection of Essays.* Garden City: Doubleday.

Osburn, C. Dixon, and Michelle M. Benecke. 1997. "Conduct Unbecoming: Second Annual Report on 'Don't Ask, Don't Tell, Don't Pursue.'" In *Wives and Warriors: Women and the Military in the US and Canada*, ed. Laurie Weinstein and Christie C. White. Westport and London: Bergin and Garvey, 151–177.

Parker, Andrew, Mary Russo, Doris Sommer, and Patricia Yaeger. 1992. *Nationalisms and Sexualities.* New York: Routledge.

Passerini, Luisa, ed. 1992. *Totalitarianism and Memory: International Yearbook of Oral History and Life Stories*, vol. 1. Oxford: Oxford University Press.

Pateman, Carole. 1988. *The Sexual Contract.* Stanford: Stanford University Press.

1989. *Feminism, Democracy and Political Theory.* Stanford: Stanford University Press.

Payne, Michael, ed. 1997. *A Dictionary of Cultural and Critical Theory.* Oxford: Blackwell.

Pearson, Ruth. 2004. "The Social is Political: Towards the Re-politicization of Feminist Analysis of the Global Economy." *International Feminist Journal of Politics*, 6, 4: 603–622.

Perks, Robert, and Alistair Thompson, eds. 1998. *The Oral History Reader.* London: Routledge.

Peterson, V. Spike. 1990. "Whose Rights?: A Critique of the Givens." *Alternatives* 15: 303–344.

   ed. 1992a. *Gendered States: Feminist (Re)Visions of International Relations Theory.* Boulder: Lynne Rienner Publishers.

   1992b. "Transgressing Boundaries: Theories of Knowledge, Gender, and International Relations." *Millennium* 21, 2: 183–206.

   1993. *Global Gender Issues.* Boulder: Westview Press.

   2003. *A Critical Rewriting of Global Political Economy: Integrating Reproductive, Productive, and Virtual Economies.* London: Routledge.

Peterson, V. Spike, and Anne Sisson Runyan. 1993. *Global Gender Issues.* Boulder: Westview Press.

Peterson, V. Spike, and Anne Sisson Runyan. 1998. *Global Gender Politics.* Second ed. Boulder: Westview Press.

Peterson, V. Spike, and Jacqui True. 1998. "New Times and New Conversations." In *The "Man" Question in International Relations*, ed. Marysia Zalewski, and Jane Parpart. Boulder: Westview Press, 14–27.

Pettman, Jan Jindy. 1996. *Worlding Women: A Feminist International Politics.* New York: Routledge.

Phillips, Anne. 1991. *Engendering Democracy.* University Park: Pennsylvania State University Press.

Phoenix, Ann. 1994. "Practising Feminist Research: The Intersection of Gender and 'Race' in the Research Process." In *Researching Women's Lives from a Feminist Perspective*, ed. Mary Maynard, and June Purvis. London: Taylor and Francis, 49–71.

Pin-Fat, Véronique. 2000. "(Im)possible Universalism: Reading Human Rights in World Politics." *Review of International Studies* 26, 4: 663–674.

Pin-Fat, Véronique, and Maria Stern. 2005. "The Scripting of Private Jessica Lynch: Biopolitics, Gender and the 'Feminisation' of the US Military." *Alternatives: Local, Global, Political* 30, 1: 25–53.

Poe, Steven C., Dierdre Wendel-Blunt, and Karl Ho. 1997. "Global Patterns in the Achievement of Women's Human Rights to Equality." *Human Rights Quarterly* 19, 4: 813–835.

Pollock, Griselda. 1992. "The Gaze and the Look: Women With Binoculars – A Question of Difference." In *Dealing With Degas: Representations of Women and the Politics of Vision*, ed. Richard Kendall and Griselda Pollock. New York: Universe.

Porter, Marilyn, and Ellen Judd. 1999. *Feminists Doing Development: A Practical Critique.* London: Zed Books.

Prasad, Bimal. 2001. *The Foundations of Muslim Nationalism.* Dhaka: The University Press.

Price, Richard, and Christian Reus-Smit. 1998. "Dangerous Liasions: The Constructivist-Critical Theory Debate in International Relations." *European Journal of International Relations* 4, 3: 259–294.

Prügl, Elisabeth. 1999. *The Global Construction of Gender: Home-based Work in the Political Economy of the Twentieth Century.* New York: Columbia University Press.

Prügl, Elisabeth, and Mary K. Meyer, eds. 1999. *Gender and Global Governance.* Lanham: Rowman and Littlefield.

Radhakrishnan, Raj. 1992. "Nationalism, Gender, and the Narrative of Identity." In *Diasporic Mediations: Between Home and Location*, ed. Raj Radhakrishnan. Minnesota: University of Minnesota Press, 185–202.

Rahman, Hasan Hafizur, ed. 1984. *Bangaladesher Shadhinata Judhyo: Dililptro*, vol. 8. Dhaka: Tothyo Montronaloy, Gonoprojatontri Bangaladesh Sharkar.

Randall, Vicky, and Georgiana Waylen, eds. 1998. *Gender, Politics and the State.* London: Routledge.

Rathgeber, Eva M. 1995. "Gender and Development in Action." In *Feminism/ Postmodernism/Development*, ed. Marianne H. Marchand, and Jane L. Parpart. London: Routledge, 204–220.

Rawls, John. 1993. "The Law of Peoples." In *On Human Rights: The Oxford Amnesty Lectures 1993*, ed. Stephen Shute, and Susan Hurley. New York: Basic Books, 41–82.

   1999. *The Law of Peoples.* Cambridge, MA: Harvard University Press.

Razavi, S., Pearson, R., and Danloy, C., eds. 2004. *Globalization, Export-Oriented Employment and Social Policy: Gendered Connections.* Basingstoke: Palgrave-Macmillan.

Reardon, Betty. 1985. *Sexism and the War System.* New York: Teacher's College Press.

   1993. *Woman and Peace: Feminist Versions of Global Security.* New York: SUNY Press.

Reed, Evelyn. [1970] 1984. "Women: Caste, Class, or Oppressed Sex?" In *Feminist Frameworks: Alternative Theoretical Accounts of the Relations between Women and Men*, ed. Alison M. Jaggar, and Paula S. Rothenberg. New York: McGraw-Hill, 170–173.

Reinharz, Shulamit. 1993. "Neglected Voices and Excessive Demands in Feminist Research." *Qualitative Sociology* 16, 1: 69–76.

Reinharz, Shulamit, with Lynn Davidman. 1992. *Feminist Methods in Social Research.* New York: Oxford University Press.

Ricks, Thomas. 1997. "The Widening Gap Between the Military and Society." *The Atlantic Monthly* 280, 1: 66–78.

Risman, Barbara J. 1993. "Methodological Implications of Feminist Scholarship." *The American Sociologist* 24, 3/4: 15–25.

Risse, Thomas, Kathryn Sikkink, and Stephen Ropp, eds. *The Power of Human Rights.* Cambridge: Cambridge University Press.

Robertson, Geoffrey. 1999. *Crimes Against Humanity: The Struggle for Global Justice.* New York: New Press.

Robinson, Fiona. 1999. *Globalizing Care: Ethics, Feminist Theory, and International Relations.* Boulder: Westview Press.

2003. "Human Rights and the Global Politics of Resistance: Feminist Perspectives." *Review of International Studies* 29, special issue: 161–180.

Rodrik, Dani. 1999. "Governing the Global Economy: Does One Architectural Style Fit All?" *Brookings Trade Forum*, 1: 105–140.

2001. "Trading in Illusions." *Foreign Policy* 123: 54–64.

Rosenau, James N., ed. 1993. *Global Voices: Dialogues in International Relations*. Boulder: Westview Press.

Rowell, Margit. 1997. *Objects of Desire: The Modern Still Life*. New York: Museum of Modern Art.

Ruddick, Sara. 1989. *Maternal Thinking: Towards a Politics of Peace*. Boston: Beacon Press.

1990. "The Rationality of Care." In *Women, Militarism, and War*, ed. J. B. Elshtain and S. Tobias. Savage: Rowman and Littlefield.

Rycenga, Jennife, ed. 2001. *Frontline Feminisms: Women, War, and Resistance*. New York: Routledge.

Said, Edward W. 1993. *Culture and Imperialism*. New York: Knopf.

[1978] 1994. *Orientalism*. New York: Vintage Books.

Sandoval, Chela. 1991. "US Third World Feminism: The Theory and Method of Oppositional Consciousness in the Postmodern World." *Genders* 10: 1–24.

Sangari, Kumkum, and Sudesh Vaid. 1994. *Women and Culture*. Bombay: Research Centre for Women's Studies.

Sangster, Joan. 1998. "Telling our Stories: Feminist Debates and the Use of Oral History." In *The Oral History Reader*, ed. Robert Perks, and Alistair Thompson. London: Routledge, 87–100.

Scarry, Elaine. 1985. *The Body in Pain: The Making and Unmaking of the World*. Oxford: Oxford University Press.

SCB Statistics. 2002. Statistics from the Swedish Central Bureau of Statistics. Available online at <http://www.scb.se>.

Schnall, David J. 1979. *Radical Dissent in Contemporary Israeli Politics: Cracks in the Wall*. New York: Praeger Publishers.

Scott, James C. 1985. *Weapons of the Weak*. New Haven: Yale University Press.

1990. *Domination and the Arts of Resistance: Hidden Transcripts*. New Haven: Yale University Press.

Scott, Joan. 1992. *Gender and the Politics of History*. Princeton: Princeton University Press.

Seager, Joni. 2003. *The Penguin Atlas of Women in the World Completely Revised and Updated*: Harmondsworth: Penguin.

Security Dialogue, 2004. vol. 35, 3.

Seidman, Steven. 2001. "From Identity to Queer Politics: Shifts in Normative Heterosexuality." In *The New Social Theory Reader*, Steven Seidman and Jeffrey Alexander. New York: Routledge: 353–360.

Seifert, Ruth. 1993. *War Rape: Analytical Approaches*. Geneva: Women's International League for Peace and Freedom.

Seigfried, Charlene Haddock, ed. 2002. *Feminist Interpretations of John Dewey*. University Park: Pennsylvania State University Press.

Sen, Amartya. 1990a. "Gender and Cooperative Conflicts." In *Persistent Inequalities: Women and World Development*, ed. Irene Tinker. New York: Oxford University Press, 123–149.
———. 1990b. "More than 100 Million Women Are Missing." *New York Review of Books* 37: 61–66.
Sen, Gita, and Caren Grown. 1987. *Development, Crisis, and Alternative Visions: Third World Women's Perspectives.* New York: Monthly Review Press.
Seu, Bruna I., and Colleen M. Heenan. 1998. *Feminism and Psychotherapy: Reflections on Contemporary Theories and Practices.* Thousand Oaks: Sage.
Sevenhuijsen, Selma. 2000. "Caring in the Third Way: The Relation between Obligation, Responsibility and Care in *Third Way* Discourse." *Critical Social Policy* 20, 1: 5–37.
———. 2001. "South African Social Policy and the Ethic of Care." Paper prepared for the annual meeting of the American Political Science Association, August–September, 2001.
———. 2003. "The Place of Care: The Relevance of the Feminist Ethic of Care for Social Policy." *Feminist Theory* 4, 2: 179–197.
Sharoni, Simona. 1994. *Gender and the Israeli–Palestinian Conflict: The Politics of Women's Resistance.* New York: Syracuse University Press.
Shaw, Martin. 1994. *Global Society and International Relations: Sociological Concepts and Political Perspectives.* Cambridge: Polity Press.
Sikkink, Kathryn. 2000. "Restructuring World Politics: The Limits and Asymmetries of Soft Power." In *Restructuring World Politics: Transnational Social Movements, Networks, and Norms*, ed. Sanjeev Khagram, James V. Riker, and Kathryn Sikkink. Minneapolis: University of Minnesota Press, 301–318.
Sission Runyan, Anne, and V. Spike Peterson. 1991. "The Radical Future of Realism: Feminist Subversion of International Relations Theory." *Alternatives* 16: 67–106.
Smith, Dorothy E., 1987. *The Everyday World as Problematic: A Feminist Sociology.* Boston: Northeastern University Press.
———. 1990a. *Texts, Facts, and Femininty: Exploring the Relations of Ruling.* New York: Routledge.
———. 1990b. *The Conceptual Practices of Power: A Feminist Sociology of Knowledge.* Boston: Northeastern University Press.
———. 1999. *Writing the Social: Critique, Theory, and Investigations.* Toronto: University of Toronto Press.
Smith, Linda Tuhiwai. 1999. *Decolonizing Methodologies: Research and Indigenous Peoples.* London: Zed Books.
Smith, Neil. 1997. "The Satanic Geographies of Globalization: Uneven Development in the 1990s," *Public Culture* 10, 1:169–189.
Smith, Steve, Ken Booth, and Marysia Zalewski, eds. 1996. *International Theory: Positivism and Beyond.* Cambridge: Cambridge University Press.
Snider, Lauren. 2003. "Constituting the Punishable Woman." *British Journal of Criminology* 43, 2: 354–378.
Sobhan, Salma. 1994. "National Identity, Fundamentalism and the Women's Movement in Bangladesh." In *Gender and National Identity: Women and*

Politics in Muslim Societies, ed. Valentine M. Moghadam. London: Zed Books, 63–80.

Sommer, Doris. 1991. "Rigoberta's Secrets." *Latin American Perspectives* 18, 3: 32–50.

SOU 1965: 68. *Värnplikten*. Stockholm: Försvarsdepartementet.

SOU 1977: 26. *Kvinnan och Försvarets Yrken*. Stockholm, Försvarsdepartementet.

SOU 1984: 63. Homosexuella och samhället. Stockholm: Socialdepartementet.

SOU 1984: 71. *Värnplikten i Framtiden*. Stockholm, Försvarsdepartementet.

SOU 1992: 139. *Totalförsvarsplikt*. Stockholm: Försvarsdepartementet.

SOU 2000: 21. *Totalförsvarsplikten*. Stockholm: Försvarsdepartementet.

Spelman, Elizabeth V., 1988. *Inessential Woman: Problems of Exclusion in Feminist Thought*. Boston: Beacon Press.

Spivak, Gayatri Chakrabarty. 1988. "Can the Subaltern Speak?" In *Marxism and the Interpretation of Culture*, ed. C. Nelson, and L. Grossberg. Basingstoke: Macmillan Education, 271–313.

Srinivas, M. N., A. M. Shah, and E. A. Ramaswamy. 1979. *The Fieldworker and the Field: Problems and Challenges in Sociological Investigation*. Delhi: Oxford University Press.

Stacey, Judith. 1988. "Can There be a Feminist Ethnography?" *Women's Studies International Forum* 11, 1: 21–27.

Stack, Carol B. 1996. "Writing Ethnography: Feminist Critical Practice." In *Feminist Dilemmas in Fieldwork*, ed. Diane L. Wolf. Boulder: Westview Press: 96–106.

Staeheli, Lynn, and Richa Nagar. 2002. "Feminists Talking Across Worlds." *Gender, Place and Culture* 9, 2: 167–172.

Stanley, Liz, ed. 1990. *Feminist Praxis: Research, Theory and Epistemology in Feminist Sociology*. London: Routledge and Kegan Paul.

Stanley, Liz, and Sue Wise. 1990. "Method, Methodology and Epistemology in Feminist Research Processes." In *Feminist Praxis*, ed. Liz Stanley. London: Routledge and Kegan Paul, 20–60.

1993. *Breaking Out Again: Feminist Ontology and Epistemology*. London and New York: Routledge.

Steans, Jill. 1997. *Gender and International Relations: An Introduction*. Oxford: Polity Press.

2003. "Engaging from the Margins: Feminist Encounters with the 'Mainstream' of International Relations." *British Journal of Politics and International Relations* 5, 3: 428–454.

Stephens, Julie. 1989. "Feminist Fictions: A Critique of the Category 'Non-Western Woman' in Feminist Writings on India." In *Subaltern Studies*, VI: *Writings on South Asian History and Society*. Ranajit Guha, ed. Delhi: Oxford University Press.

Stephenson, Carolyn M. 1988. "The Need for Alternative Forms of Security: Crises and Opportunities." In *Alternatives: Social Transformation and Humane Governance* 13, 1: 55–76.

Stern, Daniel. 2004. *The Present Moment in Psychotherapy and Everyday Life*. New York: Norton.

Stern, Maria. 2001. *Naming In/security – Constructing Identity: Mayan Women in Guatemala on the Eve of Peace*. Göteborg: Padrigu Thesis Series.

2002. "Doing Feminist International Relations: A Discussion on Methodology." Paper presented at International Studies Association Annual Conference, New Orleans.

2005. *Naming Security – Constructing Identity: Mayan Women in Guatemala on the Eve of "Peace."* Manchester: Manchester University Press.

Sternbach, Nancy, Marysa Navarro-Aranguren, Patricia Chuchryk, and Sonia E. Alvarez. 1992. "Feminisms in Latin America: From Bogotá to San Bernardo." *Signs* 17, 2: 393–434.

Stiehm, Judith Hicks, ed. 1983. *Women and Men's Wars.* Oxford: Pergamon Press.

ed. 1996. *It's Our Military Too! Women and the US Military.* Philadelphia: Temple University Press.

1999. "United Nations Peacekeeping: Men and Women's Work." In *Gender Politics and Global Governance*, ed. Mary K. Meyer, and Elizabeth Prügl. Lanham: Rowman and Littlefield, 43–57.

Stienstra, Deborah. 1994. *Women's Movements and International Organizations.* London: Macmillan.

1994-5. "Can the Silence be Broken? Gender and Canadian Foreign Policy." *International Journal* Winter: 103–127.

Stiglmayar, Alexandra, ed. 1994. *Mass Rape: The War against Women in Bosnia-Herzegovina.* Lincoln, NE, and London: University of Nebraska Press.

Subramaniam, Banu. 2001. "Snow Brown and the Seven Detergents: A Metanarrative on Science and the Scientific Method." In *Women, Science and Technology*, Mary Wyer et al. London: Routledge, 36–41.

Suleri, Sara. 1992. *The Rhetoric of English India.* Chicago: University of Chicago Press.

Svedberg, Erika, and Annica Kronsell. 2003. "Feministisk metod, teori och forskning om identiteter." In *Identitetsstudier i praktiken*, ed. Bo Petersson, and Alexa Robertson. Malmö: Liber, 53–69.

Sylvester, Christine. 1987. "Some Dangers in Merging Feminist and Peace Perspectives." *Alternatives* 12, 4: 493–509.

1992a. "Feminist Theory and Gender Studies in International Relations." *International Studies Notes* 16/17, 3/1: 32–38.

1992b. "Feminists and Realists View Autonomy and Obligation in International Relations." In *Gendered States*, ed. V. Spike Peterson. Boulder: Lynne Rienner Publishers.

1994a. *Feminist Theory and International Relations in a Postmodern Era.* Cambridge: Cambridge University Press.

1994b. "Empathetic Co-operation: A Feminist Method for IR." *Millennium* 23, 3: 315–334.

1996a. "Picturing the Cold War: An Eye Graft/Art Graft." *Alternatives* 21, 4: 393–418.

1996b. "The Contributions of Feminist Theory to International Relations." In *International Theory: Positivism and Beyond*, ed. Steve Smith, Ken Booth, and Marysia Zalewski. Cambridge: Cambridge University Press, 254–278.

1998. "Handmaids' Tales of Washington Power: The Abject and the Real Kennedy White House." *Body and Society* 4, 3: 39–66.

1999. "(Sur)Real Internationalism: Emigrés, Native Sons, and Ethical War Creations." *Alternatives* 24, 2: 219–247.

2001. "Art, Abstraction, and International Relations." *Millennium* 30, 3: 535–554.

2002. *Feminist International Relations: An Unfinished Journey.* Cambridge: Cambridge University Press.

2004. "Woe or Whoa! International Relations Where It's Not Supposed to Be." *Brown Journal of World Affairs* 10, 2: 57–68.

Taylor, Charles. 1996. "A World Consensus on Human Rights?" *Dissent* Summer: 15–21.

1999. "Conditions of an Unforced Consensus on Human Rights." In *The East Asian Challenge for Human Rights*, ed. Joanne R. Bauer, and Daniel Bell. Cambridge: Cambridge University Press, 124–144.

Terriff, Terry, with Stuart Croft, Lucy James, and Patrick M. Morgan. 1999. *Security Studies Today.* Cambridge: Polity Press.

Tessler, Mark, and Ina Warriner. 1997. "Gender, Feminism, and Attitudes toward International Conflict: Exploring Relationships with Survey-data from the Middle East." *World Politics* 49, 2: 250–281.

Thompson, Paul. 1998. "The Voice of the Past: Oral History." In *The Oral History Reader*, ed. Robert Perks, and Alistair Thompson. London: Routledge, 21–28.

2000. *The Voice of the Past: Oral History.* Oxford: Oxford University Press.

Tickner, J. Ann. 1988. "Hans Morganthau's Principles of Political Realism: A Feminist Reformulation." *Millennium* 17, 3: 429–440.

1992. *Gender in International Relations: Feminist Perspectives on Achieving Global Security.* New York: Columbia University Press.

1994. "A Feminist Critique of Political Realism." In *Women, Gender and World Politics: Perspectives, Policies and Prospects*, ed. Peter R. Beckman, and Francine D'Amico. Westport: Bergin and Garvey, 29–40.

1997. "You Just Don't Understand: Troubled Engagements Between Feminists and IR Theorists." *International Studies Quarterly* 41, 4: 611–32.

1998. "Continuing the Conversation. . ." *International Studies Quarterly* 41, 4: 205–210.

1999. "Why Women Can't Run the World: International Politics According to Francis Fukuyama." *International Studies Review* 1, 3: 3–12.

2001. *Gendering World Politics: Issues and Approaches in the Post-Cold War Era.* New York: Columbia University Press.

Tilly, Charles. 1990. *Coercion, Capital and European States AD 990–1990.* Oxford: Blackwell.

Tinker, Irene. 1999. "Nongovernmental Organizations: An Alternative Power Base for Women?" In *Gender Politics in Global Governance*, ed. Mary K. Meyer, and Elisabeth Prügl. Boulder: Rowman and Littlefield, 88–106.

Tong, Rosemarie. 1989. *Feminist Thought: A Comprehensive Introduction.* New York: Routledge.

Toulmin, Stephen. 1996. "Concluding Methodological Reflections: Elitism and Democracy among the Sciences." In *Beyond Theory: Changing Organizations through Participation*, ed. Stephen Toulmin, and Bjorn Gustavsen. Amsterdam: John Benjamins Publishing Company, 203–225.

Traweek, Sharon. 1988. *Beamtimes and Lifetimes: The World of High Energy Physics.* Cambridge, MA: Harvard University Press.

Tronto, Joan. 1993. *Moral Boundaries: A Political Argument for an Ethic of Care.* New York: Routledge.

1995. "Care as a Basis for Radical Political Judgment." *Hypatia* 10, 2: 141–149.

True, Jacqui. 1999. "Expanding Markets and Marketing Gender: The Integration of the Post-socialist Czech Republic." *Review of International Political Economy* 6, 3: 360–89.

2001. "Feminism." In *Theories of International Relations, Second Edition,* ed. Scott Burchill, and Andrew Linklater, with Richard Devetak, Matthew Paterson, and Jacqui True. New York: Palgrave.

2002. "Engendering International Relations: What Difference Does Second Generation Feminism Make?" Department of International Relations Working Paper, RSPAS, Australian National University. Available online at <http://rspas.anu.edu.au/ir/working%20papers/02-1.pdf>.

2003. *Gender, Globalization, and Postsocialism: The Czech Republic after Communism.* New York: Columbia University Press.

2004. "Engendering Social Transformations." In P. Goff, and K. Dunn, eds. *Identity in International Relations.* New York: Palgrave.

True, Jacqui, and Michael Mintrom. 2001. "Transnational Networks and Policy Diffusion: The Case of Gender Mainstreaming." *International Studies Quarterly* 45, 1: 27–57.

UNDP (United Nations Development Programme). 1994. *Human Development Report 1994.* New York: Oxford University Press.

1996. *Human Development Report 1995.* New York: Oxford University Press.

1999. *Human Development Report 1999.* New York: Oxford University Press.

2000. *Human Development Report 2000.* New York: Oxford University Press.

United Nations News Agency. 1999. "14 Women Foreign Ministers Seek to End to Human Trafficking." October 15.

Van Creveld, Martin. 2001. *Men, Women and War.* London: Cassell.

Venturi, Robert, Denise Scott Brown, and Steven Izenour. 1972. *Learning from Las Vegas.* Cambridge, MA: MIT Press.

Viola, Bill. 2003. "Sources." In *Bill Viola: The Passions,* ed. John Walsh. Los Angeles: Getty Publications, 223–255.

Wade, Robert. 2001. "Winners and Losers: By Invitation Robert Wade on Global Inequality." *The Economist,* April 8, 1–5.

2002. "Letter to Martin Wolf." *Prospect Magazine,* January 22.

Wæver, Ole. 1995. "Securitization and Desecuritization." In *Security and the Nation State,* ed. Ronnie Lipschutz and Beverly Crawford. New York: Columbia University Press, 46–86. Also printed as Working Paper no. 5/1993, Centre for Peace and Conflict Research, Copenhagen.

Wägnerud, Lena. 1999. *Kvinnorepresenation: Makt och möjligheter i Sveriges riksdag.* Lund: Studentlitteratur.

Wahl, Anna, Charlotte Holgerson, Pia Höök, and Sophie Linghag. 2001. *Det ordanar sig: Teorier om organization och kön.* Lund: Studentlitteratur.

Walker, Margaret Urban. 1998. *Moral Understandings: A Feminist Study in Ethics.* New York: Routledge.

Walker, R. B. J., 1993. *Inside/Outside: International Relations as Political Theory.* Cambridge Studies in International Relations. Cambridge: Cambridge University Press.

1999. "Forum on the Transformation of Political Community." *Review of International Studies* 25, 1: 139–142.

Waller, Marguerite R., and Jennifer Rycenga, eds. 2000. *Frontline Feminisms: Women, War and Resistance.* New York: Garland Publishing.

Waltz, Kenneth. 1998. "Interview with Ken Waltz, Conducted by Fred Halliday and Justin Rosenberg." *Review of International Studies* 24, 3: 371–386.

2001. *Man, the State, and War: A Theoretical Analysis.* Revised ed. New York: Columbia University Press.

Wapner, Paul. 1996. *Environmental Activism and World Civic Politics.* Albany: State University of New York Press.

Waring, Marilyn. 1988. *If Women Counted: A New Feminist Economics.* San Francisco: Harper and Row.

Weber, Cynthia. 1994. "Good Girls, Bad Girls and Little Girls: Male Paranoia in Robert Keohane's Critique of Feminist International Relations." *Millennium* 23, 2: 337–349.

2001. *International Relations Theory: A Critical Introduction.* London: Routledge.

Weeks, Kathi. 1998. *Constituting Feminist Subjects.* Ithaca: Cornell University Press.

Weibull, Louise. 2001. *Tjejmönstring: Lyckad rekrytering eller lockad rekryt?* Försvarshögskolan, L1, Serie F:18.

Weldes, Jutta, Mark Laffey, Hugh Gusterson, and Raymond Duvall, eds. 1999. *Cultures of Insecurity: States, Communities and the Production of Danger.* Minneapolis: University of Minnesota Press.

Weldon. S. Laurel. 2002. *Protest, Policy and the Problem of Violence Against Women: A Cross-national Comparison.* Pittsburgh: University of Pittsburgh Press.

Forthcoming, 2006. "Inclusion, Solidarity and Social Movements: The Global Movement Against Gender Violence." *Perspectives on Politics.* March.

Welton, Katherine. 1997. "Nancy Hartsock's Standpoint Theory: From Content to 'Concrete Multiplicity.'" *Women and Politics* 18, 3: 7–24.

Wendt, Alexander. 1991. "Bridging the Theory/Meta-theory Gap in International Relations." *Review of International Studies* 17, 4: 383–393.

1999. *Social Theory of International Politics.* Cambridge: Cambridge University Press.

Weston, Kath. 2002. *Gender in Real Time: Power and Transcience in a Visual Age.* London and New York: Routledge.

Westwood, Sallie, and Sarah Radcliffe. 1993. *"Viva": Women and Popular Protest in Latin America.* London: Routledge.

1996. *Remaking the Nation: Place, Identity and Politics in Latin America.* London: Routledge.

White, Stephen K., 2000. *Sustaining Affirmation: The Strengths of Weak Ontology in Political Theory.* Princeton: Princeton University Press.

Whitebrooke, Marianne. 2001. *Identity, Narrative and Politics*. London: Routledge.
Whitehead, Tony Larry, and Mary Ellen Conaway, eds. 1986. *Self, Sex and Gender in Cross-Cultural Fieldwork*. Urbana: University of Illinois Press.
Whitworth, Sandra. 1989a. "Gender and International Relations: Beyond the Interparadigm Debate." *Millennium* 18, 2: 265–72.
    1989b. "Gender in the Inter-paradigm Debate." *Millennium* 18, 2: 265–72.
    1994. *Feminism and International Relations: Towards a Political Economy of Gender in Interstate and Non-governmental Institutions*. Basingstoke: Macmillan.
    1997. "Theory as Exclusion: Gender and International Political Economy." In *Political Economy and the Changing Global Order*, ed. R. Stubbs, and G. Underhill. Basingstoke: Macmillan.
    2001. "The Practice, and Praxis, of Feminist Research in International Relations." In *Critical Theory and World Politics*, ed. Richard Wyn Jones. Boulder: Westview Press, 149–160.
Williams, Melissa. 1998. *Voice, Trust and Memory: Marginalized Groups and the Failings of Liberal Representation*. Princeton: Princeton University Press.
Williams, Patricia. 1991. *The Alchemy of Race and Rights*. Cambridge: Harvard University Press.
Williams, Patrick, and Laura Chrisman, eds. 1993. *Colonial Discourse and Postcolonial Theory: A Reader*. New York: Harvester Wheatsheaf.
Wolf, Diane L. 1996. "Situating Feminist Dilemmas in Fieldwork." In *Feminist Dilemmas in Fieldwork*, ed. Diane L. Wolf. Boulder: Westview Press, 1–55.
Wolf, Eric. 1969. "American Anthropologists and American Society." In *Concepts and Assumptions in Contemporary Anthropology*, ed. Stephen A. Tyler. Proceedings of the Southern Anthropological Society no. 3. Athens: University of Georgia Press, 3–11.
Women's Caucus for International Studies. 1998. *New Agenda Recommendations: For Implementation by ISA*. Formulated by the Women's Caucus for International Studies and submitted to the ISA Governing Council in March 1998. <http://www.isanet.org/wcis>.
Women's Environment and Development Organization. 1998. *Mapping Progress: Assessing Implementation of the Beijing Platform 1998*. New York: WEDO.
Young, Iris Marion. 1990a. *Justice and the Politics of Difference*. Princeton: Princeton University Press.
    1990b. "The Ideal of Community and the Politics of Difference." In *Feminism/Postmodernism*, ed. Linda J. Nicholson. New York: Routledge, 300–323.
Young, Iris Marion. 2000. *Inclusion and Democracy*. Oxford Series in Political Theory. Oxford University Press.
Youngs, Gillian. 1999. *International Relations in a Global Age: A Conceptual Challenge*. Cambridge: Polity Press.
Youngs, Gillian, Debbie Lisle, and Marysia Zalewski. 1999. "Three Readings of GI Jane." *International Feminist Journal of Politics* 1, 3: 476–481.
Yuval-Davis, Nira. 1994. "Identity Politics and Women's Ethnicity." In *Identity Politics and Women: Cultural Reassertions and Feminisms in an International Perspective*, ed. Valentine M. Moghadam. Boulder: Westview Press, 408–424.
    1997. *Gender and Nation*. London: Sage Publications.

Yuval-Davis, Nira, and Floya Anthias, eds. 1989. *Woman–Nation–State.* London: Macmillan.

Zalewski, Marysia. 1993a. "Feminist Theory and International Relations." In *From Cold War to Collapse: Theory and World Politics in the 1980s*, ed. Mike Bowker, and Robin Brown. Cambridge: Cambridge University Press, 115–144.

1993b. "Feminist Standpoint Theory Meets International Relations Theory." *The Fletcher Forum of World Affairs* 17, 3: 13–32.

1994. "The Women/Women Question in International Relations." *Millennium* 23, 2: 407–423.

1995. "Well, What Is the Feminist Perspective on Bosnia?" *International Affairs* 71, 2: 339–356.

1996. "'All These Theories Yet the Bodies Keep Piling Up.' Theories, Theorists, Theorising." In *International Theory: Positivism and Beyond*, eds. Ken Booth and Marysia Zalewski. Cambridge: Cambridge University Press, 340–353.

1998a. "Introduction: From the 'Woman' Question to the 'Man' Question in International Relations." In *The 'Man' Question in International Relations*, ed. Marysia Zalewski, and Jane Parpart. Boulder: Westview Press, 1–13.

1998b. "Where is Woman in International Relations? 'To Return as a Woman and Be Heard'." *Millennium* 27, 4: 847–867.

2002. "Feminism and International Relations: An Exhausted Conversation?" In *Critical Paradigms in International Studies*, ed. F. Harvey, and M. Brecher. Michigan: University of Michigan Press.

2003. "'Women's Troubles' Again in IR." *Forum on Gender and International Relations in International Studies Review* 5, 2: 291–294.

Zalewski, Marysia, and Jane L. Parpart, eds. 1998. *The "Man" Question in International Relations.* Boulder: Westview Press.

Zonabend, François. 1993. *The Nuclear Peninsula.* Cambridge: Cambridge University Press.

Zur, Judith N., 1998 *Violent Memories: Mayan War Widows in Guatemala.* Oxford: Oxford University Press.

Index